Cynics

Ancient Philosophies

Created especially for students, this series of introductory books on the schools of ancient philosophy offers a clear yet rigorous presentation of core ideas. Designed to lay the foundation for a thorough understanding of their subjects, these fresh and engaging books are compact and reasonably priced, with illustrative texts in translation.

Published in the series:

1. *Stoicism*, by John Sellars
2. *Presocratics*, by James Warren
3. *Cynics*, by William Desmond

Forthcoming in the series:

Ancient Commentators of Plato and Aristotle, by Miira Tuominen

Ancient Scepticism, by Harald Thorsrud

Aristotle, by Vasilis Politis

Classical Islamic Philosophy, by Deborah Black

Confucianism, by Paul Goldin

Epicureanism, by Tim O'Keefe

Neoplatonism, by Pauliina Remes

Plato, by Andrew Mason

Socrates, by Mark McPherran

Cynics

William Desmond

DISCARD

University of California Press
Berkeley   Los Angeles

University of California Press, one of the most distinguished university presses in the United States, enriches lives around the world by advancing scholarship in the humanities, social sciences, and natural sciences. Its activities are supported by the UC Press Foundation and by philanthropic contributions from individuals and institutions. For more information, visit www.ucpress.edu.

University of California Press
Berkeley and Los Angeles, California

© 2008 by William Desmond

Published simultaneously outside North America by
Acumen Publishing Limited.

Library of Congress Cataloging-in-Publication Data

Desmond, William D., 1974–.
  Cynics / William Desmond.
     p.   cm. — (Ancient philosophies ; 3)
  Includes bibliographical references and index.
  ISBN 978-0-520-25835-8 (cloth : alk. paper)
  ISBN 978-0-520-25861-7 (pbk. : alk. paper)
  1. Cynics (Greek philosophy)   I. Title.

B508.D46   2008
183'.4—dc22   2008008262

Manufactured in the United Kingdom

15   14   13   12   11   10   09   08
10   9   8   7   6   5   4   3   2   1

The paper used in this publication meets the minimum requirements of
ANSI/NISO Z39.48-1992 (R 1997) (*Permanence of Paper*).

Contents

Acknowledgements

For support which in sundry ways has contributed to this book, I would like to thank the following: John Cleary, John Dillon, Vasilis Politis, Santiago Sia, Andrew Smith, James Thorne, and all my colleagues at the Department of Ancient Classics at NUI Maynooth. I am also grateful to the anonymous readers for Acumen, whose suggestions have collectively been very helpful.

Introduction

According to legend, Alexander the Great had heard reports of a particular philosopher who professed a strange sort of wisdom. Owning little more than the clothes he wore, this man lived in the open in cities such as Athens and Corinth. At night he might sleep on the ground, or in porticoes or the entrances of temples, while during the day he wandered about, passing remarks about the people he met and the foolish things he saw them doing. This philosopher was said to have been exiled from his native city of Sinope, far to the north on the Black Sea, but he did not care, he said. His home was the whole earth, and he could live anywhere he liked. He was happier than kings, he said, and freer, more courageous, more just and better in all ways. In fact, everyone should become an exile like him, he said, and give up property, jobs, citizenship: everything. All these simply tie people down and make them unhappy, as they work and save for things that they do not need. If they lived like the birds or animals, they would have everything they want and be like gods. Such things the philosopher used to say to everyone he met, sometimes with a joke or a wry word, sometimes shouting, or rolling on the ground to make his point. In any case, he was quite a show and although his name was Diogenes, he was generally called by his nickname, "the Dog". Some people just laughed at this "dog-philosopher", others grew indignant, some thought him clever, and a few even followed him around as their teacher. Alexander himself had been taught by the great Aristotle, who had been taught by Plato, and Plato in turn by Socrates. But this Diogenes was said to be a "Socrates gone mad", so eccentric was he. Throughout his life Alexander would often show interest in the experience and wisdom of other peoples and he may possibly have wondered whether Diogenes had insights worth hearing. In any case, the story is that Alexander took the time to visit Diogenes "the Dog". He found him lolling in the sun but when the king generously offered him his choice of gifts, Diogenes replied dismissively, "Stand out of my sun".

So goes the story at least and, regardless of its historical accuracy, it does encapsulate many of the ideas of ancient Cynicism: elemental good and wise simplicity trumps the passing vanities of kings. This book will be about these ideas, the Cynics who lived them and the various contexts in which they appear. But first we must backtrack, and begin with the word itself. For although the word "cynic" derives from ancient Greek, Cynics such as Diogenes were rather different from their modern namesakes. When we think today of a "cynic", it is usually of someone who has a low opinion of other human beings. In the cynic's perspective, people are greedy, materialistic, manipulative and hypocritical. They act only out of self-interest. If they claim otherwise, and pretend to be acting out of love, honour, patriotism, piety, a sense of right or of duty, or from any such idealistic motive, then they are lying. For the modern cynic, politicians, for example, are not "public servants" but unscrupulous individuals who crave attention and power and, when they have them, use them to benefit themselves and their allies. Moreover, for the modern cynic there is no public good or universal standard of morality. There is only *my* good, and therefore I can only act out of self-interest. Such self-interest may involve a certain cunning manipulation of ideals, for if one is clever, one hides one's egoism behind attractive phrases, fooling others with the appearance of respectability. This Machiavellianism is often associated with a ruthless sort of cynicism: the end justifies any means. For related reasons, cynicism can be equated with nihilism, that is, the rejection of all ideals and shared meaning; and with pessimism, that is, the view that life ultimately is not good, and has no point. Thus, George Bernard Shaw's definition of the pessimist could well apply to the cynic: "a man who thinks everybody is as nasty as himself, and hates them for it". Some feel that cynicism is pervasive in contemporary Western societies, bringing with it a malaise and a damaging sense of futility.

Yet many of these negative associations should be put aside in considering ancient Cynicism. The ancient Cynics could be many things, but they were not ruthless Machiavellians or destructive nihilists. They were often pessimistic about human motivation, and they could satirize their own contemporaries mercilessly, exposing the greedy self-interest that lurked beneath fine appearances. This debunking type of satire is one common link between ancient and modern varieties of cynicism. But while it is an aspect of ancient Cynicism, it is not the only, or even the most important one. Far from being pessimistic or nihilistic, ancient Cynics were astonishingly optimistic regarding human nature. For them, ultimately, human beings are good: very good. They may have been corrupted by the bad customs and needless artificialities of "civilization", but all this can be cured. A little satire, a little humbling, and lots of frugality, a simplification of one's life, a renunciation of all unnecessary possessions and desires, a renewed living in the present moment, and one will regain one's natural goodness and happiness. The best of the Cynics tried to live these ideas themselves. They renounced possessions and attachments, went about almost naked (with just one worn cloak), wandering from city to city, living off the land and trusting in good fortune, sleeping where they could, and preaching in the streets to all and sundry that by having little one needs little and can be as happy as a "king". Theirs was a philosophy of radical individual freedom, but freedom won at the cost of a hard, ascetic lifestyle and a shameless flouting of social conventions.

It was as a result of their shameless, open-air lifestyle that Diogenes and his followers were called "dogs", dog-philosophers, *kynikoi* or Cynics. The English word "cynic" derives ultimately from the Greek *kyōn*, "dog", and the similarity is justified. If we think of cynicism in negative terms, so the nickname "dog" was generally a pejorative one for the Greeks. The dog was seen as a shameless animal, and for many the Cynics were shameless misfits. But if some called them "dogs", others called them "kings", for the Cynics claimed to have all that a person needs: clean air, healthy food, water, sunshine, freedom. The Cynics were often resolutely optimistic in their belief that everyone can be cured of false desires and that all can attain the self-contained happiness of a Diogenes. Because of this optimism, ancient Cynicism is ultimately very different from, even opposite to, its modern namesake. To highlight this, German writers distinguish ancient *Kynismus* from modern *Zynismus*, a contrast that can be preserved in English by distinguishing ancient Cynics (capitalized) and modern cynics (lower case). We shall follow this custom here.

Ancient Cynicism, then, is a far more specific phenomenon than modern cynicism. Yet it is no less complex. Its mixture of shameless-ness and idealism, anti-nomianism and radical optimism, could be developed in many different ways. As a result, it would become a creative and influential philosophy in the ancient world. It has been described as "arguably the most original and influential branch of the Socratic tradition in antiquity" (Bracht Branhan & Goulet-Cazé 1996: 1). This is quite a conclusion, given that the "Socratic tradition" includes Plato, Aristotle and the Stoics. Even stronger is the claim that ancient Cynicism is "one of the most challenging intellectual phenomena in the history of the Western world" (Navia 1996: 1). And even stronger still is Nietzsche's judgement: Cynicism is "the highest one can reach on earth" (*Ecce Homo*: "Why I Write Such Good Books", §3). When judgements like Nietzsche's are to be found in the writings of an Epictetus (*Diss.* 3.22) or a Shakespeare (*King Lear*), one must take pause. The ancient Cynics cannot be dismissed as mere shame-less "dogs" who had nothing to do with the "glory that was Greece and the grandeur that was Rome" (Poe 2006: 409). This is essentially the conclusion of nineteenth-century scholarship, which, following Hegel, tended to scorn Diogenes as a "mad Socrates" and sidelined Cynicism as one of the "minor Socratic schools" and a lifestyle rather than a serious philosophical outlook. The changing outlook of phi-losophers and classical scholars alike has, however, led to dramatic re-evaluations of Cynicism. Formerly in the dog-house, as it were, the Cynics have been let loose, and their importance reassessed.

In surveying ancient Cynicism, one must bear in mind not only its mix of shamelessness and idealism, but also the fact that it was both a single outlook and extraordinarily varied. Diogenes was the first to be called "dog" in the fourth century BCE; the last known Cynic, Sallustius, lived in the late-fifth century CE. There may well have been others after him, but that period alone covers some nine hundred years. During this long stretch of time, Cynics were present at the eclipse of the independent Greek city-states, the rise of Hellenistic kingdoms, the coming of Rome, the *Pax Romana* and its slow decline, and the rise of Christianity and of a new, Christian culture. Placed in so many different environments, Cynicism took on a wide variety of forms. It is common to categorize these forms into ascetic and hedonistic strains of Cynicism. At its purest, the "true" or "hard" or "rigorous" or "ascetic" Cynics lived as poor wanderers, with only a cloak, staff and satchel, carrying some food and maybe a book. These lived as frugally as possible and asked little from others, except that they reform their own extravagant ways. Hardy, sardonic, moral and in their own right generous, these Cynics were often admired, and at least wondered at, as if they were superior sorts of beings who had freed themselves from the usual, all-too-human desires for pleasure, money, power and status. What such individuals represented could impress some observers forcefully, but not enough to convince them to take up the Cynic cloak and staff themselves. Many, then, admired Cynic ideas from a distance, and incorporated them into their writings, but not into their own lives. As a result these have been termed "literary", "soft" or "hedonistic" Cynics.

There are extant some fragments of "true" Cynics such as Diogenes and Crates, but in general Cynicism is known mainly through its more "literary" adherents and inheritors. The most important sources are: Diogenes Laertius' *Lives of the Philosophers*, Book 6; Epictetus' *Discourses*, 3.22 and 4.8; various dialogues of Lucian, especially the *Cynicus* once (erroneously) attributed to him, perhaps the most eloquent single summary of the Cynic outlook; Dio Chrysostom's *Orations* 4 and 6–10; the anonymous *Cynic Epistles*, probably composed mainly in the first century CE but purporting to be written by figures such as Diogenes or Crates; Orations 6 and 7 of Julian, "the Apostate" Emperor; Oration 36 of Maximus of Tyre; the fragments of Teles, Bion and others that are preserved in the anthology of John Stobaeus; and many fragmentary quotations referenced in Athenaeus, Strabo, the Church Fathers and other authors of diminishing relevance. In addition, if one searches, Cynic-like ideas appear in the most unexpected places, from Petronius to the Gospels to Marcus Aurelius.

Because the evidence for Cynicism is so fragmentary, scattered and variously located, it can be difficult to assess the movement as a whole. Each Cynic was an individual, even a world unto his defiant self, and so categorizations such as "hard" and "soft" Cynicism are imprecise. Furthermore, it is difficult to reconstruct the exact views of "true" Cynics such as Diogenes, who, being wanderers, could not write very much and are known mainly at a remove. This book will take ancient Cynicism as a body of loosely related ideas that, as a whole, remained *fairly* constant from Diogenes to Sallustius. There is an overall continuity of theme and the main ideas of Cynicism seem to endure from the early Greek Cynics to the last known representatives under the late Roman Empire. Yet although its fundamental ideas endured, they also took on many local variations, for as Cynicism was adapted by different personalities from different areas over a period of nine centuries, each observer selected and emphasized certain ideas over others, and so lent his own style to the underlying Cynic outlook. It is a challenge to recognize both the variety of ancient Cynicism, and the unity that underlies this multiplicity.

This introduction to Cynicism will attempt both tasks. In Chapter 1, "Ancient Cynics and their Times", and Chapter 6, "Cynic Legacies", we shall survey a colourful parade of Cynics ancient and modern, "hard" and "soft", from Diogenes to Nietzsche and beyond. These pages will introduce many of the more important Cynics, their writings and characteristic ideas and the cultural contexts in which they lived and thought. The treatment will be chronological, from the Greek classical period through to the end of pagan antiquity (Ch. 1), and then from early Christianity through to contemporary times (Ch. 6). Chapters 2–5 turn from Cynics to Cynic themes, from personalities to enduring ideas. Here we shall interpret the basic assertions of Cynicism not as a series of paradoxes or hallowed platitudes but rather as notions that are both challenging in themselves and deeply implicated in various cultural and intellectual contexts of the ancient world. In Chapter 2, "Renunciation of Custom", Cynicism is distinguished by its thorough rejection of conventional beliefs and customs, from dietary practices to athletics to burial rites. Here Cynicism is at its most negative or "cynical", criticizing customs (*nomoi*) as corrupting and evil. In Chapter 3, "A Life According to Nature", this negative attitude gives way to an optimistic one, as the Cynics advocate living "according to nature". The best life is an "all-natural" one, with no artificial ingredients added, and here the Cynics add their own voice to ancient debates about the concept of nature. In Chapter 4, "Chance, Fate, Fortune and the Self", the Cynic sets to "work", for one must struggle through pain and ascetic training to be able to live naturally. Asceticism is the best way to become self-sufficient, invincible before fortune, and unperturbed by any chance events. In Chapter 5, "Anarchists, Democrats, Cosmpolitans, Kings", the Cynics appear as political animals of sorts. Thus in these central chapters we shall approach Cynicism as a whole from a variety of perspectives: Cynics' critique of convention, praise of natural simplicity, advocacy of self-sufficiency, freedom and defiance of fortune. Some of these themes will recur in modern varieties of cynicism, most notably freedom, which makes ancient Cynicism of continuing interest today.[1]

But first, we must meet the main characters: Diogenes, Crates, Hipparchia, Metrocles, Onesicritus, Cercidas, Bion, Menippus, Meleager, Oenomaus, Demonax, Peregrinus and the rest. Here one can only select the major names, quote some of their ideas or sayings, evoke the spirit of their times and sketch general lines of development. It is a ragtag group of individuals, yet what a group! Rebellious, self-willed and ornery, but also witty and imaginative, the "dog-philosophers" are indeed some of the most colourful personalities from antiquity. As a result, one can well believe the story that Alexander did seek out Diogenes to meet him for himself. We cannot resurrect the Cynics to interview them directly, but must piece together a mad jigsaw of ancient fragments. The resulting picture is clear at least in outline. It is an influential picture, interesting in its own right. And who knows, perhaps we too may gain some wisdom from Diogenes, and even learn to step into *his* sunshine.

ONE

Ancient Cynics and their times

Historical overview

Of the philosophies of antiquity, Cynicism was one of the most varied and enduring. Although Diogenes was the first to be nicknamed "the Dog", earlier Greeks such as Antisthenes and Socrates at least in part shared his views on social rebellion, the natural life, and indifference to fortune, with which his name would be associated. After him there are individuals known as Cynics down at least to the fifth century CE, possibly with minor gaps. Over these nine centuries, battles were fought, leagues joined and disbanded, empires won and lost. The battle of Chaeronea (338 BCE) made the Macedonian kings leaders of mainland Greece. The battles of Granicus, Issus and Arbela/Gaugamela (331 BCE) placed Alexander on the throne of Asia. The battle at Ipsus (301 BCE) effectively settled the division of Alexander's empire into Antigonid, Seleucid and Ptolemaic kingdoms. A generation later, Pyrrhus won victories of sorts against the Romans but by the end of the century, after the first two Punic Wars, the Romans ruled Italy, including the old Greek cities in the south and in Sicily, and were looking further afield. The Seleucid Empire was whittled away, especially after the battle of Magnesia (190 BCE). Antigonids and Ptolemies bowed out of history after Pydna (168 BCE) and Actium (31 BCE) respectively. Victorious everywhere, the Romans established their famous peace and so secure was this *Pax Romana* that for a time it might seem divinely ordained and everlasting. But Roman legions and emperors were eventually worn down also: Germans on the Rhine and Danube, Parthians on the Euphrates. Most of all, the idea of Rome declined and gave way to the power of new, spiritual "kingdoms", such as those of Mithras, Isis and, most significantly, Christ.

Through all these changes, there were individuals who called themselves Cynics. They came with many accents and degrees of conviction. The typical Cynic was seen in the city streets of Athens, Alexandria or even Rome, preaching to passers-by: "I am a rival follower of Antisthenes, Crates and Diogenes.[1] Reject wealth and the gifts of fickle fortune! Have the courage to be free, like me!" But there were also Cynics on the country roads, travelling between cities, drifting about the countryside, and even staying with country people.[2] Sometimes Cynics appeared in public assemblies, as when Peregrinus spoke before the Parians. At rare moments, Cynics might associate with kings, as did Onesicritus, Bion and Demetrius. Cynicism even reached to the throne itself: Dio Chrysostom may have lectured to Trajan about true kingship, the Stoic emperor Marcus Aurelius practised the Cynic ideal of labour (*ponos*), and Julian "the Apostate" emperor considered Cynicism part of the divinely ordained philosophy. There is a great gulf between being a beggar and a Roman emperor, but such was the elasticity of Cynic ideas that they could appeal across the divide. The "true" Cynic, again, was seen as someone like Diogenes, who lived as a wanderer, from day to day, with almost nothing, and who made it his business to chastise mankind for not imitating him. Others might take their Cynicism on and off like a coat, yet the experience often changed them, and changed others who knew them. The variety of styles of Cynicism ensured that it was always controversial, at once praised for its virtues and reviled for its shamelessness.

Marie-Odile Goulet-Cazé, one of the foremost scholars of Cynicism, has compiled a "Comprehensive Catalogue of Known Cynic Philosophers", which includes over one hundred persons: eighty-three Cynics "whose historical authenticity is confirmed", fourteen "anonymous Cynics", and ten others "whose link with Cynicism is uncertain" (Bracht Branham & Goulet-Cazé 1996: 389–413; cf. Navia 1996: 146). Of course, out of the millions who lived from Diogenes until the end of antiquity, one hundred names is not very many. But numbers alone do not tell a story, and in periods like the first and second centuries CE, it would seem from the tone of many literary works that Cynics constituted a strong presence in many cities and in the collective consciousness at large.[3] Among the hundred known, and many more anonymous, Cynics, can one find any broad patterns that allow one to categorize these individuals? As we have seen, some commentators distinguish between "hard", ascetic Cynics like Diogenes and "soft", hedonistic Cynics like Bion. Perhaps more useful is the pattern that several historians of Cynicism have emphasized. Goulet-Cazé, Luis Navia and others follow Donald Dudley in marking out "two unequal stages" in the history of Cynicism: the first from Antisthenes and Diogenes to the mid-third century BCE is exclusively Greek and contains the most creative and compelling Cynics; the second extends from approximately 250 BCE to 500 CE, and includes figures from across the Mediterranean, most of whom blend Cynic ideas with a medley of other influences. Navia's discussion is worth quoting at length:

> The history of Cynicism can be divided into two unequal stages. The first stage includes the early Cynics, from the beginnings of the movement to the middle of the third century BC, specifically, Antisthenes, Diogenes, Onesicritus, Monimus, Crates, Hipparchia, Metrocles, Bion, Menippus, Cercidas, and a few others. The second stage embraces the later Cynics, that is, from the middle of the third century BC to the end of Cynicism in the fifth century AD. To this second stage belong innumerable Cynics, not only Greek in origin and in language, but individuals representing many of the nations that integrated the Hellenistic world and the Roman Empire: Romans, Syrians, Palestinians, Phoenicians, Alexandrians, Pagans, Jews, Christians, and others. The first stage is historically short – about one hundred and fifty years,

linguistically homogeneous, and dominated by the influence of the Antisthenes-Diogenes succession. The second stage is historically long – over six centuries, heterogeneous in language and tradition, and often intermingled with non-Cynic philosophies and with religious currents such as Judaism and Christianity.   (Navia 1996: 12–13)[4]

This approach tends to idealize origins, as if the first leaders of the movement were somehow superior to their more mediocre successors. This may not be entirely just, either to later Cynics such as Oenomaus, Dio Chrysostom or Peregrinus, or to the scanty historical record, which makes any final evaluations very difficult. As a result we shall here introduce a few more divisions to highlight the sheer variety of Cynicism, and to place its evolution in the context of the "great events" of kings and battles that shaped the Cynics' worlds, as they proceeded from the egalitarian cities of classical Greece to the great cosmopolitan cities of the Hellenistic and Roman monarchies:

- The pre-Cynic Greek period includes many figures (both legendary and historical) who have at some point been regarded as proto-Cynics, notably Socrates and Antisthenes.
- The Greek Classical period of the fourth-century BCE witnesses the canonical figures of Diogenes and Crates, as well as followers such as Hipparchia and Metrocles.
- The Hellenistic period (c.300–50 BCE) includes Cynics considered important mainly for their literary influence – Onesicritus, Cercidas, Bion, Teles, Menippus, Oenomaus and Meleager.
- The Roman or Imperial period (c.50 BCE–500 CE) is, as Dudley and Navia write, an eclectic one, and throws forth a burgeoning diversity of Cynics and Cynic admirers, such as Agathobulus, Demetrius, Epictetus, Dio Chrysostom, Lucian, Demonax, Peregrinus, Marcus Aurelius, Julian, as well as critics such as the Christian Apologists and Church Fathers, to whom we shall return in Chapter 6.

"Cynics" before the Cynics?

Just as there were many varieties of Cynicism after the ancient Cynics, so too there were many proto-Cynics in Greece before the appearance of Diogenes "the Dog". In keeping with the circumambient intellectual fixation with origins and foundations, classical scholars of the nineteenth and early-twentieth centuries asked whether the precise origins of Cynicism lay with Antisthenes or Diogenes. Erudite arguments were presented repeatedly on both sides. In general, nineteenth-century writers (e.g. Hegel, Zeller, Ueberweg, Gomperz, Windelband and Grote) tended to follow the unanimous ancient tradition that Antisthenes was the first Cynic and a teacher of Diogenes. But in the first full-length study of Cynicism, Dudley ([1937] 1980) made it one of his central contentions that Antisthenes was not a true Cynic like Diogenes, that he probably did not even know the man, and that their relationship was a fiction promulgated by later Alexandrian genealogists. Given the available evidence, the question is probably undecidable. On the one hand, Antisthenes was a Sophist, teacher of rhetoric, admirer of Homer, sometime logician and author of books titled *On Nature*, indicating an intellectual curiosity and virtuosity that the Cynics rejected. On the other hand, he also advocates a simple, frugal and ascetic lifestyle, for poverty is the only "wealth"; he may be sympathetic to the ideal of cosmopolitanism, and in Xenophon's depiction, he is a somewhat gruff moralist. Was he the first Cynic or not? In the end, the very question may tacitly rely on a false dichotomy, and on an assumption that Cynicism was a school with its own founder, doctrine and canonical writings, just like the Academy of Plato, the Lyceum of Aristotle, the "Garden" of Epicurus or the Stoa of Zeno. But because the fundamental ideas of Cynicism were simple and adaptable, they often appear piecemeal, here and there, long before the appearance of a Diogenes or even an Antisthenes.

It is possible, then, to discern many proto-Cynics before the first real Cynics took up the staff and *pēra*. Some of the names of these proto-Cynics were proposed by the ancient Cynics themselves, as they reinterpreted old mythologies for their own purposes, while others have been suggested by modern scholars. First and most important is Heracles, son of Zeus, who completed the Twelve Labours and was therefore made into a paradigm of endurance, self-sacrifice, virtue, philanthropy and philosophy generally. Heracles was the Cynics' favourite hero.[5] But there were others too who could be idealized as Cynic exemplars: Theseus and other heroes of Heracles' generation, because they walked through the world without shoes or many clothes but with mighty beards and kingly hearts (ps.-Luc. *Cyn.* 13–14); Homer's Thersites, because he spoke up boldly and shamelessly, like a "Cynic demagogue" against the stupid greed of the Achaean generals (Luc. *Demon.* 61, *Fugitivi* 30; cf. Bracht Branham 1989: 57–63); Odysseus, versatile, adaptable and *polytropos* (like Bion and Peregrinus Proteus), who, when he returned to an Ithaca ruled by ruffians, was persuaded by Athena to put on a beggar's rags in order to regain his kingdom.[6] There were still others, historical figures, who touched on one Cynic theme or other: the poet Hesiod, who praised justice and a hard life over the wealth of kings, who claimed that "half is more than the whole", and who wrote lines on toil and virtue that were favourites among later philosophers (Luc. *Nec.* 4, referring to Hes. *Op.* 286–92); the satirist Archilochus, who preferred virtue over wealth and status (D. Chr. 33.14, 33.17–18, on Archil. Fr. 114); the Pythagorean Diodorus of Aspendus, who may have been the first to "double his cloak", wear a long beard, carry a staff and knapsack, and thus distinguish himself by a quasi-Cynic "uniform" (DL 6.13); Heraclitus, who criticized his contemporaries and Greek polytheism, and then (in legend at least) withdrew in disgust to the mountains where he lived on water-cress (Kindstrand 1984); Democritus, who may have drawn wisdom from the animal world, and in later allegories, laughed manically at mankind's follies (Stewart 1958; Temkin 1991: 61ff.); Gorgias, who (according to Hellenistic genealogies) taught Antisthenes, who taught Diogenes, who taught Crates (DL 6.1); Protagoras, whose view of man as "the measure of all that is" may anticipate the Cynics' stress on radical individual autonomy; and the Sophists generally, who tended to subordinate human custom (*nomos*) to the necessity of nature (*physis*).

Some even look as far east as India for influences on the Cynics: many have compared them with the ancient Indian worshippers of Shiva, the *Pāśupatas* (Ingalls 1962; Syrkin 1998; Hulin 1993; Navia 1996: 20–21), while Farrand Sayre mused that they resembled the Jains (Sayre 1948).[7] This is not an exhaustive list, but it serves to explain the attitude of Oenomaus when he writes that Cynicism is "neither Antisthenism nor Diogenism". To this Julian adds: "there were always men who practiced this philosophy. For it seems to be in some ways a universal philosophy, and the most natural" (Jul. *Or.* 6.187c–d).

Socrates

Whether or not there were *always* people who practised "Cynicism", with Socrates (469–399 BCE) we definitely draw closer to the first Greek Cynics. For in quasi-Cynic fashion, Socrates neglected his social duties for philosophy: he spent little time at home with his wife and sons, or at his trade of sculpture, or at the assembly and courts where Athenian citizens were expected to make their contribution. He did fight with distinction as a hoplite at Potidaea, Amphipolis and Delium, but most of his energies were spent in the marketplace or on the streets talking with passers-by about human questions, particularly the nature of morality and the good. Like the Cynics, Socrates walked about the streets barefoot, talking with rich and poor alike, for free. His conversations were dialectical, not polemical, yet like the Cynics Socrates exhorted his interlocutors not to idolize wealth or honour. *The* good of life is not money, pleasure, status, power or even scientific knowledge, but rather virtue and the philosophy that underlies it. For his stinging remarks Socrates was called the "gadfly of Athens" (Pl. *Ap.* 30e–31a) and, like later Cynics, could be both admired for his asceticism and uprightness and hated for his individualistic questioning. Most redolent of Cynicism is his statement that he was poor *because* of his philosophy (Pl. *Ap.* 23c; cf. Desmond 2006: 56–7, 155–6, 163–4).

For all this – his asceticism, voluntary poverty, indifference towards and sometimes contempt of public opinion, relative neglect of social duty, focus on ethics, and even his ironic detachment – Socrates seems to look forward to the Cynics.[8] They took these traits to greater extremes, of course, and in an oft-quoted phrase Diogenes was said to be a "Socrates gone mad": the stinging gadfly becomes a biting dog. Such similarities may lie behind attempts by Alexandrian scholars to make Socrates the great-grandfather of Cynicism, as it were: in the genealogies of scholars such as Sotion of Alexandria, Crates "listened to" Diogenes who "listened to" Antisthenes who "listened to" Socrates. That is, Socrates "taught" Antisthenes who "taught" Diogenes who "taught" Crates, who in turn "taught" Zeno of Citium, the founder of Stoicism. Along such lines of direct personal influence, Socrates becomes the ultimate progenitor of Cynicism, as well as of Stoicism, Plato's Academy and Aristotle's Lyceum. Yet these genealogies may reveal more about cataloguers' desires for neat maps than about the complex interplay of influence, counter-influence and free philosophical imagination. Dudley, therefore, is right to doubt these Hellenistic genealogies, if only because they are too precise.[9] Moreover, there are important philosophical differences between the Cynics and Socrates. The Cynics seem far more self-assured in their scepticism. They seem to *know* that ideas and traditional customs are all corrupting, that nature and the external world cannot be understood and that all one can know is the present. Socrates, on the other hand, seems not to have rejected natural science or social mores so unequivocally. His highest statement is not the Cynics' "I alone am king", but the more humble "I only know that I do not have any true knowledge". Nor did Socrates end in scepticism: rather, his resolute search for the undiscovered truth made him an intellectual hero for Plato and many others.

Antisthenes

One such admirer was Antisthenes (*c*.445–*c*.365 BCE), a student, friend and companion of Socrates, inseparable from his master, and present at his side even at his death as he drank the hemlock. As the son of an Athenian man and Thracian woman (DL 6.1), he was considered an illegitimate "bastard" (*nothos*), who by law could not enjoy the privileges of full Athenian citizenship. One of these privileges was the use of regular gymnasia and so Antisthenes used the Cynosarges, the gymnasium reserved for non-citizen metics. The name "Cynos-arges" may mean "Bright Dog", and as a result, according to one version at least, Antisthenes was nicknamed "the pure dog" (6.13) and so became the first "Cynic" in the eyes of later ancient writers.

In addition, many aspects of Antisthenes seem Cynic in tenor. Scenes in Xenophon's *Symposium* depict him as a vehement personality, more cantankerous than Socrates, as if he too were a sort of "mad" Socrates. In Cynic fashion he takes up various Socratic themes and exaggerates them. Socrates acknowledges that philosophy made him poor but Antisthenes boasts that his poverty is his "wealth" (Xen. *Symp.* 3.8, 3.34–46): being frugal and simple in his desires, he lacks nothing and so is superlatively rich. The paradoxical formulation, and wilful overturning of conventional expectations, looks forward to later Cynic shock tactics. Other sayings seem to anticipate Cynic asceticism and cosmopolitanism: *ponos* (labour, pain) is good, as the cases of Heracles and Cyrus prove (DL 6.2); luxury is a curse (6.8); it is better to be mad than to have pleasure (6.3); the Athenians are foolish for withholding citizenship from people like him, because the mother of the gods is Phrygian (6.1); the Athenians' pride in being autochthonous is stupid, because snails and locusts are also born from the soil (6.1).

Yet any anticipation of Cynic themes on Antisthenes' part was complicated by other aspects of his life and thought. Although proud of his "wealth" of poverty, he owned a house. Although he praised virtue above all, he did not scorn rhetoric, logic and literature. On the contrary, he seems to have been remarkably versatile. He is thought to have first studied with Gorgias, the great Sicilian rhetorician and Sophist. He taught rhetoric himself, but when he met Socrates he is said to have burned all his compositions, just as Plato is said to have burned his tragedies. Some of them survived the conflagration though, including speeches in the voices of Ajax and Odysseus. Diogenes Laertius (6.15–18) lists titles of works

17

that filled some ten volumes: an astonishing *oeuvre* that would put Antisthenes on a par with Democritus or Aristotle. Many of these titles have Homeric themes (such as "On Circe" or "On Odysseus, Penelope, and the Dog"), which he may have treated allegorically. Volume 6, however, contains titles such as "Truth" and "Satho or of Contradiction". Here Antisthenes' rhetorical interests may have led on to logical investigations, for both rhetoric and reasoned argument are means of persuading others. To judge from references in Aristotle, Antisthenes as logician echoed the Megarian view that predication and contradiction are impossible: one cannot say "*A* is *B*" (predication) or "*A* is not *A*" (non-contradiction) but only that "*A* is *A*". Such a view may look forwards to the most important of Cynic ideas, the notion that one can only know the present, and should therefore live fully in the present, not distracted by memories, anticipations of the future, by universal ideas, or by the complex predications that underlie the sciences and most philosophies; rather, one must attend to this thing, here, now – this *A*, which is *A* and nothing more. But if Antisthenes' logical ideas might be associated in this way with the Cynics' carefree attitude, he himself does not seem to have made the link. In fact, Antisthenes' flirtation with logic and his wide-ranging intellectual interests seem positively un-Cynic, as even later Cynics thought: Timon complained that he wrote too much (DL 6.18), and Diogenes is said to have compared him with an overly loud trumpet (D. Chr. 8.2). For such reasons too, some scholars have refused to categorize Antisthenes as a Cynic: according to this view, Antisthenes may have graduated from a sophistic/rhetorical period (when he studied with Gorgias), to a Socratic phase (when he would walk eight kilometres every day, from the Piraeus to Athens, in order to be with Socrates), but he did not have a third, Cynic phase. Other scholars, however, find a personal link with Diogenes less problematic and argue that Antisthenes took Socrates' example in a decidedly Cynic direction; he may have inspired Diogenes directly, as many later anecdotes claim. Suffice it here to emphasize that the question of Antisthenes' relation to the Cynic movement has been and remains a controversial one.[10]

Cynics of the classical period: Diogenes, Crates, Hipparchia, Metrocles

The first undisputed Cynics appeared around the middle of the fourth century BCE. This first generation includes Diogenes of Sinope and his followers: Crates of Thebes, Monimus of Syracuse, Onesicritus of Astypalaea, Menander the "Oakwood", Hegesias the "Dog-Collar" and Philiscus of Aegina (DL 6.84). In this little group, Crates seems to have played second fiddle to the maestro Diogenes, but he had his own "students" also: Hipparchia and Metrocles of Maroneia, Theombrotus, and Cleomenes (6.95).[11] They hailed from across the Greek world, from Sinope on the Black Sea, Maroneia on the Thracian coast near Abdera, and Syracuse in the west. Cities in Cyprus and Cyrene are not represented, but "old" Greece is, in Crates' Thebes and Philiscus' Aegina and the Astypalaea of Onesicritus. The social backgrounds of these first Cynics vary widely also: from wealthy (Crates and Hipparchia) to commercial (Diogenes) to slave (Monimus), while Onesicritus became essentially a mercenary adventurer in the employ of Alexander and the Macedonians. His travels as far as India prefigure the spread of Cynic ideas across the Hellenistic kingdoms in succeeding generations.

Diogenes

To begin with "the Dog" himself, if any one name is associated with Cynicism it is that of Diogenes of Sinope (*c*.412–*c*.323 BCE). The name itself was a common one, and like many Greek names is theophoric (cf. Hera-cles, Apollo-dorus), meaning "born of Zeus". Later writers would play on the etymology to suggest that the true Cynic is closer to God than other mortals, just as Diogenes was the "offspring of Zeus" and "the heavenly dog".[12] But if Diogenes had a divine parent then, like Heracles, he led a double life, for the earthly Diogenes was born the son of one Hicesias in Sinope, an important Greek city in northern Turkey on the Black Sea. Sinope was far from being a backwater. It stood at the end of a trade route stretching from Mesopotamia across the central Anatolian plateau to the Black Sea. With a good harbour roughly equidistant from the Hellespont and the Caucasus Mountains, and looking north to Scythia and the Crimean wheat fields, Sinope was well situated as a trading city and local power. As a "mother-city" with surplus population of its own, it sent out colonies around the Black Sea (e.g. Apollonia), and became important enough for Pericles to lead a fleet of ships at least once to the area, to bolster Athenian influence in this important grain-producing region, and perhaps to escort Athenian colonists. In his wide-ranging study of the ancient city, David M. Robinson (1906a,b) argues plausibly that geographical position must have made the Sinopeans (like Thucydides' Athenians) energetic, enterprising, quick-witted, irreverent and cosmopolitan, traits that are most evident in her most famous son, Diogenes of Sinope.[13]

Diogenes' philosophical career, at least in legend, begins with his exile from Sinope. It would seem, from both the literary tradition and numismatic studies of Sinopean coins from *c*.360–320 BCE, that Diogenes' father Hicesias worked in the city's mint but (to give one of several plausible courses of events) struck the faces off a number of coins, thus putting them out of circulation. For this Hicesias was prosecuted, and either imprisoned or exiled. Diogenes too was implicated somehow and went into exile. But far from ruining him, exile made Diogenes a philosopher, as he claimed later (DL 6.49). Lore has it that when he was banished from Sinope, he travelled to Delphi to consult Apollo on how to live in his new situation. The god's reply was *paracharattein to nomisma*, a riddling phrase probably meaning "deface the coinage". Later Cynics would adopt the phrase as their motto and construe it metaphorically as a command to decommission the "coinage" of social custom (6.20–21). Diogenes may have drawn the same conclusions, and so he is depicted travelling through the Greek mainland, everywhere claiming to be putting current customs out of circulation, "barking" at the Greeks for their vices and lack of freedom. For his homelessness, shamelessness and satirical snarls, he was called "the Dog", a nickname that Aristotle uses without explanation (*Rh*. 1411a24), implying that he was a well-known character in the Greece of his day.

To make a name for himself like this and to gather together his band of merry men and one woman, he must have been a forceful personality. The historical individual is fairly lost in legend, and "Diogenes" quickly became a name, symbol and one of the most popular stock-characters in all antiquity. According to one estimate, there are over one thousand anecdotes (*chreiai*) that involve Diogenes, more than for any other philosopher.[14] The following are some of most famous. (i) Alexander the Great heard stories about Diogenes and took time to consult this strange sage in Corinth. Diogenes happened to be sunning himself when Alexander stood over him, putting Diogenes in the shade. "Make a request", Alexander said, to which Diogenes replied, "Stand out of my sun" (DL 6.38; Cic. *Tusc.* 5.92; Plut. *Alex.* 14). (ii) One day Diogenes went into the marketplace at noon with a lighted lantern – "seeking a human being" (DL 6.41). This is the Greek wording, but what has passed into Western fable is that he was seeking "an honest man". In both cases, however, the implication is that "he will not find him".[15] (iii) Diogenes did not have a regular house and one day crept into an empty, overturned *pithos* and slept there (6.23). A *pithos* was a large storage jar for wine, grain or olive oil; modern variations place Diogenes in a "barrel", "tub", "vat", "wine-vat", "jar" and even "kennel", but the original Greek is *pithos*. (iv) Diogenes once saw a child drinking from his hands, and immediately threw away his own cup saying, "A child has conquered me in frugality" (*euteleia*) (6.37).

Other legends were celebrated in antiquity, although less so later. First is the story that Diogenes was captured by pirates and sold into slavery. At the slave market in Corinth, one Xeniades was interested in buying him. "What can you do?" Xeniades asked. "Rule men", was Diogenes' reply. And so Xeniades bought this natural "king", made him tutor to his sons, whom Diogenes taught to ride, shoot a bow, use a sling, throw a javelin, hunt and walk in a dignified way. To educate the mind, he had them learn poetry, histories of heroes such as Agesilaus and Epaminondas, and his own works. In Eubulus' version, Diogenes lived out his life in the house of Xeniades, and was buried by his sons (DL 6.28–31, 6.36, 6.74). If all of this were true, it would make for a far more staid existence than that of a

homeless wanderer, and could hardly have earned him the nickname "Dog". It may well be the case that as an exile Diogenes was
enslaved at some point, but later writers cared less about precise facts
than the thematic possibilities of a "king" in chains. Such a scenario
was too delicious to pass by and so the "Sale of Diogenes" became
almost a subgenre of philosophical fiction: works entitled "Sale of
Diogenes" are attributed to Menippus, Hermippus and Eubulus; and
perhaps in imitation of Menippus, Lucian wrote *Sale of Lives*, where
Pythagoreans, Platonists and other slave philosophers are put on the
auctioneer's block, to uproarious effect.

Other rumours impute various writings to Diogenes but, once
more, it is difficult to separate fact from fiction. According to
Diogenes Laertius, thirteen dialogues, a set of letters, and seven
tragedies are attributed to Diogenes. Some of these titles are tanta-
lizing – *The Fish-Head, The Fart, The People of Athens, On Wealth,
On Death* – and one wonders what unusual perspective Diogenes
might have brought to tragedies such as *Heracles, Helen, Achilles,
Odysseus* and *Medea*.[16] But on the other hand, if Diogenes threw
away his cup and had only his cloak, staff and "tub", how did he get
the papyrus, ink and reed pens (or even the cheaper wax tablets) to
write so much? And if he scorned human customs, would he not
also have despised such conventional activities as writing, as some
anecdotes imply he did? Possibly with such questions in mind, some
say that Diogenes wrote nothing at all, and assign the Cynic tragedies (which evidently did exist) to Diogenes' friend, Philiscus or
to one Pasiphon.[17] In any case, the most notorious book attributed
to Diogenes was a *Republic (Politeia)*, a common title for books on
political utopias, and not peculiar to Plato. In addition, some poetic
lines attributed to Diogenes are extant, but the most secure of all
is one of Diogenes' metaphors, which his contemporary Aristotle
quotes: "Bars are the Spartan barracks of Athens" (*Rh.* 3.10.7).

Perfect precision about Diogenes' sayings, writings, movements
and life is not attainable. What is more important, however, is the
personality of the man, for it is this personality that took on a life
of its own in later anecdotes and legend. What was this "Diogenes"
like? His detractors speak of his pride and ambition, a common

accusation against Cynics. For instance, Diogenes is said to have asked the Delphic oracle, "What should I do to become famous?" His own conclusion was that he could be remembered only by becoming notoriously outrageous (DL 6.21, 6.41). Others speak of a likeable character. Diogenes Laertius claims that Diogenes had "wonderful", even magical powers of persuasion, "so that he could easily vanquish anyone he liked in argument". He "vanquished" Onesicritus and his sons, for instance, and made them all Cynics. Onesicritus of Aegina sent one of his sons to Athens, perhaps on business, but when the son, Androsthenes, heard Diogenes talk, he decided to stay in Athens with him. Onesicritus then sent his second son, Philiscus, to retrieve his brother, but the same thing happened. Finally, when the father himself came to Athens, he too was mesmerized by this philosophical Siren, and joined Diogenes' group (6.75–6).[18] Many anecdotes suggest that he was actually liked by his peers, and some of his jokes are quite funny: Dudley ([1937] 1980: 29 n.2) and others have found the Diogenes-*chreiai* "decidedly funnier" than others, as if still reflecting Diogenes' wit. Given this, one might imagine Diogenes as a rogue, perhaps like Shakespeare's Falstaff, mischievous, self-interested, opportunistic, but larger than life, bursting with energy and wicked good humour. Epictetus says of the ideal Cynic that he should be witty, perceptive and eloquent enough to comment significantly on any situation, to the surprise and delight of his hearers (*Diss.* 3.22.90–92). In such characterizations, there may be some distant folk memories of the historical Diogenes himself.[19]

It is said that Falstaff died either discoursing about virtue, or drinking "sack", and so too there are different versions of Diogenes' death. He died holding his breath; he died from eating raw octopus; he died from a dog bite; he died of old age; he died of a fever on his way to the Olympic Games; or he died in Corinth on the same day as Alexander the Great died in Babylon, that is 10 June 323 BCE (DL 6.76–9). He left no "famous last words" of his own, but many epitaphs were written later for him. These play on his name, "son of Zeus"; on the notion that he brings to the Underworld all that he had in life and so will not overburden Charon's little boat; or on how Diogenes the

Dog finally gets to meet Cerberus, the three-headed dog of Hades.[20] In *Menippus*, Lucian even pictures him in the Underworld itself, badgering Sardanapalus, Midas and other tycoons, roaring out in laughter and song at their miserable fate. He left behind various students (or "hearers"), admirers and friends, including Phocion "the Good" of Athens, Stilpo of Megara, Menander the "Oakwood", Hegesias "the Dog-Collar" from Sinope, Onesicritus of Aegina and his two sons Androsthenes and Philiscus, another Onesicritus of Astypalaea, Monimus of Syracuse, Pasiphon and Crates of Thebes (DL 6.76, 6.84). He had no family but them.

Crates

Crates of Thebes (*c*.360–*c*.280 BCE) was the most important of Diogenes' "heirs". He was from a rich, landowning Theban family but he gave up everything for philosophy. One tradition is that he began to turn to philosophy when he saw the tragedy of Telephus (DL 6.87). Telephus was a son of Heracles and king of the Mysians who fought against the Greeks when they landed on his kingdom's shores, lost on their way to Troy. Achilles wounded him, the wound would not heal, and an oracle declared that Telephus could only be cured by the one who had injured him. In desperation Telephus travelled to Argos and, disguised as a beggar, stole into the Greek camp to beg Achilles' help. It was a famous myth, treated in tragedies by Aeschylus, Sophocles and Euripides, but whichever rendition Crates saw, he was so moved that he sold his lands and effects, and distributed the money to the Theban people: a characteristic Cynic act of renunciation. Whether true or not, the anecdote might remind one of Gautama (the Buddha), who gave up luxury and status when he saw an old man, a sick person, a corpse, a monk and realized that life is suffering – or, in a word, tragedy.

Unlike the handsome Gautama, however, Crates is said to have been ugly, a cripple and, in old age, a hunchback (DL 6.91–2). The classical Greeks could be competitive, hard and even cruel: Crates was often mocked for his appearance. Menander and Philemon mention him in their comedies, probably mainly as a butt of jokes. And yet he seems to have been liked also, and in modern scholarship is often contrasted with Diogenes, as if he represented Cynic kindness in contrast to Diogenes' truculence. He became famous, at least in legend, for his *philanthrōpia*, and was nicknamed "the Door Opener", because he used to visit people in their homes to talk philosophy (6.86). The name is ambiguous but it seems more likely that the doors were opened for him than that he beat his way in since he was also called "the Good Daimōn" (Jul. *Or.* 6.201b–c; cf. Apul. *Flor.* 22), as if his house calls were thought to bring prosperity and good luck. Certainly he was loved by the well-born Hipparchia, who married him despite the scandal caused, and with whom he had a son Pasicles (DL 6.88)[21] and possibly a daughter (6.93). Plutarch wrote a *Life of Crates* (now lost; Jul. *Or.* 6.200b), an exceptional fact given that his other *Lives* are about "noble Grecians and Romans" such as Pericles, Alexander and Caesar. One can guess his reasons: Crates was a fellow-Boeotian and Plutarch was quite patriotic; Crates, like a Phocion or Cato, exemplified heroic superiority to fortune and life's vicissitudes; and Crates was a good writer, with Diogenes Laertius even comparing his style to Plato's (DL 6.98) – quite a compliment.

Crates was indeed a versatile and inventive writer, composing elegies, hymns, tragedies, parodies of Homer and of Solon, letters and literary diaries and wills: essentially inventing new literary forms. He seems also to have been a wit and free thinker, to judge by titles and extant fragments, particularly his *paignia* ("frolics" or "caprices"), such as his "Praise of Lentil Soup" (lost), or the "diary-book of a profligate", whom he portrays balancing his budget:

> For the cook, reserve ten minae, for the doctor a drachma,
> For the flatterer five talents, and smoke for the counsellor,
> A talent for the whore, and for the philosopher, three
>   obols.   (DL 6.86)

There were six obols in a drachma, one hundred drachma per mina, and sixty minae per talent. That makes 36,000 obols in a talent, and so the profligate would pay 12,000 times more for a prostitute than for a philosopher, and even more for a yes-man. Of course one should not be overly fussy about Crates' numbers. What is amusing is Crates' ironical assumption of a persona, and his fantastical exaggeration that shows up the waster's misplaced priorities: three obols was a proverbially paltry sum, and so the "profligate" spends least on what is most important. Ancient readers must have enjoyed the poem, as Diogenes Laertius says that it was "celebrated" (6.86).

Another famous poem is Crates' description of the Cynic utopia, or *Pēra*:

> There is a city, *Pēra*, in the middle of wine-dark smoke (*typhos*), beautiful and with rich soil, washed by dirt, possessing nothing. To it sail no fools or parasites or lechers drooling at some whore's behind. Instead it brings forth thyme and garlic and figs and loaves of bread. For such things nobody fights wars, and here they do not arm themselves to battle for coin or glory. (DL 6.85)

It is a clever adaptation of the epic style, with ingenious substitutions for Homer's "wine-dark sea" and "sea-washed island". More generally, it parodies Homer's description of Crete, home of king Idomeneus. Crete was mountainous, poor and fairly marginal, on the outskirts of the Greek world and so it was here that the older Plato would locate his second-best utopia of Magnesia, isolated by mountains and sea, happy in its isolation from the entangling alliances and foreign wars of the outside world. Crates' parody has similar implications. It locates "utopia" on an island that has no great wealth to attract invading armies or pimps from the "sex industry". Crates' Pēra is rich in simple goods and, like the medieval land of Cocaigne, abounds with the simple foods of a Cynic diet, if not with milk and honey. Most of all, Pēra is not so much an external place as a state of mind. The word Pēra sounds like the name of a city but it simply means "traveller's bag", and so the hobo-Cynic carries his little sack of utopia along with him, and wherever he goes across the wide-wayed earth, he is at home. If these richly imaginative lines are representative of Crates' language, it is clear why he attracted "settlers" to his "city" and became a sort of second leader among the early Cynics. His followers included Metrocles, Monimus, Menippus, Cleomenes, Theombrotus (DL 6.95) and Zeno of Citium. Zeno went on to found the Stoic school, arguably the most influential in antiquity. But Crates had his greatest influence over one person, a woman: Hipparchia.

Hipparchia

Hipparchia is portrayed by Diogenes Laertius as a very marriage-able young woman who, when the important moment came, dismissed all her parents' practical concerns and fear of scandal. No, she would not marry for money, pedigree or even good looks, and all the suitors would have to be sent away. Hipparchia would have Crates only; Crates was "her everything", and if she could not have him, she would kill herself. When her parents asked Crates to persuade her to see reason, he presented himself naked to her and said curtly, "This is the bridegroom, here are his possessions, decide on this basis" (DL 6.96). But Hipparchia was not to be scared off. She married poor, lame, ugly Crates and henceforth they were inseparable. Hipparchia would appear with her beloved in public: she ate meals with Crates outdoors, and later denigrators sneered that they had sex in public.[22] She must have been a forceful woman if any or all of this is true, for upper-class women especially were expected to stay at home, hidden in the women's quarters. She was probably intelligent also. The *Suda*, a tenth-century Byzantine encyclopaedia, says tantalizingly that she wrote books entitled *Philosophical Subjects*, *Explorations* and *Questions for Theodorus the Atheist* (*Suda* I.517); Diogenes Laertius attributes some clever syllogisms to her. Unfortunately, however, Laertius includes only a few of the "myriad" stories told about this very free spirit (DL 6.98). There were only a handful of female philosophers in antiquity but Hipparchia, with her "dog-marriage" (*kynogamia*), was certainly the most colourful.

Metrocles

Hipparchia's brother was Metrocles of Maroneia. Little is known about the man, although Diogenes Laertius includes the story that he was "converted" to the "dog-philosophy" by a fart or, to be precise, a pair of farts. Metrocles had been studying with Theophrastus, the successor to Aristotle as head of the Lyceum, a taxonomist and classificatory thinker with a specialty in botany. Once while declaiming, Metrocles farted audibly and was so ashamed that he shut himself away from public view and thought of starving himself to death. But Crates visited him, fed him with lupin-beans, and advanced various arguments to convince him that his action was not wrong or unnatural, and had been for the best in fact. Then Crates capped his exhortation with a great fart of his own. "From that day on Metrocles started to listen to Crates' discourses and became a capable man in philosophy" (DL 6.94). Such is Diogenes Laertius' laughable, deadpan conclusion, and this is the Cynic's point: everything is laughable, there is nothing serious in mortality and one should not wrinkle one's brow with Aristotelian jargon or be ashamed of any natural functions. Other philosophers may write their *Exhortations to Philosophy* (*Protreptikoi Logoi*, a common genre), but Crates makes his point more concisely. In any case, Metrocles was a changed man: he burned his poetic compositions as "imaginings of underworldly dreams", or, by other accounts, his notes from Theophrastus' lectures (6.95). All this was *typhos*, cleared away by Crates' philosophical flatulence.

Hellenistic period (*c.*300–50 BCE): Onesicritus, Bion, Menippus, Meleager, Oenomaus and others

Onesicritus

Onesicritus' (*c.*380–305 BCE) conversing with the Indian "gymnosophists" is symbolic of the new cultural and political situation of the "Hellenistic" era. From the 350s BCE, Philip II of Macedon had gradually expanded Macedonian power, now by cunning, now by open force, until in 338 in the momentous battle of Chaeronea, he defeated the allied forces of Athens and Thebes, effectively making himself leader of all mainland Greece. His son Alexander consolidated these gains in brutal fashion when he razed Thebes in 335 BCE. Henceforth, the old Greek cities would rarely enjoy their traditional political freedoms but would have to learn to pay court to Alexander's Successor kings, in Macedon, Asia and even Egypt. Yet, the new order brought many opportunities too for individual Greeks. Alexander had conquered territory from Macedonia to the Indus River, founding Alexandria in Egypt, as well as many other Alexandrias and Greek-style cities in lands as distant as northern Afghanistan. In subsequent generations, many Greeks and Macedonians emigrated to colonize these new cities, particularly in Ptolemaic Egypt and Seleucid Syria. Some of these foreign cities became new centres of Hellenic culture, notably Alexandria, Tarsus (later the birthplace of St Paul), Antioch, and Gadara (home to the Cynics Menippus, Meleager and Oenomaus). As individuals went to and fro between cities and kingdoms, and Greeks from the old cities mixed in foreign capitals, a new "common dialect" of Greek appeared (the *Koinē*), old tribal loyalties became less important, and people increasingly tended to identify themselves less by their place of birth than by their interests, patrons, language, philosophy and religion. It was a more cosmopolitan age: here Cynicism could flourish and proliferate.

Many of the Hellenistic Cynics are little more than names to us: Theombrotus, Cleomenes, Demetrius and Timarchus of Alexandria, Echecles of Ephesus, Menedemus and Menippus. Others, such as Onesicritus, are somewhat more accessible. Onesicritus was an islander from Astypalaea. At some point in his life he associated with Diogenes in Athens, but at some later point (again details are lost), he joined Alexander's army. He must have distinguished himself in various ways, because he was chosen as head pilot of Alexander's flagship (or perhaps even the whole fleet) as the Macedonian forces travelled down the Hydaspes and Indus Rivers and out into the Indian Ocean on their long return journey to Babylon. In this journey, Onesicritus saw and recorded many "wonders" in books such as his *Periplus* and overly encomiastic biography of Alexander. After Alexander's death, Onesicritus eventually settled in Thrace, in the court of King Lysimachus, whom he sometimes bemused by reading from his fabulous histories (Plut. *Alex.* 46). For these, he would often be remembered as a teller of sailors' tales.

Yet one of Onesicritus' reports is probably true in outline at least. In India, it was Onesicritus, former student of Diogenes, who was chosen by Alexander to head the delegation in spring 326 BCE to meet certain Indian sages, who had much influence among their warlike people. Onesicritus calls them "gymnosophists" (literally, "naked sophists") because they lived naked, outdoors and in complete poverty, meditating, conversing and offering advice to those who consulted them. The passage from Strabo is worth quoting in full, as it may echo Onesicritus' own words:

> Onesicritus says he was sent to converse with these soph-
> ists. Alexander had heard that they went naked, that they
> practiced endurance, and that they were held in great honor.
> They were not wont to come when summoned, but urged
> those who intended to profit by their deeds and conversa-
> tions to seek them out. Accordingly, Onesicritus was sent,
> as it seemed improper for Alexander to go himself, or to
> force them to violate their custom unwillingly. He found
> fifteen men twenty stades from the city, one in one posture,
> one in another – standing, sitting or lying naked until
> evening. In the evening they would return to the city. The
> sun was so hot that anyone else could hardly endure touch-
> ing the ground with his bare feet. He addressed one of their
> number, Calanus, the man who later followed the King as far
> as Persia, where he met his end in accordance with ancestral
> custom, dying on a funeral pyre. At the time this man was
> lying on some stones. Approaching, and addressing him by
> name, Onesicritus said that he had been sent by the King
> to hear and report their wisdom. If no one objected, he was
> anxious to hear them discourse. Observing that Onesicritus

wore a cloak, a broad-brimmed hat and high boots, Calanus burst out laughing. "In the olden days," he said, "barley and wheat and flour were as common as dust is now. There were springs of water, of milk, of honey, of wine and even some springs of olive oil. From surfeit and luxury man fell into indolent ways. Zeus, despising the state of affairs, took everything away, offering man a life of hardship (*ponos*). Moderation and every other virtue becoming common, there was again an abundance of good things. But now, once more, the condition of satiety and insolence draws near, so probably everything will be taken away again."

When Calanus had finished he told Onesicritus to remove his clothes if he wanted to listen, and to join in their conversation lying naked on the stones. While Onesicritus hesitated, Mandanis, the oldest and wisest of them, rebuked Calanus for being an insolent fellow, even though he had been declaiming against insolence. But he called Onesicritus, and said that he praised the King, because he still sought after wisdom, despite the fact that he ruled such a large empire; for he was the only man he knew who played the philosopher in arms. The best thing that could happen would be for such a man, who had the power, to persuade the amenable to practice self-control, and to force the recalcitrant to do so. He hoped that he might be excused if he failed to give a profitable demonstration, for he had to speak through three interpreters, who, except for languages, knew no more than the rabble. It was like expecting clean water to float through mud. Mandanis' remarks, Onesicritus said, tended to show that the best doctrine was that which freed the soul from pleasure and pain. Pain and hardship are different, the one being hostile, the other friendly to man. Bodies are exercised by hardship (*ponos*) so that the understanding (*gnōmē*) may be strengthened. Civil strife may then be ended, and good counsel prevail in public matters and in private matters. Mandanis said he had advised Taxiles [i.e. an Indian war-leader] to submit to Alexander, for if Alexander were the better man he ought to obey him, and if he were not he might improve him. When Mandanis had finished speaking, he asked whether such doctrines were held by the Greeks. Onesicritus replied that Pythagoras held such views and that he had enjoined abstinence from living things, and that Socrates and also Diogenes, whom he had heard himself, held such views. Mandanis said that while in all other respects he thought they seemed wise men, yet that they had made an error in placing law (*nomos*) before nature (*physis*). Had they not done so they would not be ashamed to go naked like him, living a simple life; that the best house was the one needing the least furnishings. Mandanis said that they (i.e. the Indian sages) had made a study of nature – about prognostications, clouds, droughts and diseases.

When they returned to the city the sophists dispersed in the market places. Whenever they met someone carrying figs or grapes, they helped themselves without payment, or if it were oil that was being carried, the oil was poured out and they were anointed. The door of every rich man's house was open to them, even the women's apartments. Entering, they shared in the dinner as well as in the conversation. Bodily illness they regarded as very shameful. A man who feared that he had such an ailment would remove himself with fire. Heaping up a pyre, anointing himself and sitting on the pyre, he would order it to be kindled, and then remain motionless while he was burned.

(Strabo 15.1.64–5; trans. in Brown [1949] 1981: 38–9)[23]

In Onesicritus' description, the Indian sages differ from the Cynics in their study of nature and in the high honours they enjoy from their people. But in other respects, they are depicted almost as perfect Cynics: they insolently denounce human insolence and luxury; they have fully transcended *nomos* to live fully in accordance with nature; they embrace ascetic hardship (*ponos*) as a means of self-perfection, and as a means of quelling social strife between the "haves" and "have-nots"; they are superior to kings, who must come courting them for advice; and when they grow too old, they end their lives voluntarily.

Bion

Bion of Borysthenes (*c.*335–*c.*245 BCE) led a colourful life too, although one quite different from Onesicritus. According to Diogenes Laertius, Bion was born in Borysthenes, on the northern shore of the Black Sea, the son of a fish-seller and a prostitute. When his father fell into debt, the whole family was sold and separated and from this moment Bion would be jerked about by fortune, sometimes prosperous, and sometimes not. Bought by an orator, he lived as his slave and student, but when the orator died he left Bion everything, thus enabling him around 314 BCE to travel to Athens, where he turned philosopher: a rags-to-"riches" story? Bion may have indeed described himself as a modern Odysseus, for he quoted Odysseus' boasts as if his own, gaining the epithet *polytropos* ("many-wayed") from Diogenes Laertius. As a philosophical Odysseus, his intellectual wanderings in Athens made him in turn a student of Xenocrates the Academic, of the Cynics, of Theodorus "the godless" (one of the few ancient atheists), and of Theophrastus the Peripatetic. From this varied philosophical education he moved on to an illustrious career, teaching in Rhodes, proclaiming speeches in many Greek cities, and eventually living under the patronage of the Macedonian king Antigonus Gonatas as a sort of adviser and court philosopher. Obviously talented enough to gain the respect of Antigonus, he also won himself many enemies who would portray him as a "cynical" self-promoter. In their eyes, he flouted all accepted philosophical precepts by living extravagantly, charging fees like a sophist, gathering students to himself as lovers and bodyguards, and in Rhodes even paying sailors to dress up as students and follow him around like retainers. Bion's detractors also vilified him as a shameless hypocrite: in life (they said), he followed Theodorus "the atheist" in attacking the gods, but when the moment of truth came and Bion himself faced death, he proved himself a superstitious coward – he "allowed an old woman to put a charm round his neck, and in full faith bound his arms with leather and placed the rhamnus and the laurel-branch over the door" (4.56–7). So his enemies reported the death of this "many-coloured sophist" (*sophistēs poikilos*) (4.47). He was many-coloured indeed, but the fragments of his writings seem closer to Cynicism than other philosophies, with their criticism of luxury, wealth and pleasure, their recommendation of self-sufficiency and living in the present, their praise of individual freedom and scorn for intellectual pursuits such as mathematics and metaphysics. As a result, J. F. Kindstrand concludes that Bion "proves to be mainly a Cynic" (1976: 67), even though his Cynicism is largely of the literary variety, for clearly Bion made some accommodations with the world, taking fee-paying students, and himself accepting the patronage of a king.

Bion is perhaps most important for his shaping of the diatribe, a style of writing that has been closely associated with the Cynics and Stoics. Originally, the word *diatribē* had the general meaning of "a way of passing the time"; it later came to mean more specifically a conversation, and then a philosophical conversation. In the hands of successors of Bion, the diatribe style seems to have been a way of talking aloud in writing: the speaker "shadow-boxes" with an imaginary interlocutor, throwing out punchy questions or objections on the interlocutor's behalf, and then moving in to answer them himself. The traditional scholarly view was that Bion "invented" the diatribe as a new genre but more detailed research throws doubt on this overly exact judgement.[24] In any case, Bion's style is thought to have impressed many later authors: Roman satirists such as Lucilius, Horace[25] and Juvenal; Stoics such as Aristo, Seneca and Epictetus; late sophists such as Synesius and Themistius; and Christian sermon-writers such as Gregory of Nazianzus. Most of all, they provided models for the seven fragmentary diatribes of the Cynic Teles of Megara (*c.*250 BCE): *On Appearance and Reality, On Self-Sufficiency, On Exile, That Pleasure is not the Goal, Comparison of Wealth and Virtue, On Circumstances* and *On Comfort.*[26]

If Bion did inspire such a range of later authors, Greek, Roman and Christian, this would give an idea of the talent of this "many-coloured sophist", and of the literary creativity of Cynics in the Hellenistic period. We have seen instances of Crates' inventiveness, and shall see more in the works of Menippus, Meleager and Lucian. Other more minor Cynics also testify to this remarkable flowering that helped reinvigorate and reshape Greek literature. Cercidas of Megalopolis (c.290–220 BCE) was a highly individual figure: respected leader and legislator for his Megalopolitans; a general who led his citizens in the battle of Sellasia (222 BCE) where Sparta's power was crushed by Macedonia and the Achaean League; a littérateur who admired Pythagoras, Hecataeus and most of all Homer; and most importantly for our purposes, a "dog" who espoused Cynic principles as he wrote blistering satires of the wealthy, arrogant Peloponnesians of his day, poems that recalled the fire of an Archilochus and Hipponax, but in a metre that was of Cercidas' own making, the so-called meliambus. Other lyric poets of the third and second centuries BCE were not Cynics themselves (like Cercidas), but nevertheless seem to register some Cynic influence. Leonidas of Tarentum celebrates peasants, fishers and decent, hardworking, frugal folk, in a way that looks forward to Dio Chrysostom's *Euboean Discourse*. Sotades of Maroneia (home also to Hipparchia and Metrocles) was known for his foul language and unrestrained satire of kings such as Lysimachus and Ptolemy Philadelphus, and for his invention of the Sotadean metre. He speaks sometimes of the unpredictability of fortune, which he had to suffer himself when, because of his mocking *parrhēsia* towards Ptolemy, the king had him pursued, arrested, locked in a leaden chest, and thrown into the sea. Phoenix of Colophon is a moralistic poet whose fragments have been regarded as Cynic in tone, at least by Gerhard in his lengthy commentaries. The work of writers such as these, and the proliferation of Cynic themes generally, have inspired various observers to make some strong claims: "Among philosophers and moralists, it's the Cynics who show the most literary enterprise" (Parsons 1993: 167). Another commentator argues that: "a great deal (though not all) Hellenistic gnomic poetry may be attributed, directly, or indirectly to the Cynics" (Wilson 1991: 64). And yet another describes Cynicism as "the most literarily inventive philosophical movement

... The map of Greek literature simply wasn't the same after the Cynics" (Bracht Branham 1996: 82–5).[27]

Menippus

Perhaps the most important of the "literary" Cynics was Menippus of Gadara (flourished first half of third century BCE). He was the first of three famous Cynics from a city in eastern Syria that has been called a "city of philosophers" and was an important centre of Hellenic culture. Refounded by Seleucus Nicator in the Greek style with an acropolis and agora, Gadara would go on to acquire baths, two theatres, a hippodrome, colonnaded streets and, under the Romans, aqueducts (see Weber & Khouri 1989: 17–18). It would also become part of the Decapolis, a league of ten cities that banded together after the decline of their Seleucid protectors to ward off Jewish and Arabian influence. The strong Greek presence in these cities is clear from some of their Macedonian names: Pella, Dion, Philadelphia, Hippos and Gadara (Macedonian Gadeira). Gadara itself would become the birthplace of three Cynics (Menippus, Meleager, Oenomaus), an Epicurean (Philodemus), a mathematician (Philo), and two orators (Theodorus, who taught Tiberius, and Apsines). Its warm and cold baths were famous: the neo-Pythagorean Iamblichus performed a wonder there; the empress Eudocia, wife of Theodosius II, praised them in Homeric verse; and the city's name was associated with one of Jesus' miracles, to which we shall return in Chapter 6.

Despite his great influence, Menippus of Gadara is a wraithlike figure about whose life little is really known. His dates are approximately 300–250 BCE and indeed even his place of birth is sometimes disputed, for some say he came from Sinope, not Gadara.[28] According to Diogenes Laertius, he returned to the Black Sea at some point, when he was enslaved to Batus of Pontus. Later again, he made it to Thebes, where he met Crates (DL 6.95; cf. Luc. *Fugitivi* 11). Diogenes Laertius clearly disliked him, calls him a "Cretan dog", and slanders him as a money-lender, or, more precisely, a *hēmerodaneistēs*,

one of the petty usurers who lent money for a single day and typically charged extortionate rates. According to Diogenes Laertius,
Menippus lost all possessions to a thief and committed suicide
in despair (DL 6.100). Even more dubious is the statement in the
Suda:

> Menippus the Cynic went to such a degree of marvel-
> mongering that he adopted the get-up of a Fury, saying that
> he had come up from Hades as an inspector of sins and would
> go down again to report them to the powers there. His cloth-
> ing for this included a grey (*phaios*), ankle-length cloak, tied
> with a purple belt, an Arcadian cap on his head, interwo-
> ven with the twelve signs (i.e. of the Zodiac), tragic boots, a
> massive bead, and a staff of ash in his hand.   (*Suda*)

When, where, why, for how long or even if Menippus pulled this
prank is unknown. All we have is the *Suda* entry, which is actually
an entry for the word "grey" (*phaios*), not for Menippus himself.
And Diogenes Laertius tells the same story about Menedemus, in
almost identical terms (DL 6.102). Joel Relihan (1993: 45–6) takes it,
however, as "a very important testimonium" concerning Menippus
and links it to a fragment from Varro (F539); to the motley attire
of Lucian's Menippus, who returns from the underworld with
Odysseus' hat, Orpheus' lyre and Heracles' lion skin; and to the
general association of Menippus with journeys to the underworld.
If then, as Relihan suggests, it contains the shadow of some truth,
the *Suda* entry depicts Menippus in the pose he may have typically
adopted: an observer of human failings, a messenger from another
world, even a representative of the gods, this Fury-Menippus has the
Cynic's beard and staff, but he wears an *Arcadian* cap (like a poor
traveller), a *purple* belt (like a king), and the twelve Zodiacal signs
(like a Magus).

Equally elusive is what Menippus wrote, how he wrote, for whom,
in what tone and with what precise effect. Diogenes Laertius quotes
various sources for Menippus' writings, but he is clearly uneasy with
the thirteen titles that he finally lists: "*Nekyia, Wills, Clever Letters*

from the Gods, Against Natural Scientists and Mathematicians and Grammarians, Birthday of Epicurus, The Epicurean Reverence for the Twentieth Day, and others" (DL 6.101). Among these unspecified "others" may be the *Sale of Diogenes* (6.29), *Arcesilaus*[29] and a *Symposium* (Ath. 629e=14.27.18). Diogenes Laertius claims that "there is no seriousness" in Menippus' books, which are filled with mockery. Marcus Aurelius also places Menippus at the forefront of the "mockers of the mortal and ephemeral life of mankind" (*Med.* 6.47). Others summarize Meleager as *spoudogeloios* and Lucian admires Menippus because he was "truly a dog" who "laughed while biting" (Luc. *Bis Acc.* 33), thinking perhaps of the way a dog's lips curl up when it is biting, as if in a grin.[30]

For whom Menippus wrote is unclear, and many important works that seem to bear his influence survive only in fragments. Foremost among these are Varro's *Saturae Menippeae*, whose very title inaugurated a literary genre of sorts. These *Menippean Satires* were written in the general style of Menippus and, from Mras's study (1914), the Cynic themes visited by Varro (e.g. criticism of the rich and of luxury, promotion of water-drinking) would seem to be so extensive that one can understand the later nicknames given to Varro: the Menippean, the Roman Cynic (*Romanus Cynicus*) and Diogenes with a Roman pen (*Romani stili Diogenes*).[31] Lucian's favourite character is Menippus, whom he puts centre stage in the *Menippus, Icaromenippus* and many of the *Dialogues of the Dead*.[32] The mixture of prose and verse in Seneca's *Apocolocyntosis*, Petronius' *Satyricon*, Boethius' *Consolatio Philosophiae*, Apuleius' *Metamorphoses*, and Martius Capella's *Wedding of Philology and Mercury* might all hark back to a similarly prosimetric style in Menippus. Altogether, it seems to be a very variegated legacy, which will grow even more motley in the medieval and modern worlds (see Chapter 6). In the historical Menippus we have the curious situation of a person whose life and works were obscure even by the time of Diogenes Laertius (perhaps *c.*200 CE) but whose writings somehow inspired a wide variety of authors, both Roman and Greek. It is not for nothing then that Menippus has often been likened to the grinning Cheshire Cat of that latter-day Menippean, Lewis Carroll.[33] His grinning cat is more grin than cat, and so too with Menippus: the original is lost amid a hall of mirrors, a kaleidoscope of shifting and proliferating images.

Meleager

A fellow-citizen of Menippus was Meleager of Gadara (*c.*135–50 BCE). He acknowledges his debt to Menippus several times, for he wrote certain "Menippean Graces" (*Menippeae Charites*) (Ath. 157a; cf. *AG* 7.417, 418) and perhaps a *Symposium* (Ath. 502c) under his influence. Diogenes Laertius couples the two Gadarenes, carping that Meleager's writings are as filled with mockery as those of Menippus (DL 6.99). Meleager himself claims to mix laughter and seriousness (*AG* 7.421.9–10) and stresses that "grace" or charm (*charis*) is the distinguishing mark of his writing, which blends the Muses, the Graces and wisdom (7.421).[34] These more properly Cynic works are now lost, and what remains are Meleager's contributions to the *Anthologia Graeca*, an anthology of Greek verse collected and augmented by different hands over many centuries. In fact, Meleager was one of the first to begin to weave this "garland" of poetic flowers and he remains one of the most important poets in the final collection. Meleager himself dedicated his collection to "glorious Diocles" (4.1.3), the same Diocles who was a major source of information on Cynicism for Diogenes Laertius, and thus indirectly for us.

Yet, despite Meleager's clear affiliation with the movement, in his poems Cynic themes have all but faded away. The most notable exception is the note of Cynic cosmopolitanism in his own epitaph. Here he summarizes his life, saying that he was born in Gadara ("Athens in Syria"), grew up in "holy Tyre", and became a citizen of the island of Cos, where he died a contented, chatty old man (*AG* 7.417–419). To Aramaic-speaking passers-by, this friendly Meleager says "Salam!", to Phoenicians "Naidios!", and to Greeks "Chaire!" (7.419.7–8). Thus, differences of nationality and speech make no difference: it is "the one Chaos that has made us all" and the cosmos as a whole is "one fatherland" (7.417.6–7). Other poems, however, are positively un-Cynic in their sentiments, and so Meleager has often been counted among the "soft" or "hedonistic" Cynics, who avoid the hard asceticism of a Diogenes. His love epigrams and verse epitaphs, especially, have little of the typical Cynic's steely scorn for fortune and contempt for romantic entanglements. In one, for instance, he curses Fate (*Moira*) as an "evil maiden", barren and careless of a mother's grief, for *Moira* killed young Charixenus, aged eighteen, leaving his friends and parents in despair (7.468). Meleager himself mourns the death of Heliodora, who was his lover and torturer, troubling his dreams, ruining his sleep, scorching his soul (7.476) – and altogether destroying any sense of self-sufficiency, one might add. Zenophila, Timarion, Demo and other lovers also subjected him to the erratic fortunes of a lover, so that in two poems he even begs a cicada and locust to sing, so that he might sleep and forget the *ponoi* of love (7.195–196). Tender imagination even leads Meleager to write epigrams on the long-eared hare that Phanion nursed with spring-flowers (7.207); or on Pan, who will go to live in the city now that his Daphnis is dead, for what pleasure can he have in dancing on the mountains when Daphnis is there no more (7.535)? One might hear faint Cynic echoes in the facetious lines to a mosquito: fly, mosquito, to Zenophila's bed, and if you can wake her (without waking my rival) and bring her to me, then for your heroic deed, I will honour you with Heracles' club and lion skin (5.152). But in general, Meleager's delicate, witty and graceful poems betray few hints of why he was known as a "dog".

Oenomaus

This is not the case with the final Gadarene Cynic, Oenomaus. Oenomaus lived over two hundred years after Meleager, in the second century CE, when philosophy and Hellenism generally were enjoying the imperial favour of emperors such as Hadrian. Oenomaus' books include *On Cynicism, Republic, Concerning Homer's Philosophy, Concerning Crates, Diogenes and the Rest, Oracles directly from the Dog* and some tragedies.[35] Most well known, however, is his bitter

Detection of Impostors, which Eusebius quotes at great length in his own refutation of the pagan oracles. Eusebius' quotation runs over seventeen chapters, and makes clear that at least in part of his book, Oenomaus rampaged through the most celebrated oracles of Greek antiquity, mocking and debunking them all as foolish, tautologous, idiotic and unworthy of a god (Euseb. *Praep. evang.* 5.18–36). In Eusebius' selection, these include the oracle that the Athenians send fourteen youths each year as punishment for the murder of Androgeos, Minos' son; the oracle to the Heracleidae; the oracle that Croesus would destroy a great empire if he crossed the Halys river; the two oracles to the Athenians during Xerxes' great invasion, and before the battle of Salamis; the oracle to the Spartans before Thermopylae that either their city would be besieged, or they would mourn a king killed; the oracle to the Cnidians besieged by Harpagus; the oracles to the Lacedaemonians against the Messenians, and to the Messenians against the Lacedaemonians; the oracle to Lycurgus, giving him Sparta's mythic law code; and so forth in a treasure trove of oracular responses, public and private through the centuries. With all of these, Oenomaus will have no truck. All are discredited for some reason: they are stupid, obvious, irrelevant, deceitfully ambiguous, or mere poetic highfalutin. The oracle to the Athenians, for example – "O Holy Salamis, you will destroy the off-spring of women,/ When men scatter the seed, or when they gather in the harvest" – only says the obvious, because in a battle "children of women" will die, but Apollo did not specify whether they would be children of Persian or Greek women. Furthermore, a naval battle cannot occur in the winter, so by mentioning spring and summer, the Delphic priests effectively covered the rest of the year. As for the correct prognostication about the "wooden wall", that, Oenomaus carps, was "advice", not prophecy. From such fevered denunciations of the "sophists of Delphi and Dodona", Oenomaus generalizes that the oracles have brought only obscurity, deceit, unprofitable wars and suffering (Euseb. *Praep. evang.* 5.25). To Oenomaus, they were human, all-too-human, institutions driven by the greed of the priests and Delphians. One must remember that the oracles reflected the belief in the gods' providential oversight of mankind, and the

Delphic oracle was especially revered. Therefore, for Oenomaus to launch such a cynical and violent polemic against it would have been highly offensive, even at a time when the oracles were in decline.[36] Two centuries later, the emperor Julian was offended, and said that Oenomaus' tragedies and other writings were full of similar blasphemy. Julian for one abominated him as a "shameless dog" and claimed that Oenomaus did not reflect the spirit of the true Cynicism of Diogenes and Crates (Jul. *Or.* 7.209b–c, 7.210d–211a). This probably reflects Julian's own ardent religious temperament, however: Oenomaus may in fact be fairly representative of the Cynics' loud criticism of traditional pagan religion and its paraphernalia.

Roman Period (*c.*50 BCE–500 CE): Favonius, Demetrius, Dio Chrysostom, Epictetus, Lucian, Demonax, Peregrinus, Julian and others

Oenomaus' attack on prophecy is an interesting one, not least because it seems to stand at a great crossroads in the ancient world. In itself, it is almost wholly retrospective, as it quotes the oracles of old archaic and classical Greece, which were by then many centuries in the past. Yet we can read Oenomaus only thanks to Eusebius, Bishop of Caesarea. Eusebius, writing in the early 300s CE in the time of Constantine the Great, found Oenomaus' polemics useful for dividing the pagans, discrediting the old religion, and promoting Christianity, which had its own prophets. Thus, Oenomaus' backward-looking tirade unwittingly looks forward to the decline of the pagan world itself. Furthermore, in reading Oenomaus' fragments, one would hardly realize that Oenomaus lived in times quite different from those of Croesus, Diogenes or even his fellow-citizens Menippus and Meleager. For their Gadara was now ruled by western "barbarians" called Romans, and Oenomaus' ultimate overlord was not a Greek-speaking Seleucid king, but a Latin-speaking emperor named Hadrian. The world had changed, externally at least, since Meleager wrote his poems to Zenophila, and Cercidas fought at Sellasia. Let us retrace our steps, therefore, and survey some of the events that had profoundly affected the cities around the Cynics' Mediterranean.

By the middle of the first century BCE, the Romans were consolidating their power over much of the Mediterranean and gradually learning to call it *mare nostrum*, "our sea". Contact between Romans and Greeks had intensified from the third century BCE onward: in 280 BCE Pyrrhus landed with his elephants and phalanx to defend Greek Tarentum from the Romans. He won his "Pyrrhic victories" at Heraclea and Ausculum, but in 275 at Beneventum the Romans had their revenge and took the old Greek cities in southern Italy. A generation later, Rome's eventual victory in the First Punic War (264–241 BCE) gave it Sicily as a province. To this during the Second Punic War was added Syracuse, one of the greatest Greek cities, home to Theocritus and Archimedes. In the next two centuries, Roman legions won major victories over all the Hellenistic kingdoms: over Macedonia at Cynoscephalae (197 BCE) and Pydna (168 BCE); over Seleucid Syria and Asia at Magnesia (190 BCE); and, finally, over Ptolemaic Egypt at Actium (31 BCE). The Attalid kingdom of Pergamum, with its library and altar to Zeus, was bequeathed to the Roman senate and people by its last king (133 BCE) and made a province.

Thus, one by one the Greek kingdoms fell. The Romans themselves were sometimes ambiguous about all their success, which seemed sanctioned by some divine fate, and yet brought arrogance, greed, laziness and decadent hedonism along with wealth and power. In particular, empire brought new influences into Rome and Latium, among which were those strangest of creatures, so bafflingly free-spirited and argumentative, the Greek philosophers. Roman ambiguity towards philosophy is encapsulated by the events of 155 BCE. In that year, the three leading Greek philosophers came as ambassadors from Athens to Rome, where the senate and people welcomed them. One of the three, Carneades – head of the Academy, now home to a sceptical philosophy – gave a speech in praise of justice that was well received. But the next day he gave a speech praising injustice and argued that the Roman Empire was based on it. A dubious sort of encomium this, and Carneades' dialectical display did not fully impress frank traditionalists such as Cato the Elder, who moved that the philosophers be banished from the city (Plut. *Cat. Mai.* 22). Although Cato did not utterly reject Greek learning – he studied Greek himself – he did fear the social effects of Greek ideas if popularized. His was a typical response among the traditionally cohesive Romans: the Greeks are fascinating, but fickle, undisciplined, quarrelsome, cunning and therefore dangerous. In Virgil's *Aeneid*, for example, the Greek Sinon swears false oaths on family and the gods, and betrays the trust of the Trojans, to the destruction of a whole city; well did Laocoon "fear the Greeks, even when bearing gifts"; later, Juvenal damningly portrays the "hungry Greekling" who can talk his way into anything; Seneca's father reportedly "hated philosophy". Cato feared that Greek philosophy would corrupt the youth and weaken the unity of the state and although he did not succeed in having Carneades expelled from Rome, on various later occasions philosophers were banished, and for similar reasons of state: in 161 BCE by the senate (Suet. *Gram.* 25.1; Gell. *NA* 15.11), in 65 CE by Nero, between 71 and 74 CE by Vespasian, in 89 and 94 CE by Domitian (Suet. *Dom.* 10.3; Cass. Dio 65). Individual philosophers were also targeted. In 173 BCE (Ath. 12.547a) as well as 154 CE some Epicureans were banished from Italy, and in 157 CE Peregrinus Proteus was ordered to leave Rome by the city prefect.[37]

Yet there were other responses, diametrically opposed to Cato's. From 98–180 CE, philosophy enjoyed the highest official respect among the Roman elite and was promoted as a unifying social force. The empire was regarded, in Stoic fashion, as a single "city" that mirrored the completeness and self-sufficiency of the universe. Hellenic culture was encouraged as a unifying spirit for this cosmic empire, and so, for example, Hadrian promoted Greek art, Marcus wrote in Greek and all the emperors took to wearing beards like the philosophers. Philosophical theories of kingship too may have inspired the "good emperors" to abandon the Julio-Claudian and Flavian principle of heredity and choose their successors on the basis of talent and merit: that is, the best man should be king.[38] This trend reaches its climax in the reign of Marcus Aurelius, Stoic and emperor, philosopher and king. In 176 CE, Marcus endowed two chairs in Athens for each of the four major schools (Academics, Peripatetics, Stoics, Epicureans). With such official support, philosophy enjoyed a surge in popularity, or at least Cassius Dio writes that many proclaimed their love of wisdom simply because the emperors were doing so (71.35).

This admiration for philosophy did not develop overnight, however, but was present alongside its opposite from the beginning. In 155 BCE Cato could propose banning the Greek thinkers only because he saw how awed the "Roman youth" were by their eloquence. To Cato's old guard, one can oppose figures such as Scipio Aemilianus and his circle (often made interlocutors in Cicero's philosophical dialogues), Brutus, Cicero, Lucretius, Seneca, Musonius Rufus, Annaeus Cornutus, and Marcus Aurelius. Roman poets from Horace and Virgil to Lucan and Persius read their Greek philosophers. Many young, rich Romans travelled to Athens, Rhodes or other Greek centres to study philosophy with the masters, in its native setting. And the masters in turn journeyed to Rome, to lecture publicly (e.g. Pliny the Younger *Ep.* 1.10), to act as tutors in wealthy houses[39] or, in the case of the Cynics, to rail against the vices of mankind in those places where they were most concentrated. To its critics, Rome was the new Babylon, the great "whore", who would do anything for power, wealth and pleasure, where "everything was for sale" (Sall. *Iug.* 8.1) and nothing was sacred. If previous Cynics attacked Athenian magistrates or Hellenistic kings, now Cynics would shift their aim to their Roman overlords.

This is one reason why Cynicism never took firm hold among the Romans and remained a phenomenon primarily of the Greek-speaking provinces of the East. Other reasons are that traditional Roman virtues could not accommodate the Cynics' anarchic individualism: Cynic shamelessness was incompatible with Roman *gravitas* and *decorum*; Cynic irreverence with Roman *pietas*; Cynic contempt for custom with Roman respect for the *mos maiorum*. In brief, high-minded but worldly Romans might find Cynicism antisocial, even cynical, self-indulgent, unpatriotic and ineffective. If one wants to be a hedonist, then be a proper hedonist. If one wants to revive the tough frugality of Cincinnatus, Horatius and the old Republic, then take up the new, politicized version of Stoic ethics. Thus Cicero, for all his inclusive eclecticism, warns categorically against listening "to the Cynics or those Stoics who are almost Cynics". Their primary sin is shamelessness, which violates not only the Roman virtues of *decorum* and *verecundia*, but contradicts nature itself (Cic. *Off.* 1.128). Significantly, Cicero's criticism is repeated almost exactly, four hundred years later, by Augustine, a North African Latin-speaker: Cynic shamelessness is not only unsocial, but positively unnatural (August. *De civ. D.* 14.20). Roman distaste for Cynic antics is reflected in poems such as Martial's contemptuous 4.53,[40] and in the fact that there were hardly any Roman Cynics, although judging by their Latin names, some have speculated that the Cynics Peregrinus and Crescens may have been Roman citizens.[41]

Favonius

Some Romans did play-act as Cynics, however. Favonius was a friend of Cato the Younger; aedile in 52 BCE, praetor in 49 BCE, but never consul, he was awarded the nickname "absolute dog" (*haplokyōn*) by Brutus owing to his abusive way of speaking (Plut. *Bru.* 34.7).[42] This Cynic-like *parrhēsia* would ultimately prompt his execution after the battles of Philippi (42 BCE). Given his political status, Favonius can hardly be called a Cynic in the fashion of Diogenes or Crates, and his Cynicism was probably more of a pose, a gesture towards the old Republican frugality that, in traditionalists' minds, had made Rome great. Thus, Plutarch records how Favonius entertained the Romans as aedile, with Cato's help:

> Afterwards, when Favonius was made aedile, Cato administered the duties of the office, including the theatrical spectacles, where he gave to the actors not gold crowns but crowns of wild olive (just as at the Olympic Games); and to the Greeks he gave not expensive presents but beets, lettuces, radishes, and pears; and to the Romans, he gave

earthen jars of wine, pork, figs, cucumbers, and bundles of wood. Some people laughed at the frugality (*euteleia*) of all this, others quietly enjoyed seeing Cato's austere intensity relax. Finally, Favonius threw himself into the crowd, sat down in the theatre, and started applauding Cato, shouting to him to honour the audience with gifts and at the same time calling on the spectators to honour Cato – for he had given all his authority over to Cato. In the other theatre meanwhile, Curio (fellow-aedile with Favonius) was putting on an extravagant display. But the people left him to go to Favonius' theatre where they joined in the game enthusiastically, as Favonius acted the part of a private person and Cato that of superintendent of the shows. He did this to ridicule the practice of giving lavish games, and to teach the people that when relaxing one ought to remain playful and conduct the spectacles with unconceited (*a-typhos*) grace rather than with extravagant preparations, by which one expends huge thought and concern on things that are in themselves worth nothing.   (Plut. *Cat. Min.* 46)[43]

Plutarch ends the story with a bit of heavy Cynic moralizing about the *typhos* of the Roman games but Favonius himself must have used a lighter touch. Certainly he must have had some charisma to pull a stunt like this among a Roman crowd that had grown used to being bribed with ever more lavish spectacles of gladiators, *venationes* and huge naval battles.

The name of "Cynic" would not enjoy popularity like this again in Rome. For if under the Republic high-minded Romans such as Brutus had frowned at Favonius' *parrhēsia*, the principate would bring conditions even more inhospitable for outspoken Cynics. Cynic *parrhēsia* arose first in the more egalitarian Greek cities of the classical period, but Roman society was highly aristocratic and unequal. The patron–client relationship had been a dominant one in the Republic and retained its hold under the principate, as the emperor himself served as chief patron, setting a standard for gift-giving and lavish display, in the form of games, baths, aqueducts and

other public works. Given the great inequalities in power, depend-
ents might hesitate to speak their minds openly and had to seethe in
private, like Juvenal in his *Satires* or Tacitus in his histories. Epictetus
makes this observation when he writes that it was safer to speak
bluntly to a fellow citizen in democratic Athens than to an ex-consul
in Rome (Epict. *Diss.* 2.12.17–26). Criticizing an emperor could be
particularly dangerous, to be punished as a crime against the majesty
of the empire itself (see Morford 2002: 161, 216).

Yet despite a sometimes stifling atmosphere, Cynics still pop
into the historical annals as public hecklers. When Nero was going
through the streets of Rome, the Cynic Isidorus passed a comment:
"You sing the misfortunes of Nauplius well, but behave badly yourself" (Suet. *Ner.* 39.3). Nero responded by banishing Isidorus from
Rome and Italy. In 75 CE one Diogenes, "a dog-sophist", stepped forth
in a packed Roman theatre to mock Titus and his mistress Berenice;
in punishment, he was flogged. When one Heras stepped up to take
his place and said "many strange things in Cynic-style", Titus had
him beheaded (Cass. Dio 65.15.4). Lucian tells the story of the Cynic
in Athens who stood up on a stone and started to mock a Roman
proconsul, saying that he was a passive homosexual (*kinaidos*)
because he used to remove all his bodily hair. The Roman official
debated whether to have him beaten, put in the stocks or exiled.
But Demonax, a Cynic of the kindlier sort, advised him to pardon
the man: he was only exercising his *parrhēsia*, he said, "according to
the customary law" of the Cynics, but if he did it again, he should
himself be depilated (Luc. *Demon.* 50).[44]

The "Stoic Opposition"

All of these were petty subversives in comparison with the majesty
of Rome, but at times the trouble spread higher, even to the point of
worrying several Roman emperors, notably Nero and the Flavians
(Vespasian, Titus, Domitian). Through their reigns, a so-called "Stoic
Opposition" formed against the principate and the principle of one-
man rule. This group over some two generations included such names

as the stoicizing senators Rubellius Plautus, Thrasea Paetus, Barea Soranus, Helvidius Priscus, Hostilianus, Paconius Agrippinus, and others such as the tribune Arulenus Rusticus as well as philosophers proper, Musonius Rufus, Annaeus Cornutus (teacher of Persius and Lucan), and one Cynic, Demetrius. As a whole, the Stoic Opposition may have had less to do with Stoicism than with power politics: these aristocratic men hated the principate as a disguised tyranny, with its centralization of decision-making, its perceived abuse of power, and its humiliation of the senatorial class. For them, old Republican Rome was the true Rome, with its competitive pursuit of political honours and military glory. This Rome had been founded by the killing of a king, but was now foundering in its adulation of tyrants. Here, the Opposition could call on Cynic–Stoic notions of *parrhēsia*, ascetic frugality (with its quasi-Republican aura) and individualistic freedom. Such language succeeded in nettling the emperors. Nero hated Thrasea Paetus and Soranus, seeing their discipline and simple lifestyle as a slur on his own self-indulgence: "Having butchered so many distinguished men, Nero at last lusted to extinguish virtue herself by killing Thrasea Paetus and Barea Soranus" (Tac. *Ann.* 16.21). Vespasian hated Thrasea's son-in-law Helvidius Priscus less for personal than for political reasons:

> Vespasian hated him because he was a trouble-maker and appealed to the mob, always condemning monarchy and praising democracy, and, in keeping with this, gathering some supporters – as if it were the function of philosophy to throw muck at rulers, stir up the masses, overthrow the established system and bring on a revolution.
>
> (Cass. Dio 65.12)

Contrary to this caricature, the senator Helvidius was hardly a democratic revolutionary or anarchist agitator, for all his quasi-Cynic rhetoric of freedom and truth-telling. In any case, a pattern emerges in the emperors' treatment of such opponents: in 65 CE, after the Pisonian Conspiracy, Nero forced Thrasea Paetus (and Seneca) to commit suicide, purged his government and exiled the philosophers;

between 71 and 74, Vespasian executed Helvidius Priscus, and exiled the philosophers; perhaps in 89 (after the conspiracy of Antoninus Saturninus) and again in 94, Domitian executed suspected political enemies and exiled the philosophers from Italy.[45] Among these, in 94, was Epictetus, a Stoic who for all his admiration of Cynicism was less incendiary than his master, the famous Cynic Demetrius of Corinth.

Demetrius

Demetrius seems to be the first "true" Cynic after a hiatus of some two hundred years.[46] Most of his austere life was lived in Rome, as a tutor of philosophy, friend of senators and scourge of emperors. His first reported act of "resistance" was his refusal of Caligula's gift of 200,000 sesterces (Sen. *Ben.* 7.11). To Nero he said, "You threaten me with death, but Nature threatens you" (Epict. *Diss.* 1.25). When baths were dedicated by Nero and the senate in 66 CE, he appeared in a loincloth and lambasted the bathers, saying that they were "dirtying themselves". For this, Nero's Tigellinus drove him out of Rome (Philostr. 4.42). But he had friends in high places too, not least Seneca, who praises him in extravagant terms. For Seneca, "our Demetrius", "that half-naked man", is "the best of men", eloquent, constant, sublime, appointed by divine providence and nature herself to be a model, and a reproach for the times; he is not merely a teacher, but a sage, and a witness to the truth that the poor Cynic is truly rich (e.g. Sen. *Ben.* 7.8, *Ep.* 20.9, 62.3). In Cynic style, Demetrius seems to have crusaded especially against wealth, and Seneca includes a passage that may well echo Demetrius' own "diatribes" against the evil and frivolity of riches: the embroidered tortoiseshells, crystal goblets, heavy pearl earrings, the *vomitoria*, and the transparent silk dresses of adulterous upper-class women; men dig iron from the earth to kill each other, and gold and silver for mutual self-deception; they deceive each other with all the unnatural instruments of finance, the letters of credit, promissory notes, bonds, all so many "empty phantoms of property, ghosts of sick Avarice".

The diatribe concludes with a glance at the *latifundia* and the vast villas of the super-rich such as Trimalchio, home to undeserved suffering and frenzied pleasure-making alike:

> Wretched is he who can take pleasure in the size of the audit book of his estate, in great tracts of land cultivated by slaves in chains, in huge flocks and herds which require provinces and kingdoms for their pasture ground, in a household of servants, more in number than some of the most warlike nations, or in a private house whose extent surpasses that of a large city! After he has carefully reviewed all his wealth, in what it is invested, and on what it is spent, and has rendered himself proud by the thoughts of it, let him compare what he has with what he wants: he becomes a poor man at once. Let me go: restore me to those riches of mine. I know the kingdom of wisdom, which is great and stable: I possess every thing, and in such a manner that it belongs to all men nevertheless. (Sen. *Ben.* 7.10; trans. Stewart)

The vehement language of the passage may well echo Demetrius' own speech. If so, one may appreciate why Nero, Vespasian and Domitian did not spare him when punishing Stoicizing senators and their philosopher friends. More particularly, Demetrius was a close advisor of Thrasea Paetus, and when the Pisonian Conspiracy was uncovered and Thrasea forced to commit suicide, Demetrius was there with him to the very last. Curiously, his name is the word with which Tacitus' *Histories* breaks off: "with the slowness of his [Thrasea's] death giving him terrible pain, he turned to Demetrius ...". After this catastrophe of fortune, Demetrius' movements are obscure. He may have gone to Greece but, wherever he took himself, he was back in Rome by 70 CE when he controversially defended Egnatius Celer, who was being prosecuted as an informer by the Stoic Musonius Rufus. Shortly afterwards, Demetrius did not show Vespasian the proper deference due an emperor. Unlike Nero, however, the soldierly Vespasian was untroubled, confident in his power: "You are doing everything to make me kill you, but I will not murder a barking dog" (Cass. Dio 65.13 ; cf. Suet. *Vesp.* 13). Eventually, in 71 CE, Vespasian did exile him, and from then on Demetrius, the scourge of three successive emperors (Caligula, Nero, Vespasian), disappears from view.

People can be banished, but ideas cannot, and many quasi-Cynic ideas crop up through Roman literature, as they had in Hellenistic literature. We have mentioned the possible influence of Bion on Roman satire and Seneca; and of Menippean satire on Varro, Seneca, Petronius, Boethius and others. We shall return in particular to Petronius' treatment of fortune in Chapter 4. Nor are Cynic ideas confined to the savage indignation of the satirists. To mention a single example: Horace's "Maecenas Ode" (*Carm.* 3.29) is, in Mark Morford's judgement, "perhaps the best place in which to study the poet's philosophy in the Odes" (2002: 145). But if so, then the whole is coloured by the Cynic critique of wealth, the city of Rome, the seductions of fortune and all that *typhos*. One may enjoy *present* good fortune, but should not hope for anything more. In brief, Horace advises Maecenas to "stop wondering at the smoke, the riches, and the noise of wealthy Rome" (ll.11–12) and instead to "live content in the moment" (ll.32–3). The poem ends by praising poverty as the best way to weather fortune. For when the storms of circumstance whip up the waters, Horace would prefer to ride it out safe in a little rowboat rather than in a ship loaded down with "Cyprian and Tyrian merchandise" (ll.57–64). Or, in another image, Fortune is like a cruel, winged god, and Horace would prefer to marry Poverty than her:

> Fortune, happy in her cruel work and obstinately playing her insolent game, changes her unsteady favours, now favouring me and now another. I praise her when she stays; but if she shakes her swift wings, I renounce her gifts, wrap myself in my virtue, and seek honest Poverty, even without a dowry.
> (ll.49–56)

Thus, the "Maecenas Ode" is strongly Cynic in flavour and here at least, Cynic ideas have not been wholly "exiled" from the Roman consciousness. The image of a man abandoning the corrupt city of Rome for the simple, virtuous Italian countryside is a favourite one in Latin literature. Parallel themes appear in Greek literature of the first and second centuries CE as orators like Dio Chrysostom contrast the rich and poor city: Troy versus Ithaca; Tarsus or Alexandria versus their humble neighbours; or, most emblematic of all, Rome versus Athens. In this moralistic dichotomy, Rome is big, wealthy, powerful, filled with opportunity, but also with opportunists, philistines, criminals great and small. Athens, on the other hand, is small, poor, weak, but its people are intelligent, imaginative and well-salted with Attic wit.[47] "I'd rather lick salt in Athens" is Diogenes' defiant phrase (DL 6.57), which must have been echoed by those Cynics who did not always find a welcome in the West. But in Greece, Asia Minor, Syria, Egypt and other eastern lands in which Greek was the *koinē glōssa*, the common tongue and *lingua franca*, where Cynics such as Demetrius, Epictetus, Peregrinus and others had returned after various banishments – here Cynicism flourished.

From references in Lucian, Dio and others, the first two centuries CE would seem to have been the heyday of ancient Cynicism, at least in terms of numbers. Elis, Corinth, Athens, Tarsus, Antioch, Gadara, Alexandria: many important cities had Cynics in their midst as a vocal and sometimes unsettling presence.[48] Cynics' birthplaces span the eastern Mediterranean: Agathobulus of Alexandria, Demonax of Cyprus, Dio "Chrysostom" of Prusa (in northwestern Turkey), Peregrinus of Parium (in the Propontis), and Demetrius of Corinth are major names, but there are many others. Important admirers of Cynicism include Epictetus from Hierapolis (in Phrygia in central Turkey), and Lucian of Samosata (in eastern Syria, on the Euphrates). The first Cynics had already been fairly cosmopolitan, hailing from Sinope in the northeast to Syracuse in the southwest, but the *Pax Romana* and good Roman roads enabled Cynics and Cynic ideas to travel even more widely. The memory of some of these Cynics survives only in their curious names. In first-century Athens, we hear of an Honoratus who wore a bear-skin (Luc. *Demon.* 19), and of the anonymous Cynic who swaggered about carrying a club instead of a staff and shouting out, "I am the successor of Antisthenes, Crates and Diogenes" (48). At the same time, Sostratus the Boeotian was (according to Lucian at least) a sort of wild man who lived rough on Mount Parnassus and who would sally forth to clear the countryside of robbers, to "make rough places smooth and bridge deep waters". For such benefactions, he was called, and believed to be a latter-day Heracles, and Lucian himself claims to have "seen and marvelled" at this giant of a man (1). Other names include Antiochus of Cilicia, "the Renegade" who joined the campaign of Severus and Caracalla against the Parthians in 197 CE, performed feats of asceticism by rolling in the snow during one cold winter, and eventually fled to the Parthian king (Cass. Dio 78.19). In the fourth century, the emperor Julian met a Cynic near Besançon in eastern Gaul, and does not express any particular surprise at the fact (Jul. *Ep.* 26). Stories like this suggest that there may have been other Cynic tramps, hobos and wanderers who drifted quietly west, fairly unnoticed by officialdom and the book-writing classes.[49] Similarly, Cynics tended to congregate in cities, but they did have to pass through the countryside when travelling and they may often have welcomed these sojourns, as a return to elemental nature. This is reflected in the travels of Dio Chrysostom, who spent fourteen years wandering the countryside of northern Asia Minor, Greece and Thrace.

But before turning to Dio, we revisit the typical pattern of response to Cynicism: an ambivalence that alternates, sometimes quite wildly, between adulation and disgust. Many observers claim to admire Cynicism itself and lionize its early proponents (Antisthenes, Diogenes, Crates) as higher beings, embodiments of virtue itself. Yet these same observers can revile contemporary Cynics as cynical fakes. In their eyes, these impostors are living off the reputation of their ancestors: they take up the philosopher's coat and staff, grow their beards long, wander the streets and marketplaces, begging, shouting at passers-by that they are "rich", "kings", and followers of Antisthenes and Diogenes, heckling magistrates about virtue, but all the while angling for an obol, a bite to eat, some cheap sex. For all their protestations, these cunning hypocrites do not practise Cynic ideals of self-sufficiency, superiority to fortune, the natural life, *parrhēsia*, freedom from false conventions and liberation from all hopes and fears. On the contrary, they live on handouts, complain endlessly, flatter shamelessly, and love finery and gold more than any. They live for their own pleasure only and have no real ideals, these scoffers, parasites and anarchists. Most common of all is the charge that contemporary Cynics are motivated by vainglory (*philodoxia*), as if all they sought was fame through infamy.[50] Because of them, it is said, normal people can despise all "philosophers" and associate philosophy just with laziness and professional mendicancy. This schizophrenic view – loving the "ancient" Cynics and the idea of Cynicism, but hating contemporary Cynics – is pronounced in Epictetus (*Diss.* 3.22.50), Dio Chrysostom (D. Chr. 33), Lucian (e.g. *Fugitivi* 16), Gregory of Nazianzus (*De Vita Sua* 1033ff.), Augustine and others. It is an ambiguity that would persist through Christian responses to Cynicism, and ultimately form the backdrop for the emergence of the modern notion of an immoral, wholly self-serving cynicism, in which the idealism of its ancient namesake has been excised.

The most concentrated example of this ambivalence – "past good, present bad" – can be found in Lucian's *Runaways* (*Fugitivi*). Here, Philosophy herself is the main character as she narrates her glorious past to the gods, and complains about the present. After enlightening most of mankind, especially the Greeks, she was persuaded to stay on earth for just a little longer by Antisthenes, Diogenes, Crates and Menippus, admirable men all (*Fugitivi* 11). But now, she cries, there is a group intervening between true philosophers and the people. These are the show philosophers, conmen who abandon their workbenches and honest trades, put on shabby clothes, and learn stock phrases and insults, which they bawl out everywhere shamelessly. By doing so they claim to be philosophers, but beneath it they are pederasts, adulterers, parricides, gluttons, hedonists, liars, flatterers, brawlers, drunkards, and so the common people now hate the very word "philosophy" (18). To save the day, Zeus sends Heracles down, along with Hermes and Philosophy herself, to perform the "Thirteenth Labour" of cleaning the world stables of the dung of contemporary Cynicism (23); they begin by rounding up one Cantharus (i.e. "Dung-Beetle"), a runaway slave and false Cynic, return him to his master, and set him working again.

Thus Lucian's *Runaways* paints in broad strokes of black and white, like any morality play. But stray comments remind one that there was another perspective, and that there must have been compelling reasons for so many to become Cynics:

> So every city is filled with these do-nothings who enter the names of Diogenes, Antisthenes, and Crates and enrol in the army of the dog ... You will soon see what will happen. All the craftsmen will rush out of their shops and abandon their trades when they see that by labouring and toiling, bent over their work from dawn to dusk for a paltry wage, they are hardly able to survive. But then they see these lazy charlatans living in abundance, demanding service like tyrants, getting it easily, flying into a rage if they don't, and if they do, not even saying, "Thanks". All this would seem like the life of Cronus (i.e. Eden) to these craftsmen, as if honey itself were to flow from heaven straight into their mouths.
>
> (Luc. *Fugitivi* 16–17)

Lucian absurdly exaggerates the profits made by Cynic beggars, particularly when he writes that many of them eventually buy farms, slaves, and loll about in luxury, which is all that they ever wanted anyway (20). But despite Lucian's unsympathetic polemics, the quoted passage alerts one to the malaise that was beginning to fester under the *Pax Romana*: with little hope of self-advancement and without a compelling patriotic cause, it is understandable why some would drop their tools, say farewell to drudgery, and take up the philosopher's cloak, believing that as a "philosopher" one could live almost as well materially as a craftsman or oppressed peasant, and have a measure of freedom and even adventure to boot.

Dio of Prusa, or Dio Chrysostom

If many self-styled Cynics came from the lower classes there were always exceptions, and in the restless personality of Dio of Prusa (*c*.40–115 CE), one finds an exception to all rules. Aristocrat, student of the Stoic Musonius Rufus, Cynic wanderer, Sophistic orator, enemy of one Roman emperor (Domitian) and adviser to another (Trajan), local dignitary and sometime rogue, Dio is perhaps best understood as a phil-Hellene who campaigned for a rejuvenation of Greek culture. He was born to a wealthy family in Prusa, Bithynia; lived in Rome under Titus, whom he criticized for having a homosexual relationship with a boxer; angered Domitian also, and was banished in 82 CE from both Italy and Bithynia. According to legend, he went to the Delphic Oracle, where Apollo advised him "to do the thing in which [he] was engaged, with undivided energy, as if it were some fine and useful affair, until [he] reached the ends of the earth" (D. Chr. 13.9). And so he did, following his nose through Greece, Thrace, Pontus, Moesia and the lands of the Getae on the banks of the Danube, almost at the limits of Roman power at the time, and thus, it would seem, to the ends of the earth. In his travels, "some used to call him a wanderer, others a beggar, and some even a philosopher" (13.11) and it was owing to this last group that exile made him a philosopher, since they would ask him big questions, as if he were the bearer of higher wisdom. And so Dio became used to speaking about good and evil and basic human concerns, both privately and in public. Later, in his major orations to Trajan and to city assemblies and councils, he would often refer back to those Cynic years, as if they gave him a definite moral authority among the Athenians, Tarsians, and others (7; and see Swain 1996: 232). In the same breath, Dio often compares himself to Odysseus – for to be a Cynic is also to be a "king" in rags. One passage is typical of many:

> When I happened to be wandering in exile once … I went to as many places as possible, now travelling among Greeks, now among barbarians, in the dress of a beggar "asking for crusts rather than fine cauldrons and swords" [=*Od.* 17.217]. And so I came to the Peloponnese, where I tended not to visit the cities but spent my time in the countryside – because there was so much to see there – mingling with herdsmen and hunters, with their noble, simple habits. And

> so I was walking along the Alpheus River on my way from
> Heraea to Pisa until …   (D. Chr. 1.50–51)

And so Dio goes on to tell the story of how an old peasant woman enlightened him with a prophetic version of Prodicus' "Choice of Heracles". At times during his exile, Dio must have despaired of ever returning to his former status and, if what he writes in his *Encomium of Hair* is true, at one point even his own hair was a catastrophe, as "wild and tangled as the fleece hanging between the legs of a sheep". But his fortune changed in 96 CE when Domitian died. Nerva came to power and pardoned Dio, who now gave up the drifter's life and returned to more public responsibilities. Speech-making was an important aspect of his new role and for his eloquence and many orations (of which eighty survive) he was nicknamed Chrysostom or "of the golden mouth". Several of these speeches are strongly Cynic in content and style, notably Orations 1, 3 and 4 (on kingship), 6 ("Diogenes or on Tyranny"), 7 ("Euboean Discourse"), 8 ("Diogenes or on Virtue"), 9 ("Isthmian Discourse") and 10 ("Diogenes or on Servants"), while many others touch on Cynic themes in unexpected ways: those fourteen years clearly left their mark on the man. We shall return to his Kingship Orations (1–4) in more detail in Chapter 5.

Epictetus

Epictetus (*c.*55–135 CE) was a near contemporary of Dio, but was less versatile and more earnest. He was originally a Phrygian from Hierapolis in central Asia Minor, but at some point was enslaved, and ended up working for Epaphroditus, Nero's powerful freedman. Even while a slave, however, he studied philosophy under the Stoic Musonius Rufus. At some unspecified time, he was emancipated and became a Roman citizen. But citizen or not, the banishment order of 94 CE drove Epictetus out of Italy along with Demetrius. He did not go far. Just across the Adriatic, in Nicopolis, Epirus, he established a school (his "hospital", as he called it) where he taught Stoic philosophy and lived in profound frugality. Among his many spiritual "patients" and admirers was Arrian of Nicomedia, himself remarkably versatile and sometimes known as the "second Xenophon": soldier, governor of Cappadocia, consul, writer of various histories (including an *Anabasis* of Alexander), and, most famously, a compiler of Epictetus's discourses or *diatribai*. In them Epictetus can use the heavy Stoic vocabulary of "cataleptic assent" and "preferred indifferents", and he recommends logic as propaedeutic (*Diss.* 1.7). But in his conversational tone and his focus on ethics, he steers closer to the Cynic practice of philosophy.

Moreover, Epictetus' own central vision is strongly Cynic: *Discourses* 3.22 and 4.8 idealize Cynicism as the highest, and hardest, human calling. A young person (Epictetus argues) should consider very carefully before growing a beard and taking up the staff, for the true Cynic will have no wife, child or home, nor any possessions. If in his voluntary homelessness, he remains as materialistic and attached to this world as he always was, then he will be an utter failure, "hateful to God". But if he succeeds, then he will be transformed into something miraculously free, happy, and powerful:

> And how is it possible that a man who has nothing, who is naked, houseless, without a hearth, squalid, without a slave, without a city, can pass a life that flows on easily? Look – God has sent you a man [i.e. Diogenes] to show you that it is possible. Look at me, I am without a city, without a house, without possessions, without a slave; I sleep on the ground; I have no wife, no children; no little mansion, but only the earth and heavens, and one little cloak. And what do I lack? Am I not without pain? Am I not without fear? Am I not free? When did any of you see me failing to get what I desired? Or ever falling into what I wanted to avoid? Did I ever blame either God or man? Did I ever accuse anyone? Did any of you ever see me with a glum face? And how do I face those whom you fear and admire? Isn't it as if they were slaves? Who, when he sees me, does not think that he sees his own king and master? (*Diss.* 3.22.45–9)

Alluding to idealized figures such as the God-sent "Diogenes", Epictetus holds that a human being *is* capable of being self-sufficient and perfect. The Cynic wanderer is the "thing itself": there is nothing higher on earth.[51]

Lucian

Epictetus was a revered and influential personality in his own time, and after it one of the most authoritative champions of Stoicism. Yet the earnest lessons that he gave from his "hospital" would probably have drawn down only the sardonic laughter of another observer. Lucian (*c*.120–185 CE) would eventually become *the* Greek author whom Renaissance scholars and satirists sought to emulate, but in his own time he seems to have been, essentially, a nobody, and certainly not as famous as Epictetus or Dio. Hints gleaned from his own writings suggest that he hailed from Samosata on the western bank of the Euphrates, at the edge of the Mediterranean world. He refers to himself as "Syrian", even "Assyrian", and a "barbarian in speech", so that his native language may have been Syriac. But he left Syrian Samosata behind to become a zealous phil-Hellene. In the *Life of Lucian*, he writes that as a boy he was faced with a choice: to go with Lady Sculpture or Lady Rhetoric, that is, to become a mason chiselling stone in his workshop, or an orator travelling the world and declaiming to rapturous, fee-paying audiences. Lucian chose Rhetoric, who took her latest bridegroom to Ionia, mainland Greece and Italy, and even as far as Gaul. With her, presumably, he learned the classical Attic dialect of Lysias and Plato, which was cultivated in the "Second Sophistic" as proof of one's education, taste and culture. But Rhetoric was a fickle companion (according to the *Life*) and so he left her for a steadier consort, Philosophy.

As a philosopher of sorts, Lucian's main innovation was to combine comedy and the dialogue form (traditionally a philosophical genre) into satirical conversations that often feature different thinkers and an almost allegorical play of ideas. This is perhaps in the tradition of Bion's *spoudogeloion*; indeed, many dialogues introduce the Cynics Diogenes, Crates, Bion and, especially, Menippus.[52] Throughout, Lucian shows the age's typical ambivalence towards Cynicism. Towards contemporary Cynics, such as Peregrinus, he is ferociously hostile. Demonax is the great exception here yet, curiously, Lucian seems anxious not to call Demonax a Cynic directly, or to associate him with those unholy hypocrites. This is one example of how slippery and protean a writer Lucian is. Nevertheless, one possible overall interpretation is to regard him as a "literary" Cynic and a cynical critic of mankind: that is, he is a Cynic in his adulation of a Diogenes or Menippus, and cynical in his self-assured contempt for his ignoble contemporaries. One can gain a flavour of this ambivalence by looking briefly at a few of the dialogues.

First, the *Sale of Lives* may be a clever extension of the legend of Diogenes' sale into slavery, and of Bion's possible treatment of it. Indeed, Lucian implies at one point that he "dug up" Bion, as if reviving him from obscurity (*Bis. Acc.* 33). In any case, Lucian extends the Diogenes legend to satirize all the major philosophies, from Pythagoreanism to Scepticism. He proceeds fairly chronologically, with the exception of Diogenes, who steps on to the block as Lot #2, the "dirty Pontian" (*Vit. auct.* 7). Asked about his skills, Diogenes says that he will teach his masters/charges how to strip everything away and learn to batten on the "wealth" of nothing. Above all, he will teach them how to be "aggressive and bold, ready to abuse everyone in turn, both kings and commoners". Diogenes will train his students to scowl and snarl, and to banish dignity and moderation. They will live openly in the most crowded places but will have no friends. They will be openly sexual and in the end will die by eating octopus or cuttlefish. This is Cynic happiness (*eudaimonia*), and in Lucian's depiction, it is a stupid thing and the Cynic little more than a foul-mouthed bully (*hybristēs*), interested just in getting attention and "glory" (*Vit. auct.* 9.22–11.15). Lucian satirizes other philosophers too, but the Cynic may come out the worst of all: he does not have the golden thigh of Pythagoras, the merriment of Aristippus, Aristotle's erudition, or the Stoics' jargon and world-famous, all-conquering syllogism. It is true that the "twins", the laughing Democritus and weeping Heraclitus, find no buyers, but they are the teachers of Epicurus, who fetches a good price, while the gods are eager to get rid of the Pontian for a measly two obols.

The dramatic sequel to the *Sale of Lives* is the *Fisher*, in which a mob of philosophers gangs up to take revenge on one Parrhēsiast ("Truth-Speaker"). It becomes quickly clear that this character is Lucian himself *in propria persona*: Parrhēsiast describes himself as a Syrian from near the Euphrates, a barbarian who learned Greek, and turned from rhetoric to philosophy. But his slanderous *Sale of Lives* has the philosophers in a lather and a posse (led by Plato) is on the point of stoning him to death. Parrhēsiast persuades them to be reasonable and just (as philosophers should be) and to give him a proper trial. And so it comes to pass. Philosophia herself presides from her tribunal, assisted by Truth, Freedom, Demonstration and others. Diogenes, particularly nettled at having been sold off for only two obols (*Pisc.* 23), demands the right to conduct the prosecution on behalf of all the philosophers:

> This fellow [Parrhēsiast] calls together the aristocrats, medi-
> tates and prepares for a long time, writes his invectives in
> a fat book, and then with a loud voice starts to abuse Plato,
> Pythagoras, Aristotle here, Chrysippus there, me and in
> short, all of us, even though he doesn't have the licence of
> festival-time or any private grievance against us: he would
> have some excuse for the affair if he did it in self-defence
> and didn't start it himself. What's worst of all is that he does
> these things in your name, Philosophy, seducing our servant
> Dialogue to act in partnership against us, and even persuad-
> ing our companion Menippus to join him in his mockery.
>
> (*Pisc.* 26)

In defence, Parrhēsiast claims that he never slandered the philoso-
phers themselves. Far from it: he learned everything he knows from them and has used his knowledge to wage war against the mob of (namely Cynic) impostors who grow their beards, wear rags, shout about virtuous poverty, but are always begging, stealing and flattering the rich. Their profession of "a life according to nature" is a

sham, and these self-styled "philosophers" are no better than the orators and sophists among whom Parrhēsiast wasted his earlier years. They resemble asses imitating lions, or apes pretending to be Heracles (31–2):

> The strangest thing of all is that most of them are perfectly precise in adopting your [the philosophers'] language, and then live as if they had read and studied simply to live in the opposite fashion. For the book says that one must despise money and honour and consider good only what is noble – being without passion and scorning finery and talking with their owners as equals – all fine statements, by the gods! and wise and amazing, really. But they teach these things for a fee, gawping before the rich and panting after money, more bad-tempered than dogs, more cowardly than hares, more imitative than monkeys, more self-willed than donkeys, more thieving than cats, more competitive than cocks. So they become ridiculous as they elbow each other, jostling around the doors of the rich, sitting down at crowded dinners, boorishly praising their hosts, guzzling more than what's polite and still complaining loudly, miserably philosophizing over their cups and hardly able to take the unmixed wine: all the ordinary folk present openly laugh and spit at philosophy if it indeed spawns such slime.
>
> (*Pisc.* 34)

As soon as Parrhēsiast declaims these plain truths, Diogenes drops his case, utterly convinced. In fact, Diogenes embraces Parrhēsiast as his "noble" friend, and Judge Philosophy not only acquits him but authorizes him to be the official prosecutor or "fisher" for false philosophers. And so the allegory ends with Parrhēsiast hunting down the fake philosophers. He announces that all "philosophers" in Athens should report to the Acropolis for a generous distribution of sesame cakes, fig rolls and two *minae* per head. At this, they come swarming like bees to honey: "the Acropolis is full of them as they settle with a clatter, and everywhere it's *pēra*, flattery, beard, shamelessness, staves, lust, syllogism and avarice" (42). From this great crowd, one "Cynic" comes forth, but what does his *pēra* contain? Not beans, a book or barley crusts but gold, perfume, a barber's blade, a mirror and dice (45; cf. *Fugitivi* 31). Wealth, vanity and the unpredictable gifts of fortune are what these phoneys want. And so Lucian the Fisher sits over the edge of the Acropolis, dangling his rod baited with figs and gold, in order to lure the hypocrites to their doom.

With such edifying discourses, Lucian pours out his scorn on contemporary "Cynics" and "philosophers". On the other hand, he maintains that Cynicism itself remains a noble and necessary calling. It is Diogenes who represents the philosophers before Philosophia's tribunal. It is the Cynic ideals of Freedom and *Parrhēsia* who are the closest companions of Truth (*Pisc.* 17). It is Menippus who aids Parrhēsiast in his exposure of contemporary fakes. And it is Lucian himself who is "Parrhēsiast, son of Truthful, son of Refutation" (19), as if he were a sort of Mr Honest smoking out pretence with every word he wrote. Cynic in fashion also is Lucian's schizophrenic blend of strident hatreds and loves: he hates boasters, fakes, falsehood and *typhos* but loves truth, beauty and simplicity (20).

Lucian's tendency to paint in black and white becomes even more pronounced in the dialogues about Cynics in Hades. In the *Menippus*, Lucian depicts the Cynic talking with an Athenian, Philonides, just after his return from Hades. Menippus had been searching for the meaning of life, because neither the poets nor the common laws nor the philosophers were consistent in what they said. Eventually, he had gone to a Zoroastrian Magi (cf. the *Suda*'s description of Menippus), who gave him instruction, culminating in preparations for a journey to Hades to consult Tiresias. Copying the three great heroes who had made this dangerous journey before – Orpheus, Heracles and Odysseus – Menippus armed himself with a lyre, lion skin and sailor's cap, and off he went. Among the dead he learned many things, most notably that the senate, assembly and other authorities in Hades were preparing legislation for the improvement of the living. Foremost in this legislation was a decree against the rich, who were seen as the most reprehensible party, guilty of "violence, ostentation, pride, injustice" (*Nec.* 19) and other vices. The rich people whom Menippus saw below were not impressive specimens: "Pale, pot-bellied, and gouty" (11), they would infuriate the local magistrates with their whining, arrogant demands for special treatment.

But even they too eventually learned the truth: that death is the great leveller, stripping away wealth, power, erudition, everything, so that among the shades all are equal. Best not to strive for any temporal vanity is Menippus' implication. This is confirmed to him in the end by Tiresias, who whispers to him an almost forbidden wisdom:

> The life of the common people is the best and most prudent one, freed from philosophico-jibber-jabber about purposes and examination of axioms – and so, spitting on all those clever syllogisms as so much nonsense, seek out this one single thing before all else: arrange the present well and jog on, laughing a lot and taking nothing seriously. (*Nec.* 21)

Thus, Tiresias counsels a carefree living in the present. As the dialogue opens, it is with Tiresias' words ringing in his ears that Menippus appears. He has just returned from his journey to Hades and is ecstatic to see his "home" again: the earth, the sky, the bright sun. He is bursting to tell the world of his experience and starts with Philonides and, through him, Lucian's readers.

Lucian seems to have especially enjoyed this notion of the Cynic in the Underworld. Thus, in the *Descent to the Underworld*, the rough and ready Cyniscus uses his cudgel to help Hermes herd the unwilling souls across the river Styx, and does even better service later when he prosecutes the tyrant Megapenthes. He becomes fast friends with a humble cobbler (Micyllus), and when the two of them go before Judge Rhadamanthus, they are the only souls who are entirely free of the marks that sin leaves on the soul, for their philosophy and plain living have cleaned all stains away (*Catapl.* 24). In *Dialogues of the Dead*, Menippus appears often, terrorizing tyrants such as Midas, Croesus, Sardanapalus (*Dial. mort.* 2) and Tantalus (#17; cf. #24); or embarrassing prophets such as Trophonius (#3) and Tiresias (#28) with his searching questions; or witnessing the confusion of philosophers such as Pythagoras (who, abandoning old principle, begs for some of Menippus' beans!) or Socrates (who keeps asking what the Athenians are saying about him) (#20). "Dog" speaks to dog when Menippus converses with Cerberus and is told that Socrates cried like a baby when he entered Hades; of all the dead, it was only Diogenes and Menippus who "came in of [their] own free will, without compulsion, laughing away" (#21). Menippus was also the only passenger who crossed the Styx in Charon's boat for free. He did not even have the token fare of a single obol, but at least he was honest about it, and made up by rowing, baling water and drowning out the others' complaints with his own laughing, singing and mockery (#22; cf. *Catapl.* 19).

Repeated many times in these dialogues is the notion that Hades is a "democracy" in which all are equal. Death, again, is the great leveller. Thus, in Lucian's Hades, there are no tyrants, governors or usurers, but only indigent, powerless shades. There are no beautiful women such as Helen and Leda for a Hesiod to catalogue: beauty is now but a heap of bones (#18; cf. #25). The eschatological myths of Plato are haunted by a vision of the sublimity of the end of things. But this is absent in Lucian's cynical picture of the afterlife, where everything is blighted. Or, not quite everything: in the midst of universal despair, the Cynic is enjoying himself, roaring out in laughter at other suffering wretches, for he alone (along with honest Micyllus) was happy with nothing in life and can remain so in death. None of the other philosophies prepare the soul for this great levelling, claim Lucian's characters; nor do the religions that promise some kind of posthumous divinization. In his *On the Death of Peregrinus*, Lucian sniggers cynically at the people called "Christians" who worship a "crucified sophist" (13). Equally smug is the speech of his Diogenes to Alexander. This speech sums up the often violent tone adopted by Lucian's characters towards wealth, authority and religious hope, for Alexander as king, favourite of fortune, son of Ammon and self-proclaimed "god" symbolizes all these:

Shouldn't I [Diogenes] laugh, Alexander, seeing that even in Hades you foolishly hope to become an Anubis or Osiris? Surely you shouldn't hope for these things, o most divine one! For this is not lawful for those who have sailed over the infernal lake and entered this gate: Aeacus is not careless nor Cerberus easily dismissed. But I would gladly learn from you – how can you bear it when you consider all the happiness you left behind in coming here, the bodyguards and crack-troops and satraps and all that gold and the fawning nations and Babylon and Bactria and the big elephants and the honour and the glory and being seen as you drive about crowned with a white diadem and wearing a little purple cloak. Doesn't it pain you to remember all this? Why are you weeping, you fool? Didn't wise Aristotle train you for this – to regard the things of *Tychē* as unstable?

(*Dial. mort.* 13.3–4)

Demonax

In the *Demonax*, Lucian reclaims something of the profession of love for mankind that he made in the *Fisher*, for he here admires Demonax as a paradigm of *philanthrōpia*. Demonax (*c*.70–170 CE) was born in Cyprus, of a wealthy and influential family, but abandoned money, power and all-too-human goods for philosophy (Luc. *Demon.* 3). At some point, he left Cyprus and travelled, to Rome perhaps (for he was a sometime student of Demetrius), to Alexandria (where he studied with Agathobulus), and eventually, perhaps around 120 CE, to Athens, where he was first received as a kind of second Socrates. That is, he was at first hated for his seeming impiety: he disregarded religious custom by not sacrificing to Athena or the gods, and he alone refused to be initiated in the Eleusinian Mysteries (11). But he talked the Athenians round to his side and, in Lucian's account, went from being accused of impiety to becoming something of a holy man in his adopted city. He spent his time in moral exhortation, criticizing public figures such as Herodes Atticus (24, 33), and crossing swords with other philosophers, particularly Peripatetics (29, 31, 54, 55; Herminus) and rival Cynics (19, 48). But his style was more akin to Crates' than Diogenes': genial rather than harsh. Lucian welcomes the fact that Demonax was *homodiaitos* with others: he was not interested in flaunting his difference, and so did not sport the dirty beard and single cloak of other Cynics.

But if Lucian distances Demonax from contemporary "dogs", the ideas that he attributes to him cannot be described as anything but Cynic. According to Lucian, Demonax spent his life wandering around Athens, telling the people to be happy simply in the present. Nothing – neither wealth, poverty, health nor sickness – will last long and so one should live free from hope and fear (8, 19). Only the free are happy (19). Cheerfulness is all and Lucian's Demonax was cheerful, always laughing and poking fun. His genial humour was contagious (6), and perhaps this partly explains why Demonax was such an effective peacemaker. He would reconcile quarrelling brothers and spouses, and brought the assembled people back to a sense of decorum whenever they got rowdy (9). Once, as an old man, he presented his person without a word to the assembly, and they fell silent, suddenly ashamed of their wrangling (64).[53] In the spirit of the age, he made friendship (*philia*) and *philanthrōpia* the highest ideals: he loved almost all mankind, because, he said, each person was intimately related to him (10). Indeed, this good will extended even to animals, for he would have been glad if his corpse did some good as food for fish, dogs and birds (35, 66–7). It would be too much to compare him to St Francis of Assisi, who stressed more explicitly the unity of all life in Christ. Yet several statements do sound positively Christian: Demonax would hate the sin (*hamartēma*) but forgive the sinner, saying that it is human to sin, but divine to correct faults (7). Throughout his long life of approximately one hundred years, he was helpful to his friends, but never ever acquired an enemy (63), thus breaking with the traditional heroic ideal of helping friends and harming enemies. In old age, he would go uninvited and unexpected from house to house, where he would always be given food and a bed: the hosts welcomed him in as a "good *daimōn*" (shades of Crates!), as if his visit were "the manifestation of a god" (63). Bakers' wives would compete for the honour of giving him bread. He died not only universally beloved in Athens and Greece, but revered almost as a holy man. The Athenians gave him a public burial (an honour traditionally reserved for war heroes), and the stone on which he used to rest they would kiss and decorate like a sacred thing (67). Thus the outsider to Athens who was first suspected of impiety ends almost as its tutelary saint. Indeed, he had taught the Athenians what true piety is (11).

Demonax also seems a Cynic in his relations with other philosophers. He was a student of Agathobulus, Demetrius, Epictetus and Timocrates (3) and himself admired Socrates, Antisthenes and Diogenes above all other philosophers (62). Was he an Epicurean? In Lucian's account, Demonax does not mention Epicurus or his books. A Platonist? Again, no mention of the Academy. A Peripatetic? He mocks them regularly and uses none of their terminology. A penchant for plain Cynicism, on the other hand, would explain why he singles out Cynics – like Honoratus in his bear skin or the unnamed Cynic bawler who carried a club rather than a staff (19, 48) – as fakes: they are rivals to be discredited. His greatest rival was Peregrinus. In one exchange, Peregrinus criticized Demonax for laughing too much: he was not serious enough to be a Cynic. "You are no dog", said Peregrinus. "And you", Demonax retorted, "are no human being" (21), as if to imply that Peregrinus' Cynicism was all too harsh. Such duels suggest that Demonax was a Cynic after Lucian's own heart: modest, cheerful and an enemy of all cant. Yet Lucian hesitates to call Demonax a Cynic outright, for fear that the word would conjure up the wrong associations in some people's minds.

Peregrinus

If good humour and *philanthrōpia* endeared Demonax to Lucian as the "best of the philosophers" whom he knew (*Demon.* 2), it may have been a perceived self-righteousness in Peregrinus that made Lucian hate him so viciously. One of Lucian's most important pieces is his *Death of Peregrinus*, which describes the actual events at Elis and Olympia in the years leading up to 165 CE. At the Olympic Games of 161, the Cynic Peregrinus "Proteus" and his sidekick Theagenes announced to the gathered multitudes that in the same place, in four years' time, Peregrinus would have himself burned alive in a bonfire, thus demonstrating to mankind that death is not to be feared. Peregrinus fulfilled his promise and in 165 he did indeed die on a pyre. People arrived from all quarters to watch the spectacle. This sort of thing had been heard of before: Calanus the gymnosophist had committed suicide in this way in Susa before Alexander and the Macedonians in 324 BCE; a "Brahman" had burned himself alive publicly in Rome during the reign of "the divine Augustus" (Plut. *Alex.* 69.6–8).[54] Such things had happened also in even more ancient times. The philosopher Empedocles had thrown himself into the volcano of Mount Etna, and Heracles had burned himself on a pyre on the top of Mount Oeta in Thessaly: slain by the dead in fulfilment of the prophecy, it is said, for Deianeira had innocently sent him a shirt poisoned with the centaur's blood. And does not the Phoenix die in fire every few centuries, only to rise at once from the ashes again? Would Peregrinus too prove that death is not an end to be feared?

Peregrinus' death certainly brought an end to a varied and exciting life that well justified his nickname of Proteus – the Old Man of the Sea, who could change shape at will, becoming human, seal, lion, tree, water, fire. Peregrinus was born in Parium in the Propontis, a Roman colony, and his name is curiously Roman, meaning "traveller, foreigner". At some point, after his father's death, he left home, went to Palestine where he converted to Christianity, and became a well-respected member, even a leader, of the community. Following a brief imprisonment by the Roman authorities, he returned to Parium and attempted to recover his patrimony. But once home, something happened: he "converted" to Cynicism, renounced his property, gave it to the Parians and left home for a second time, this time to go to Alexandria to study with Agathobulus. Agathobulus was a famous Cynic and critic of Roman rule, teacher of Epictetus and Demonax, among others. We know little about him, but St Jerome mentions him as one of the notable philosophers of his day.

One may speculate about his attitudes towards Roman rule: the Alexandrians, and Alexandrian Cynics, were notoriously subversive throughout the second century and beyond.[55] After his time with Agathobulus, Peregrinus became an outspoken agitator in his own right. He travelled to Rome where he criticized the emperor Antoninus Pius, only to be banished by the city prefect. He retreated to Elis and Olympia, where he criticized the Eleans and the tycoon Herodes Atticus. He may even have helped incite the rebellion in Achaea during Pius' reign.[56] Eventually, he announced at the Games of 161 CE that he would burn himself alive in the following Games and in 165 this came to pass. For a few years afterwards he had followers who revered him with shrines and prayers.

Such seem to be the main facts of Peregrinus' life, extracted from Lucian's account, which is our main source. But if these are the facts, then Lucian peppers them with salacious allegations and a slander that knows no bounds. Not only is his Peregrinus a fake (materialistic, cowardly, vainglorious), but he seduced a married woman (for which he was punished by having a radish stuffed up his anus, a punishment borrowed from classical Athens), corrupted an innocent, poor boy (whose parents he then bought off), and finally, to cap it all, strangled his father, a sacrilegious crime that precipitated his first flight from Parium (*De mort. Peregr.* 9–10). In Palestine, he overawed the naive Christians with his eloquence, and battened in luxury at their expense (16). As a Christian he was imprisoned by the Roman authorities (i.e. for treason in not worshipping the emperor's image) but eventually freed. He returned to Parium to recover his inheritance, but when this proved impossible he appeared in the assembly with long hair, a dirty cloak and *pēra*, and generously bestowed all his money on the people: thus, Proteus changed shape again and made the best of a bad situation, but his motives, Lucian writes cynically, were as selfish as ever. Then with Agathobulus in Alexandria, he learned such philosophical lessons as how to shave half his head and cover his face with mud.[57] In Rome he lashed out at everyone, including the gentle Antoninus Pius (18), who otherwise respected philosophers. Peregrinus also turned his banishment by the city prefect to good use. This made him an exemplar of *parrhēsia* and free-spiritedness, he claimed; he had been punished for his truth-telling by a cruel tyrant, just like Musonius, Dio, Epictetus and others (18). In Greece, he continued with his cantankerous "barking", attacking the Eleans (perhaps for hosting the Games) and Herodes Atticus (for generously building a fountain, the Nymphaeon, for the spectators of the Games) and, in particular, inciting armed rebellion against the Romans. Eventually he ran out of insults and, changing shape once more, came up with a final stunt to gain notoriety. He pretended that he was about to become a god, and so proclaimed his imminent self-immolation. But when so many showed up and encouraged him to do it, he saw that he could not escape his promise, and, coward though he was, Peregrinus had to die.

Lucian does a hatchet job on Peregrinus and his vilification of the man is obviously exaggerated. In fact many moments in Lucian's narrative suggest a less cynical interpretation of the underlying events. Peregrinus' interest in Christianity, Cynicism, Pythagoreanism and other systems indicates a man who for many years searched restlessly for "meaning"; that he committed suicide in the manner Lucian describes, with attendants and a solemn ritual, suggests that he found that meaning, at least in his own mind. That he had attendants and many followers makes one suspect he was not entirely mad but an impressive individual, to some at least. He had impressed the Palestinian Christians, a more closely knit and less cosmopolitan group than the Syrian or other Churches, even though he was a Greek-speaker with a Latin name, from near the Black Sea. He persuaded the Roman governor to free him without punishment. Finally, some observers have recorded their admiration for the man: Aulus Gellius says that he visited Peregrinus regularly in Athens, and was impressed by him as a *vir constans et gravis*, "steady and authoritative" (Gell. *NA* 12.11), not protean and vain, *pace* Lucian.[58]

In any case, Peregrinus was a controversial figure, and he went up in a fiery death. After him, there are no great names in Cynicism and we know little substantial of the movement until the reign of Julian some two centuries later. But in the interim, there is the significant figure of Marcus Aurelius, the Stoic emperor (121–180 CE; emperor 161–180). In his *Meditations* Marcus often recalls Epictetus, the greatest influence on his thought, and just as Epictetus was a Cynicizing Stoic, so Marcus too occasionally expresses admiration for Diogenes (8.3, 11.6), Crates and Monimus (2.15).[59] Most of all, in Marcus' remembrance of his first tutor in philosophy, Diognetus, one hears echoes of Cynic precepts regarding religious superstition, luxury, *parrhēsia* and self-imposed simplicity:

> From Diognetus, [I learned] not to be serious about vanities; and not to believe the words of the conjurors and magicians concerning incantations and banishing demons and the like; and not to keep quails or to get excited about such things; and to endure plain speaking (*parrhēsia*); and to grow intimate with philosophy and to study first with Baccheius, then Tandasis and Marcianus; and to write dialogues in boyhood; and to be ambitious for the pallet-bed and leather-coat and all the things that go with the Greek regimen.　(*Med.* 1.6)

The "Greek regimen" is an ascetic one and, for a Roman emperor, Marcus lived very frugally. In his conscientious attendance to his political duties, he practised the Stoic–Cynic ideal that the good king does not use power for his own enjoyment but endures many "toils" (*ponoi*) to serve his people and, through them, all mankind.

Julian

Almost at the end of pagan antiquity, Julian the "Apostate" emperor (331–63 CE; emperor 361–63 CE) looked back to Marcus as one exemplar to imitate. He too sought out the "Greek regimen", lived austerely, worked extremely hard at the task of being king, and wrote feverishly at night or in spare moments, in Greek, about religion and literature. He is known most for his suppression of Christianity, a policy that also recalls Marcus, but more than any predecessor, Julian made this his *raison d'être*. What drove him on to this zealous crusade? He was educated in the Greek classics, but saw Homer being gradually replaced by the Bible. He grew up in the imperial family of the Constantines, but was alienated partly by their self-serving use of a politicized Christianity. In addition, his teacher, the philosopher Maximus, prophesied that Julian would found a third empire (after the Pagan and Christian empires) and so he may well have believed that he was appointed by Zeus and Helios to restore the old, pagan ways (e.g. *Or.* 7.229c–234c). Driven thus by a complex blend of motivations, Julian pursued his course single-mindedly. He closed Christian churches, and tried to turn ambitious people away from Christianity by forbidding Christians to teach the Greek classics or to join the army. In addition to his all-consuming practical duties as emperor, he conducted a literary campaign, snatching free moments at night to write orations, epigrams, letters and occasional pieces, enough to fill three Loeb volumes. Included among these are his two orations on Cynicism, "To the Uneducated Cynics" (Oration 6) and "To Heraclius the Cynic" (Oration 7).

In the first, Julian writes that Cynicism is "a branch of philosophy, and by no means the most insignificant or least honourable, but rivalling the noblest" (*Or.* 6.182c; cf. 7.236b). "Philosophy" for Julian signifies a synthesis of the ideas of the Pythagoreans, Plato, Aristotle, the Stoics and others. This is in the style of "the divine Iamblichus" (Julian's hero) and other contemporary Neoplatonists who sought to capture the essential unity of philosophy, and of Being as a whole. For them, Being is one, and so wisdom is to know the One so intimately that one becomes identical with the totality. Therefore, philosophy too must be one, and even if there might seem to be many, different philosophies, they only approach and articulate the same truth from different perspectives (6.182c–186b). Cynicism too is one branch of philosophy, intimately related to the others, and not merely a series of discrete clichés or capricious paradoxes. It was not founded by Diogenes or Antisthenes, but by Apollo himself (6.188a–b, 7.211b), for it was Apollo who told Diogenes to "put the currency out of circulation", a commandment that Julian closely links to the more famous "Know Thyself". Indeed, in places Julian assimilates Cynicism to many key notions of the philosophical Schools. For instance, he quotes Plato's *Phaedo* to assert that Cynicism too is a "preparation for death" (6.191c). He asserts that the goal of philosophy is, at once, the *apatheia* of the Stoics, the Platonic ideal of "becoming like God" (6.192a), Aristotelian *eudaimonia* as well as the "life according to nature" (6.193d) – and Cynic asceticism serves all these goals. The resulting Oration 6 has been praised as a remarkable work of synthesis, or a laughable mishmash.[60] In any case, it does serve Julian's own purpose: to enlighten the "uneducated Cynics" of his day in the main points of ancient philosophy and to inspire them to view Cynicism not as a way of shirking social duty but as one of the steps by which one may become truly virtuous, happy, wise and god-like. Cynicism, then, is integral to Julian's Neoplatonic programme and he adopts various images to illustrate the point. Cynicism is like Socrates, as praised by Alcibiades in Plato's *Symposium*: rough and ugly on the exterior, but on the soul-side, beautiful and golden (*Or.* 6.186d–187b). Or, in a second image, philosophy is likened to a great city: the uneducated Cynics of Julian's day are like travellers who come to this city, but remain among the outer slums and never penetrate to the temples at the centre. Their squalid lifestyle may have some worth, but it must be deepened by further philosophical study. Otherwise, as happens now, Cynics become materialistic hypocrites who in their disillusion with all ideals have the effect of destroying other people's idealism (6.198a–d). Searching about for insults harsh enough for these shallow Cynics, Julian can find none more damning than that they are like his worst enemies: the *apotaktitai*, the hermits revered by Christians (7.224b).

In his zeal to educate the uneducated Cynics, Julian remakes Diogenes and Crates into models of decorum, even more pious than Epictetus' ideal Cynic or Lucian's Demonax. Julian's Diogenes respects the gods, oracles, temples, mysteries and other sacred things. His exemplary Cynics do not act shamelessly and they lose their impish mischief.[61] Rather than running into Plato's lectures with plucked chickens, they become disciplined students of Neoplatonic mysticism. Rather than mocking magistrates, they become the foot soldiers in the social campaigns of a Roman emperor. Julian would thus seem to make room for Cynic asceticism in the training of his new philosophical priesthood, whose task would be to rival and replace the disciplined, talented Christian bishops.

With the knowledge of hindsight, many have seen in Julian's work a Trojan effort to restore the old ways. His learning, idealism and restless energy, all his legislation and furious writing at night could not stop the tide. When he died of a wound after victories over the Sassanids in Mesopotamia, his life's work was quickly undone. "You have won, Galilaean!" are his legendary last words, and in the generations after him such figures as Basil, Gregory of Nazianzus, Theodosius, Jerome, Ambrose, Augustine and others ensured that Christ would "win". Yet at the same time, for at least 150 years after Julian, there were Cynics. Maximus Hero (late fourth century) was both Christian and a Cynic. The pagan Sallustius of Emesa is the last known "dog", born *circa* 430 CE and living at least until the end of the fifth century. A generation later, in 529 CE the Emperor Justinian closed the Academy, a stronghold of pagan sentiment, but in the same year St Benedict founded the first Western monastery at Monte Cassino. In such places, Cynic austerity and voluntary poverty would live on in a new guise that Julian had perversely refused to honour. A new culture was maturing, with its own beliefs and customs, such as Communion and fasting. Julian's idealistic efforts to recreate and purify pagan culture had much in common with this new religion, but he rejected it, and in this one respect, he does recapture something of the spirit of Diogenes and the classical Cynics, who made it their first task to renounce their society's prevailing customs.

TWO

Renunciation of custom

The most obvious activity of the ancient Cynics was their renunciation of traditional proprieties, and since antiquity observers have
been alternately inspired and disgusted by their brazen protests.
The Cynics' rejection of custom is an interesting cultural phenomenon in its own right, and to understand it in detail would take one
through the whole gamut of Greek social usages. First, then, what
are customs? Customs are the practices and expectations that guide
the life of an individual and community. Generally they are habitual,
and sometimes so engrained in routine that they are hardly noticed.
One takes customs for granted, forgets their origins, as if they had
always existed, and rarely questions them. The classical Sophists did
question their societies' *mores*, however, as did many ancient philosophers after them. Most radical of all in their scepticism were the
Cynics. From Diogenes until the last "dogs" of the ancient world,
the Cynics defined themselves first by "snarling" at the institutions,
rituals, beliefs and assumptions by which their contemporaries lived.
To list their different acts of critique would be to compose a long
priamel: "Not this, not that, and definitely not that", says the Cynic
in his scorn for all things merely conventional. In his seemingly
universal nay-saying, the Cynic avoids traditional clothes, jewellery
and bodily adornments for his own "uniform"; he restricts his diet;
does not live in a house; derides bathing, sports, the Games; scoffs at

festivals, sacrifice, prayer and religious life generally; does not marry, dodges work and steers clear of the courts, assembly, army and other arenas of political participation. He even strives to bust out of old patterns of talking, and tosses up for himself a wild new language.

All of these, from food and physical needs to politics and religion and language, we shall describe in turn, under four headings: customs for the individual, customs for the family, customs for the city and customs for the soul. In attacking a broad array of Greek conventions, the Cynic often claimed to be following Apollo's order to Diogenes: *paracharattein to nomisa*, "deface the currency of custom". At worst, this amounts to a perverse contrariness. At best, it becomes synonymous with critical reason and the refusal to live according to mere habit and entrenched opinion. Thus Julian compares Cynic renunciation with Socrates' practice of *elenchus* in a passage that foreshadows modern Enlightenment ideals:

> [J]ust as Socrates said of himself that he embraced the life of cross-examining (*elenchus*) because he believed that he could perform his service to the god only by examining in all its bearings the meaning of the oracle that had been uttered concerning him, so I think Diogenes also, because he was convinced that philosophy was ordained by the Pythian oracle, believed that he ought to test everything by facts and not be influenced by the opinions of others, which may be true and may be false …. What then was it right for him to do who had been appointed by God like a general to abolish the common currency (*exelein to nomisma*) and to judge all questions by criteria of reason and truth?   (6.191a–192c; trans. Wright)

Customs for the individual: clothing, housing, food, pleasure

Clothes and beard

"Clothes maketh the man", and the Cynic was no exception, differentiating himself most obviously by the clothes he wore – and did not wear. From Diogenes to the time of Julian, the Cynic was easily recognizable by his staff, travelling bag (*pēra*), beard, single thin cloak (*tribōn*) and nothing else except his dirt. Let us take each aspect of the Cynics' "uniform" in turn. The staff (*baktron*) had many possible uses: for walking and travelling, for self-defence, for offence (e.g. threatening hecklers who might interrupt a street sermon), and eventually just for the sake of tradition. The staff became to the Cynic what the club was to Heracles: the weapon of a superior being entitled as if by divine right to beat a way through the evils of the world. Some Cynics actually carried clubs, just as at least one wore bear skin, in imitation of Heracles' lion skin (see Luc. *Demon.* 19, 48; cf. *Vit. auct.* 8.9; Voss 1967). Most Cynics, however, wore the common *tribōn*. The word is derived from *tribein*, "to rub away", and so the *tribōn* was a thin, much-used, worn-down covering usually worn by slaves and the poor. Thin and "rubbed away", it was not normally winter gear and the Cynic is typically said to have folded it in two for warmth in the colder months. This may mean that the *tribōn* was wrapped about the upper torso twice, thus keeping the chest, waist and groin warm while leaving legs and arms exposed to the elements.[1] The feet were bare too, for Cynics rejected the custom of shoe-wearing and went about barefoot, like Socrates. Plato often speaks of Socrates as "shoeless" as if it were a remarkable thing,but one should remember that Plato was an aristocrat and that for many throughout antiquity, shoes were a luxury, kept for travel or the best occasions. Thus Socrates proudly sports his "slippers" when sallying forth to the *symposium* to celebrate Agathon's first victory, but normally he just walks around without any footwear.[2] Finally, the Cynic *pēra* or travelling bag (rendered "wallet" in older translations) was a knapsack in which the Cynic put his few possessions: the true Cynic, Lucian comments, might carry beans, barley bread and a book, but the false one has mirrors, razors, dice, gold and perfume (*Pisc.* 45; cf. *Vit. auct.* 9.12; DL 6.22, where Diogenes' *pēra* holds food). This note by Lucian is unusual and highlights the fact that extant literature does not bother to explain the Cynic *tribōn*, staff or *pēra* in detail: how big was a typical *pēra*, for instance?

But perhaps questions like this are beside the point. By limiting themselves to one thin cloak and a bag, the Cynics would seem to have come as close as possible to going about naked (*gymnos*). This was the ultimate consequence of the agenda of rejecting merely human artifice, since no animal makes or wears clothes, and so human beings should not either. This seems to be Onesicritus' line of reasoning when he inserts his sly critique of the Cynics, who rightly rejected custom but did not pursue the principle as far as Calanus and the Indian gymnosophists in order to live as naked as nature made them. The assertion that one should forgo protective clothing is more plausible for inhabitants of the littoral cities of Greece, Asia and South Italy, where one could brave the temperate winters with relatively few clothes. Still, one would have to be fairly tough and so the Cynics often argue that going about half-naked is invigorating, while clothes are corrupting and make one soft.

Worse, they make one vain and deceitful. Most forms of clothing are designed not to protect against the elements, but to impress others and to make the body seem more beautiful than it is. Many anecdotes, therefore, feature Cynics ridiculing others for their fancy costumes. The Cynics do not seem to have been particularly upset by women's fashions, but the sight of a foppish man would call down their thunder. Thus, when Diogenes sees a man who had "done himself up", he asks him to pull up his cloak to show him whether he was a man or a woman (DL 6.46). When he sees a young man "beautifying himself", he says that for men to do this is unfortunate, and for women unjust (6.54). A law for Zeno's ideal city was that men and women wear the same dress and that no part of the body be completely covered (7.33); perhaps the idea was that scanty uniforms would banish vanity. In a later Athens, Demonax mocked an Olympian victor who wore flowery clothes and he ridiculed the effeminate son of a Roman senator (Luc. *Demon.* 25, 18). Worst of all were purple clothes. Purple dye was made with much labour by squeezing juice from the *Murex brandaris* (a mollusc), and so expensive was it that it became synonymous with power and ultimately royalty: Athenian archons, Roman senators and generals wore bands of purple on their official garb; babies born into Byzantine royal families were titled *porphyro-geniti*, "born in the purple". The rich connotations of purple could only attract much Cynic criticism.[3] In just one example, Demonax quipped that one could wear purple wool, but the sheep before wore the same wool, and remained nothing but a sheep (Luc. *Demon.* 41).

But if he got rid of his purple and finery, the Cynic would feel positively exposed without his beard. No self-respecting Cynic could appear in public without his whiskers, and this is the final part of the Cynic "uniform". The beard is an almost universal symbol of experience and strength, distinguishing men from boys, and wise old men from callow "striplings": rabbis, Orthodox priests, mullahs and ancient philosophers typically wear beards. From the time of Homer, Greek men wore beards, but Alexander seems to have done much to change this fashion, almost single-handedly. Alexander shaved, perhaps to reinforce his image as the new Achilles, perpetually young, energetic and beautiful. This set the fashion for Alexander's Macedonians, as well as for the Seleucids, Ptolemies, Antigonids and Greek elites who divided his empire. At around the same time, the Roman elite also began to shave (according to Varro and Pliny), and from about 300 BCE, a clean face, or at least a short, tidy beard, was *de rigueur* among senators and equestrians. Even Aristotle surrendered to fashion (DL 5.1), but philosophers in general held out and wore beards so flamboyantly that they could be called *pōgōnotrophoi* ("beard-growers"), and thoughtful commentators sometimes felt compelled to remind readers that "beard-growing alone does not make a philosopher" (e.g. Plut. *De Is. et Os.* 352c; Luc. *Demon.* 13). Most fashion-unconscious of all were the Cynics, who, with their long, thick, matted beards, must have seemed to emerge from a different world altogether. Dio Chrysostom in his "Encomium of Hair" says that at one point his own coiffure was "wild and tangled as the fleece hanging between the legs of a sheep" (*Encomium Comae* 2.3–7), and his beard must have been just as tangled. Julian exaggerates for comic effect when he mocks his own beard as a thicket filled with lice and old food and so tough that one could "twist ropes from it". On the other hand, however, he considers his goatish beard to be more manly than the soft chins of the pretty boys of Antioch (Jul. *Mis.* 3). Thus Emperor and Antiochenes traded insults during Julian's visit to the city in 361–2 CE.

As Julian implies, the beard could be seen from opposite perspectives, now leonine and sexy, now goatish and repulsive. The Cynics' considered view was that beards are natural, masculine, mane-like, a frugal form of self-beautification, even God's gift to men. Therefore they bellowed at their pathetic contemporaries for grooming themselves before the mirror, shaving, depilating their bodies, waxing, and making themselves "like women" (see esp. ps.-Luc. *Cyn.* 14). In Lucian's life of Demonax, for instance, a Roman proconsul in Athens had the custom of removing his body hair with hot pitch. When news of this got out, an unnamed Cynic stood up on a stone and started slandering him, shouting to passers-by that the Roman was a *kinaidos*, a passive homosexual. The proconsul was livid and would have had him beaten, put in the stocks or exiled, had not Demonax been there and advised him to pardon the man, saying that he was only practising freedom of speech (*parrhēsia*), "according to the customary law of the Cynics".[4] But if he did it again, Demonax advised, he should be depilated himself in punishment. For a Cynic, such luxurious treatment would be punishment indeed: to be stripped of his hair would be tantamount to stripping him of his identity, self-respect, his citizenship in the "city of Diogenes". Indeed, it would make him the very antithesis of a Cynic: a smooth, "metrosexual" type. At the same time, with his advice Demonax also slyly reproves the proconsul, who seeks out this "punishment" as a regular treat.[5]

Housing

In addition to his simple clothes and bristling virility, the Cynic was most obviously distinguished by his homelessness. The classical and Hellenistic Greeks were, of course, a non-nomadic people: they lived in settled cities, they lived in houses, and the ideal was not to rent, but to live in one's own house on one's own land, to own property (*ousia*) and so to be a person of substance and solid respectability. Oppositely, to be without land, hearth, house and city was one of the worst fates. Aristotle echoes Greek expectations when he defines the human essence in terms of having a fixed abode: the human being is the "political animal" or, more precisely, the "polis-animal", the "animal who by nature tends to live in cities". The city, in turn, is first approximated by the *oikos*: for Aristotle, human beings naturally live in pairs, male and female, in a house with productive land. But the Cynics rejected all this as mere cultural prejudice. They claimed to be "citizens of the cosmos", and to make the whole earth their hearth. They found shelter where they could: sometimes squatting in temples and *gymnasia*, "the most beautiful and healthful houses"; sometimes sleeping in the baths; and sometimes just in the open air, "under the *aithēr*", that is, "under Zeus". Most celebrated of all is Diogenes' *pithos*.[6] A *pithos*, again, was a very large earthen jar, often well over a metre high, used to store wine, olive oil or grain: as the usual storage vessels of the ancient world, used as far back as the Minoans, *pithoi* were very common. And so Diogenes would not have had very far to look if the story is true that he crawled into a *pithos* when he grew tired of waiting for a house to be built. It was from a *pithos* that Diogenes is often pictured talking with Alexander. Other stories make Diogenes a nomad: like the Persian kings, or storks and cranes, he migrated from summer quarters in Athens to his wintering grounds in Corinth (D. Chr. 6.1–7). Nomads keep their furniture and household items to a minimum, and so too Diogenes is said to have thrown away his own cup when he saw a child drinking with his hands. On a similar occasion he tossed away his bowl (DL 6.37). For the Cynics, one needs neither a house for shelter, nor household implements to eat.

Food and diet: lentils, dessert, meat, wine, symposia

But what is one to eat? The Greek diet was traditionally simple, dominated by bread, grapes, wine, olives and olive oil: that is, the "Mediterranean triad" of grain, grapes and olives. The Cynics' diet overlapped with this to a certain extent, although they gravitated towards wild, uncultivated plants: they are usually depicted eating figs, lupin beans, lentils, olives, lettuces, garlic, thyme, mint and other herbs, as well as loaves of barley bread, or even wheat loaves and honey cakes if they were there for the taking. Sometimes they are said to have grown vegetables themselves. At other times, they picked them by the roadside, and one should not forget that the Greek cities (even Athens) were small. The countryside was not far off, and *that* countryside would have been richer in flora and fauna than polluted or denuded modern landscapes.[7] Lentils, in particular, became something of a joke among and about the Cynics, as if the Cynics' diet consisted of lentils, lentils and more lentils. Thus one of Crates' play-pieces (*paignia*) was an "Encomium of Lentil Soup". Meleager followed suit by writing a "Comparison of Thick and Clear Lentil Soup", and in the *Cynics' Symposium* of Parmeniscus, what is on the menu? Nothing but lentils, and the main interlocutor, the "dog-leader" Carneius, stuns Parmeniscus, Cebes the host, the other five Cynic guests, and even the courtesans (one of whom, Nicion, is nicknamed "the dog-fly") with his amazing erudition about the lentil: food of heroes, theme of tragic and comic poets alike, *summum bonum* of philosophers![8] Judging from Parmeniscus' *Symposium*, these pieces on lentils played on the comic tradition in which Heracles was a mad eater of pea and lentil soup. The comparison may be somewhat appropriate, for lentils and legumes were to the Cynics what spinach is to Popeye: a source of strength and power. Thus Crates can boast, "A quart of lupin-beans, and you worry about nothing!" (Stob. 4.33.31). In this school of thought, a cheap natural diet makes one independent of the market and the labour of others, and so heightens one's sense of self-sufficiency. It has other benefits too: the food is healthy, non-fattening and does not fill one with unnecessary aggression, as meat does; and the philosopher enjoys his beans with gusto, because hunger is indeed the best sauce: "I swear to you that I would rather live this life, slurping down sweet lentils without fear, than have all the excess of Seleucus the king" (Ath. 4.44, quoting Antiphanes).[9]

With an attitude like this, the Cynic can only hold up his hands to dessert too, and say no to honey cakes, fig cakes, dried fruits, sweetmeats and all tasty *opsa* and *tragēmata*. Once when Diogenes was eating his breakfast, he found a honey cake among his figs, which he picked out and flung away, saying "Away from the presence of the tyrant", as if the honey cake were some impudent intruder in the royal court (DL 6.55). However, the Cynic will often enjoy luxuries if they are free: Demonax eats honey cakes with a clear conscience, because "bees do not make honey for fools only" (Luc. *Demon*. 52). But in general dessert is *not* free, and comes with costs that limit one's freedom in some way or other. Callisthenes, for instance, court-philosopher to Alexander, can only eat breakfast when Alexander allows (DL 6.45). By contrast, Diogenes "would rather lick salt in Athens" than sit at the well-stocked table of a tyrant such as Craterus (6.57).[10]

But cooked meat was one luxury that the Cynics seem to have avoided on principle. Meat was more expensive than grains or legumes, and most ancients ate meat rarely, most typically on a day of sacrifice. Then oxen, goats, sheep, even horses might be offered to the gods, and most of the meat offered to the happy citizens in the ensuing feast. Pythagoreans were vegetarians because they regarded all life as interconnected; early Christians rejected sacrificial meat because it was an *anathēma*, an unholy offering to demons and idols. The Cynics had a different reason for renouncing meat: it was cooked, and cooking, whether boiling, roasting, frying or fricasseeing, is a merely human invention. It involves fire, the basis of all arts and crafts, and hence represents the primal evil, the crime of Prometheus, that separated man from nature, bringing with it warm baths and warm houses, as well as sinister inventions such as the forge, metal-working, gold-mining, money and weapons of war. With this in mind, the myth-makers were right to envisage Prometheus punished. In particular, Prometheus' fire transformed eating into dining, and so introduced an endless array of luxuries and the corresponding appe-tite for them (see e.g. D. Chr. 6.25).[11] Gourmands are never satisfied and, in Cynic literature, the cook can appear only to minister to vice; we have seen how in Crates' parodic "diary", the profligate sets aside ten *minae* for the cook (DL 6.86). The main item that cooks cook is meat, and according to one body of ancient medical opinion, meat-eating makes one stupid and ill-tempered. Again, not many Greeks ate meat regularly, but the semi-professional athletes who competed at the pan-Hellenic Games did. The Cynics often mock them for their bulk and mental sloth, "made only of pork and beef" as they are (6.49). By the same token, Diogenes ridiculed the mad stupidity at the festivals when a whole city might gorge itself for a few hours on the free sacrificial meat (6.28).

But if one should not eat cooked meat, there was no reason not to try it raw and, according to legend at least, the Cynics were not ideological vegetarians. Notorious stories tell of Cynics eating raw flesh (DL 6.34), especially raw octopus (6.76), to demonstrate to mankind that one does not need fire to eat well.[12] But if dogs can eat raw meat, human beings usually cannot, and in these stories, the Cynic gets sick or even dies. Even more notorious are the rumours of cannibalism: Diogenes "saw nothing wrong in … eating any animal; and nothing unholy even in eating human flesh, as is obvious from the customs of other peoples" (6.73). The underlying thought is that if other peoples practise cannibalism, then surely it is only local prejudice that keeps the Greeks from doing the same. The Greeks, of course, abhorred the custom: in Homer it is the savage Laestrygonians and Cyclops who are man-eaters; Pindar cannot quite credit the old myth that the gods ate Tantalus' shoulder and replaced it with an ivory one (Pind. *Ol.* 1.52); Herodotus tells a story of Greeks appalled to meet Indian cannibals (Hdt. *Hist.* 3.38). Diogenes may have argued that such prejudices are myopic, disrespectful to foreign customs and ignorant of scientific fact; according to Diogenes Laertius, Diogenes held that each type of substance contains elements of every other, and that "in bread there is meat and in vegetables, bread". To eat lamb, then, or barley is ultimately no different from eating human flesh, because there are elements of human flesh in all other foods (DL 6.73; cf. D. Chr. 10.29–30). That everything is contained in everything is a somewhat common reflection, made not only by Anaxagoras, but revisited, for example, by Demetrius (Sen. *Ben.* 7.3.3), and by Stoic monists such as Marcus Aurelius (*Med.* 4.36). It would not be surprising, then, if Diogenes were to argue along these lines. It is unknown whether certain Cynics did actually try to eat human flesh, or whether this was a slander concocted by their detractors. One can only note that to be consistent, a man-eating Cynic would have to eat it raw.

Cercidas avoids all these unpleasant thoughts when he eulogizes Diogenes as one who soars aloft, "feeding on ether" (DL 6.77). Such idealizations would make the Cynics, "heavenly dogs", "sons of Zeus" who only drink nectar and ambrosia, the wine of the gods. But on the contrary, it seems that many of them did not even drink earthly wine, that quintessentially Greek drink. Many anecdotes portray the Cynics as resolute water-drinkers. Crates drank water and refused wine, and according to some reports, so did Diogenes (6.90). In one of Teles' fragments, Poverty says that she always provides for people's needs, for "aren't the springs full of water?" (Stob. 3.1.98) Varro coins a word, *Hydrokyōn*, "water-dog" (Varro *Sat. Men.* fr. 575 [= Gel. *NA* 13.31]), probably in reference to an abstemious Cynic.[13] Best of all, once more, is Parmeniscus' *Cynics' Symposium*, in which the Cynics sit around washing down their lentils with draughts of water, and discoursing expertly about the merits of different regional drafts. They seem to be enjoying themselves but, for others, the very word "water-drinker" connotes a killjoy who will not join in the fun. As with meat, however, the Cynics were not ideological abstainers. They did not anathematize wine as the devil's drink, cause of lies, brawls, fornication, poverty and despair. If certain Cynics renounced wine, it is must have been mainly because wine was an artificial product, obtained by unnecessary labour and itself a cause of unnecessary desires.

This is just extrapolation from the Cynics' general orientation towards custom, however, for the Cynics were not apostles of temperance who made wine one of their main targets. In fact, many stories portray the Cynics not only drinking wine and going to the *symposia*, but even entering those dens of disrepute, the *kapēleia* and *pandokeia*, to do it (DL 6.66; cf. 6.50). What type of wine does Diogenes like to drink best? Someone else's (6.54). On one occasion, Diogenes asked Plato for some figs and wine, but when Plato sent back a whole jar of each, Diogenes scolded him for sending too much – although not for sending them altogether (6.26). How then should one interpret Diogenes' enigmatic metaphor: the taverns of Athens are its *phiditia* (Spartan barracks) (Arist. *Rh.* 1411a24)? Does he here condemn the Athenian pubs as lairs of luxury and unnatural vice, far removed from the hardy Lacedaemonian virtues that thrive on the cold waters of the Eurotas?

The Cynics' ambiguous disapproval of wine is reflected also in their shameless antics at *symposia*. The *symposium*, literally a "drinking together", usually took place after the dinner; then the wine, flute-girls, dancers, jugglers, acrobats and other entertainment would be brought out and the real partying got underway. In the archaic and classical periods, the *symposium* was associated with the aristocratic and upper classes, and here was one of the first hotbeds of Greek music, song, poetry and decorative art. What place could the "Dogs" have in such cultured society? Many anecdotes portray them as gatecrashers who broke in to mock the perfumed degenerates as they reclined drunkenly around their tables. Thus, Metrocles tells the story of Diogenes going to a *symposium* with one half of his head shaved. The other symposiasts must not have liked this and he reportedly "took blows". But he got his revenge by writing the names of the perpetrators on a board, slinging the board around his neck and walking about town, thus publicizing their *hubris* and shaming them (DL 6.33). Or in another story, it is implied that Diogenes once went to a *symposium* (literally, "went to dinner") but would never go again, because "his host had not expressed the proper gratitude" (6.34). Of course, Diogenes may not have behaved himself on such an occasion; in one anecdote, when the diners began to throw bones to him, as if to a dog, Diogenes responded in kind, by lifting his leg like a dog and urinating on them (DL 6.46). Such expectations make Parmeniscus' *Cynics' Symposium* a witty juxtaposition of incommensurables: the Cynics should not be at a *symposium* at all, still less should they have one of their own, and even less should they indulge in erudite disquisitions on the bibliography of the lentil, to which even their prostitute, Nicion the "Dogfly", has something learned to contribute (Ath. 4.45).

The *symposium* occurred indoors, and the Greeks' custom was to eat and drink indoors. In fact, it was somewhat shameful to be seen eating in public. Diogenes, however, made it *his* custom to do "the works of Demeter" out of doors, regardless of what others thought (DL 6.69). To this outrageous spectacle people would sometimes flock, and mock Diogenes as a shameless dog (6.61). But to such criticisms, he replied rationally enough: "Why not eat in the agora? I was hungry there too" (6.58). Some might call this attitude shamelessness, but the Cynics called it freedom: the Cynic eats where and when he is hungry, while most others hide away in their houses, and eat according to schedule, customary mealtimes and the dictates of others.

Sex, baths and pleasure-spots

In fact, Diogenes boasted of being willing to use any space for any natural purpose (DL 6.22), and this might include sex. If eating was customarily seen as an indoor activity, then *a fortiori*, sex was even more private. Through pagan antiquity, both Greek and Roman, there were no strict taboos against pre-marital sex, the use of prostitutes or homosexuality. In such an atmosphere, Cynic attitudes towards sex can be seen as at once more shameless and more moralistic than the norm. On the one hand, sex is a natural activity, and so one should not be ashamed of any genuine sexual urges; one can learn this from the animals (the Cynic says), for they know simple remedies for their simple desires. Fish wisely rub themselves on rough surfaces when in need (D. Chr. 6.18), and so Diogenes was notoriously said to "use his hand", and to perform "the works of Aphrodite" (DL 6.69) in public.[14] If only, he exclaimed, one could relieve a hungry belly also just by rubbing it (6.46).[15] Pagan attitudes towards sex, Aphrodite, Eros and Priapus may have been more easygoing than those publicly espoused during the Middle Ages, say, but public masturbation was going too far, and in describing such phenomena, Diogenes Laertius is too embarrassed to use anything but euphemistic language. On the other hand, many sexual desires are not natural, and Cynics fear that one can easily become a slave to needless sexual pleasure.[16] Therefore, taking prostitutes is a bad thing (DL 6.66); good-looking women are dangerous, for their beauty ensnares (6.61); lovers "take pleasure in a misfortune" (6.67); and Cynic Heracles might have loosened Hippolyta's girdle but he had the self-control to wander on afterwards, despite all the beautiful Amazon's efforts to keep him for herself (D. Chr. 8.32). Similarly, Diogenes frowns upon the activities of Didymon the adulterer (DL 6.68), not, one imagines, because he revered the marital vow or deplored the effect on the woman's family, but because serial adultery only stokes sexual appetite, which is endless, unnecessary and often highly destructive:

> That for which people have the most problems, spend the most money – for which many cities are destroyed and many nations miserably ruined – this Diogenes thought was the least labour-intensive and the least expensive. For he didn't need to go anywhere for sex, but joked that Aphrodite was present for him everywhere, and for free … He was astonished at people's not wanting to pay money to have a foot scratched or a hand or any other part of the body, and that even the extremely wealthy would not pay out a single drachma for this, but on the other hand for that one member they would pay many talents again and again, and some even risk their lives to boot. He joked that this type of sex was Pan's discovery. For when he fell in love with Echo but could not catch her and was wandering among the hills day and night, it was then that Hermes taught him, out of pity and because he was his son. And so on learning the technique, Pan was released from his distress, and it was from him that the shepherds learned how to do it.
>
> (D. Chr. 6.16–20)

But if for some Cynics, masturbation and "free love" was natural, wise and god-like all at once, homosexuality was definitely not. Many anecdotes clearly express Cynic disapproval of "Greek love". Diogenes quotes the *Iliad* to warn a good-looking young man who was sleeping unguarded, "rise up, so that someone does not fix a spear in your back as you sleep" (DL 6.53). Or again, he tells a good-looking young man going off to a *symposium* that he will return "worse" (i.e. buggered) (6.59).[17] Crates mocked Menedemus for being an *erōmenos* (the passive partner) (6.91). Demonax ridiculed a handsome young man who had not yet lost his *daktylion* (ambiguously, either his ring or his anus), despite being well on the way, since he is happy to take the *daktylion* (i.e. the ring) of someone else (Luc. *Demon.* 17, cf. 15). Bion "said in censure of Alcibiades that as a boy he drew away the husbands from their wives, and as a young man the wives from their husbands" (DL 4.49). In his public speeches, Dio Chrysostom condemned homosexuality on many counts: it is unnatural, unmanly, unGreek.[18] Such statements may reflect a change in sexual *mores* in the Hellenistic and Roman period, or, when attributed to a Diogenes and Crates, may reflect how those early, classical Cynics allied themselves with the more homophobic attitudes of the non-aristocratic classes.

In all periods (particularly the classical), homosexual liaisons could be made in the *gymnasia*, *palaestrai* and baths of the Greek cities, and so it is not surprising to read of Cynics targeting these places as hotbeds of vice and degeneracy. The baths were particularly reprehensible on this score. The Romans were proud of their baths, of course. Private and public, men's baths and women's baths, there were hundreds of *balneae* in Rome itself. Baths were built throughout the Empire, from Britain to Morocco to Syria, and in all the lands in which Cynics appear during their "Imperial" period. Demetrius criticized the bathers in the baths newly dedicated by Nero and the Senate: he did so half-naked, with only a girdle on, and he said, paradoxically, that the bathers were "dirtying themselves" (Philostr. *V S* 4.42). Bathing was a Greek custom too, which went back to Homeric times, when Briseis bathed Achilles, and Eurycleia Odysseus, but from the beginning also, there were grumblers who carped that *warm* baths were corrupting.[19] The Cynics added to this chorus, as Diogenes and others emerge from the public *balaneia* with sharp words for the *cottabus* (a popular drinking game) played there (DL 6.46), the dirt of the places (6.47) and the "mob" that frequent them (6.40). "What does a dog have to do with the baths?" is a proverb that could be easily transferred to the Cynics (Luc. *Ind.* 5.30; cf. Jul. *Or.* 6.181a). The Cynics did not go to the baths to bathe themselves but to "bark" at vice: baths, with their homosexuality and self-indulgence (DL 6.52), are incompatible with physical toughness, temperance and sexual integrity. One wonders too whether some Cynics reflected also on the hidden costs of the baths, on how some pleasures are purchased with much pain: did they think of the despised *balneatores*, and the hundreds of slaves in the Roman hypocausts, working through steam and darkness so that Trimalchio-like figures could seduce boys in the *tepidaria* just above?[20] There are other customs of personal care and hygiene, notably medicine, the renunciation of whose drugs, poultices and the like coheres only too well with the Cynic principle of avoiding all artifice. But let us move on to a different set of conventions: those concerning family, friendship, business and social interaction generally.

Customs for the household: marriage, children, property, wealth, work, games

Marriage, wives and children

Regarding the family, marriage, spouses and children, servants and slaves, if a Cynic did not have a house (*oikos*), neither did he have any of its appurtenances. In the first place, Cynics disapproved of traditional marriage as an unnecessary burden, an impediment to freedom, the old "ball and chain". Diogenes called the mistresses of kings "kingesses", because they "make the kings do their bidding" (DL 6.63). When Bion was "consulted by someone as to whether he should marry, he answered, with cruel logic: if your wife is ugly, you'll have your punishment; if she is beautiful, you won't have her" (literally, "if you marry a beautiful woman, you will have to share her") (4.48).[21] In other words: don't marry! Many philosophers did not marry, of course: Socrates, Aristotle and Cicero did, but Thales, Heraclitus, Empedocles, Plato, Zeno, Epicurus, Plotinus and others did not. Given their radical individualism, it is not surprising that most of the known Cynics did not "tie the knot". The exception proving the rule is the famous "dog-marriage" (*kynogamia*) of Crates and Hipparchia, which bore a "pup" in Pasicles and perhaps also a daughter (DL 6.88, 93). Epictetus would ideally recommend a marriage like this for Cynics: marriage, cooking meals, cleaning babies, taking children to school and the like all distract one from philosophy, but if one marries another free-spirited Cynic, has a Cynic father-in-law, Cynic babies and so forth, it might not be so (*Diss.* 3.22.67–82). Epictetus sees this arrangement as fairly unlikely, however, and so in general his ideal Cynic will not marry: the marriage of Crates and Hipparchia was unrepeatable, for here Crates married "another Crates" (3.22.76). In all this, however, it would seem that Epictetus was outwitted by his student Demonax. For when he advised Demonax to get married (i.e. not to become a Cynic?), Demonax laughed it off and said that he would follow his advice but only if Epictetus would give him one of his own daughters (Luc. *Demon.* 55). Epictetus, of course, had no daughters and never married, so why should Demonax settle for second best? He would either marry Epictetus' daughter, or be like the master himself; either scenario would be perfect. With regard to Crates and Hipparchia, it would seem that they were genuinely in love, an unlikely couple to add to the famous lovers of antiquity, like Helen and Paris, Penelope and Odysseus, Aspasia and Pericles, Cleopatra and Antony. But even this "dog-marriage" was a flouting of convention, given that Hipparchia had to overcome her parents' desires for a more mainstream, lucrative match.[22]

But with this one exception, marriage is regarded by the Cynics as a battleground and an uneasy truce. In one cryptic anecdote a newlywed man wrote above his door: "The son of Zeus, victorious Heracles dwells here; let nothing evil enter". When he read this, Diogenes quipped, "after war, alliance" (DL 6.50). What did he mean by this? Perhaps Diogenes is comparing the period of "courting" to a war, in which the grooms' and brides' families manoeuvre and scheme for maximum advantage before coming to close quarters, as it were. Affection and love were less important considerations than material gain: the status of the partners, their wealth, land, the dowry that the bride would bring to the husband's house, the security that he would provide her. Thus, after a struggle for advantage, the groom wins his bride, like some conquering Heracles, and the two then unite for the further promotion of their household: a marital, if not martial, alliance. More cryptic still is the story of how Crates took his son to a brothel, saying that this was how his father was married (6.89). Whatever the precise implication here, it is obviously not a positive one. In all this, the Cynics did not share Aristotle's view that marriage is natural, indispensable both to one's basic humanity and to the "good life". Far less did they regard it with romantic eyes, as if to meet "the one" and share all one's days together were the consummation of happiness, devoutly to be wished. On the contrary, marriage breeds attachments, quarrels, trivial worries and, at best, a conventional happiness, that is, a complacent habituation to daily routine. A married person is not free, and if he seeks escape through adultery, he may risk being killed (6.4, 6.89).

Given such an uncompromising rejection of family values, one wonders how the Cynics regarded children. Is the desire for children natural or merely conventional? Some ancient thinkers regarded this desire as one of the most basic: for the Stoics, it is one aspect of the drive to self-preservation, and so too for Plato and Aristotle, sexual desire is not simply as an urge "to discharge" or to get some passing satisfaction but is rather nature's means of continuing the species and of allowing the individual to live on after death. In Plato's *Symposium*, Socrates envisions sexual desire as a *daimōn* that mediates between time and eternity: through sex, one reproduces oneself, lives on through one's child, and so cheats death for at least a few more generations. The atmosphere is very different in perhaps the main passage that propounds Cynic ideas in this regard, Epictetus' *Dissertations* 3.22.77–82. Here Epictetus asserts that the true Cynic is also a true "father", because he treats and loves all human beings as his children:

> "How then", asked the young man, "will a Cynic preserve society"? In the name of God, man, who is the greater benefactor to mankind? Those who bring forth two or three ugly-snouted children to take their place, or those who watch over all mankind as best they can, observing what they do, how they spend their time, what they care for, and what they disregard contrary to their duty? (*Diss.* 3.22.77)

The tone and argument is tendentious, as is the Cynic stance as a whole. Indeed, it may not have been wholly consistent. For if the sexual drive is natural, as is the desire to satisfy it, then having children is natural. But if children will be born, who will raise them? Human children cannot be laid and abandoned like insects' eggs; long nurturing is natural to the human animal. Extant literature suggests, however, that the Cynics were not overly bothered by the issue. One *Cynic Epistle* answers that the extinction of mankind would be no worse than that of wasps or flies (*Ep. Diog.* 47 [Malherbe]). Or, in the *Republic* attributed to him, Diogenes advocated a community of women (and men), with children being raised together, all in a gaggle (DL 6.72, 7.131). This is reminiscent of Plato's *Republic*, of course, in which Socrates regards the nuclear family as a mere convention, to be legislated out of existence for the common good. If Diogenes did advocate such a "reform", he may have been inspired by reports of polygamous or even polyandrous societies in which children from different parents were reared as a group. Centuries later, Lucian repeats such ideas but with a venom all his own. In his *Runaways*, three "bad" Cynics share one adulterous woman, who has not yet "bitched from them" and brought forth Cerberus-like Cynic children into the world (Luc. *Fugitivi* 18, 31–33). Lucian's language suggests that such *ménages à quatres* and Cynics "packs" were not uncommon, and that individualistic Cynics were not greatly concerned about the responsibility of children.[23]

Property and slavery

More uplifting is the Cynic rejection of that other important element of the ancient household, slavery. Aristotle again articulates conventional "common sense" when he writes that the slave is a part of the household in the way that furniture, animals and property generally are. For Aristotle, a household consists of husband, wife, children and property, with some property being inanimate, such as land, buildings and tools, and other property alive, such as oxen, horses and human chattel, the slaves, whom Aristotle defines as "living tools", in distinction from inanimate implements such as ploughs. Before coming to this infamous definition, Aristotle felt the need to address the contemporary debate as to whether slavery existed by "custom or nature". Aristotle's own view was that there are natural slaves, and natural masters. In these arguments, Aristotle only gives his own philosophical structure to "common sense". Slavery was a commonplace in the classical Greek cities, and hardly anyone questioned it. By some estimates, the typical small-time Athenian farmer might have two or three slaves (as in Aristophanes' plays, for instance). Slavery would become more industrial in scale during the Hellenistic and Roman period when larger cities, more extensive markets, greater concentrations of wealth, greater contact with foreign peoples, and bigger wars would only facilitate the slave trade. As a result, by the first century BCE slave markets at, for example, Rhodes, Delos and Rome were extremely busy, and the *latifundia* with its terrible chattel slavery was entrenched in large parts of Italy.

In the face of such institutional facts, very few, as mentioned, questioned the right or value of slavery. But one can surmise that the Cynics' orientation drove them to sympathize with these few. For the Cynics rejected property, money and the convention of wealth: after all, what can one own except the ground under one's feet,[24] and if one cannot really own things, then far less can one possess another human being.From a different angle, the Cynics did not recognize the label "slave" as applicable to themselves, for regardless of his situation, the Cynic remains free and is in fact freer than any masters. This is one moral of the popular story of the "Sale of Diogenes": Diogenes comes up for sale as a slave, but when asked about his skills, proclaims that he can "rule others". Thus, in chains Diogenes is still a "king"; despite changes in external fortune, the Cynic's freedom is inalienable. The Cynics shouted such egalitarian notions from street corners, broadcasting a message of liberty to all, and thus contributing, in their own way, to the gradual trend through ancient philosophy of locating freedom in the inner will and soul.[25]

In their own defiant pride, then, the Cynics reflect the burgeoning respect for the inherent dignity of the human being, an important theme for Socratic thinkers generally, and later for Christian anthropology. But if some aspects of Cynicism weakly anticipated the abolition of slavery, the Cynics themselves seem to have argued *explicitly* against slavery less because of the injustice done to the slaves than because of the dangers to the masters themselves. Most notable here is Dio's oration "On Slaves". In it Diogenes consoles a man whose slave has run away. No matter, he argues: slaves entail unnecessary and unnatural labour; having to feed, clothe and guard them, the master cannot leave home for fear of problems arising, and when he does stay at home, he is bound to monitor the slaves. Worse than this loss of leisure is the loss of virtue. For the more an owner depends on his slaves' labour, the less self-sufficient and capable he himself becomes. Relying on others for even the smallest tasks, he grows lazy, arrogant and peevish, and so paradoxically, rich masters "are often worse off for help than are the poor who keep no slaves" (D. Chr. 10.3–13, esp. 10.10). The thought is reflected in other passages and anecdotes. Pseudo-Lucian's Cynic portrays masters hardly able to walk, carried about by their porters "like freight", and still complaining about everything. Fearing such a fate perhaps, in one anecdote Diogenes is reputed to have said that he would no more allow a slave to put on his shoes than to wipe his nose (DL 6.44). In another, as *paidagōgus* to Xeniades' sons, Diogenes taught the boys to wait on themselves and not rely on slaves (6.31; cf. D. Chr. 10.13). In yet another anecdote, Diogenes is said at one point to have had a slave, Manes. But Manes ran away and Diogenes did not bother trying to catch him, saying: "if Manes can live without Diogenes, then Diogenes can live without Manes" (DL 6.55).[26] The quip is typical of the Greek view that the ruler should be *better* or more "virtuous" than the ruled, but it implies also a Cynic critique of slavery as an institution debilitating to the master-class. This echoes Cynic reservations about the enervating effect of baths, and in its own way anticipates Hegel's master–slave dialectic, according to which forced labour gradually makes the slaves freer and more capable of being masters than the masters themselves, until they eventually switch positions.[27] Moreover, there are moments when the Cynics express positive sympathy for the slaves themselves. According to Diogenes, some masters are "evil" (DL 6.39), and when they are gluttons, slaves are justified in stealing from them (6.28). When Dio's Diogenes consoles the owner of the runaway slave, he wonders aloud whether the slave had good reason to flee (D. Chr. 10.3–4, 10.7). Pseudo-Lucian's Cynic berates his interlocutor for treating slaves like wagons and beasts of burden, and considering this to be happiness (ps.-Luc. *Cyn.* 10). Such statements are not surprising given the tradition that many Cynics (Diogenes, Monimus, Menippus; cf. Epictetus) endured slavery at some point in their lives. Such experiences might lead those Cynics to look past circumstances and external appearances, to accord human beings an inherent dignity and freedom.

Wealth, money, coins and gold

Slavery in the ancient world was one form of wealth, and Cynic grumblings about slavery rise to a deafening shout when it comes to money, gold and wealth beyond one's daily needs. As we have seen, the Cynic motto was to "deface the coinage" (*paracharattein to nomisma*). The word *nomisma* is related etymologically to *nomos* and can be used as a near synonym for it. The particular formulation of the motto therefore suggests the identity of the two, as if customary relationships (*nomoi*) were, in the Cynics' view, dominated by coins (*nomismata*), money and greed. The Cynics reserve their most violent and most blanketing criticisms for money and the rich, condemning them wholesale for avarice, hubris, arrogance, injustice, profligacy and so forth. The unequivocal statement in the New Testament that "The love of money is the root of all evil" (1 Timothy 6:9–10; cf. Luke 16:13, Mark 6:24, 10:17–26; Colossians 3:5) was probably originally a Cynic saying: "The love of money he [e.g. Diogenes] declared to be the mother-city of all evils" (DL 6.50).[28]

Numerous anecdotes bear a tinge of this critique of wealth. Diogenes tells Alexander to stand out of the sunshine, and refuses his gifts: the best things are free, sunshine is the golden shower of Zeus, and the Cynic does not want Alexander's conventional gold, for what good is a shiny metal? Again, Diogenes goes with a lamp at noon into the marketplace looking for a human being: but he will find only wolves there in the marketplace, where people go to cheat each other by buying too low or selling too high, swindling each other for petty profit. Or again, Diogenes throws away his cup so as not to be beaten by the child in frugality (*euteleia*), the virtue that is the basis of the Cynic's "wealth". Other anecdotes include Diogenes spitting in a rich man's face, "because he could find no place better to do it" (DL 6.32); Diogenes calling an "ignorant rich man ... 'the sheep with the golden fleece'" (6.47); or calling temple officials "bigger thieves" than the thief who stole a bowl (6.45). Wealth is also a source of fear and loss of happiness: gold is pale, as if from fear and worry because so many people are plotting against it (6.51); according to Bion, it is those who want to be rich who suffer the most anxiety (4.48), but when a rich person acquires a fortune, it is actually the fortune that acquires him, for he becomes enslaved to his things (4.50).

One could multiply such examples many times over, in illustration of the simultaneous Cynic attack upon *nomos* and *nomisma*, custom and money, the twin corrupters of nature. There are direct attacks on the rich also, which are not so subtle. Diogenes is said to have struck Meidias, the richest man in Athens (DL 6.42). He says that Harpalus, happy with the huge wealth he stole from Alexander's treasury, provides testimony against the gods, for how could they allow such a criminal to be happy (Cic. *Nat. D.* 3.83)? The genial Demonax criticizes rich Herodes Atticus (Luc. *Demon.* 24, 33), as does his firebrand rival, Peregrinus (Luc. *De mort. Peregr.* 19).[29] The *Cynic Epistles* often feature philosophers rejecting the financial offers of one king or another. At the Isthmian Games, Dio's Diogenes has a put-down for everyone, but he is especially harsh towards those made arrogant by wealth and pedigree (D. Chr. 9.8–9). Dio's Diogenes also interprets the labours of Heracles as part of the perennial Cynic war on wealth: Heracles wandered the world, half-naked and hungry, toppling arrogant lords such as Diomedes (rich in horses) and Geryon (rich in cattle), and gladly giving the apples of the Hesperides to the tyrant Eurystheus. "Keep them and go hang [this Heracles says], for apples of gold are of no use to a man" (8.29–

34). The rich are probably *the* target of Lucian's satire too, as we have seen, particularly when they appear in the underworld, stripped of all their finery. Lucian's Menippus, for instance, says that Minos:

> was particularly harsh towards those made arrogant by their wealth and status and who expected others to kowtow before them – for he [Minos] loathed their short-lived bravado and snobbishness and obliviousness to the fact that they were mortal themselves and had merely stumbled upon passing goods. Stripped of all that finery, they – and by them I mean those rich in pedigree and power – stood naked, with downcast looks, as if revisiting their happiness like some dream. On seeing all this, I was absolutely delighted and if I recognized any of them, I would go up quietly and remind him of what he used to be in life and how conceited he was once. (Luc. *Nec.* 12)

In another passage, when Menippus sees various tyrants begging and cobbling shoes, he dances about with glee. His *schadenfreude* knows no bounds and he is positively beside himself when the assembly of the dead pass a decree condemning the rich on many counts, "including violence, ostentation, pride, injustice" (19–20). Their punishment (in addition to infernal tortures) will be to return to live as donkeys, to bear the burdens of the poor for twenty-five myriads of years (i.e. 250,000 years). Many such scenes and statements in Lucian are too bitter and venomous to be seen as ironic or a merely literary sport, and, as some have argued, they may well reflect the growing division between classes in the outwardly prosperous years under the "Good Emperors".[30]

Other Cynics took a somewhat gentler attitude. Monimus says that money is harmful unless used right (DL 6.95). The position might recall Aristotle's doctrine of right use, except for the fact that for Monimus, money is primarily "harmful" (not neutral), and that the condition of right use is a significant one: how often is wealth used wisely (many Cynics ask, e.g. D. Chr. 10.14–15; ps.-Luc. *Cyn.* 8–10) and not on fattening foods, alcohol, gambling, prostitutes, conspicuous consumption, bribery and political machinations, and most of all, for war and the business of killing?

Here one might take a short diversion to examine the continuity between Cynic and Stoic attitudes towards wealth, and the pleasures that wealth facilitates. Both sets of attitudes have struck many as strangely ambiguous, and so have inspired a welter of interpretations. The Stoics officially located wealth among the "preferred indifferents", but could be accused of hypocrisy or blatant self-contradiction when figures such as Seneca were fantastically wealthy. Analogously, the Cynics embraced an ascetic poverty and criticized both wealth and the wealthy, yet many anecdotes depict them enjoying honey cakes, *symposia* and expensive luxuries: are such Cynics here convicted of hypocrisy? Just as some ancients admired Cynic frugality but hated contemporary Cynics' materialism, so some modern scholars have regarded the Cynics as genuine "ascetics" who lived rough and warred against pleasure, while others (notably Sayre) interpreted them as "hedonists" who indulged freely while hiding behind a pretence of temperance. Thus, as with the Stoics, one may ask whether the Cynics were *really* indifferent to wealth and pleasure, or did they really "prefer" to have them, while feigning a sham indifference?[31]

In the Cynics' case at least, the dichotomy of hedonism versus asceticism may often be a false one if it is true that the Cynics did not stand under the empire of pleasure or pain (Jeremy Bentham's "two masters") but rather served their own easy freedom, as *opportunists*.[32] That is, their good was immediate freedom: they sought to live fully in the present moment, and therefore "preferred" what was immediately available but remained indifferent to everything that was not, that is, to whatever was troublesome to acquire. Thus, they might "prefer" wealth and luxury, if present. But generally these commodities are not within easy reach, and so the Cynics simply enjoyed whatever was at hand, even if it were only lentils and sunshine. But to be able to enjoy the chance occurrences of the present is very difficult, and such a radical simplicity requires both physical and psychological discipline. Hence *askēsis* was central to the Cynic lifestyle, although theirs was a cheerful and hedonistic, not a world-denying, asceticism.

That is, they paradoxically welcomed pain as a necessary condition of elemental pleasure. *Askēsis* made them true hedonists, to such an extent that they might even get pleasure in their self-chosen pains: "the scorn of pleasure is the greatest pleasure" (DL 6.71). That *askēsis* is the key concept of Cynicism is the important thesis of Goulet-Cazé (1986a: esp. 17–92), but one can find a similar view adumbrated in Julian: the true Cynic must first practice *askēsis* to free himself from the desire for pleasures, but once he is able to "trample" on them at will, then "he may permit himself to dip into that sort of thing *if it come his way*" (Jul. *Or.* 6.200d, emphasis added).

This attitude of living opportunistically in the moment ensures that the Cynics, theoretically at least, are truly indifferent to wealth and money, for these are abstract entities without any immediate reality. As a result of their dedication to the present moment, Cynics often reminded the conventionally minded how useless money actually is. Crates, for example, writes that he does not want to "heap up the wealth of the beetle" (Jul. *Or.* 6.200a, 7.213c). One must here read between the lines: he may well mean the dung beetle, which gathers and eats dung – as human animals should not.[33] Again, gold and silver are as valuable as "pebbles on a beach", a common refrain (Luc. *Pisc.* 35). Or again, most people will pay three thousand drachmas for a statue, but only two coppers for a *choenix* (i.e. two pints) of grain: that is, they spend a fortune on what is useless, but hardly anything for their daily bread (DL 6.35). Again, when Bion asked for three obols from Antigonus Gonatas, the king gave him a whole talent, which Bion proceeded to give to a baker in exchange for the loaf of bread that he really wanted. Such gestures contrast Cynic simplicity with the complicated web of trust and deception that make an economic system possible. Lucian's Demonax compares financial dealings to wizardry: one can go into a bakery and with the spell of a few coins bewitch the baker to hand over loaves (Luc. *Demon.* 23). Money casts its spell over the fools of the world, so that ultimately many forget what is of true value, and sacrifice all in their mania for a soft, inedible metal. Even more basic is the thought that one cannot really possess anything external. One owns only what one can hold in one's hand, as it were: only what is *here* is real. Therefore, Epictetus makes bodily need the measure of wealth while all else belongs to fickle fortune.[34]

To inoculate themselves against the destructive mania for wealth, the Cynics made it almost a rite of passage to renounce all one's possessions. Thus Diogenes "defaces the coinage" (DL 6.20). Monimus upsets the table of his master, a banker, and starts to throw the coins around the marketplace (6.82). Crates sells his land and gives the money away, or throws it in the sea, or lodges it with a banker, telling him to give it to his sons if they grow up to be conventional citizens, but to distribute it among the people if they become philosophers (6.88). Hipparchia rejects a wealthy marriage to Crates (6.96) and Peregrinus gives all his property and money to his fellow citizens of Parium (Luc. *De mort. Peregr.* 15). Throwing one's money into the sea becomes a common image for the Cynics' irreversible choice (e.g. DL 6.87). In fact, in the Hellenistic and Imperial periods, it became a widespread expectation that the philosopher will reject money, or excessive money, as a matter of course. Diogenes Laertius projects these quasi-Cynic expectations as far back as the Seven Sages. His Solon, for instance, forgives a large debt owed to his father (1.45) and his Pittacus refuses advancement from Croesus (1.76, 1.81; cf. Luc. *Fugitivi* 29, of Orpheus).

Work and begging

If one has no money, it might seem that one must work to live, but surprisingly the Cynics did little work and were known as idlers. How then did they live? We have seen how they scraped by, foraging and gathering, but they were also dependent on the human landscape, despite protestations of self-sufficiency. Later Cynics are said to have taken food left at crossroads as offerings to Hecate. This custom of leaving "Hecate's dinners" belonged to the classical period also, and so it is possible that these dinners for the goddess fed earlier Cynics as well.[35] Scholars have generally overlooked how Diogenes' mischievous syllogism may half-seriously justify the opportunistic theft of such sacred offerings: all things belong to the gods (Diogenes reasoned), the wise are friends to the gods, but friends hold all things in common, so therefore all things belong to the wise (DL 6.37).[36] The inference is that Hecate is morally obliged to give me her supper. This sort of roguish logic must have served many Cynics well as they lived by their wits from moment to moment. Most characteristically, Cynics begged (*aitein*) from strangers and friends. Or, as Diogenes preferred to put it, they only asked their due (*apaitein*), or took "gifts", or permanently "borrowed" items such as cloaks (e.g. 6.45, 6.49, 6.56, 6.62, 6.66). Or, as later Cynics said, they were only "collecting tribute" and "shearing the sheep", for do not kings collect taxes, and aren't sheep better off unburdened by their wool? And if their subjects and flocks hesitated to contribute, they roared and shouted and satirized, shaming them into paying up (Luc. *Fugitivi* 14, 20). Once more, from depictions in Lucian, Dio Chrysostom and Julian, it would seem that many later Cynics were little more than professional beggars (e.g. Mart. *Ep.* 7.64.8), as materialistic as any, and maybe more so. This might explain why some were quicker to give money to the blind and lame than to "philosophers" (DL 6.56), who were a source of both awe and distrust to the conventionally minded (Luc. *Fugitivi* 12, 14, 18).

Less hypocritical Cynics, however, claimed not to work because they had very few needs, which were easily satisfied. Most people work for unnecessary things, and are miserable as a result since their greatest fear is to lose their house, food and life itself. They fear poverty and death. But one cannot control one's fortune, or know the hour of one's passing. Chance rules all. Therefore, Dio Chrysostom argues, human beings only multiply their own sufferings by trying to avoid them (D. Chr. 6.31–4). Or, from a different perspective again, weeds and thistles will cover all one's labours, so why bother working? Demonax repeats the line of Homer's Achilles: "they both died, the lazy man and the busy-body" (Luc. *Demon.* 60). Or, from a different perspective again, neither gods nor animals work. The Homeric gods enjoy perpetual ease, and dogs lie contented in the sun. Why, therefore, should one slave and toil, often at sordid jobs and for trivial or pernicious wants? One should remember of course that Cynic laziness was less reprehensible in a culture that knew no rigid work ethic, never mind all the instruments that drill industry into modern labour forces: alarm clocks, regimented days, production schedules and quarterly reports. On the other hand, Cynics such as Dio Chrysostom and Lucian's Cynicus did work for their daily bread. Dio was at times an agricultural labourer and gardener, and when shipwrecked off Euboea, he helped a hunter skin a deer: the immediate task at hand (D. Chr. 7.2–5). Lucian's Menippus did not have the obol fare to cross the River Styx but he earned his passage by rowing and baling (Luc. *Dial. mort.* 22). Thus the Cynic-tramp does whatever needs doing, but he is not bound by any long-term duties, and works only when and where he needs.

Play, games and the Games

If the Cynics rejected work, one might expect them to have liked playing, and in a way this was true. They claimed to treat life as a festival and each moment was for them a time for joking. Lucian's dialogues are full of Cynics laughing at others and taking nothing seriously and usually, in Lucian's presentation, this is the right attitude. Crates was said to have gone through life laughing, and in this he recalled the humours of Socrates who was also something of a joker, ironist and buffoon.[37]

But in another sense, the Cynics did *not* play along when others were in the mood. That is, there is evidence of them ridiculing Greek pastimes, and in particular the Greek mania for games and sports. This frenzy took many forms. One Greek game was *cottabus*, in which a player would flick drops of wine from his cup into a bowl. When Diogenes saw a young man playing *cottabus* in the baths, he said paradoxically, "So much the better, so much the worse", meaning that the better you can play this game, the greater fool you are (DL 6.46). Drinking games, dicing, cock-fighting and the like were relatively harmless compared to the premier Roman sport, the gladiatorial games. Significantly, during the imperial period, mainland Greece was one of the few places in the Empire where gladiatorial games never really took hold. Commercial Corinth was exceptional

and had an arena, and out of local rivalry Athens might have followed suit if Demonax had not stepped forward to argue against it
as a pitiless custom (Luc. *Demon.* 57; cf. D. Chr. 31.122; Philostr.
V A 4.22). In Alexandria, one sees Dio Chrysostom mocking the
populace for their unnatural addiction to the hippodrome (D. Chr.
32.31, 32.46).

Before gladiatorial games and hippodromes, however, and indeed
before everything, the Greeks loved athletics. Nothing was more
important for the life of the people as a whole than the Games,
and it was the custom for families and cities to send athletes to
Olympia, Delphi, Nemea and the Isthmus at the traditional times,
in the summer of every fourth or second year. The Olympics, in
particular, were celebrated continuously from 776 BCE (the traditional date, when Coroebus won the foot race) until 394 CE (when
the Christian Emperor Theodosius abolished them and closed the
sanctuary). For the Games were also a religious occasion, an offering
to Zeus himself, who watched in delight and at whose temple the
Olympic victors were crowned with a wreath of sacred olive leaves.
It took independence of spirit to question these exciting and sacred
Games, yet many philosophers and intellectuals did. Xenophanes,
Euripides, Isocrates and others doubted whether so much energy
should be devoted to watching naked men throw things, wrestle and
run around a field. True to form, the Cynics joined in this chorus.
According to legend, Antisthenes went to the Isthmian games to
praise and criticize the Greeks, but didn't bother when he saw the
size of the crowd, perhaps realizing that one could do nothing with
that mob (DL 6.2). Diogenes called athletes sheep-like and wres-
tlers stupid (6.49, 6.61). Demonax mocked the effeminate clothing
of one athlete, who responded by beating him on the head until he
bled (Luc. *Demon.* 16, 39). At another time, when the pancratiasts
started to bite each other (contrary to the rules) Demonax praised
them dubiously, saying that their admirers were right to call them
"lions".[38]

And yet, the atmosphere and prestige of the Games were such
that for all their mockery, the Cynics too could not escape their
allure. In them they found perhaps their richest source of meta-

phor and moral inspiration. The athletes, ideally, trained for years and then came out to struggle in the dust under a pitiless July sun, and for what? For nothing more than the honour of winning, and a crown of leaves. Many Greek writers express their astonishment and pride that their people would compete for something as intangible as honour, as if this were yet one more proof of the Hellenes' nobility and superiority to other nations. For their part, the Cynics might mock this crown of leaves as something that only goats would want to nibble, but, they too felt the magic of the Games, the glory of so many centuries. And so they tried to appropriate some of that glory for themselves, by claiming to be true Olympic victors. Thus, they too had their own *askēsis*, their years of lonely labour (*ponos*, *athlos*) worthy of Heracles himself, the mythic founder of Olympia (e.g. Epict. *Diss.* 3.22.51–2; Jul. *Or.* 6.195a–b). For all this, their only reward was virtue, and yet this virtue was more sufficient for happiness than any withering wreath. A common anecdote sees Diogenes proclaiming his superiority to Pythian, Isthmian or Olympic victors, for they only defeat slaves while he overcomes real men, or real dangers like pleasure, pain, desire and folly (e.g. DL 6.33, 6.43; D. Chr. 9.12). In one story, he crowns *himself* at the Isthmus with a sprig of pine (D. Chr. 9.10–13). In another, "To those who said, 'You are an old man, take it easy from now on', Diogenes replied 'What? If I were running the *dolichos* [i.e. the distance event, *c*.2400m] and were near the end, should I slow down and not rather speed up?'" (DL 6.34). Thus, the Games provided a venue for Cynics to advertise their superiority. In this they were typically Greek, and for all the rhetoric of rejecting custom, they too followed the custom of so many other orators, poets, historians and sculptors who went to Olympia to give speeches, read their compositions aloud and display their statues (e.g. D. Chr. 8.9). The greatest display of all was brought to the assembled Greeks by Peregrinus in the Games of 165 CE: it is a fitting culmination of the Cynic rejection of athletics that Peregrinus chose to kill himself at Olympia, where for over 900 years already the Greeks had gathered at the customary time to celebrate strength, speed and endurance – in a word, life.

Customs for the city: politics, war, citizenship

Politics

"Man is a political animal", or more precisely, Aristotle defined a human being as the animal that naturally belongs to the *polis*. Bees have their hives, fish their shoals, wolves their packs, and mankind their city-states, in the Greek style. For (Aristotle argues) it is only in these relatively small[39] communities that everyone can know everyone, and can participate directly in all the decisions affecting the city: the assemblies, courts, magistracies, sacrifices, festivals and military campaigns. Only in such an environment can the human animal actualize all its potentialities as a social, rational and even god-like being. Living in cities is not merely a Greek convention, or an accident of history, but an extension of human nature itself.

The classical Greeks tended instinctively to recognize the profundity of Aristotle's remarks; or, rather, Aristotle's theory is deeply indebted to the Greek custom of living in cities, and of identifying the individual closely with the city of his or her birth. That is, in classical Greece, a person was not seen primarily as an autonomous agent rationally maximizing his or her utility; nor as a free being drifting through the abyss of freedom; nor as a creature made in God's image and likeness, an earthly pilgrim seeking a heavenly home. Rather, a person was a son, daughter, father, mother, husband, wife, friend, neighbour or fellow-tribesman, all of which relations were completed in citizenship, because a person was felt to be first and foremost a citizen of a city. Hence individuals were often identified by their city of birth – Parmenides of Elea, Herodotus of Halicarnassus, Socrates of Athens, Diogenes of Sinope, Crates of Thebes, Monimus of Syracuse, Bion of Borysthenes, Menippus of Gadara, Demetrius of Corinth, Dio of Prusa – and this identification continued even when (like Diogenes) they had long since left it. In the classical period especially, the citizen's life was fairly dominated by the consuming life of the *polis*. All the great experiences (even religious ones) were public experiences and so the Greek man typically spent most of his time outdoors, working, buying and selling in the market, or politicking in the assembly and courts. In this environment, not to join in was to risk being called "useless" – or woman-like, for women tended to be kept sequestered indoors, except for special occasions such as festivals or family gatherings.

For the men, however, such an outdoors life, and the smallness of the city-state ensured that basically everyone talked about everyone and everything, and therefore every act was a potentially political one. There was no real privacy. What one ate for dinner, whether one liked women or boys, whether one carried a stick, how one wore one's hair, whether one let one's *himation* flow down or tied it up more severely, how much of one's arm was kept outside one's cloak, whether one ate fish and what kind, how loudly one talked: all the myriad details of a personality and lifestyle could be interpreted in a myriad ways, depending on who was observing and spinning them into a particular narrative. As a result, the Greeks have been called the "political people" and, collectively, their political experience was incredibly broad, ranging from absolute tyrannies to radical democracies to federations of cities and even the beginnings of representative democracy. The democratic Athenians, with their frequent assemblies and large court-sittings, were regarded as more politically aware than most and, among them, figures such as Alcibiades and Demosthenes surpassed all others as true "political animals". More than others, they lived for the excitement of affairs.

But, like so much else, the classical Cynics rejected this bustling involvement and stood aside from elections, juries and daily politics. Diogenes waved his middle finger at Demosthenes and called him the "demagogue of Athens" (DL 6.34). He mocked Anaximenes, a fat orator (6.57). He called demagogues generally the "lackeys of the people" and the crowns awarded to them "the efflorescence of fame" (6.41). Once when Diogenes saw Demosthenes eating in an inn (*pandokeion*), Demosthenes recoiled further inside, afraid of scandal, but Diogenes sang out that this would only shame him more (6.34): as a "receive-all", the *pandokeion* might be a rough place where customers could get cheap wine, prostitutes, fleas, black eyes and worse. The Cynics express even more distaste at aristocratic and monarchical politics. Diogenes told Plato not to visit the tyrants in Sicily, because he could eat olives just as well in Attica; if Plato washed his own lettuces, he would not need to flatter tyrants like Dionysius (6.25, 6.58). The Athens of the older Plato, Aristotle and Demosthenes was also the Athens struggling against Philip and Alexander, and the Cynics appear in many anecdotes like gadflies, stinging those mighty figures with their sharp quips. Later kings such as Perdiccas, Craterus and others felt the sting too, at least in legend. In one of the better exchanges, Antigonus Monophthalmus ("the One-Eyed") wins a rare victory of wit over the Cynic Thrasyllus. "Give me a drachma!" says Thrasyllus. "No, that is unworthy of a king." "Give me a talent then!" "No", says the king, "That is unworthy of a Cynic".[40] This tradition loves to see the anti-political Cynic crossing swords with whole phalanxes and legions of politicos: orators and magistrates of democratic Athens, Hellenistic kings and generals, and eventually Roman consuls (*hypatoi* in Greek) (e.g. Luc. *Demon.* 30), proconsuls (*anthypatoi*) (e.g. Luc. *Demon.* 16, 50), and even emperors (*basileis*) (e.g. Cass. Dio 65.15.4 on Titus). In these last examples, as well as in the cases of Peregrinus Proteus and the early Dio Chrysostom, it seems that some Cynics routinely criticized Roman rule, perhaps even with calls for the Greeks to reassert their ancestral freedom in arms.

This rejection of political life could sometimes make the Cynics seem like utter misanthropes, as if they were at war with all mankind. Thus, Antisthenes scorns the Athenian pride in being autochthonous, the only people to be born from the soil on which they lived; in this, he said, they are no more noble than snails and locusts (DL 6.1). Diogenes said darkly that it would make no more difference if the whole human race died out, because they are no better than flies and wasps (*Ep. Diog.* 47 [Malherbe]). He also used the term "human" as a synonym for "wretched"', when he played with words to call orators "thrice human" rather than the more customary "thrice wretched" (DL 6.47).[41] So too Diogenes may have thought that few people were really human: most belonged to the mob (*ochlos*) (6.40, 6.60) and in the famous image, Diogenes lit a lantern during the day and went around the city looking "for a human being" as if, under the bright

Mediterranean sun, there would not be enough light to find this rare and elusive creature (6.41).

War

If war is an extension of politics, then the Cynics extend their renunciation of conventional politics to include the pointlessness of war. For the archaic and classical Greek city-states, war was a commonplace, almost part of the traditional fabric of life. In the spring or summer, the men of the city might take their weapons and march out to fight the men of neighbouring cities, on a level plain where the massed hoplite armies could line up properly. There were casualties but there were rarely wholesale massacres; fleeing soldiers were not generally cut down or even pursued far, for the victorious army stopped at that point of the field where the route began. This was the "turning point" and there the winners customarily set up a *tropaion* or "trophy" to mark it, heaping up captured spoils and weapons. The dead were exchanged, and prisoners ransomed in the aftermath. Vengeance rarely extended to inflicting casualties on women and children; battles were not fought in the winter, until the ambitious Philip broke with tradition. Thus, war was rarely the "total war" of the twentieth century. It remained something both terrible and sublime: Greek men could still enjoy the *Iliad* and catch something of that old heroic glory in the battles of their day. So engrained was war in customary life that some scholars regard the classical *polis* as effectively a political entity organized for war, dominated as it often was by its citizen-fighters: the aristocratic cavalry of archaic cities, the hoplites of later ones, or the sailors and rowers of Periclean Athens. By one reckoning, between roughly 511 and 320 BCE, democratic Athens was at war for two years of every three, and the greatest document of the democracy is Pericles' *Funeral Oration*: an oration praising the fallen dead. Statutes, poems and histories were made to celebrate heroes and patriots. War, then, was a custom whose influence was nearly all pervasive.

As with slavery, very few seem to have questioned the need for war. There were no dreams of a "perpetual peace" or of the end of all wars. Even the calls for Greeks not to fight other Greeks were late in coming and never really heeded. Eventually it took the efficient Roman legions, and terrors such as Mummius' razing of Corinth (146 BCE), to shock the cities into a jealous peace. Local rivalries continued but no longer escalated into open war. Before the *Pax Romana*, however, Herodotus was one of the few to question Greek customs of war, but he puts his ideas into the mouth of a Persian (*Hist.* 7.9.2). Philosophers such as Plato and Aristotle were more explicit, envisaging ideal cities that fight no unnecessary wars. In their vision, the natural condition is one of peace and rest, while war with its agitated commotion is unnatural.[42]

The Cynics concurred that war is unnatural, for what other animals dress themselves in metal and line up to kill each other, with no benefit to anyone? In a famous quote, Crates played on words to compare generals with mule-drivers: in Greek, the word "general", *stratēgos*, means literally "army-driver", and so Crates pictures them like Homer's "shepherds of the people", herdsmen who drive their men forwards like so many senseless brutes (DL 6.92). In another anecdote, all Corinth was in uproar preparing for an attack by Alexander. So as not to be the only one doing nothing, Diogenes started rolling his *pithos* up and down a hill, a pointless, Sisyphean task underscoring the stupidity going on around him (Luc. *Hist. conscr.* 3). Such anecdotes may cohere with a larger critique of the pointlessness of war. For the Cynic, war must have appeared especially stupid: all the usual motivations, such as honour, revenge, glory, wealth, ancestors, fatherland are false abstractions, mere "smoke" (*typhos*) that mean nothing *now*. For if one lives in the present moment, then why spend it wearing heavy bronze armour on a dusty plain, shoving blindly, pushing one's spear forward, and perhaps being gored oneself in the neck or groin? Those who fight wars fight for nothing (cf. Max. Tyr. 36.5–6; Schofield 1991: 51–2). This complex of ideas is related to many aspects of Cynic renunciation: their criticism of kings, one of whose main duties was to fight, and who were often motivated by desire for glory; their acceptance of dishonour, poverty, slavery and exile as nothing evil, and their refusal to fight to escape them.

Yet as with the Games, war was so prominent in the Greek consciousness that the Cynics could not completely avoid its glorious associations. Just as he is the true "athlete", so the Cynic also boasts of being the true "king". He has armed himself with unassailable syllogisms and with virtue, a "weapon that cannot be taken away" (DL 6.12). As a citizen of *Pēra* and of "Poverty unsacked by Fortune" (6.93), he cannot be exiled or harmed by Fortune. The arrows of Fortune cannot hit him and towards her, he is "invincible". Or as a foot soldier in the "army of the dog" (Luc. *Fugitivi* 16), need the Cynic fear a tyrant's armies, for what can they take from him, and how can they harm him who carries all his goods with him at every moment?[43]

Citizenship and exile

The Greeks would indeed have regarded the Cynics' willingness to accept the destruction of their home cities as the definitive proof of their misanthropy. Indeed, the renunciation of custom is capped by the voluntary renunciation of citizenship, and the acceptance of exile and nomadism as the only way to live. Traditionally citizenship was treasured, as much for the material benefits it afforded as for the sense of belonging and pride it brought. Oppositely, the deprivation of civic rights and protections – *atimia* – was a major punishment second only to execution, and sometimes not even to that. The punishment of *atimia*, generally speaking, prevented the condemned person from using the law courts, temples, agora, assembly and public buildings: that is, he could not buy and sell in the marketplace or transact business; he could not vote; he could not defend himself in court, and so could be convicted more easily, and thereafter attacked with impunity; and even worse, he could not offer sacrifice to the gods, thereby angering them also. All of this would make life fairly intolerable, and so a punishment of *atimia* was tantamount to exile. Exile was not easy either, for metics in foreign cities would have fewer civic rights, and would suffer the typical fate of immigrants everywhere: greater friction with the city's natives;

difficulties in doing business, making friends, finding representation in court and assembly, and the like.

And yet, in some cases, exile could be the making of a person. Pindar's twelfth Olympian ode celebrates Ergoteles for winning the distance race in 466 BCE, and for his three other victories at Delphi and the Isthmus. He would never have gained such glory if "Saviour Fortune (*Tychē*), child of Zeus the Liberator", had not exiled him from Knossos in Crete. The Cretan cities did not participate in the Games, and so a seemingly bad fate turned out to be the best one. More famously, Herodotus and Thucydides might not written their histories without going into exile: travel allowed Herodotus to see the world, while exile for twenty years from his native Athens is often thought to have made Thucydides a more impartial and penetrating observer of the Peloponnesian War. All this could corroborate the Cynic in his proud isolation, an attitude diametrically opposed to the Aristotelian understanding of man as a citizen. This attitude is summed up in one extremely significant saying of Diogenes: *exile made me a philosopher* (DL 6.49; cf. Plut. *De tranq. anim.* 467c).

This statement has many exemplifications and ramifications. Other Cynics also renounced their citizenship, took to the open road and became "citizens of the cosmos"; some spoke or wrote works "about exile" (e.g. Bion, Teles, Dio Chrysostom), and more argued that it should not be feared and could even be a benefit in disguise. The renunciation of house, wife, children and property; the renunciation of work, either on the land or in a particular craft; the renunciation of money and the coinage of a particular city; the renunciation of war and fighting for some *polis*, king, mercenary leader, or "army-driver": these little renunciations are all moments in the great renunciation by which the Cynic refuses a life tied to particularity. He says no to a life bound up with the idiosyncrasies of a place and people, their peculiar habits and traditions, which are comforting because familiar and settled. Exile rips through this comfort and was one of the most feared fates in the ancient world. Exile is painful, yet from the restrained words of the Cynics one must listen carefully to hear how they too suffered exile: they speak simply, but always, of the *ponos* of their lifestyle. In keeping with this, Epictetus tries to dissuade a young man from "turning dog" because a Cynic life is too hard, both physically and spiritually (e.g. Epict. *Diss.* 3.22.45–52). Of course, the Cynics were not the only philosophers who embraced exile. The Sophists were well travelled, by classical standards. Plato's Socrates, who hardly ever left Athens and chose to be executed there, understood philosophy as a kind of exile from the physical world itself. But, as usual, the Cynics were the most radical in their claims of difference. More than others they stressed that exile frees one from the particularities of received custom. It throws one back on one's own unaided resources. It forces one to doubt and to wonder about the immense number of possible paths that one may follow.

Customs for the soul: religion, language, death rites

Fear of the gods, prayer, sacred space, Mysteries, oracles

Where to go? What to do? How to live? Social and political customs provide much guidance to these fundamental questions. Equally important in giving a sense of direction are religious customs. Religion is rarely wholly separate from the rest of the life of the community, and in ancient cultures religion pervaded everyday life in a way that can be difficult for us to appreciate. Particular days were holy to different deities, and many festivals punctuated the year as the city, or sections of it, worshipped a god or goddess with processions, games, sacrifices, feasting and the like. Classical Attica is thought to have had as many as 180 festivals in the year. Particular places too were consecrated to their tutelary deities: a grove of trees, a cave, a river might be felt to be charged with the numinous presence of a god, and in the more significant of these holy places worshippers might erect an altar, shrine, temple or even a complex of temples and other buildings to honour and delight the deity. Similarly, they might hold contests for the gods to watch and enjoy: the pan-Hellenic games, like the Panathenaea, were primarily religious occasions. Thus, many of the distinctive triumphs of

Greek culture – athletics, temple architecture, statuary, tragic and comic drama – have an essential religious colouring. The Cynics seem to have been less troubled by this complex religious heritage than were thinkers like Plato and the Epicureans. Yet they too could criticize such religious phenomena as fear of the gods, and the consequent desire to propitiate them through prayer, sacrifice and offerings; they could reject oracles and the attempt to predict the future; and they ridiculed hopes regarding the afterlife. In general, classical and Hellenistic Cynics, such as Diogenes, Bion and Menippus, tend to take a negative attitude towards religion. The later Roman age, however, was more cosmopolitan, syncretistic and eclectic, and often less confident in human power unaided by the gods. This later, more pious atmosphere is thought to have affected individual Cynics and their admirers: Peregrinus, for instance, was a sort of philosophical holy man to his followers; Lucian writes an almost hagiographic life of Demonax; Epictetus and Julian transform Cynicism into a quasi-religious calling, as if the Cynic were literally, and not just metaphorically, the "scout of God" who is "born of Zeus".

With regard to the earlier Cynics, we can mention some anecdotes representative of their religious nay-saying. First, *deisidaimonia* or "fear of the gods" was a common target of philosophical criticism. Plato, for example, takes it as axiomatic that God is good and is therefore not to be feared. Epicurus makes it one of his "principal doctrines" that one should not fear the gods, because they inhabit the distant spaces between worlds and do not care about us. Taking up the theme, Diogenes cajoled a superstitious person by threatening to sneeze out of his *left* nostril (DL 6.48): it was as if he asked, "Is thunder much different from a big sneeze?" Bion is said to have spent his life lampooning temples, sacrifices, holy hearths, altars, incense-sniffing gods, amulet-wearers and the like (4.54–7): was he an atheist (there were only a handful in all antiquity), and did he write a book on *deisidaimonia* that Plutarch might have used later for his own book on the subject?[44]

If one does not fear the gods, then one may not feel the need to sacrifice or pray to them either. In one story, someone pointed to the many offerings in Samothrace as a proof that the gods listen to prayers and save their adherents (e.g. from drowning), but Diogenes replied that it would be stranger if the drowned had made offerings there (DL 6.59).[45] Nor do sacrifices automatically betoken piety or holiness; according to Diogenes, even a prostitute can offer golden statues to Apollo, as when Phryne dedicated a statue of Aphrodite in the sanctuary of Delphi (6.60). Lucian's Demonax does not sacrifice to Athena because she needs nothing from him: it would be impious to offer sacrifices to the gods (Demonax argues), for that either implies the gods are not self-sufficient, or they can be controlled, as by magic (Luc. *Demon.* 11). True piety means praying for the *right* things, and not merely for things; therefore, parents should pray not for the birth of a son, but for the birth of a good son (DL 6.63). Unfortunately, people tend to pray for things that seem good, but are not really so (6.42).

The Greek pagans might pray or sacrifice anywhere and religious activities were not at all confined to special places. In some ways, the whole land was sacred: the earth itself was *Gaia*, oldest of the gods and mother of all things; on her surface were scattered sacred stones, trees, groves, caves and other natural features that were felt somehow to be charged with some uncanny power, often because a god had been there once. This numinous power was stronger in some places than others, and so in these special locations human beings might leave piles of stones, a roadside shrine, an altar or, eventually, a temple or temple complex adorned with beautiful carvings, statues, altars and gold. It was felt that such gifts pleased the gods and might persuade them to linger a little longer in their favourite sacred haunts, where they might look kindly on their human worshippers and impart some of their blessed power. Delphi, Olympia and the Athenian Acropolis were some of the more important of these holy places, but each city had its own, and indeed each individual might have his or her own.

Often Cynics seem to have played on the rich ambiguity of this feature of paganism: if every place is sacred (some Cynics argued), then all places are equally sacred, therefore no place is more sacred than another, and therefore Delphi is no more sacred than my armpit. Many Cynic sayings of this kind seem designed to shock customary pieties. Diogenes, for example, calls it stupid to fall down before images of the gods, as if these were especially holy and the gods' presence not everywhere (DL 6.37); or to believe that temples are particularly sacred spots from which one should not steal, and in which one should not eat (6.73). So Diogenes ate his dinner in a temple, and said that his belly was the true holy place – let no impure loaves enter here (6.64)! Even harsher, a temple is no more holy than a "shit-hole", and Diogenes would not scruple to visit "unpurified" places, for the (divine) sun also peeps down into cesspits without being sullied (6.63). Nor is sprinkling oneself with water purify-ing (6.42). Such ideas were revisited by Cynics such as Bion and Demonax. When one of his companions said, "Let's go to the shrine of Asclepius", Demonax answered that he must think Asclepius deaf if he could not hear them from where they are (Luc. *Demon.* 27).

Such sayings are essentially the equivalent of smashing idols: so much for the civic religion of altar, temple and sacrifice, and so much for the Greeks' beautiful statuary. Nor were the Cynics sympathetic to the different sort of religiosity offered by the Eleusinian and other Mysteries. Little is known about these Mysteries, but they may have promised a kind of blessed immortality after death. Certainly, they seem to have offered the individual a deeper sense of cosmic meaning and belonging than did the festivals and sacrifices to the Olympian gods. As a result perhaps, the Eleusinian Mysteries became highly respected in classical Athens, and through the Hellenistic and Roman periods their fame spread to the far ends of the Mediterranean. Even Romans such as Cicero and Marcus Aurelius might be initiated. The Mysteries were revered until Alaric the Goth sacked Eleusis in 396 CE, and in the aftermath they could not be revived given the hostility of Theodosius, the reigning Christian emperor. Ancient Christianity was a mystery religion too, of sorts, and it had to triumph over many rivals, for in the Roman period, Mysteries multiplied and many new mystery religions appeared.[46]

But it would seem that the Cynics on the whole were not impressed. When the priest of the Orphic mysteries told Antisthenes about the blessings that the initiate enjoys in Hades, Antisthenes replied, "Why then don't you die?" (DL 6.4).[47] The Athenians (it is said) honoured

Diogenes by asking him (a Sinopean and non-citizen) to be initiated into the Mysteries. He refused contemptuously: Agesilaus and Epaminondas were not initiated, yet who can believe that these virtuous men wallow in mud and filth while other mediocrities enjoy a blessed afterlife, just because they went through some ritual (6.39; Jul. *Or.* 7.238a)? Using a different argument, Lucian's Demonax refused to be initiated because he would not be able to keep the Mysteries secret: if they were bad he would have to warn everyone, and if they were good he would want to enlighten everyone (Luc. *Demon.* 11). Demonax also pointed to the cosmopolitan foundation of the Eleusinian Mysteries: given that the Mysteries' founder was Eumolpus, a Thracian king, the Athenians should not be so exclusive and tribal (34).

The Cynics reserved perhaps their most biting commentary for the oracles, and all attempts to know the divine will and predict the future. When Diogenes saw dream interpreters, soothsayers and their followers, he thought man to be the stupidest thing (DL 6.24; cf. Cynic Didymus in Plut. *De def. Or.* 413a–b). Hence, he did not agree with Homer that "dreams are also from Zeus" (DL 6.43). Demonax criticized prophets and seers: either they can change the future or they cannot; if they can, then they are charging too little for their services, but if they cannot, then what are they doing (Luc. *Demon.* 37)? Most thorough in his denunciation of oracles was Oenomaus of Gadara, who, as we have seen, rampaged through the famous oracular responses of the past, debunking and mocking all as ambiguous or inane. Oenomaus also offered arguments against the very notion of oracles, and the very possibility of predicting the future: one has only one's sense-perception and sense of self-consciousness, and therefore one can know only present realities; the rest is *typhos*, ruled by chance (*tychē*), and should be ignored, if one is wise. In this way, Cynics such as Oenomaus take up one extreme position on the debate as to whether the future is determined or not, and whether it can be known or not.

Oenomaus' discussion is unusually intellectual for a Cynic. More representative are the mocking dismissals that one finds in, say, Lucian's dialogues. In the *Dialogues of the Dead*, for example, Menippus satirizes the procedure at oracles:

> Unless I go to Lebadea and creep through a narrow passage
> into a cave, decked out ridiculously in linen and holding a
> loaf in my hands – before this, I could not know whether
> you [Trophonius] are a corpse too, differing from us only by
> your mumbo-jumbo. But by your powers of prophesy, what
> really is a demigod (*hērōs*)?   (Luc. *Dial. mort.* 10.2)

Taking up this theme in a different dialogue, Diogenes puzzles over how Heracles can be man, god, and shade: is he two selves put together, like a Centaur, or three, or how many (*Dial. mort.* 16)? In Dialogue 28, Menippus embarrasses Tiresias with awkward questions: was he ever pregnant when he was a woman? And when he changed back to a man, did it happen in an instant, or did it take a while for his beard to return? Thus the smart-aleck Menippus sardonically dismisses the possibility of oracles: for him, the whole rigmarole of prophets, human-gods and ritual hocus-pocus is an all-too-human sham.

And yet, as with war and the Games, the Cynics often appropriated the ancient prestige of oracles and of religion for their own uses, and claimed that their philosophy had divine sanction. Julian writes that Apollo himself founded Cynicism (*Or.* 7.7), but here Julian is only reinterpreting the old Cynic lore that Apollo in Delphi had ordered Diogenes to "deface the coinage" (DL 6.20). Other oracular responses also seemed to make Cynicism a divine ordinance: Apollo told the young Zeno (first a student of Crates) to "take on the colour of the dead" (7.2). Apollo advised Dio of Prusa "to do the thing at hand, until you come to the ends of the earth" (D. Chr. 13.9). In Lucian's dialogue, the prophet Tiresias whispers Cynic wisdom into Menippus' ear when he tells him: "seek out this one single thing before all else: arrange the present well and jog on, laughing a lot and taking nothing seriously" (Luc. *Nec.* 21).[48] In such stories, it was as if Apollo, god of colonization, had sanctioned the founding of the Cynic life and "city" also, ordering Cynics to make it their law to live in the present only, and dismiss all else. Of course, such a life would involve the dismissal of oracles and Apollo too, but the Cynics do not seem to have been troubled by this possible contradiction.

More generally, self-sufficiency is a divine quality that one should emulate: the gods are self-sufficient, the animals nearly so, and humans least so (DL 6.104; Goulet-Cazé 1996: 61–4). Therefore, in the quest for divine self-sufficiency, one should not be ashamed to become first like an animal, a dog: Diogenes the "dog" thereby becomes truly "Zeus-born" (*Dio-genes*). The thought might seem counter to the anthropomorphism of Greek religion, which depicted the gods in *human* form, and not like the Egyptians' crocodile and cat gods. The notion that animals are more divine than human beings might seem, thus, to hearken back to older, "primitive" nature religions. It is more likely, however, that the early Cynics did not think of this, but rather appropriated religious language for mainly rhetorical effect, using words such as "divine" and "god-like" simply as synonyms for "very good". Yet, even if this were the case, the rhetoric was potentially ambivalent and its ambiguities were taken in a different direction by some more religiously oriented Cynics of the later Roman period. Thus, Diogenes himself is probably just being witty when he gives his famous syllogism about the gods (DL 6.37, 6.72); or when he compares the Homeric gods' life of ease with the hard idleness of the Cynic (6.44); or when he says that the Athenians should elect him Sarapis, just as they voted to call Alexander Dionysus (6.63). But Cercidas and Diogenes Laertius are more in earnest when they call Diogenes the "heavenly dog", as if he were "born of Zeus" and closer to the divine. More earnest still is a Peregrinus Proteus, who seriously promoted himself as a man-god, like Heracles or Empedocles. Demonax too was half-revered as a kind of philosophical saint. It is in this more pious atmosphere that Epictetus and Julian recast their heroes "Diogenes" and "Crates" as models of sanctity and submission to the divine, rather than as shameless "dogs" who made a cult of radical self-sufficiency and freedom from submission to anything, whether to Fortune, gods, or all-too-human religious customs.[49] If so, then one can begin to understand Cynicism's fraught relationship with early Christianity: early Christians admired Cynic asceticism as a prelude to true holiness, yet the pagan Cynics they tended to distrust as "atheists" who would not bow the knee to any god.[50] Much later, however, modern thinkers such as Rousseau, Nietzsche and even Kant would hanker to free humanity from the feeling of dependence on God and could sometimes turn to the Cynics as classical exemplars of human autonomy.

Language: gesture, wit, puns, neologisms, metaphors, genres, plain speech

One area that has been studied comparatively little is the Cynic attempt to extend their autonomy even to the way Greek was spoken. Perhaps even more than customs of work, social organization and religion, language shapes consciousness in the most subtle ways, from one's explicit creed down even to indeterminate feelings, unquestioned assumptions and general orientation towards the world. The influence of language on subjective experience is more a modern than an ancient idea, but one finds hints of it in classical literature. Isocrates, for instance, comments on the intimate connection between speaking Greek and being "Greek". Those who speak Greek well but have no Greek "blood" may be considered Greeks: a thought that phil-Hellenes such as Lucian (a Syrian) took seriously. Seemingly without exception the Cynics were Greeks or primarily Greek speakers, but for all their resolution to be self-sufficient and to reject mere inherited customs, they could no more cast off the Greek language than outrun their own shadows. And yet, if one reads carefully, many Cynics stretch the language, making puns, coining new words, cobbling new metaphors and even inventing new poetic metres and literary genres, as if they were struggling to burst through the bonds of customary speech to fashion their own, Cynic, forms of communication.

The first and perhaps most obvious aspect of this new "language" is the Cynic vocabulary of gesture. Actions speak louder than words: whistling to the crowd, eating beans noisily, farting, belching, urinating, defecating in public, masturbating, rolling about in the sand, embracing snowy statues, carrying a tuna or bowl of soup across a crowded marketplace, sleeping in a *pithos*, carrying a lantern around at noon, and innumerable other contortions, twists and shapes: all these loudly trumpet the brazen freedom and antinomianism of the

Cynics.[51] One gesture in this dialect of renunciation is sticking up the middle finger. "Flipping the bird" has not always and in all cultures been taken as a sign of contempt, but various anecdotes show that the Cynics did use it as such. Thus, Diogenes flicked the finger at Demosthenes. In scholarship on Cynicism, Diogenes is almost invariably quoted for saying that "most people … are so nearly mad that a finger makes all the difference". But this makes sense really only in the context of the full anecdote: "For, if you go along with your middle finger stretched out, some one will think you mad, but if it is the little finger, he will not think so" (DL 6.35). For Diogenes there is no reason why one should get angry at being shown the middle finger rather than the little finger. It is a crazy custom. It is crazy too to get angry at any expression of contempt or dishonour: what should one care what other people think?[52] Postmodern thinkers such as Peter Sloterdijk (1983) have been interested in Cynic gestures like this, arguing that bodily language is the best way to escape the hegemony of *logos*, science, grand narratives and all self-justifying ideologies.

Yet the ancient Cynics, although they may have distrusted *logos* as systematic reason, did not distrust language *per se*. Cynics such as Diogenes (DL 6.75–6), Crates, Bion and Menippus were well known for their eloquence and repartee; sometime Cynic Dio of Prusa was named "golden-mouthed" (*Chrysostomos*) for his fluency, some of which he must have gained in his wanderings. Epictetus (*Diss.* 3.22.90–92) makes wit a required talent for his ideal Cynic, and one imagines that Lucian would have demanded it even more stridently. Indeed, it must have been a widespread expectation, given the popularity of *chreiai* in which Cynics cleverly put down the rich, powerful and complacent. Cynic wit is evident not least in their use of puns and word-play. Crates' "Pēra" plays on the word *pēra*, a feminine noun that could well be a city name; and on *thymos* (DL 6.85), which means both "courage" (*thymós*) and "thyme" (*thýmos*), depending on the accent. Diogenes played on *pēra* also, saying that it is not the maimed, deaf or blind who should be pitied as "disabled" (*anapērous*), but rather all those who have no *pēra* and are not fortunate enough to be as poor as the Cynic. That is, Diogenes puns on *anapēros*, which normally means "lame" but which Diogenes construes as an alpha-privative (6.33). On a different occasion, Diogenes makes fun of an Olympic victor whom he sees tending (*nemonta*) sheep: how quickly, he says, you have progressed from the Olympic to the *Nemean* Games (6.49). It is a clever pun in Greek. Bion's quip about not marrying uses a clever rhyme (*poinēn* – *koinēn*) (4.48). Rhymes were not common in Greek but Bion seems to have used them more regularly.[53]

The ability to make new words from old can be a sign of a restless intelligence, and the Cynics coined their own words freely. Diogenes called the consorts of kings "kingesses", because they are the ones who tell kings what to do (DL 6.63). Bion called Fortune a "poetess" (*poietria*) (Stob. 3.1.98), because she "makes" people whatever she wants them to be, just as a playwright can make an actor play any part. Pseudo-Lucian uses an unusual antonym for *pleonexia* ("wanting more and more") – *meionexia* ("wanting less and less") (ps.-Luc. *Cyn.* 15): the Cynic prays that he may be able to persevere in his virtue of *meionexia*. Menippus coined a word when he wrote of the "brine-drinking city of Myndos" (Ath. 1.59.18 [=32e]).[54] Varro spices up his *Menippean Satires* with titles such as *hippo-kyōn* (horse-dog, i.e. Roman senator), *kyōn-rhētor* (Cynic orator) and *hydro-kyōn* ("water-drinking dog"). Most importantly, Diogenes may well have coined the word *cosmopolitēs*, "citizen of the cosmos", and ancestor of the English "cosmopolitan" (DL 6.63). There are other examples and this is not an exhaustive list.

More complex are metaphors. Because they compare two seemingly unrelated entities in unexpected ways, metaphors are often a sign of creativity and inquisitive intelligence (as Aristotle and others have argued), for only the intelligent seek for the hidden unity of apparently disparate things. The Cynic self-description abounds in metaphor. Most important, of course, is the metaphor that the Cynic is a "dog", barking at enemies, wagging his tail at friends, living naturally without shame among human beings, and so forth. Other comparisons, important especially later in the Hellenistic and Roman periods, are that the Cynic is a spy (*kataskopos*) on mankind's virtues and vices;[55] an overseer or inspector (*episkopos*); a herald, perhaps because these were holy to Zeus, armed with only a staff yet able to act as peacemakers between foreign peoples; a benefactor (*euergetēs*) and saviour (*sōtēr*) who because of his "wealth" and *philanthrōpia* performs great deeds of public munificence; a tutor (*paidagōgos*, *didaskalos*) instructing mankind in the truth; a ruler (*archōn*) and king (*basileus*) who both instructs and rebukes his inferiors; a moral inspector (*sōphrōnistēs*) and chastister (*nouthetēs*); a doctor (*iatros*) who heals sick souls (D. Chr. 8.6–9, 9.2; Luc. *Vit. auct.* 8); a mediator (*diallaktēs*) who shows that there is no need to fight; a liberator (*eleutherōtēs*) from false ideas (*ibid.*); and even a prophet (*prophētēs*) (*ibid.*), that is, a prophet and teller of "truth and *parrhēsia*", if not of the future.[56]

Metaphors are hidden in other Cynic anecdotes. Aristotle quotes Diogenes' metaphor: "Pubs are the barracks of Athens" (*Rh.* 1411a24). There are allusions to many others: "the stomach is livelihood's Charybdis" because it sucks down everything one owns (DL 6.51); demagogues are "the lackeys of the people and the crowns awarded to them the efflorescence of fame" (*doxēs exanthēmata*) (6.41); rich men are newborns who need their swaddling clothes (D. Chr. 6.16); good birth and fame are "the jewellery of vice" (*kosmēmata kakias*) (DL 6.72); the whole earth is a hearth to the wise (D. Chr. 4.13). Bion "called old age the harbour of all ills: at least they all take refuge there". Renown he called "the mother of virtues"; beauty "another's good"; wealth "the sinews of success" (DL 4.48); life is a feast; the body is an old decrepit house, and nature its landlord (Bion Fr. 68 [=Stob. 3.1.98]). For Demetrius, a life without suffering is like the Dead Sea, lifeless, and motionless (Sen. *Ep.* 67.14). Lucian's Menippus compares life to a pageant or play, "arranged and marshalled by Chance", in which each one plays a part before the costumes are switched (Luc. *Nec.* 16; cf. Stob. 3.1.98, DL 7.160]). Finally, the foundational phrase "defacing the coinage" (DL 6.20) implicitly equates *nomisma* and *nomos*: to deface a city's coins (*nomismata*) is tantamount to rejecting all that it buys, sells, sanctions and values – that is, its values, customs and *nomoi*.

Requiring more sustained powers of invention still are the new metres and genres of Cynic writers. Cercidas of Megalopolis first wrote in the meliambic metre and Sotades of Maroneia invented the Sotadean, which had many imitators, including perhaps even Ennius in Latin. One of Varro's Menippean satires, the *Cynodidascalicus*, seems to have discussed metrics, not surprising, perhaps, given some of the Cynic's innovations here.[57] Cynic authors also wrote in a wide medley of forms: dialogues, tragedies, letters, essays, poems, mock diaries. As we have seen, Bion is mainly credited with the "invention" of the diatribe. Menippus is associated with the "Menippean satire", which (at least in traditional representatives such as Seneca's *Apocolocyntosis*, Petronius' *Satyricon*, Boethius' *Consolation of Philosophy*) is distinguished by its mixture of prose and poetry, narrative and snatches of song. The *Nekyia* or *Journey to the Dead* was Homeric: it became almost a Cynic preserve owing to Menippus, Lucian (e.g. *Dialogues of the Dead*), Sotades' *Nekyia* (*Suda* S 871) and even Timon's *Silloi*.[58] Perhaps most remarkable, however, is Lucian's transformation of the dialogue, an old genre closely associated with philosophical argumentation; Lucian remoulded it into a vehicle for satirical amusement and often for Cynic-style mockery.

Another genre appropriated by Cynic authors is the *paignion* or "play-piece". Among Sophists, this could often take the form of an *epideixis*, showing off the cleverness of orators whose eloquence was so great that they could praise the unpraisable. So Gorgias wrote an encomium of the adulterous Helen; Alcidamas wrote a praise of death; Polycrates composed encomia of pebbles, mice, Clytemnestra, a pot; and with his *Phaedo*, Plato too wrote a kind of praise of death (Desmond 2006: 23). For the Cynics, the *paignion* became a light-hearted ditty with a satirical slant, praising the small and seemingly contemptible, poking fun at the grand and mighty. Thus Monimus wrote "*Paignia* mixed with hidden seriousness" (DL 6.83) and it is in this serio-comic (*spoudogeloion*) style that Crates wrote his "Praise of Lentil Soup" and "Encomium of Cheapness" (*euteleia*). Dio Chrysostom wrote a (lost) "Encomium of a Parrot" and a "Praise of a Gnat", as well as an "Encomium of Hair", which inspired the Antiochene bishop Synesius to respond centuries later with an "Encomium of Baldness", which is perhaps the harder task. Lucian wrote in "Praise of a Fly", and these are followed later by

Erasmus' *Praise of Folly*, Bertrand Russell's *In Praise of Idleness* and even my own *Greek Praise of Poverty*.

Most of all, the Cynics sometimes innovated by regressing: that is, by simplifying, scrapping jargon, archaisms and any specialized language that might keep the "mob" out of the temple of philosophy. They favoured plain speech: the *parrhēsiast* speaks plainly and he speaks true, on the assumption that technical language is too often a sort of *typhos*: mumbo jumbo to conceal ignorance and falsehoods. In the early Hellenistic period, philosophy was becoming technical in some quarters. Peripatetics and Stoics especially raised linguistic walls that fairly excluded the outsider: to be "in", one needed to be comfortable talking about substances, accidents, entelechies and sayables; one had to know how to bend one's ideas into judgements, syllogisms and other logical forms. For the Cynics, this kind of "education" is to be renounced. Not only is it a distraction from ethical concerns; worse, abstract speech too often becomes convoluted speech – one does not know what one is talking about, and by talking further, one only makes oneself more confused. Or even worse, one does not even know that one is confused and confusing. The best cure for this *typhos* is to speak simply. As we have seen, in the Imperial period, poor, witty, homely Athens could be contrasted with rich, boorish and pretentious Rome. Similar ideas are operative when a Dio or a Lucian strives to speak in the Attic dialect of some five centuries before: the earlier, "Attic style" was cultivated as a model of directness and simplicity.[59] Of course, the Cynics' demand for simple language could be extremely anti-intellectual, and *we* should not automatically mock abstract language or seemingly irrelevant diversions (e.g. into metaphysics), as these can ultimately prove surprisingly enlightening. On the other hand, however, the Cynics' exhortation to speak simply and clearly, without "smoke", is of perennial value. For all those interminable debates, in which neither side says or understands anything intelligible, Demonax provides a memorable image and a series of metaphors. One day when he saw two philosophers arguing, one asking ridiculous questions, the other giving irrelevant answers, Demonax quipped that the first seemed to be milking a goat, and the second putting the milk in a sieve (Luc. *Demon.* 28). In another anecdote, Diogenes had been listening to a very long lecture. Eventually the speaker was winding up and pointed to the blank space at the end of the roll, at which Diogenes perked up and called out to the other listeners: "Courage, lads! There's land in sight" (DL 6.38).

It is in this context that one might understand the Cynic rejection of philosophical learning and sophistication. Diogenes did not care about "music and geometry and astronomy and all those useless, unnecessary things" (6.73). They are useless because they seem to have nothing to do with the present and, as we have seen, Cynicism may be most defined by concentration on the simple present: this spot of sunshine, this *pithos*. Thinking and reason can be unreasonable in that they so often lead one astray into thoughts about what is abstract, or distant in time or space. When this happens, one needs some surprising gesture or unusual expression to jolt one back to the present. Thus, when a sophist or a Zeno "proves" that human beings have horns or that motion is impossible, Diogenes unexpectedly "refutes" them by touching his head, or walking about (6.39). In many anecdotes Diogenes disrupts the complex discussions going on in the Academy or Lyceum. In one session, for instance, when the Platonists have agreed to define man as "a featherless biped", Diogenes rushes in with a plucked chicken shouting, "Here is Plato's human being" (6.40). One can imagine the consternation in the Academy and, in response, the definition was amended to "a featherless biped, with broad nails". The (imaginary) incident is a send-up of a type of intellectualism that boasts a rigorous precision, but ultimately only produces thin, pathetic human beings – plucked chickens – scratching amid their anaemic ideas. If these are fair extrapolations, they may form the context for Bion's saying: "Conceited thinking (*oiēsis*) is a hindrance to progress" (4.50). The Cynic philosophy does not privilege cogitation in the way that a Plato does and this anti-intellectual attitude was general until the end of the tradition. Thus, Julian can only deplore contemporary Cynics' ignorance of the philosophical tradition (*Or.* 7.225b; *Or.* 6). Such "uneducated" Cynics in their own way revisit Apollodorus' epigram that Cynicism is the "short cut to virtue" (DL 7.121), to the vast exasperation of Julian, who thought that people should take the long road, as he himself did (*Or.* 7.225b–d, 7.235d).

Death rites

Unconventional in life, the Cynics were unconventional in death too. Is it natural to fear death? In the extant literature, the Cynics do not explicitly renounce the fear of death as something unnatural and merely customary. But such a final renunciation accords with many of their recorded statements and actions. For Diogenes (as for Epicurus), death is not an evil, for we do not feel it, and therefore we should not anticipate it with dread (DL 6.68). This idea would lead to a wholesale revision of burial customs. Traditional Greek custom held that the corpse should be washed, dressed, mourned and buried, often with a coin in the mouth: to pay Charon to be ferried across the Styx was one explanation. If the body were unburied, then the shade of the dead person would wander on this side of the Styx, miserably; Hades and Persephone would be displeased also, deprived of a subject who by rights belonged in their "cold halls". The funerary right was so sacred that it was respected by international truce and by armies on campaign, who after battle would pause to exchange bodies for burial. It would be deeply shocking therefore if Diogenes did actually order his body to be thrown into the Ilissus River, or left unburied for animals to eat, or at most thrown into a pit with a little dust scattered over (6.79).[60] Bion too "cast a cold eye on death", when he said that the road to Hades was easy to travel, because people do it with their eyes closed (4.49). Demonax shrugs his shoulders at the horrors of Hades, Cerberus and Tartarus. He did not fear dying at sea, and when asked, "What is in Hades?", he replied, "Wait a while, and I'll send you a letter from there". No one can see across the grave, so why fear what one cannot know? Therefore, Demonax laughs at Admetus the poet, first for believing the soul immortal, and then for writing bad poetry on the theme (Luc. *Demon.* 43, 44).[61]

The Cynics were not quite indifferent to death, however. They and their admirers were also interested in death as a final revelation of character. It was a common sentiment that the final moment, the last gestures and "famous last words" should capture the spirit of the entire life. Therefore, much attention was paid to the deaths of famous people. Foremost is Plato's Socrates, who spent his last minutes arguing dialectically, so great was his desire for knowledge. Cato the Younger fell stoically on his sword when the Republic was lost, and he was stripped of honour and purpose. Petronius, *elegantiae arbiter* and high priest of hedonism, carried out Nero's suicide orders by partying all day and then taking a warm bath, in which he periodically opened his veins, thus fading away in an untroubled, vaguely pleasant way. Oppositely, Jesus suffered the worst pain, yet spoke words of love and forgiveness from the Cross. Something of a Stoic atmosphere surrounds the death of gladiators; their struggles in the arena before an inevitable doom symbolized all lives, and so they were applauded if they met Fate with the cheerful indifference of a Stoic, the courage of a Roman. In comparison with all these, the stories of Cynic deaths are rather laughable. Diogenes died attacked by dogs, or by holding his breath, or by eating a raw "many-foot" (i.e. octopus) (DL 6.77; cf. Luc. *Vit. auct.* 10, *Catapl.* 7). Metrocles strangled himself (DL 6.95). Menippus hanged himself because a thief stole his stuff (6.100). Calanus the gymnosophist burned himself on a pyre (Arr. *Anab.* 7.4.1–6), and Peregrinus did the same at the Olympics. Demonax starved himself to death. Here some individual details may be invented: breathing is an involuntary function and one *cannot* die by holding one's breath. By contrast, the reports of Calanus and Peregrinus are no doubt true, given the thousands of witnesses present.

Regardless of particular details, however, the stories and reports collectively suggest that the Cynics not only condoned suicide but may have even encouraged it. Julian, for his part, assimilates the Cynic attitude to the argument of Plato's *Phaedo* (Pl. *Phd.* 80e–81a), in which philosophy is defined as a "practice of death" (Jul. *Or.* 6.181a, 191c–193c). Julian forgets, however, that for Plato's Socrates, we have duties beyond ourselves, our bodies and lives are not ours only to dispose of, and that we must therefore abide by our god-given destiny to the end: that is, Platonic philosophy is a "practice of death" only metaphorically. Cynics, by contrast, found different reasons for literally accepting death. In Bion's metaphor old age is the "harbour of all ills", and so a Cynic such as Demonax dreads that he will become less self-sufficient with advancing years. From a different angle, Diogenes' eating octopus is interpreted by Julian as proof of the Cynic's *philanthrōpia* and rejection of custom: Diogenes ate raw meat to free mankind from their reliance on cooking, and although he died in the attempt, his personal experiment was a benefaction to all mankind. Suicide may also be final proof of the Cynic's freedom. Rather than clinging to life desperately, the Cynic winks at fortune and says "*I* choose death". He wills his own end, often choosing one that will epitomize and crown his whole life. Similarly, the "life according to nature" finds a natural end in the Cynic's death. The Cynic transcends the merely conventional fear of death and so demonstrates that dying too is natural and a part of life. Finally, there is a point even to the reports of silly deaths by dog-bite or self-asphyxiation; having passed through life as through a festival, the Cynic will also go out with a laugh, and not even oblivion can make him glum.

All of these considerations may be operative in the philosophical death of Peregrinus Proteus. Again, it was at the Olympic Games of 165 CE that Peregrinus burned himself alive before a vast crowd, imitating Heracles, Empedocles, Calanus and the "Brahmans", in order to benefit mankind by showing death is not to be feared. He may also have felt old and his powers of self-sufficiency may have been waning after a hard and varied life. Report has it that Calanus lay calmly on the pyre, not screaming, and not even moving as the flames destroyed his body. But even if Peregrinus too had played his part unflinchingly, Lucian would still have mocked him for a poor performance. In Lucian's eyes, Peregrinus was a showman to the end and his suicide was just a final stunt to win applause. Lucian considers the whole charade ridiculous and claims to have burst his sides laughing. If so, then the grave Peregrinus may have unwittingly capped a Cynic life with a fitting Cynic death: a punchline that showed to some at least the folly of human ways.

THREE

A life according to nature

The Cynics' denunciation of custom might strike one as often cynical and pessimistic with regard to human goodness. But while a modern cynic might remain content with carping, the ancient Cynics did not *merely* say no to custom. On the contrary, they criticized in order to clear the way for a better alternative: the "life according to nature" (*kata physin*) (DL 6.71).[1] For them, the natural life is one of complete simplicity, free of all unnecessary, all-too-human contrivances. It is unburdened by needless cogitation and mental distraction. Living fully in the moment, without great hopes or fears, is for the Cynic the only way to become virtuous and happy: natural living brings the greatest pleasures, and the right pleasures. If contemporary people have forgotten elemental happiness, it is no matter: one can regain it by training oneself with much ascetic "work" (*ponos*), and Cynics could find inspiration in the thought that they were not alone, for there were many "primitive" peoples who shared citizenship with them in nature's elemental kingdom.

Images of nature

This is a summary of what is perhaps the Cynics' most important idea. But let us unravel its constituent strands in more detail. The

Cynic renounces customs in order to live in accordance with nature, but what, one may ask, is nature? The question is a large one and this single word, "nature", has been a battleground of rival worldviews. Ancient philosophers waged their wars over it also, and to understand Cynicism properly within this ancient context, one must appreciate some of the major Greek conceptions of what nature as a whole is. We may begin with the word itself. The Greek *physis* gives rise to English words such as *physics*, *physical* and *physiology* and like the English "nature", *physis* was used in a wide variety of contexts. Greeks spoke of the *physis* of fire or iron, for example, or of a geographical region, a tool, an individual, a biological species and so forth. As a derivative of the Latin *natura*, "nature" does not carry the same resonance for an English speaker as *physis* did for a Greek. In it, a Greek speaker could always detect its root, the transitive verb *phyein*, meaning "to bring forth, produce, put forth". Thus the earth "puts forth" (*phyei*) plants, causing them to grow. Plants are *ta phyta*, and this word could in turn be extended to other living things, even human beings. In Plato's *Timaeus*, for example, a human being is described as a "heavenly plant" (*phyton ouranion*) (Pl. *Ti.* 90a) whose mind is rooted in the heavens, as it were: human beings are distinguished by their upright posture, by their rationality and ability to look up at the stars as well as to desire the eternal, and thus might be regarded as planted in eternity, growing from their heads down. Other related words are those for "parents" (*hoi physantes*, or "those who caused [children] to grow"); and for natural things generally (*ta physika*). This last is the Greek title of Aristotle's *Physics*, a work mainly on mechanics and physics (in our sense). Many books on science and "natural philosophy" were ultimately given the simple title *Peri Physeōs* or *On Nature*; Lucretius' *De Rerum Natura* is an echo in Latin of this long Greek tradition. This tradition, with its rich contributions in medicine, psychology, biology, astronomy, mechanics and so forth, demonstrates the Greeks' extraordinary curiosity about the natural world. Perhaps this cultural trait was one factor that inspired Aristotle to formulate his famous generalization, "All human beings by nature desire to know" (Arist. *Metaph.* 980a21).[2] Perhaps the Cynics form an exception to this rule, or at least were far more severe in what they considered knowable, for they seem scarcely curious about the composition of the stars, the size of the earth or incubation habits of water fowl. No work titled *On Nature* is attributed to an ancient Cynic, in striking contrast to the Presocratics and the major Schools.[3]

And yet, although the Cynics did not regard nature as worthy of extensive scientific study, they did see it as the source of all good and all value, both moral and economic. Again one can ask the question: what is nature? But this time let us look at some images of nature, both ancient and modern, that are morally significant. These images in turn picture nature as a beneficent presence, and even as a kindly goddess, as a healthy organism, a work of art, a machine, and as a competition or battle. First, English speakers sometimes speak of "Mother Nature" as a wise and gentle provider whose wisdom has been maturing for millennia. She has ordered all things for the best, and her foolish children tinker with innovations, only to learn in the end that nature's devices are superior and even miraculously complex. The Greeks did not speak of *physis* as a "mother", and in any case, the Greek woman was typically expected to be more a dutiful wife than a loving mother. But with this in mind, one may detect the presence of something similar to "Mother Nature" in one of Aristotle's favourite images. Aristotle often compares nature to a good *housekeeper* (*oikonomos agathos*), that is, a conscientious wife who keeps everything in its place, wastes nothing and is clever at finding a purpose for each object, so that each thing can attain its full self-actualization (Arist. *Gen. an.* 744b16). Complementing this image is the Aristotelian maxim, "nature does nothing in vain" (*IA* 704b15; *De an.* 434a31; *Cael.* 291b13; *Part. an.* 661b23). Here, each aspect of the organic body has a purpose, and form is admirably fitted to purpose: the eye for seeing, ear for hearing, fin for swimming, wing for flying and so forth. From fingernails to the stars, nature seems pervaded by the presence of a unified intelligence. There is disorder and chance, of course, and brute matter ever resists the rationality of form. But in general, Housekeeper Nature does her job with wonderful skill, and Theophrastus, head of the Lyceum after Aristotle, will find fault with Heraclitus for stating with such gross falsehood that "the most beautiful cosmos is like a mound of stuff heaped up at random" (*Metaph.* 6b–7a, on Heracl. Fr. 24 [DK]).

Despite his personification of natural rationality, however, and despite his doctrine of God as Unmoved Mover and perfect Mind, and finally despite his insistence on purpose as a cause in all natural events, Aristotle does not argue that nature is the product of divine creation: Aristotle's cosmos is eternal but its precise dependence on God is left unclear. Many others, however, did speak of God as a cosmic maker. For them, nature becomes like an artwork of divine craftsmanship, for only some vastly powerful, intelligent and generous mind could have so bound things together to produce this world, which is so beautiful and cunningly wrought. This vision is explored perhaps most profoundly in Plato's *Timaeus*, where the natural world becomes the work of a demiurge, pictured as a divine craftsman, a blacksmith who in his eternal forge hammers together ideas and matter, triangles and chance, into a beautiful unity.

The Stoics would find different allegories for their more pantheistic vision, as when they sometimes compared nature to a chorus, and God to a chorus leader. In this image, the various strains and modulations of natural events are blended into a lovely whole by God: all discordances, all seemingly wrong or irrelevant notes, have their place within the great symphony. Disease, for example, pain, death and "all the woes that flesh is heir to", may seem evil to those suffering them, but this is appearance only. From a higher perspective these too become necessary turns in a well-tuned totality, for they too are being orchestrated by Providence, and have their rightful place. The wise person raises himself to the level of this cosmic music, and in each particular event he hears the necessity of the universe. For him, each particular, including his own body and self, is equally a part of the whole.

A very different sort of cosmology tends to strip nature of beauty, intelligence and divine presence. In the modern version of this mechanistic vision, nature is likened to a machine: a mill, clock or piston in which hammers rise and fall, wheels spin and parts move each other with inexorable motion. Nature is composed of matter and force, of material entities pushing and pulling each other with quantifiable forces, and nothing else. Nothing else exists. Therefore, if one were to know the disposition of all matter at a given time then, with the aid of the laws of motion, one could predict any future state with any desired degree of precision. One must remember, of course, that ancient scientists and philosophers did not think in terms of equations and "laws of nature", and had nothing like Newton's second law of motion ($F = ma$, or force equals mass times acceleration). Yet Newton, Boyle, Gassendi, Descartes and other "classical" mechanists of early modernity were initially influenced by the ancient atomism of Democritus. Here they found an essentially mechanistic cosmology, even though Democritus does not speak of machines. In Democritus' view, atoms push against each other and hook together to form larger and larger compounds, from minerals to plants and animals to the universe as a whole. The interactions of the atoms occur according to necessity: when an entity is caused to move in a certain way, it *must* move in that way. All that exists can and should be understood as complicated concatenations of atoms, swirling in the void. In Democritus' rough and jagged words, "by custom there exists sweet, by custom bitter, by custom hot, by custom cold, by custom colour – but in reality, there are only atoms and the void" (Democr. Fr. 9 [DK]).

Many ancients found this vision bleak and disconcerting. Perhaps even worse is the last image of nature as a sort of battlefield in which the victors enjoy the spoils of life while the losers are put to the sword. Nature is "red in tooth and claw", dog eats dog and only the fittest survive, while the weak and ill-adapted die and disappear. Nature is a realm of violence and competition, a struggle for existence. This image is applied mainly to organic nature, for the aspect of nature most obvious to us (as organisms that must fight to live and propagate) is the struggle of organisms with their environment and each other. But some thinkers have regarded this aspect of organic life as basic to inorganic nature also: here, subatomic particles, atoms, molecules, the earth as a whole, and all seemingly non-living things also demonstrate a kind of will to persist and propagate, a *conatus essendi*, or, as the neo-Cynic Nietzsche argues, a "will to power". Evolutionary thought is, of course, a primarily modern theory. But it is faintly adumbrated in the fragments of Presocratics such as Anaximander (who speculated about the origin of life in the sea) and Xenophanes (who was puzzled by fossils of sea creatures found high in the mountains of central Sicily). Anaximander also speaks of the injustice of nature: when summer comes, its heat and dryness drive out the cold and wet of winter-time; when the sun shines, it steals water from organisms, rivers and lakes; an organism lives by robbing other organisms of their lives. From this perspective, it seems that all things exist by such robbery and "injustice", and will perish by it too. At least, this is one suggested interpretation of Anaximander's enigmatic fragment: "According to necessity, existing things originate from and perish into the boundless (*apeiron*). For they pay the just penalty to each other for their injustice according to the ordering of time" (Fr. 1 [DK]).

The idea that nature is a realm of power, violence and injustice comes to the fore during the Sophistic movement, and forms one of the main foils for Cynic thought. Even darker views of nature lurk in the old myths. According to Hesiod's influential cosmology, in the beginning there was no "Mother Nature", no rational demiurge or loving God, but rather, Earth, eldest of the gods, vast and brooding, the mother of Night, the Titans, Hundred-Handers, Giants, Typhon, Chimera and other terrible beings. For the Hebrews, nature can be the Leviathan, Behemoth, the whirlwind from which He spoke his power unto Job. Similarly, for the pagan Greeks, nature is the lightning bolt, the storm at sea, the frenzy of desire in spring, the riot of green growth: nature in various guises is named Zeus, Poseidon, Dionysus and other inscrutable immortals who make and destroy at whim.

In the ancient world, myth-makers such as Hesiod or Plato often remained actively imaginative, science did not have the prestige or practical success of its modern successor, and therefore creative speculation about nature could remain more fluid. Many ideas circulated at different periods, although the ones we have outlined are perhaps the most important for the Greeks: nature as kind benefactor, as product of an intelligent god, as atoms combining in the void, and as the battleground of violence and injustice. Presented with a variety of plausible alternatives, which should one choose? Which is true? Such problems become even more urgent and important when conjoined with the ethical question: how should *I* live? For if nature is a battleground, then I would be a fool not to sharpen my sword. Or, if nature is just a swirl of atoms, signifying nothing, then I would be stupid not to enjoy myself for my little time alive. And if nature is the product of a superior being, I would be deceiving myself if I regarded trivial battles and pleasures as important. In the Cynics' view, finally, the only "nature" to be known is what one experiences here and now: this "nature" is like an ever-present treasure trove from which one can draw up endless pleasures, and so one should not be deluded into searching any further.

All of these are possible ethical complements to cosmological speculation. That is, each articulates what nature is, and then how one should live in accordance with nature. The phrase "life in accordance with nature" is thus a rich and suggestive one and can be construed in many ways. The phrase itself is associated most with the Stoics, who repeated it as a mantra, and it was almost equally hallowed as a Cynic motto. Indeed, the underlying idea is fundamental to ancient philosophy as a whole and so to appreciate the peculiarities of the Cynic "life in accordance with nature", one must juxtapose it with alternative interpretations, such as those of Platonism and Epicureanism, which jostled for attention and adherents.

Life in accordance with, against and beyond nature

What is nature? One asks the question for a third time, but this time we turn to the immediate context from which the Cynic conception of a natural life arose. The notion of living "in accordance with nature" is not one that has occurred to every people. The Greeks came to it only gradually, and the most important milestone was in the fifth century BCE, when Sophistic thinkers began to distinguish between *physis* and *nomos*. This distinction became something of a habit, and many arguments were grounded on the assumption that any entity can exist in exactly one of two ways, either naturally and spontaneously, or due to human invention and contrivance: that is, either "according to nature" or "according to custom". Therefore a typical question asked by writers of the Sophistic period is: given any entity X, does X exist by nature or custom? At worst, the question can be formulaic, but often it is quite probing. Is it natural, for example, to bury the dead, or merely customary? The classical Greeks practiced inhumation, but Herodotus claimed to meet Indians who honoured their dead by eating them, and when these cannibals heard Greeks describing their customs, they cried out in horror at such abominations (Hdt. *Hist.* 3.38). Thus, one can ask: is it *merely* a Greek custom to bury the dead and is it somehow unnatural to eat corpses? Similar questions were raised concerning incest and homosexuality: do the many prohibitions against them exist only by local custom and prejudice, or are these things crimes against nature?

Such questions can be asked about any human activity or phenomenon, and classical thinkers did in fact interrogate a great range of practices and beliefs, notably those concerning the gods, slavery, political constitutions and money. First, do the gods exist by nature, or by *nomos* only? Is Zeus, for instance, "father of gods and men"; does he throw the thunderbolt, and hold the golden scales to determine the fate of mortals? Or is God Ammon, or the Persians' fire, or the Scythians' sun? Are the gods to be identified with the sun, moon, rivers and other things useful to human beings, as Prodicus argued (Sext. Emp. *Math.* 9.18, 52)? Or, as Critias wrote, are the gods a result of human fear and desire, a cunning fiction projected onto the heavens to fool the credulous multitude (Sext. Emp. *Math.* 9.54)? Aristophanes' *Clouds* presents a variety of options: God is Zeus, or Democritus' Vortex, or vaporous cloud, or perhaps nothing at all. Such Sophistic ideas are extremely disconcerting to the traditionally minded majority.[4]

Equally shocking for a world in which slavery was routine was the question: does slavery exist by *physis* or by *nomos* only? Are some people or peoples somehow better than others and naturally entitled to rule them? Is there a master-people while others are their born slaves? Again, do political constitutions exist by nature or by custom? Are human beings free and equal by nature, or by *nomos* only? That is, do human beings naturally tend to live on an egalitarian basis, so that over time all societies tend to become more democratic? Or, on the contrary, are human beings naturally monarchical, like societies of bees and ants, so that if they are leaderless, they will clamour to have a king put above them, "like the other nations"? Or is it the case that some people live in democracies, others in monarchies, others in constitutional monarchies representing the will of the people or the nobles, and so forth in endless proliferation of constitutional customs, each based on peculiar local conditions and histories, but none "natural" and inherently right? One final question – important especially for the voluntarily poor Cynics – concerns the nature of wealth. The Persians have their *darics* and *statērs*, the Athenians their "owls", the Spartans their iron obols, while the Ethiopians hardly value gold at all because they have so much of it. Therefore, do metal coins have a natural value, or are gold and silver "no better than beach-pebbles" (Luc. *Pisc.* 35)? Does money possess only a conventional worth, as a medium of exchange guaranteed by some local authority to represent valuable things? And more generally, does value depend solely on subjective desire and the balance of demand and supply? Or is value objective, residing in things themselves, regardless of human wants?

This last extrapolation from Aristotle's discussion of money in *Politics* 1.9–11 suggests the dominant evaluation of the customary and natural among post-Sophistic thinkers. This is the view that what is natural is simply so, despite human whim: it is objective, holds everywhere and in every circumstance. "Fire burns here and in Persia", as Aristotle writes, but what the fickle Athenian assembly decrees today it may rescind tomorrow, and its laws are disregarded in Sparta, Thebes and Babylon. Faced with this dichotomy, very few thinkers would repeat Herodotus' advice to act according to local laws, wherever one happens to be. "When at Rome, do as the Romans", or as Herodotus says, quoting Pindar's adage, "custom is king of all" (*Hist.* 3.38): each people should obey its own customs as it would a king, for they have proved their worth over generations. In this respect, Herodotus is more conservative than many thinkers of the Sophistic period, who show less respect for the wisdom of local *mores*. For these thinkers, it would be capricious and irrational simply to follow accepted habits and to practice one set of customs merely because they are customary. "Men want what is better, not simply what their fathers had", writes Aristotle (*Pol.* 1269a) and when they begin to be conscious of the possibility of change, they no longer regard inherited conventions as inevitable and quasi-divine. Then custom is regarded as a "human, all-too-human" construct, something that was made at some point in the past, and that can be unmade in the future. What new, improved customs should one develop, and what criterion of worth should one wilfully adopt? Modern philosophers tend to make this criterion pleasure, utility, subjective satisfaction. The dominant classical approach was to identify it with "the natural". Customs will be right, good and profitable to the degree that they conform to nature, and if one lives "in accordance with nature", then one will gain all that is good: true wealth, true pleasures and happiness, proper community, real piety. There are at least six major conceptions of the orientation of this "natural life", each differentiated by a different understanding of nature. We shall examine them in a roughly chronological order: the Calliclean, Platonic, Aristotelian, Epicurean, Stoic and, finally, the Cynic.

Calliclean will-to-power

Social Darwinism had its forerunners among the classical Greeks too, and indeed those who glorify strength, "real" politics and amoral ruthlessness have probably existed in all cultures: the theory of evolution only gives purportedly scientific sanction to an old *idée fixe*. To all kings and strong men, Hesiod tells the fable of the hawk and the nightingale: the hawk's nature is to eat the nightingale, but human beings are *not* hawks, and among them Zeus has established justice and the right (*Op.* 202–12). Despite Hesiod's reputation as a teacher of Greece, however, his fable would often be forgotten. Perhaps most famous is a speech that Thucydides attributes to the Athenians in the summer of 416 BCE when they are besieging the little island of Melos off Sparta's eastern coast. Melos had tried to remain neutral between Athens and Sparta, but the Athenians would not allow any islanders to stay outside their empire, and so they conquered Melos, killed the men, enslaved the women and children, and sent out their own colonists to farm the land. Before these terrible events, and during the siege itself, the Athenians conducted talks with the Melians that, according to Thucydides at least, ranged across many issues, for what was at stake was literally life and death. In Thucydides' so-called Melian Dialogue, the Athenians proclaim that the highest law of nature is the law of amoral power, to which gods and human beings must alike submit:

> We surmise that the divine – and we know that the human being – everywhere and under the necessity of nature, rules where it can. We neither instituted this law nor were the first to act according to it, but simply have adopted it as a fact and will leave it as such forever, knowing that you and others in our position of power would have done the same.
>
> (*History* 5.105.1)

So for the Athenians at Melos the essence of politics is power, of religion power, of nature power; everything is power, and nothing more.

Such ferocious and cynical ideas the Cynics would reject. In the meantime, they troubled Plato too, particularly in his *Republic* and *Gorgias*, where Thrasymachus, Glaucon and Callicles argue for the naturalness of violence and inequality. Most violent in his advocacy is Callicles. In nature, as viewed by Callicles, a few are strong, while everyone else is weak. Equality is a notion false to nature. Therefore, political systems such as democracy, that are based on equality of personhood, of rights and duties, are unnatural and Callicles despises them. Instead he eulogizes tyrants such as Xerxes who act like the lions they are, unabashedly using their kingdoms to satisfy their gigantic and infinitely expanding appetites. The strong do and should prey upon the weak: this is the *nomos* and "justice of nature" (Pl. *Grg.* 483e–484b).

Similarly Calliclean remarks can be found elsewhere in Greek literature, and it is not surprising that such ideas would be common enough in a competitive, warlike culture. Such ideas appear within the Cynics' genealogy also. We have seen that in legend at least, Diogenes "listened" to Antisthenes, who once studied rhetoric with Gorgias of Leontini: the same Gorgias whom Plato depicts as the teacher of Callicles. This influential Gorgias also touched on a natural "law of power" when, in his *Encomium of Helen*, he writes that "by nature the stronger cannot be constrained by the weaker, but the weaker is ruled and driven along by the stronger, and the strong leads while the weak follows" (Gorg. *Hel.* 11.35–8). Gorgias himself will not conclude his piece on a Calliclean note, but his approach could be taken in that direction, as Plato clearly recognized when he made Callicles Gorgias' follower, and indeed his most impressive follower. But while Callicles eulogizes tyrants, the Cynics typically denounced autocrats as stunted creatures, furthest removed from the beneficent light of nature.

Platonic transcendence

Given his characterization of Callicles as Gorgias' best student, it is tempting to regard Plato's ethical thought as very much a protest against Sophistic flirtations with the will-to-power: a protest against the assumption that the "good man" is the powerful man – powerful in speech, thought, wealth, friends and influence. Plato's own chosen hero is Socrates, who disclaims technical expertise, has little power and does not seek more, ironically effaces his own personality and argues to Callicles' face that "it is better to suffer injustice than to do it". And he seems to have applied the principle to himself when in 399 BCE he remained in Athens to suffer an unjust decree of execution, rather than betray the city of his birth: better to die with honour that prove traitor to one's "mother". Furthermore, if Callicles or the Athenians of Thucydides see nature as a battleground in which the strongest rightfully take the most, Plato disagrees forcefully, pointing to other features of nature that draw the soul beyond private desire, will-to-power and even beyond the temporal order altogether, towards a higher dimension that is the real source of tangible nature. Two of these aspects of nature are: (i) the existence of universals that determine particular things for what they are, make them intelligible, and that yet themselves endure beyond the death of particulars, and draw the mind into more precise and far-ranging thought; and (ii) the beauty of things, from the symmetry of the atomic elements through the beauty of organic bodies, souls, laws and institutions, all of which charge the viewer with longing for an unconditioned Beauty existing elusively at once in, through and beyond natural things. Yet although for Plato nature is pervaded by Form and by Beauty, and is both intelligible and lovely, it is not perfect. "There will never be an end to evils *here* in this world. Therefore, flee as quickly as possible *there*; as much as possible, make yourself like unto God". Such is the radical exhortation of *Theaetetus* 176a–b, and in the *Phaedo* Socrates defines philosophy as the "practice of death" (81a), that is, the disciplined elevation of the soul out of and above the immediacy of bodily life. Here there are no perfect circles, no straight lines, no unconditionally just actions, no perfectly virtuous motives: in short, nothing perfect, but only shadows of a magnificence so rich that even its shadows can enthrall. But one should not be enthralled, Plato urges; one should not live in accordance with this shadow world, but above it, transcending it. Just as shadows gain their shape and existence from the solid object from which they are thrown, so sensuous nature depends on a more solid, transcendent realm. All natural things seek eternity, each to its own capacity, and so too a human being should seek it not through reproduction or fame alone but through the awakening of the soul's own timeless mindfulness. Through various methods (e.g. dialectical exercises of collection and division, mathematics and the deductive explication of hypothetical assumptions), one can raise one's consciousness above mere particularity and become more divine. The ultimate vision cannot be forced, but comes unexpectedly, a sudden gift from beyond. But if it comes, it will make the philosopher a stranger to the world, just as Plato's Socrates is a stranger to the Athenians among whom he lived his entire biological life. Thus, once more the striking image of the *Timaeus*: man is a "divine growth" (90a) rooted in the heavens for he grows strongest there, not in the dirt of this earth. Or to make the point more paradoxically, man's nature is for Plato rather unnatural. Human beings have a higher nature and calling: to rise above the immediacy of animal life and become pure mind. People like Callicles have not studied enough geometry, says Socrates, and so for all their blustering talk of power, they are stunted creatures, never fulfilled or truly impressive.

Aristotelian self-actualization

In moments of candour Aristotle echoes Plato's calls to transcend temporal nature for the divine, which is the source of motion and actuality, and in such moments Aristotle can betray some of the fire of Plato's writing. But in general, Aristotle does not exhort one to transcend the body and time but rather to complete one's nature, and to actualize all one's natural potencies. For Aristotle, each existent has a definite essence, which determines it as a particular type of thing, different from other types: a human being, for instance, is not a monkey, or a horse, or a stone, or a cloud. What distinguishes a human being is his or her humanity, which might in turn be equated with high intelligence, reason, self-consciousness, the ability to laugh, upright posture, or a variety of other traits that the biologist must sift and judge in order of importance.

Aristotle's own judgement leads to his famous definition of the human being as "the political, rational animal": rationality and the need to live in *polis*-like communities distinguish human beings from other animals, and even more from plants and non-living things. An essence such as "humanity" serves not only to ground definitions; it exists as the *entelechy* of a thing, that is, as its inner structure, driving force and final purpose. Thus, in this example, each human being is impelled naturally from the moment of conception to develop his or her rationality and sociality as much as possible. When this essence is brought to fruition, Aristotle claims, the human being has actualized all its potential. In Aristotle's view, this means that one lives in a well-regulated city-state such as the Greek *polis*, with family, friends and fellow-citizens, taking on a variety of roles and in particular the role of a citizen, "ruling and being ruled in turn" (*Pol.* 1277a) as one participates virtuously in all the duties of civic life. Moreover, a human being desires by nature to know, and so one is never fully content unless one learns about many things, including the natural world: that is, one must philosophize, study biology, physics and cosmology, and use one's rational intelligence to the full. To do all this is to become a really excellent human being. Aristotle even speaks of this as a god-like life, and in his more "Platonic" moments exhorts his readers to "make themselves immortal, divine" (*athanatos*) (*EN* 1177b). Contrast this life in accordance with one's rational, social nature with a different sort of life: those who live for pleasure might be likened to molluscs, which siphon in food and drink and then excrete it out. But, in Aristotle's judgement, a human being should not live in accordance with the nature of a mollusc.

Aristotle's balanced outlook leaves room for custom also in the total economy of the natural life, for, unlike the Sophists, he does not rigidly speak of *physis* versus *nomos*, or oppose the spontaneous with the artificial. Rather, Aristotle tends to regard custom, along with art and human contrivance generally, as a means of "perfecting" nature. Thus, the leather shoe surrounds the softer foot and enables one to walk over rough ground; a lever lengthens the arm and increases its effective strength; rhythm and metre enhance the expressive powers of speech. The *polis* as a whole, with all its laws, magistracies and social arrangements, is a product of human making: cities do not grow on trees! But they are at the same time an extension of the natural drive to sociality. By nature, man and woman need each other, and so the nuclear family exists naturally, and not by mere convention. So, too, all peoples at an early historical stage live in villages, although only among some peoples do villages coalesce into cities or larger groupings. The Greek-like city is the natural *telos* of this historical trend, and so, for Aristotle, the *polis* is a natural entity. Indeed, it represents the perfection of human nature, for it is only by participating in a *polis* and all its manifold customs that one can actualize one's full humanity. As we have seen, the Cynics reject this idea wholesale with their antinomian behaviour. For them, a human being is not naturally so sociable or dependent on others: therefore, to "actualize one's potential", one does not need to live as citizens of cities or subject oneself to a mass of burdensome laws, taboos and social expectations.

Epicurus' atoms and the tranquil sage

Like the Cynics, the main Hellenistic Schools tended to veer away from Aristotle's classical attachment to the city. They emphasized a more individualistic ethic, and cast about for cosmologies on which to ground it. Epicurus, for example, did not pursue Aristotle's emphasis on final causes, or immanent *entelechies* that drive an entity towards its proper goal. An acorn, for instance, usually becomes an oak, but the reason (Epicurus thought) is not some mysterious "essence" that is both final and efficient cause of its self-actualization. Rather, Epicurus regarded natural entities through the lens of Democritus' quasi-mechanistic atomism. An acorn is atoms and void: the acorn's atoms move about, hooking on to more atoms in soil and sunshine so that gradually the acorn grows into an oak. In turn, as more time passes and more atoms begin to unhook, the tree grows old and dies – and that is all! The atomic processes run on. Nothing really serious happens in nature, and so one should not be troubled by dreams of Calliclean power, or of an all-redeeming Platonic Beauty, or of an Aristotelian self-actualization. The atoms might unhook tomorrow and so one should live as free from pain as possible, today. A tranquil attitude is the best response to a nature that is nothing but a complex conglomeration of atoms. In Epicurus' vision, the gods too are bundles of atoms, isolated in some distant chinks between worlds (Lucretius' *intermundia*). They do not care about human beings, and will not punish or reward us, and so we need not fear, worship or propitiate them. But if the gods are unserious and tranquil, then human beings can do no better: best to live for the simple pleasures of today.

Therefore, in some ways, the Epicurean "life according to nature" veers quite close to Cynic views. Like the Cynic, the Epicurean is not deceived by the pretty allure of wealth, honours, status, luxuries and fancy pleasures: all of these are the product of *nomos*, not nature. One needs very little to enjoy the gods' easy pleasure, and Epicurus said that all he needed was water, plain bread, and perhaps a little cheese (DL 10.11). For Lucretius too, "there is no poverty in little" (*DRN* 5.1119). In fact, it is best to have little, for having little one is less troubled by its inevitable loss. Attachment brings the inevitable pain of separation and so the Epicurean sage adopts a stance of tranquil detachment from custom, communal life and even from life itself. Let the atoms hook and unhook remorselessly: the wise will avoid the pain of needless entanglement with external contingencies, and so claim to gain the greatest of possible pleasures (DL 10.130–31).

Stoic identification with the whole

Even closer to the Cynic ethical outlook is that of the Stoics, who also adopted a stance of general detachment from externals. Yet like the Epicureans, the Stoics sought to ground their moral ideas on a comprehensive theory of nature, and a complex, many-layered physics that the Cynics would reject as so much superfluous verbiage. To summarize this complexity is difficult, but perhaps the first axiom of Stoic physics is the unity of nature. That is, every entity exists in relation to every other, and each thing is a part of – or, rather, is a moment deeply interfused by – the universal whole. This whole can be called many names: nature, God, *logos*, providence, fate, necessity. But whatever its name, as a whole it is single, solitary, self-sufficient, and unchanging. Its parts may shift about, but the whole itself remains unaltered. Within the universal totality, human beings are remarkable parts in that they have a spark of God and *logos*, and so may raise their little minds to knowledge of the whole. That is, although as bodily beings they are parts of nature, as thinking bodies they may contemplate all nature. But the mind that thinks the totality thereby becomes like it also and so, theoretically at least, the Stoic sage is postulated as being as single, solitary, self-sufficient, and unchanging as God or nature itself.

Such wisdom is a rare accomplishment, however. There are very few like the ideal Stoic sage, and the many non-philosophers comprehend him as little as they comprehend the totality. Being self-sufficient, the sage does not need friends, community or any others. Like nature, he does not change. In particular, he does not fly into a rage, or break down in grief, or burst into laughter: he does not suffer any passion, and this quintessentially Stoic attitude is "in accordance with nature", because nature itself does not weep or rage, but continues on serenely from age to age, through catastrophes and triumphs alike, indifferent to merely human pleasures and pains. Nature does not know emotion and so for the Stoic emotions are ultimately unnatural: irrational dispositions of soul. Realizing that emotions are false judgements, the Stoic strives to extirpate them and attain a lofty indifference. Ideally, he will look down calmly on particular happenings such as exile or homecoming, punishment or enthronement, poverty or wealth, sickness or health and life or death as matters of no great importance. Neither is better or worse than the other; they are neither good nor evil in themselves. They simply happen and, being local, are not of cosmic consequence. Therefore, one of the Stoics' maxims is *nil admirandum*: "one should not be enthralled" by any particular occurrence. The only thing worthy of admiration is virtue, namely, the disposition according to which one identifies oneself with nature as a whole. So to identify oneself is to be wise (for the unity of being is the fundamental truth), courageous before contingencies (which are not to be feared), temperate in appetite (for only one thing is to be desired), just in dealing with others (for one is temperate and self-controlled), pious towards the divine (for one knows what God truly is), and thus virtuous in all ways. Moreover, untroubled by conflicting desires, the sage is at one with himself; unfazed by hopes and fears, he is at one with his external environment and "fate". This unity of the sage's being brings real happiness, so that no matter what happens, he is content. When viewed from the outside, the indifference and imperturbability of the Stoic "natural life" may seem utterly "unnatural" and inhuman, and the Stoics have been nicknamed "the men of stone". Yet it has its own inner logic, which was compelling enough to inspire many capable

Romans, as well as influence great thinkers such as Spinoza, Kant, Hegel and the neo-Cynic Nietzsche.

Cynic simplicity

When one turns from the Stoics' theories of the ideal natural life to the Cynics' kindred conception, it is a turn from complexity to simplicity. For them, "nature" is almost synonymous with a single world: simplicity. "Simplify, simplify, simplify!" says Henry David Thoreau and, in the Cynics' case, one consequence of their great simplification is the abandonment of any extended philosophy of nature: the Cynics did not study the heavens, earth or organisms in any detail. They made some observations about dogs, mice, hares, sheep, deer, lions, frogs, larks, storks and the like, but all with a view to promoting their ethic of simplifying and stripping away unnecessary desires and customs.

And yet in this they share with almost all other ancient thinkers a common analysis of desire. Democritus, Plato, Aristotle, the Epicureans and Stoics agree in rejecting Callicles' analysis: it is *not* natural to expand one's desires infinitely and to seek to satisfy every possible desire, for such an attitude would make one perpetually restless, and probably even mad. Therefore the ancient thinkers are fairly unanimous in distinguishing between the few desires that are natural and necessary, and the many others that are neither. One hungers for food and this is natural, but one's mouth will not water for two-year-old Pyrenean boar stuffed with live thrushes: this is an acquired taste, and quite unnecessary. Of course, where one exactly divides the natural from the unnatural is unclear, and none of the Schools attempts a precise division. Nevertheless, it may be foolish to ask for geometrical precision in such matters, and there is a rough sense in the distinction, which provides grounds for what could be called an ethic of moderation. Nobody *needs* to own hundreds of houses and buildings, land in various countries, armies of slaves, and gold and silver beyond measure, like Petronius' Trimalchio. Those who like Callicles are always craving more, more and ever more

– more money, more power, more sexual experiences, more types of expensive foods and wines – and are afflicted by that vice that the Greeks called *pleonexia*, fall into a life that is not only unnatural, but positively harmful and evil, both for others and themselves.

Effectively all the ancient philosophers subscribed to these ideas, but it was the Cynics who insisted on them most vehemently. They form the foundation of the Cynics' "life according to nature". This Cynic naturalism might be characterized by three main headings: (i) simplicity of natural desire; (ii) the bounty of the natural world; and (iii) man's natural fitness for his environment. As we have seen already, the Cynic boasts that he lives in utmost simplicity, without house, furniture, cups, weapons, clothes, jewellery or money: in short, without the products of human craft and technology. Unhoused, unwashed, unshaven, unshod and almost unclothed, eating figs, lupin-beans, lentils and whatever else he finds growing in the fields or hills nearby, the Cynic is an "all-natural" philosopher who would, like Thoreau, simplify everything. Eat when hungry, drink when thirsty. Seek shelter from the elements when you have to. Relieve sexual needs when they arise. Use only what is immediately available. Live here, now. All this is the wisdom of the animals that eat what is nearby, drink from the closest stream or pond, hide in a cave or hole or whatever is available and copulate when nature urges.[5] There is nothing shameful in any of this, the Cynic argues, for if the need or desire is natural, then surely the satisfying of it is natural too, no matter where one is. If the desire is spontaneous, shouldn't one satisfy it spontaneously also? In the notorious anecdote, then, when Diogenes masturbates in the marketplace, he is only living "according to nature". What is unnatural, in the Cynics' perspective, is to hide away behind thick walls, fornicating with slaves and gorging oneself on peacocks and exotic foods carried across deep seas, at great cost in money and lives.

Furthermore, nature is bountiful and will provide for all natural needs. Teles, for instance, has Poverty ask: "Surely you don't lack for anything necessary? Are not the roadsides full of vegetables? Aren't the springs filled with water, and don't I provide you with a bed wherever there is earth, and a couch of leaves?" (Stob. 3.1.98).

Or Dio's Diogenes boasts that not only does nature provide, but she provides enough for the Cynic to feast like the companions of a Homeric king:

> She is capable of providing my food – apples, millet, barley, bitter vetch, the cheapest of lentils, acorns cooked in ash, cornel-berries, on which Homer says Circe feasted the companions of Odysseus and on which even the largest animals can survive.   (D. Chr. 6.62)

On this point, Dio's Euboean Discourse is particularly illuminating of the Cynics' praise of natural living. The hunter-gatherers in Euboea, whom Dio met during his years of wandering, have no money and few implements, but they lack for nothing, with their game of all sorts, swine, "sorb apples, medlars, winter apples, and swollen bunches of fine grapes ... loaves of pure wheat, boiled eggs on wooden platters, dried chickpeas" (D. Chr. 7.74–6), and so forth.

There are some four hundred years between Teles and Dio Chrysostom, and so one recognizes the continuity in basic ideas. Plato touches on them also when he conjures up a vision of natural wealth in the "city of pigs". This Socrates suggests (perhaps with an ironic nod to associates such as Antisthenes) is the "true city", even though its citizens are "sophisticates" in comparison with the Cynics: they have houses, wear shoes and warm clothes in winter, eat barley and wheat bread and recline on reeds and leaves. In addition they have loads of "relish": "salt and olives and cheese; and they will boil roots and herbs like country people do; for dessert we will give them figs and peas and beans; and they will roast myrtle-berries and acorns on the fire, drinking in moderation" (Pl. *Resp.* 372). Implicit in such quasi-Cynic visions is the assumption that the lentils and beans *will* crowd forth by the wayside, and that the springs will *not* run dry. Nature is implicitly trusted almost as Mother Nature, the Good Housekeeper who will not forget her human children. That is, the Cynics seem not to have feared drought or famine or the lean winter months and, if they occurred, they could be endured easily in the faith that nature would provide enough. It is a simple faith, and perhaps a simplistic one, yet perhaps we should not dismiss the idea too cynically: again, previous ecosystems are known to have been fabulously wealthy in contrast with our exploited environment, and so the ancient Cynics may not have been hopelessly out of touch with their world.

Cynic adaptation to environment: *ponos* and natural toughness

Although bountiful nature easily provides for all simple needs, the Cynics stress that human beings are not immediately at home in nature, but must struggle to regain their rightful place in it. Human beings foolishly separate themselves off from the natural world, congregating in large cities, living inside houses, covering their bodies with clothes, regulating their waking hours with tyrannical clocks and an unquestioned concatenation of customs that only lull them into a different sort of sleep. The artificiality of *nomos* is perpetuated from generation to generation, as children are born and put into "swaddling clothes" of various sorts, from which many never emerge. Born into a culture and its set of proprieties, the individual can become defined, even bound, by them. In the Cynics' view, this process of enculturation and of "civilizing" the human animal only diminishes his or her happiness and freedom. To break one's chains requires struggle, and initially at least it is more painful to struggle than to sit still. This image of breaking free from the chains of custom may have been common: Antiphon describes *nomoi* as "chains of nature" (Fr. 4.29), while Plato in his allegory of the cave envisages prisoners blinking at shadows on the wall: these shadows are the city's customs, as well as all natural events – indeed, all sensible phenomena, which lie like so many fetters on the benighted consciousness, blinkering it to the higher reality outside. The Cynics switch metaphors, holding that one must endure *ponoi, askēsis, athloi* and much *talaipōria* in order to regain one's true nature.

These words are most associated with athletics, the Olympic Games and their mythic founder, Heracles. Heracles' twelve labours were *athloi*; according to Cynic and Stoic allegory, he endured them for the good of mankind. He killed the Nemean Lion with his bare hands, shot down the Stymphalian Birds, and in general cleared the earth of monsters and criminals, so great was his *philanthrōpia*. All of this was hard labour, *athlos*. The related adjective *athlos* means "wretched" and "in pain", and an athlete (*athlētēs*) is literally one who is in pain, either because he is training for competition, or competing in the hot dust at the Games themselves. Another word that the Cynics played on is *ponos*, meaning both "labour" and "pain" at once (e.g. D. Chr. 8.16; Epict. *Ench.* 29.6–7). Heracles' labours were often denoted his *ponoi*, and Plato's Socrates is one of the first philosophers to liken his own philosophical "work" to Heracles' (Pl. *Ap.* 22a6–8). The Cynics play even more extensively on this conceit, as they undergo ascetic "labours" to train themselves for the wise, natural life. These *ponoi* involve physical pain: rolling in the hot sand, embracing snowy statues, walking barefoot on snow and enduring summer heat, winter cold, hard beds and little food. Their labours also include exercises in disappointment and psychological pain. Rather laughably, for instance, Diogenes is said to have begged money from statues, so as to get used to rejection, and many Cynics-in-training shaved half their heads (DL 6.33), and carried tuna fish, pots of lentils and other embarrassing objects across a crowded space so as to get used to the whistles and jeering.[6] That is, one hardens oneself to shamelessness so as not to be overawed by the taboo-bound multitude. Such physical and psychological "labours" constitute the Cynic's *askēsis*, another word with definite connotations of athletic training but with the added notion of "perfecting". Its English derivative is "asceticism", and so the Cynic becomes an ascetic of sorts, training through pain for a hard, simple life "according to nature".

Such a natural life is possible, the Cynic argues, contrary to those sceptics who think such human products as buildings, shoes and clothes are necessary. For the Cynics, nature (like Aristotle's Housekeeper) does provide, and there is no natural thing that cannot live a spontaneous, unadorned existence. Perhaps the most complete Cynic defence of man's natural fitness for his environment is Dio Chrysostom's sixth oration ("Diogenes"). Here, echoing ideas of the classical Sophistic movement, Dio uses Diogenes to argue that human beings are as well adapted to a wild, outdoor existence as any other animal: they do *not* need clothing, houses, fires and the like, but do better without them. Some argue, falsely, that human beings are unique: they alone walk upright, have no thick skin or warm hair or fur or scales for protection from the elements; they have no natural weapons such as claws or fangs; they are not as strong as lions, or as fast as deer. Dio's treatment is reminiscent of the words of Protagoras when in Plato's dialogue he tells how Epimetheus once distributed talents to the different animals, but, in his absentmindedness, portioned them all out before coming to mankind and so left human beings defenceless. In Protagoras' myth, Prometheus intervened to save mankind with the gifts of fire and cities: technology and humanity's tendency to flock together has enabled it to survive, as well as the further divine gifts of justice and reverence (*aidōs*).

But, on the contrary, Dio argues in Cynic fashion, man is not at all naturally helpless or weak. To lack thick hair or fur is not to be hopelessly exposed to the elements, for frogs have bare skin like human beings, yet spend the whole year outdoors, most of it in cold water. Or, consider the eye. This is a delicate organ. But it does not need to be wrapped up or protected outdoors. What need then is there to bind up one's feet with shoes? People's feet are tender only because they wear shoes and if they walked about as nature made them, their feet would be tough as leather (D. Chr. 6.15, 6.26–7; cf. ps.-Luc. *Cyn.* 15). Similarly, people cannot endure heat or cold simply because in the summer they hide in the shade and in the winter they huddle indoors by the fire: such unnatural customs have ruined the species. People should pity themselves less. Frailty is not the human condition but a human choice. Weakness is not due to nature, but only to degenerate customs. Worst and most unnatural of all are the rich, because they are the most dependent on "civilization" and the customary obedience of others: Dio's Diogenes compares them to newborn babies, for both need their swaddling clothes (D. Chr. 6.15). The rich, however, are never forced to outgrow theirs and in their folly they forget the beneficent wisdom of nature, which as universal mother provides proper nourishment for all her children: "[N]o creature is born in any region where it cannot live. For otherwise, how could the first human beings have survived, since then there was no fire, houses, clothing, or any other food except what grew wild" (6.28). The first peoples were forced to adapt themselves to the environment, and in this they were only like storks and cranes, who wander on to different regions if ever it becomes too hot or cold (6.32–4; cf. 6.1–4).

This adaptation to the environment or, in the Cynic's language, adaptation to external circumstances, is not an accomplishment that happens immediately. One must train through *ponos* to recover one's natural self, but when one does return to nature, one returns to an elemental goodness. One recognizes only the present moment as real. What one experiences in the immediacy of the present is "nature": this sunshine, this shadow, this simple desire, this simple satisfaction. Those who live "according to nature", in the fullness of the present, will never be disappointed, for there is always enough. Nature provides easily for simple needs and so makes the Cynic supremely happy for she never fails to cater to his elemental desires. In addition, she makes him supremely virtuous. Those who live simply in the present will not act on unnecessary cravings. Rejecting power, honour, wealth and the like as so many delusions, the Cynic has no motive to wage war, murder, enslave, rob, deceive or commit any injustice towards others. He luxuriates in the "wealth" of owning little, yet his simple "kingdom" is surrounded (like Crates' *Pēra*) by a sea of "wine-dark *typhos*" at whose storms and ceaseless commotion he looks out with anger, dismay, amusement or pity, depending on his momentary mood. He looks out also on the delusions of the philosophers sailing this way and that, following their stars or atoms or nonexistent Ideas. None of these live "according to nature", and so none but the Cynic is truly happy or good.

Let us dwell on some of these ideas a little further. First, the injunction to live in the elemental present is fundamental to ancient Cynicism, and is consequently reflected in a great variety of anecdotes and statements, from early to late. Antisthenes, for instance, claims to satisfy his desires with whatever is present (*to paron*) (Xen. *Symp.* 4.38, 4.42). Diogenes tells Alexander to stand out of his sun, compared to which world-conquest, Persian glory and the like are unreal (DL 6.38). The Gymnosophists tell Alexander that he will never possess more than the ground he stands on, except when he dies, when he will occupy a bit more (Arr. *Anab.* 7.1.5–6). Epictetus (unwittingly) revisits the thought when he writes that the measure of property is the body and what the body can hold: one cannot own anything else. Demetrius of Corinth says that one should live in the moment, because everything is here, and nothing exists elsewhere (Sen. *Ben.* 7.2.4). Teles' advice is "to use what is present" (Stob. 3.1.98). Tiresias whispers in the ear of Lucian's Menippus, "seek out this one single thing before all else: arrange the present well and run along, laughing a lot and taking nothing seriously" (Luc. *Nec.* 21). The Delphic oracle told Dio to "do the thing at hand until you come to the ends of the earth" (D. Chr. 13.9). Julian writes that the Cynic satisfies his desires with "whatever comes to hand" (*Or.* 7.226b). More abstractly, Oenomaus argues that human knowledge is limited to sense-perception and self-consciousness: one knows oneself, and what one sees, hears and touches, but nothing else (Euseb. *Praep. evang.* 6.7). In keeping with this are anecdotes pitting Diogenes against metaphysical idealists: Diogenes rejects Platonic Ideas (like "Cupness"), because they cannot be seen (DL 6.53); he refutes Zeno the Eleatic's arguments against motion by walking around. More abstractly still, Antisthenes' denial of predication may, theoretically at least, provide grounding for the ethic of living *now*, unburdened by needless abstractions of "past" or "future", which do not exist *now*. For, again, Antisthenes seems to have argued that one cannot say "A is B" but only "A is A". If so, then this simple logic could issue forth in a simple epistemology, and an ethic of simplicity: only this "A" *here* can be known; only this lived moment is real, and so one should live in accordance with this natural immediacy, concentrate on "the thing at hand" and dismiss all else as *typhos*. Thus one might reconstruct the Cynics' general train of thought, and there must be some such line of reasoning. For why else would they adopt as a motto the phrase, "use the things that are present"?[7] This is the positive complement of the motto of "defacing the coinage": the Cynic rejects custom, the "mother-city" of ills, to return to nature, source of virtue, happiness and all goods.

One of these goods is pleasure, but how does one get it? For an answer, we must enrol briefly in the Cynic School of Hedonism. Their advice is simple really: enjoy life, now, like the animals do, for if one cannot enjoy the present moment, then one cannot really enjoy anything.[8] This is what makes the lot of the rich so unbearable, the Cynics argue. For the rich are deluded by a million unnecessary "needs": they must have their sumptuous dinners, but these require armies of servants, and after the feast one needs entertainment of all sorts, many sexual partners perhaps, and, at the end, soft beds. But one cannot really want what one does not really need, and so the happiness of these deluded hedonists is always spoiled by something. Their typical vice is *mempsimoiria*: that is, they "blame fate", and are satisfied with nothing that comes their way, like the tyrant who will behead his guests if they flatter him – and if they do not flatter him. True pleasure, the Cynics often contend, can only be had by scorning it and by welcoming its opposite, pain. There will always be pain, and so rather than escape it, or try to control uncontrollable fortune, one should grasp the serpent by the neck (Stob. 3.1.98), put out the fire with one's tongue, rush into the fray fearlessly, and fearlessly stare down the barking dog (D. Chr. 8.17–19): that is, one should welcome pains as inevitable, love them, or at least accept them as *ponoi*, preparing one for the pleasures of the satisfaction that *will* come. *Ponos*, as both "pain" and "labour", becomes the Cynics' means for maximizing his pleasure. More paradoxically, pain is the cause of pleasure, and the Cynics are a strange breed of ascetic hedonists, or hedonistic ascetics. Or, rather, theirs is the hedonism of nature itself. Pleasure can exist in conjunction with pain. Therefore, "hunger is the best sauce" (as the Greeks said also) and only *ponos* can give piquancy to experience. "Despising pleasure is the greatest of pleasures", says Diogenes (DL 6.71), as he enjoys his "tub" more than Xerxes his palace (*Ep. Diog.* 37 [Malherbe]). To the goddess Happiness, Diogenes cries out: "I will remain for you, O Happiness, drinking water, eating water-cress and sleeping on the ground. And Happiness answered him that this life is ultimately not *ponos* but pleasure" (Max. Tyr. *Diss.* 3.9; cf. D. Chr. 6.6–20, 8.20–33). Such ideas are summed up in a lecture by Dio Chrysostom:

Ponoi make themselves ever lesser and easier to bear, and make one's pleasures both greater and less harmful whenever they occur with *ponoi*. But luxury makes pains (*ponoi*) seem ever harder, and dulls and weakens one's pleasures. For the person who is always luxuriating and never touches *ponos* will end up unable to endure any pain at all, and also not able to feel any pleasure, not even the most intense. As a result the self-controlled lover of *ponos* ... lives a life that is far more pleasurable than his opposite.   (3.83–5)

If Dio did indeed deliver these words to Trajan, then one has the extraordinary scene of a one-time Cynic trying to train not just anybody, but the king of the world himself, in the notion that the natural "ascetic" is the true "hedonist" and that one will be good and happy only by living here and now. It seems that especially for later figures like Dio, Epictetus, Demonax and Peregrinus, such training was one of the ideal Cynic's *ponoi*: the Cynic "works" like Heracles ridding the land of evils, or "toils" like the sun bringing light to mankind (D. Chr. 3.73–5). Sun, hero, Cynic, king: in all cases, Dio generalizes, "the stronger naturally govern and care for the weaker" (305). If so, we have come full circle from Callicles' harsh *Machtpolitik*: the strong Cynic "king" does not "rule" others for his own interest only, but endures and teaches asceticism for their betterment. He is motivated by *philanthrōpia*, the highest virtue made possible by a natural life. Only those freed from false desires can truly "love" others. Such ideas may have been operative at the death of Peregrinus, when he sought to teach mankind that death is not an evil. In this final *ponos* of Peregrinus, his fellow Cynics compared him to Heracles and the sun (Luc. *De mort. Peregr.* 4). In the reported words of Theagenes, just as Phedias' Zeus and Polycleitus' Doryphorus were the perfection of art, so Peregrinus was the perfection of nature (6, 9).

Noble savages and the Cynic majority

Paragons such as Peregrinus were rare indeed, yet the Cynics often claimed that their ideas of the natural life were not *theirs* only. Their ideas were not simply the customary concepts of a small group of like-minded philosophers. Rather, these ideas belonged to all mankind, and in preaching them the Cynic was only reminding his hearers of truths they had forgotten. But other peoples had not forgotten them, and Cynics may have found inspiration in the thought that their philosophy was in fact the most universal of all. Looking past the small Greek cities to the hinterlands, with their farmers, hunters and fishers, and even farther still to barbarian lands beyond, Cynics sometimes surmised that by far the largest number of peoples live "according to nature" and that it is the "civilized" Graeco-Roman city-dwellers who are the decided minority. If so, nature herself had made an elemental life the norm and the Cynic philosophers were only recovering for their society a truth that other peoples had not lost. These virtuous "primitives" included the ancient Persians, the Scythians and Getae, the Indian gymnosophists, as well as peoples closer to home such as the Spartans, or even the noble poor whom Dio Chrysostom met in the wilds of Euboea and Arcadia, in the very centre of the Greek world itself.[9] A journey to the edges of the earth, or to the very heart of it, can also be a journey back in time, to the original, elemental and natural. Thus, Diogenes and Dio are said to have received their first instructions from Delphi: the "naval" and centre of the Greek universe, from which timeless truths are revealed. Among the Indians, Onesicritus finds naked men who put even Diogenes to shame. Such "primitive" peoples, the observer may speculate, must be like the first peoples, and from them one can guess what human beings were like before civilization developed. The conclusion of such primitivist thought, generally, is that "natural" peoples had little technology, science or wealth. They needed little, wanted little, and lived in harmony with their natural environment, which provided all they needed in abundance. Having everything, all were equal and lived together in peace, without strife, law suits or wars. Living according to nature, those people were free. Man is born free, but time has brought a fall, and now everywhere people are in chains. Calanus laughs at Onesicritus' clothes and hat: Onesicritus is in chains.[10]

A passage from Dio Chrysostom, again, sums up the Cynics' primitivism as well as many themes of this chapter: the simplicity of natural desire, the wealth of the natural environment, man's native fitness for his environment, the pleasure of *ponos*, and the need to renounce the chains of custom to return to our natural happiness:

> [N]o creature is born in any region where it cannot live. For otherwise, how could the first human beings have survived, since then there was no fire, houses, clothing, or any other food except what grew wild. But later generations' meddling ambition, their contriving and plotting have not helped their lives at all. For they do not use their intelligence to promote courage or justice, but to procure pleasure only. But though they pursue the pleasant everywhere, they in fact live less pleasantly and with more pains; and though they think they are providing for themselves, they are in fact ruining themselves through their vast fastidiousness. It was for this reason that Prometheus was rightly said to have been bound to the rock, with his liver torn by the eagle.   (D. Chr. 6.28–30)

Who would want to suffer the fate of Prometheus? For the Cynics, Prometheus was not the benefactor of the human race, but its seducer, corrupter and betrayer. He stole fire, and from fire came all the other crafts and technologies, from leatherworking to metallurgy, the minting of coins, carving of jewellery and forging of weapons. Prometheus is the great culture bringer according to tradition, but the Cynics reject this customary view and see him as the corruptor of nature. Those who adopt Prometheus' inventions and lead an artificial life become bound by those inventions and conventions, to their lasting unhappiness. In the myth, it is Heracles who breaks Prometheus' chains and ends his torture. So too, one of the Cynics' "labours" is to snap the hold that conventional thinking has on their contemporaries, and restore them from Tartarus to the light of the sun.

FOUR

Chance, fate, fortune and the self

When Diogenes was asked, "What have you learned from philosophy?", he responded that it had taught him self-sufficiency and the ability to bear all the twists of fortune (DL 6.63).[1] Lucian's, Demonax lived by the same creed: he made a cult of self-sufficiency, but as he grew older and more dependent on others he decided to end his life (Luc. *Demon.* 4). These two moments encapsulate concepts central to the Cynic philosophy: those of fortune, fate, chance and self-sufficiency. These ideas can easily become the stuff of cliché, but as with the notion of the life according to nature, terms such as *Tychē* and *autarkeia* arise from long cultural development and are rich with resonance. In exploring these, we shall again proceed from the abstract to the ethical, from the ideas of fate, fortune, chance and providence to the Cynic ethics of detachment and independence. The resulting Cynic synthesis was very influential, not least on Stoicism, but also in quarters as unexpected as Petronius' "Dinner of Trimalchio".

Fate, fortune, chance, providence

The interrelated concepts of fate, fortune, chance and providence should be treated in themselves before we turn to some Greek sources, as the terms can be blended in a confusing variety of ways.

There are two opposing views: either all things have a cause, or they do not. The first view that (i) all things that happen have a cause can be called *causal determinism*. This is sometimes linked closely with strict determinism, according to which all that happens must be so: the cosmos is governed by necessity, unalterable law, or fate. If these determinists tend to view events as bad, they are fatalists, for in English at least to be "fatalistic" is to think that events will march inexorably on, ending with death or some catastrophe. And so the fatalist says pessimistically, "it has to end badly" or "nothing good can come of it". Some Greek tragedies are fatalistic in this sense: whatever Oedipus does, he is doomed to suffer the decrees of fate. A different variation on determinism, however, is the belief in providence. Here what governs the cosmos is not merely a neutral fate or impersonal cosmic law. Nor is it a malign deity or crushing doom, but instead providence that "looks forward" to the advantage of each entity and event, ordering nature and history for the good, and even for the best. In this foreseeing and fore-ordering, Providence is often conceived in quasi-personal terms: originally a personal virtue, *providentia* becomes for the Romans a vaguely female deity, then a virtue of the emperors, and ultimately an attribute of the Christian God; for the Greeks, Prometheus is the "foreseeing" immortal who may know a future dark even to Zeus.

Oppositely, one may deny (i) and assert its opposite: (ii) some things do not have a cause, but happen spontaneously, randomly, unpredictably. This *causal indeterminism* affirms the existence of objective chance. What is chance? There are at least three basic views. Some hold that "chance" is only a word that refers to subjective ignorance. There are no chance events, really, but we say that things happen by chance when we do not know their causes. Thus one may say, "He hit the target by chance" or "They met by chance on the road", but, regarding the first statement, what one effectively means is, "The dart that he threw followed a complicated path which in throwing he did not intend or understand". Democritus seems to regard chance in this way: chance is not a cause or a reality, but merely a word indicating subjective ignorance of the true causes and realities. Regarding the second example, each person walks down the road with a purpose of their own. Neither intended to meet the other, and so we say that they met "by chance": their meeting was unintended, an accident. This is Aristotle's understanding of the word, and he generalizes from an example like this to the notion of the coincidence of separate trajectories of motion. There are definite causes that set two objects on their respective paths, but there is no such cause for the coincidence of their paths, if they happen to hit each other. The coincidence is not entirely uncaused, for definite causes are involved in the two separate motions, but it does not have a definite cause either. Therefore, Aristotle understands chance as an "indefinite cause".

Contrary to both of these views is a third. This is true causal indeterminism, according to which chance is not a mere word or a merely indefinite cause, but an effective aspect of objective reality. Subatomic particles pop out of nothing; atoms "swerve" or follow random paths; genes mutate; individuals suddenly veer from their entrenched habits, surprising everyone, as perhaps when Hipparchia married Crates and "ran away with the circus". According to the causal indeterminist, some events simply happen. They are not caused by some antecedent or contemporary force; nor are they caused for a reason or future purpose, as when one says "I am throwing the dart because I want to hit the target". Without efficient or final causes, chance events cannot be understood or explained and in them nature shows itself to be sometimes irregular, spontaneous, random, full of novelty and unpredictability.

To sketch in broad strokes, ancient philosophy as a whole affirmed (i), while in the wake of quantum mechanics, twentieth-century philosophy has looked on variations of (ii) with greater seriousness. For the ancients, one of the first axioms, taken often as self-evident and even necessary for experience and thought, is that "nothing comes from nothing", *ex nihilo nihil fit*: Being can only derive from Being; each happening must have its cause; each substance comes from a similar substance; each event proceeds only from an antecedent actuality; the cause must have as much or more reality than its effect. Such formulations by Parmenides, Aristotle, Lucretius and other ancients are revisited by modern physics's law of conservation (of mass and energy), by Leibniz's principle of sufficient reason or even by Einstein's conviction that "God does not play dice". On the other hand, Lucretius speaks of the random swerve of atoms, and the notion of indeterminism returns in more technical form in quantum mechanics. At higher levels of complexity, Lucretius would find a parallel to the atomic swerve in human freedom and many modern thinkers also stress the eruption of rough unpredictability in the seemingly fixed processes of nature: one prominent example is Charles Peirce according to whose *tychism* chance events are not only real but somehow "first", the most primitive and creative of all.

Thus, modern physics and postmodern philosophy can in some ways radically revise the deterministic model of Newtonian mechanics that dominated European thought from the seventeenth to the nineteenth century. According to this vision, the universe is matter in motion. Matter is inertial, stays put and, like dead weight, simply resists force. But when force is applied to an object, it accelerates according to Newton's second law of motion, $F = ma$. This "law" governs all natural motions, for instance gravitational motion: apples, oranges, raindrops, the moon, the sun and all bodies are pulled towards the earth with a quantifiable acceleration. The stars too are not "fixed" in their eternal circular orbits (as the ancients thought), but are pulled about in all directions by the hurly-burly of innumerable conflicting forces. This deterministic viewpoint was dominant through the eighteenth and nineteenth centuries, and could even inspire a fatalistic attitude that has not yet disappeared: the universe (some believe) runs on its predetermined path, and human efforts cannot change what must be; human freedom is an illusion, and we are simply self-conscious bits of matter, ruled by tyrannical "natural laws".

This quasi-scientific fatalism revisits some of the most ancient and primitive ideas of mankind, a stock of feelings and premonitions that formed one of the main contexts for Cynicism. This is the belief in fate. Modern Newtonians, Kantians and others speak of unalterable natural "law", but this essentially dresses up an age-old belief in the garb of calculus. The belief can be suggested by simple reflection on experience. A little thought reminds one how large the world is, how long time has been and will be, and how small in comparison with it all the individual is. Day follows night, winter summer. The young are born, grow old and die. The stars above circle around and after much time return to the same place. Things recur. All events and individuals recur as moments in some great recurrent pattern. And so, one imagines that if one lived long enough, one would see everything happen. There would be "nothing new under the sun". Moreover, in the face of the cosmic immensity and inevitability, it would seem that the individual's wishes and efforts, no matter how heroic, are only a small gesture, mere bubbles, or, in the Cynics' image, smoke, *typhos*. The belief in fate, then, can easily lead to a pessimistic fatalism. For if nature is determined by vast, inevitable forces, what is now had to be so, and what will be *will* be, regardless of what I do. One's life is determined in advance: the play has been written and all one does is act out one's part. No one can escape their fate.

Acceptance of fate in some form – from a general cosmic fate governing the universe in outline to a more exact fate governing the details of each individual life – is writ large over the ancient world, and existed through all the periods and places in which there were Cynics. Many Greeks and Romans, early and late, simple and sophisticated, respected the notion of fate. Its importance for the Greeks is indicated by the great number of oracles, prophets, soothsayers and eventually, in the imperial period, astrologers, who claimed to know the future that was to be. Its importance is reflected also in the great number of words and images for fate: μοῖρα, μόρος, πότμος, αἶσα, οἶτος, κήρ, ἡ πεπρωμένη ἡμέρα, αἴσιμον ἦμαρ, μόρσιμον ἦμαρ and τὸ πεπρωμένον. Furthermore, fate can be conceived as a person, as an impersonal principle or force, or as something hovering ambiguously between the two. Most vivid is the personification of fate as three old women, the *Clōthes* or Spinsters: *Clōthō* who spins the yarn of a life, *Lachesis* who measures it and *Atropos* who cuts it.[2] In other personifications, Hesiod describes the Fates as the daughters of Night and sisters of Death (*Theog.* 211–17); or, alternatively as the daughters of Zeus and Right (*Themis*), and the sisters of the Seasons (*Hōrae*) (904). The Homeric poets speak of *Moira* and the *Moirai* (plural) but it is unclear whether they are goddesses, impersonal forces or both; unclear also is their relation to Zeus, whether more powerful than or somehow synonymous with him (e.g. Hom. *Il.* 16.432–8, 8.68–74). Philosophers tend to make fate more an impersonal principle. In Plato's Myth of Er, it is true, Socrates speaks of the three Moirai as "Daughters of Necessity", but this is allegory, not true myth. More typical are the Stoics who use the greyer abstraction, *to peprōmenon*.

Roman popular attitudes were as unsystematic and varied as those of the Greeks. For the Romans, fate was conceived primarily as *Fortuna*, but also as the three old *Parcae* (imaged like the Greek *Clōthes*) and as the impersonal *fatum*. The last may be related to the word *fari*, "to say": fate is "that which has been said", and what has been pronounced by destiny is as unalterable as a king's decree. *Fortuna* on the other hand is related to *ferre*, "to carry", and so *Fortuna* from the beginning was a goddess who "carried" and brought good luck. The Romans tended to give their deities a myriad of specialized functions, and *Fortuna* was no exception. There was a *Fortuna Primigenia* (who presided over newborn children), *Fortuna Liberum* (who brought good luck to children), *Fortuna Virginalis* (for young women), *Fortuna Muliebris* (for older women) and *Fortuna Redux* (for safe homecoming), as well as various political *Fortunae*: *Fortuna Victrix* (giver of victory), *Patricia*, *Equestris* and *Plebeia* (for the three orders of society) and, most importantly, *Fortuna Populi Romani* and later under the emperor, *Fortuna Augusta*. Individual generals could call themselves *Felix* (e.g. Sulla) if previous victories showed that Fortuna as Lady Luck was on their side. Among the many others aspects of *Fortuna*, perhaps the most curious is *Fortuna Barbata*, to whom young men dedicated the shavings of their first beard: an important moment when one faces the adult world with both hope and trepidation. For this and other challenges in life, one always needs a little luck and so one might say a prayer. *Fortuna* was worshipped and propitiated in many temples, as at Rome, Antium, and especially Praeneste.[3] Trajan dedicated a temple to *Fortuna*, moved her feast day from 26 June (close to the summer solstice) to the even more momentous time of 1 January, on which day offerings were given to her on behalf of the whole empire. That a whole empire, at the height of its power, would pray for luck is not surprising, for in the Hellenistic and Roman periods *Fortuna* had come to be regarded as one of the supreme forces in the universe. Here one should note the ambiguity of these terms *vis-à-vis* the distinctions drawn above: *Fortuna* has elements of a beneficent, all-determining providence, as well as of a fickle goddess who may answer a prayer, but then again may chance not to.

A similar "fate" awaited another divine principle of the Greeks: *Tychē* (Τύχη). Etymologically, this should more closely resemble causal indeterminism, (ii) above: *Tychē* is the noun form of the verb meaning "to happen or stumble upon" and therefore might be translated roughly as "luck", as it primarily connotes chance, contingency and the unpredictable. Yet despite the etymological connotation, there were many conflicting conceptions of *Tychē*. Is it a cause, or randomness? Abstract principle or goddess? Precise resonances can differ confusingly, but the dominant trend was to regard her as a goddess, benevolent but with mysterious ways. One should propitiate her with sacrifice, but her favours are not guaranteed. Thus, when Aeschylus and Pindar refer to *Tychē*, they can address her hopefully as "saviour". Indeed, Pindar in one ode makes her the enigmatic cause of almost all that happens:

> It is you who on the sea guides swift ships, and on land rapid battles and assemblies that render counsel. As for men's hopes, they often rise, while at other times they roll down as they voyage across vain falsehoods. No human has yet found a sure sign from the gods regarding an impending action; their plans for future events lie hidden from view. Many things happen to men counter to their judgment, at times to the reverse of their delight, but then some who have encountered grievous storms exchange their pain for great good in a short space. (*Ol.* 12.3–12; trans. Race)

Ideas such as this become more prevalent in the Hellenistic and imperial periods, when *Tychē* was definitively personified as one of the most important deities. Classical Thebes had a temple to *Tychē* and she was later followed by Argos, Elis, Megalopolis, Athens and Syracuse; Pausanias tells of shrines in Messenian Pharae, Sicyon, Smyrna, Achaean Aegeira, Lebadeia and Olympia. It was a clear proof of her popularity when the great successor to Alexander, king Seleucus Nicator, built a temple to her in Antioch, and that city would be especially dedicated to *Tychē* until it became the seat of a Christian patriarch.[4] Eventually in the syncretistic culture of the Roman East, *Tychē*, *Fortuna* and the Egyptian goddess Isis were blended together into one goddess of prosperity, who carried a "horn of Amalthea", a globe and a rudder: the horn of plenty symbolized her potential beneficence, the globe her unsteady nature (analogous to our "wheel of fortune") and the rudder her control of affairs and the fact that she might unpredictably steer a different course, veering from prosperity to cruel adversity, or vice versa.

The resonance of the word *Tychē* is hard to overestimate, but also hard to specify, for this goddess impressed different people in different ways. She might be conceived alternatively as unpredictable chance, as necessary fate or even as all-seeing Providence. Thus, recent history in Polybius' view is governed by *Tychē* in the sense of Providence: the Romans were *destined* to acquire their empire, and so it would be futile, even impious, for the Greeks to continue to resist.[5] At the other extreme, comic poets such as Menander and Philemon depict *Tychē* as a stormy and capricious woman (e.g. Menander Fr. 630 [Kassel]): suitors beware! There is a sense of this too in Petronius' *Satyricon*, in which Trimalchio is Fortune's darling, raised undeservedly from penniless slave to glorious *sevir Augustalis*, and Trimalchio is just as whimsical and unpredictable as his patroness.

The *Satyricon* is worth dwelling on briefly, both because of its many quasi-Cynic elements, and its witty play on notions of fortune. It is often classified as a "Menippean satire" because of its mixture of prose and poetry. Add to this a host of manic characters, unsparing satire of a full spectrum of social custom, and a sheer delight in life, and one has in many ways a Cynic novel. To judge from the remaining fragments, it is a picaresque novel. Its feckless heroes Ascyltus and Encolpius move from moment to moment, adventure to adventure, as they wander about a city – a "Greek city" and "*colonia*"[6] – living by their wits because they have lost their money. The only episode that survives in full is the Dinner of Trimalchio, but what a dinner it was! The host, Trimalchio, is a big, bald, boastful freedman, larger than life in all ways, bursting with money and fat and mischief. Various moments of this dinner sound a Cynic note. Ascyltus sings a song in which he uses the word *pēra* (by now a "low" Latin word) and laments how in these corrupt times "money rules supreme and poverty can win no victories" and even former Cynics often "sell the truth for coins" (Petron. *Sat.* 14). When the two enter Trimalchio's house, they pass a painted dog that is so lifelike that it seems chained to the wall, and under it are the words *cave canem*, "beware of dog" (29).[7] Trimalchio also has a real guard dog, Scylax ("puppy" in Greek), which he says loves him more than anyone else in the household (64), and on his tombstone he plans to have a dog carved, among other things (72).

Perhaps the cleverest quasi-Cynic touch is the treatment of Trimalchio's relation to his wife. Her name is Fortunata, and he dotes on her as his "*Topanta*", his "everything". Herein may lie a brilliant spoof on prevailing beliefs about Fortune and *Tychē*, which Trimalchio encapsulates when he comments breathlessly about his wife's decisive manner: "Those whom she likes, she likes, and those whom she doesn't, she doesn't" (37). Such comments may play cleverly on typical characterizations of Fortune, according to which one plays for all or nothing: either Fortune loves one or she does not; one is either rich or poor, a king or a beggar, but rarely a middling trader, centurion or small farmer holding his own. So too Trimalchio was once a slave and is now a petty tyrant, king of his household and business empire. His beloved Fortunata was only a minute ago a woman "from whose hands you would not even take a crust of bread", but now she is … the wife of Trimalchio. One suspects a sly reversal of roles here: Trimalchio, raised by fortune from slavery, has raised Fortunata from the gutters. And yet, reversals abound, for who is really in charge? Has Trimalchio really tamed the lady, or is he only boasting idly? For his Fortunata has a sharp tongue and when she whispers in her darling's ear, he immediately goes quiet, as if his *Topanta* were the real master of the household.

In other ways, Trimalchio is the opposite of a Cynic philosopher. Fat, rich and obsessed with wealth, reputation, titles, novelties and other things of fortune, this Trimalchio plans to fill his epitaph with lists of his offices and monies, and end it all with the words, "He never listened to a philosopher" (72). And yet, in Petronius' wily satire, Trimalchio does play the "philosopher" as one of his party tricks. At one point in the dinner, he assumes the guise of an astrologist or "mathematician", loftily teaching his guests about the zodiac and explaining how he was born under the crab, for, like a crab, he "stands on many feet and has possessions in the sea and many lands" (39). Such good fortune is denied to others as the "circle of the world turns like a mill and always brings some evil, as people are born or perish" (39). Contemplating this great truth with momentary solemnity, Trimalchio strikes the pose of an imperturbable philosopher, or even a god, for he too "does nothing without a reason" in this universal banquet of his. The diners leap up crying out, in Greek, "Bravo! What wisdom!" (*sophōs*) (39–40), and such ironic touches would seem to make Trimalchio all that the Cynics hated in the degenerate, arrogant rich. Trimalchio arrived from Asia with nothing, not even his freedom, but was eventually liberated, made heir to his master, increased his fortune as a merchant and then as a (ruthless) moneylender. Whatever he touched grew "like a honey comb" (66) and he is now worth thirty million sesterces. He was a frog and is now a king; he lived in a hovel but now inhabits a "temple" (77), surrounded by slaves and clients who pamper him like a god. With all this wealth, Trimalchio boasts about his self-sufficiency. Like a god, he has everything he needs, and his party is an unending stream of surprises. To supply it all, his possessions stretch across Italy and beyond. All his slaves are born within the "household" (rather than being bought) and he even organizes them into "legions", as if he were a king commanding an empire of his own. Of course, Petronius exaggerates for effect, and Trimalchio redeems himself, like Shakespeare's Falstaff, by being so open, funny and full of life. But the guests begin to weary of his boastfulness and, suddenly, Ascyltus and Encolpius decide they must escape. The two Cynic-like wanderers flee the house of Trimalchio, the anti-Cynic.

The political, moral and religious ideal of self-sufficiency

Trimalchio's claim to have conquered fortune and to have made Fortunata a part of his self-sufficient household is one response to an important question: what to do in the face of the *uncontrollable*, whether this be unpredictable fortune or iron-clad fate? The question is similar to the previous question of how to live in relation to nature and, like it, elicited many responses in antiquity. One may deny that there is anything uncontrollable, strive to increase one's power and the extent of what one can control (cf. Plato's Callicles). At the other extreme, holding that everything is uncontrollable, one may let go, either in despair or in joyful abandon and trust, saying "what will be, will be". Between these extremes of will-to-power and detachment are at least two other responses. First is the personification of the uncontrollable as a divinity that can be propitiated and won over, if not fully controlled: the dominant response in the Hellenistic and imperial periods, as the cults of *Tychē* and Fortuna progressed rapidly across Greek and Roman lands. Quite different in tenor is the attempt to make oneself immune to the external, resolutely deciding to increase one's inner power. This is the Cynic option, to be as self-sufficient as possible and not to feel the need for anything beyond oneself. External events belong to *Tychē* and are uncontrollable, but the Cynic lets them go as unimportant. He concentrates on his present self, and affirms that nothing evil can happen to one now, if one truly lives according to nature. Before turning to some characteristic Cynic statements regarding self-sufficiency *vis-à-vis Tychē*, we must again look at the cultural and intellectual contexts that influenced these statements. The Greek word for self-sufficiency is *autarkeia*, literally being sufficient (*arkein*) to oneself (*autos*). It is one of the most important ideals in Greek philosophy, and has roots deep in the customary life of the archaic and classical cities. Self-sufficiency was first a political ideal, but it was momentous enough to be applied later to the individual life, to the divine and to the cosmos as a whole.

To begin with the political expression of the ideal, a city-state is self-sufficient if it has all that it needs. It has its own springs or rivers for water, its own land rich for grazing, grain, olives and vines, its own timber, metals and other resources. It has its own traditions, its own gods, holy places, festivals and rites, its own laws, magistrates and political bodies, its own coins, its own armies. If it looks abroad, it does so to export goods, merchants, settlers, travellers, soldiers, ideas. But it does not need to export anything, and still less does it need any imports. In this strict sense, it is clear that no Greek city of any period was fully self-sufficient. Classical Athens and many Aegean islands did not produce enough food and needed to import grain from the Black Sea area or Sicily. In the periods of colonization, cities sent forth settlers partly because they could not feed them all. The import of grain and the export of people show how many city-states were not economically self-sufficient. Furthermore, the need for leagues (e.g. Amphictyonic, Delian, Peloponnesian, Aetolian, Achaean leagues) as well as the increasing use of mercenaries after the Peloponnesian War testifies that even the most powerful cities were not self-sufficient militarily. It could even be argued that the regularly warring city-states needed each other for war: the excess energy of young men needed some outlet, and it was better released on a plain between two cities than in the streets of the individual cities themselves. Finally, in terms of ideas, no city was an island or isolated in itself. A *polis* might pride itself on the yearly festivals and lavish attention on its temples and shrines – as Athens, for instance, did on the spring Dionysia and on its Acropolis, sacred to Athena herself – but this religious inheritance was part of a larger pan-Hellenic network of overlapping customs and beliefs. Furthermore, the historically conscious observer realizes that each city was shaped by innumerable past influences, and was in continual change. Even the faces of the gods change, as do religious aspirations. As Plato's *Republic* begins, for instance, Socrates has gone down to the port in Piraeus to see the torch races and festivities to the goddess Bendis, newly imported from Thrace; later in the dialogue, Socrates exiles the old gods from his ideal city, and subjects religious language to the control of philosopher-kings, who know the divine Good.

Nevertheless, in a less exacting sense, many archaic and classical city-states were self-sufficient enough for *autarkeia* to be regarded as a practical ideal. There were generally two views on how the state could be self-sufficient. First, it might do so by becoming large, embracing a wide variety of terrains and soils, and a large population capable of doing many tasks. Wheat could be produced on the plains, for instance, grapes in the foothills. Each region could exchange its products for others it lacked – bread for wine – and so internal trade between the parts would enrich the whole, and no part would lack for anything. This ideal self-sufficiency seemed roughly to fit various empires: the Persian and Roman empires, the mythical empire of Atlantis in Plato's *Critias*, and even the Athenian "empire", which Thucydides' Pericles describes as "the most self-sufficient" (2.36.3). Here, Pericles may be implying that the "city" of Athens now includes all its subject cities and islands as parts of itself; Athens ships out silver, settlers, magistrates, soldiers and ships, and receives mainly tribute and grain in return. Nevertheless, all this counts only as the internal trade of a newly expanded "city". If so, then one might compare Pericles' statement with a similar trend in the Romans' conception of their city and empire: Rome was first a local city, then the capital of an empire, but gradually the term *Roma* became ambiguous, referring both to the original city and to the empire as a whole. The *urbs* had metamorphosed into the *orbs terrarum* (circle of lands) for Rome had made the *orbs* like a single city, as if everything were now "Rome". The Stoics go even further, speaking of the whole cosmos as a single "city" of gods and mortals (e.g. Cic. *Nat. D.* 2.154; Epict. *Diss.* 2.5.26; Euseb. *Praep. Ev.* 15.15). The individual therefore becomes self-sufficient only to the degree that he identifies himself with the whole: a paradoxical notion.

If some thought that the state (and individual) might become more self-sufficient by expanding to incorporate more of the world, others such as Plato, Aristotle and the Cynics disagreed fundamentally. In their view, the *polis* must simplify, contracting its needs and borders. "Much wants more": imperial states pursue power relentlessly, and the result is dissatisfaction, internal division and external war. The mania for more is dangerous, and should be controlled. Like the individual person, the state should focus on its real needs: simple food, shelter, the safety, health, education, and true well-being of its citizens. Such an arrangement is best procured if the state is small, remote and content with necessities, either humbly wealthy or modestly poor. Variations on this shared idea can be found in Plato, the Cynics, the Stoic Zeno, and even Aristotle. In the *Republic*, Plato's Socrates calls the "city of pigs" the "true city" (372e), and whether he is being facetious here or not, it is clear that later his ideal philosophical city, with its elite communism, will not be a mercantile oligarchy or commercial empire. It is not oriented to maximizing wealth, and it fights only defensive wars, as in the *Critias*, when a version of it battles successfully against Atlantis, which is self-sufficient in the first sense above. Similarly, in the *Laws*, Plato would locate his second-best city on Crete, inland, away from external wars and "entangling alliances". Aristotle too would make the state as self-sufficient as possible, but because this may not be practically possible, it may need a harbour to import necessities. But Aristotle would limit luxuries and the transit trade: the ideal city should not be a market for other peoples, for being a "middle-man" like this is a form of "unnatural" money-making that detracts from the good life. Furthermore, Aristotle's city itself would be located somewhat inland, at a safe distance from the port, in order to insulate itself from the contagions – the brawling sailor-types, avaricious merchants, the stew of superstitions and barbarisms – that tend to ferment in harbour areas (*Pol.* 1327a). The vision of the island-utopia is one that Crates revisited in his *Pēra*, that *polis* "in the middle of wine-dark *typhos*, beautiful, fertile, girdled in dirt, possessing nothing" (DL 6.85).

Utopias are not quite earthly places, and often have a religious tinge to them, as being somehow closer to the divine order. It is not surprising then that the ideal of self-sufficiency infiltrated religious ideas also. All the ancient philosophers agree that the divine must be self-sufficient, for we could not regard as superior a being that hungers, thirsts, feels pain or needs helpers, friends or anything beyond itself. Need implies weakness, and to be weak is miserable, but surely God is not miserable.

Nor can God be jealous, angry or sad, or have any human emotions, all of which signify some sort of lack and need, and again surely a needy God cannot be God? Indeed, all change, motion and becoming signify a need and lack: a lion moves across the plain to kill a deer because it is hungry; an Alexander moves across Asia to win glory, that is, others' applause, because he is not satisfied with himself. In contrast, God cannot be afflicted by movement and the restlessness of becoming. God does not change or become, but simply is. This vision of an eternal, timeless divinity takes on different variations from the Eleatics to Aristotle and the Hellenistic schools. For instance, Aristotle argues that God must be a perfect, self-thinking thinking (*Metaph.* 1074b). Thinking is the most self-sufficient activity known to man: one can sit quietly and think of many things, for nothing is faster than the mind, or more wide-ranging. One can therefore imagine a mind that could think of everything in an instant: "Somehow the soul is all things" (*De an.* 431b21). Therefore, for Aristotle, if God is self-sufficient, his activity must be self-sufficient thought. But if it is self-sufficient, it must not progress beyond itself: God will think about itself, and Aristotle's God becomes the activity of thinking as it thinks thinking, νοήσις νοήσεως. In Neoplatonic and Hegelian developments of this vision, the world in all its details evolves or emanates as a moment in this self-thinking of God or the One: all things become an aspect of the infinite, all-inclusive Mind. Such a God is truly self-sufficient, because in truth nothing exists external to it. Ostensibly, of course, the Cynics reject ideas like this as "smoke" (*typhos*) and seem generally to have been less interested in religious questions than other philosophers. On the other hand, they often invoke the ideal of a self-sufficient divinity. Antisthenes, Diogenes and others stated that it was peculiar to the gods to need nothing, and of the god-like to need little (DL 6.44, 6.104; D. Chr. 6.31; Luc. *Cyn.* 12). On this point, the Cynics are in essential agreement with other philosophers.[8]

This brings us to the ethical expression of the ideal: the individual should make himself like God or the perfect state, and strive for self-sufficiency. Thus, typical of Hellenistic philosophers is the claim not to need others, whether family, teachers, friends or fellow citizens. The philosopher is passionless, serene, content in himself, and fairly indifferent to externals. Detachment is the basic attitude shared by Epicureans, Stoics, Sceptics and Cynics. It has many corollaries. For example, with regard to education, often the best thing is to have taught oneself (as Epicurus claimed), or to be like Socrates (Xen. *Symp.* 2.2.3) or Dio Chrysostom a "peasant-farmer of philosophy" (D. Chr. 1.9): that is, one who does one's own thinking rather than taking ideas from others or from books.[9] Or, in another example of ethical self-sufficiency, philosophers often claim not to *need* others for companionship. If they have friends, it is because they have chosen to have them, not because they are too weak to live without them. Such discussions of friendship can become rather strained, as philosophers like Aristotle or Seneca sense the incompatibility of the ideals of self-sufficient solitude and of friendship, but cannot jettison either. The Cynics, by contrast, choose self-sufficiency. Even when surrounded by astonished, amused or angry onlookers, the Cynic is essentially a solitary figure, without friends, and wilfully so: Lucian's Diogenes advises the would-be Cynic to "find out the most crowded places, stand there alone and unaccompanied, welcoming neither friend nor stranger – for these would destroy your kingdom" (Luc. *Vit. auct.* 9.22).[10] So too the Cynic did not welcome marriage or citizenship, fearing that these ties would "destroy" his *autarkeia*.

Without friends, family, city, customs, formal learning and most of all without wealth or possessions that would tie them to the marketplace and a wide social net, the Cynics were the most resolutely self-sufficient. They pursued the ideal down to the smallest details, as when Diogenes throws away his cup. Ultimately, it was a false ideal, of course, for no individual can be self-sufficient, not even those as solitary as a Robinson Crusoe or as multi-talented as Hippias of Elis.[11] They need air to breathe, water to drink, plants and animals to eat, sunshine for warmth and life and so forth, in a circle of dependency that broadens to the utmost edges of the universe, if one were to trace every link. Monistic philosophies recognize this unity of being. Thinkers such as the Stoics, Hegel and Alfred North Whitehead stress that each entity is constituted and shaped by its internal relations to all other entities. For them, the notion of self-sufficiency, that any absolutes can exist in splendid isolation, is a lie. If so, ancient Cynicism was partly grounded on an impossible ideal. Indeed, they are often criticized for failing to live their ideal. They profess self-sufficiency, yet are still partly dependent on others for alms and protection. Some Cynics in their lucid moments also recognized this fact, as when Tatian notes that the Cynic needs the services of the weaver for his cloak, and the leather-worker for his *pēra* (*Ad Gr.* 25).

Nevertheless, one could argue that at least the Cynic lie was a noble one, and that the ideal of self-sufficiency, although impossible, was yet a necessary one for the ancients. For its proponents encouraged others to be self-reliant, and not to wait in vain for external help. One should not rely passively on the assistance of friends, neighbours, a generous benefactor, the government, kings, lucky Fortune or the gods. There are no saviours, and one can only save oneself. But can one save oneself? Here the Cynics are resolutely optimistic in their conviction that each individual can, unaided, endure the worst tragedies, and even laugh his way through them. This ideal of an invincible cheerfulness before fortune and of a secular self-sufficiency may, again, be fundamentally a lie. Yet, again, it may have been a beneficial one, especially when broadcast among fatalists whose courage too easily drops, who quickly lose heart and say despondently: "All is fated. We are puppets of relentless forces. We can do nothing". The pull towards fatalism was all too strong in the ancient world but by obstinately preaching an impossible self-sufficiency, the Cynics helped to reaffirm faith at least in humanity's own native powers. It is an affirmation that has made Cynicism of especial interest to modern thinkers such as Nietzsche (Chapter 6).

Conceptions of the self

If self-sufficiency is an ideal, and thought to be a possible ideal, then one may ask a series of basic questions. What is the self? What is it to be an individual self? Who am I? Such questions often occur in times of crisis. But to continue to ask them takes courage. Sometimes self-examination leads straight to self-contempt and even a cynical despair. "But to think is to be full of sorrow / and leaden-eyed despairs", writes Keats (2007). Man is the "dream of a shadow", "straw", "dust and shadow", the "quintessence of dust",[12] and thus we often flee self-knowledge, because "in much wisdom is much grief, and he that increaseth knowledge increaseth sorrow", as the Preacher says (Ecclesiastes 1:18). If so, then perhaps the best thing is not to know, and not to try to know oneself. Better to forget these questions, and live as merrily as one can in blissful oblivion.

Such a hedonistic self-forgetfulness can be one response to an emerging self-awareness. Work can be another. By work one tries to extend one's power over the external environment and tries to reshape the external world as an image of one's own desire and will. Strength of will and the desire to leave one's stamp on the world has perhaps never been so manifested as in Alexander. Ancient writers on kingship often make him *philodoxotatos*, the greatest lover of glory, as if Alexander wanted to be honoured by all his contemporaries, Greek and barbarian, by the dead, by the yet unborn, and even by unspeaking animals (D. Chr. 4.4). Yet the Cynics reject this response to human fortunes also, and we have seen already how the Gymnosophists said to Alexander that he would never possess anything more than the land under his feet, except, that is, when he was dead, when he would occupy a little more (Arr. *Anab.* 7.1.5–6).[13] It is a sobering thought, but one that cannot be explained, or worked away. No matter how hard one works, what external thing can one *really* possess? A figure such as Alexander is most ignorant of himself, precisely because he tends to identify his self with external possessions, which are in fact farthest from the self.

The Cynics draw a sharp dichotomy between the self and externals governed by *Tychē*: what I am truly is wholly divorced from outside things and events. Yet one might question where exactly the boundary lies. In fact, the notion of self is expandable, and the boundary between "me" and "not me" is porous and variable. Is my property part of myself? But I can sell or "alienate" my possessions without losing myself. Are my friends, family and loved ones part of myself? Horace calls Virgil *dimidium meae* (half of myself) (*Carm.* 1.3.6); Alexander calls Hephaistion "another Alexander";

and in the ancient proverb, a friend is "another self", an *alter ego*. But one can leave all one's loved ones. Is my body *me*? But I can cut my hair and trim my nails. Can I do the same to fingers, arms or legs? Can I not cut off all these if I choose? People have sometimes done so voluntarily; indeed, some people have taken their own lives willingly. Of all animals, only human beings commit suicide: a revealing fact. But if one strips away everything external, from land and money to clothes and life itself, then what is left? The true self is the inner person that cannot ever be considered as an external object. Philosophers of various traditions have called this by many names – soul, mind, the Stoic "ruling principle" (*hēgemonikon*),[14] Cartesian *cogito*, transcendental apperception (Kant), or infinitely self-reflexive subjectivity (Hegel) – but the underlying ideas have a family resemblance. The true self is the thinking subject: all else is a contingent object of thought. Thus, the Cynics' dichotomy between self and fortune looks forward to the Stoic contrast of the controllable and non-controllable, and perhaps even further, to the post-Cartesian dichotomy between subject and object, experiencing ego and experienced phenomena.

Somewhat reminiscent of Cartesian dualism also is the Cynic suggestion that the true self is not in any way shaped or determined by external phenomena. On the contrary, their overriding conception is that the self is a *substantial* thing, impenetrable and solid. A substance is that which endures through change. A tree, for instance, can be seen as a substance: it may be green in summer, bare in winter, small as an acorn, gnarled and huge as an oak, yet through all this change, it is still somehow the same entity that directs its own growth and adapts its environment to its needs. From such examples, Aristotle tends to conclude that individual things are "primary substances": a tree, a horse, a dog are substances, while all else that a thing experiences or becomes, such as "green" or "big" or "standing", are attributes and "accidents" of substances. Greenness, for example, can exist only as an attribute of green things. A similar line of thought can apply to the human self. I may be sad or happy; I may laugh, or cry; I may be young or old, poor or rich: yet through it all, I am myself, the same person regardless of my accidental qualities. Similarly, the mind may wander through many thoughts, and yet beneath this stream of consciousness remains itself; to access it is, according to the Platonic tradition, for instance, to access one's true self.

The notions of the self as substantial and as self-sufficient are clearly related, and in the typical Cynic outlook, the political, ethical and even religious senses of self-sufficiency are blended with the conviction that the true self is utterly independent of externality and its random occurrences. Life throws one into a medley of surprises and accidents: no one can know or control what will happen. But according to the Cynic, one should bitterly resist the power of *Tychē*, assert one's native freedom and self-sufficiency, and refuse to be conquered by her. Such a dichotomy between fortune's crazy mutability and a secure inner virtue would become a commonplace of Hellenistic and Roman literature. But the Cynics insisted on it most uncompromisingly, and found some vivid images for their own attitude of "invincible" defiance. The Cynic self is a warrior, battling against fortune with weapons of virtue, syllogisms and reason. The self is a fortress, impregnable and stout; or an island, rising high above fortune's waves; or even a rock, the immovable foundation of truth. Homer often uses this image for heroes like Ajax, upon whose mighty strength the waves of the enemy break like so much water. Similarly Marcus Aurelius exhorts himself to "be like a headland of rock on which the waves break incessantly". Because of their unchanging demeanour, the Stoics were sometimes referred to as "men of stone". Finally, later Cynics and Cynicizing Stoics commonly speak of "the god within" who remains the same through life's changes. The true self is as unflinching before fortune as a warrior, a cliff-face or god.[15]

Very different in tone, yet stemming from the same basic idea, is the comparison of the self to an actor. This metaphor is first attributed to Bion but becomes very prevalent, and is used by Lucian, Seneca (*Epistle* 77), Marcus Aurelius (*Med.* 3.8, 12.36) and others.[16] Actors tended not to be revered as artists but were distrusted as bohemian types, particularly by thinkers such as Plato, who thought that playing many roles made an actor deceitful and flighty, incapable of playing one part well in life itself. The arguments that Socrates presents in Plato's *Republic* stem from the notion that the true self is a single, substantial thing, which can only be corrupted by frivolous plurality. But the same underlying idea is taken by some later Cynics in the opposite direction. For if the self is substantial and secure in itself, then, like a good actor, it can put on and off many masks, playing many roles without dissipating or compromising itself, just as a good actor can appear in many guises while remaining the same person beneath. Thus, for Lucian, Peregrinus was rightly nicknamed Proteus because he was as adaptable and many-masked as the Old Man of the Sea. He took on many shapes and professed not to be changed by any. Lucian scoffs, but Peregrinus' own intention in his last "role" as a latter-day Heracles may have been to demonstrate that external flames and a melting body cannot harm "the god within".

Peregrinus may have acted in a tragedy of sorts, but others, such as Lucian, regarded life as a comedy in which one might as well enjoy oneself. Thus, his Menippus sums up the argument in a passage worth quoting at length:

> So as I contemplated these things, it seemed to me that human life resembles a great procession where *Tychē* choreographed and arranged each detail, giving different and varied roles to the performers. She would take one and get him up as a king, for example, putting on a tiara, granting him bodyguards and crowning his head with a diadem. But on another she would put the appearance of a slave. One person she makes beautiful, another ugly and contemptible – for the spectacle, I think, must have variety of all sorts. Often even during the procession itself she switched the roles of some, not letting them finish the procession as they had started. She forced Croesus to take up the gear of a slave and war-captive; Maeandrius (who till then marched as a slave) she re-clothed in the tyranny of Polycrates. And when the procession was over, each gave back his costume, took off his persona with his body and became just like he was before, no different from his neighbour. Then some, whenever *Tychē* demands the costumes back, in their igno-

rance grow angry as if they were being deprived of their own things and were not returning what they had borrowed for a short time. I imagine that you have often seen tragic actors changing due to the requirements of the play, now being Creons, now becoming Priams or Agamemnons; and the same man, for instance, just a moment ago played the figure of Cecrops or Erechtheus very grandly but a little later comes back out as a slave, when so ordered by the poet. When the drama ends, each takes off that gold-laced clothing, removes the mask, descends from the high tragic boots, and goes forth, a poor humble individual – no longer Agamemnon son of Atreus or Creon son of Menoeceus, but Polus son of Charicles from Sounion or Satyrus son of Theogeiton from Marathon. Such is the condition of human beings, as it seemed to me then. (Luc. *Nec.* 16)

In Lucian's description of life as a tragicomedy, it is unclear whether the *Tychē* who distributes the clothes and takes them back is random Chance or relentless Fate. From the human perspective, this metaphysical question may not matter and certainly the Cynics were not bothered by abstract speculations about determinism and indeterminism. For them all such cogitation is *typhos*. One cannot answer these questions, and does not need to. For if one is content and self-sufficient now, all will be well. Therefore the Cynics can laugh at other philosophers for the quarrelsome part they play in the grand comedy. Cynic laughter is most pronounced in Lucian's dialogues, but it is evident too in Dio Chrysostom's Cynic speeches, in Oenomaus, in Timon's quasi-Cynic *Silloi*, and elsewhere. The Cynic's good humour before uncontrollable fortune, his cheerful poverty and jaunty self-sufficiency all resonate in a comic line that one writer offers as a type of Cynic blessing and farewell: "may the lentil be your guardian-daemon, and may a lentil-fate take you" (Ath. 4.45)![17]

FIVE

Anarchists, democrats, cosmopolitans, kings

Renouncing custom, living wild among their urban peers, and boasting that they were wholly self-sufficient amid the ups and downs of life, the Cynics could often be a strong and disturbing presence in their societies. How should one assess this presence, and how should one understand them in relation to the political communities of which they were a part? There are several interconnected questions here. To what extent were the Cynics interested in politics? Were any of them political actors who joined in contemporary debates and struggles? Were any of them political theorists, and can various stray comments about the Athenian people, Hellenistic kings, Roman consuls, the city, law and the like add up to a recognizable political philosophy? More generally, what kind of political rhetoric did they favour? What political implications could the Cynic way of life have for their contemporaries? Once more, the issues involved are complex and can be approached from a variety of perspectives. As a result, there have been at least four main ways of judging the Cynics as political animals: they are at once anarchists, democrats, "kings" and cosmopolitans. We shall examine each in turn.

Anarchists

The most convenient label for the Cynics is that they were anarchists. The word "anarchy" is itself a Greek one: anarchy is a state without hierarchy or government. But the idea is really a modern one. The modern anarchist's creed is that all forms of coercive power are evil; individuals should make their own decisions freely, and hence all instruments of social control should be encouraged to wither away. When government by force has dissolved, then individuals will be free to regroup into purely voluntary associations, from friendships and contractual arrangements between individuals to larger cooperatives and syndicates. Anarchism thrived especially in the nineteenth and early twentieth centuries, and at one point seemed even to compete with Marxism for the leadership of the Left. The great theorist of modern anarchism Peter Kropotkin was originally a Russian aristocrat and accomplished biologist, but he turned to anarchism partly in moral revulsion against social inequality, partly in the scientific belief that species progress more by cooperation than competition. In his *Encyclopaedia Britannica* article on anarchism, Kropotkin (1910, 2005) makes the significant claim that the early Zeno – a Cynic student of Crates – was among the first precursors of modern anarchism.

Is it true that the Cynics were anarchists? Kropotkin's suggestion is an insightful one in many respects. As we have seen, the Cynics tended to define themselves in opposition to established authority of all sorts. "Defacing the coinage", they renounced the authority of officialdom and of social tradition: not marrying; not claiming citizenship in their native or adopted cities; not holding political office; not voting in the assembly and courts; not exercising in the gymnasia or marching with the city militia; and not respecting political leaders, whether Athenian orators, Hellenistic kings, or Roman emperors and proconsuls. Figures such as Oenomaus ridiculed the authority of Delphi and other oracles; self-sufficient Cynics rejected the gods' jurisdiction over them altogether. To be free is to have no master, whether that master be a god, political assembly, magistrate, general or spouse. A Cynic may claim to be a "citizen of Diogenes" or a "citizen of the cosmos", but really he was only a citizen of himself, following his own laws, wandering about as free as a dog. The Cynic might have friends or even (in Crates' case) marry, but these associations were freely made and not socially coerced (e.g. DL 6.72). At a larger level, the *Republic* attributed to Diogenes could well be understood as prescribing an anarchist society. The precise content of the book (and its relation to the subsequent *Republics* of Zeno and Chrysippus) is not fully clear, but the consensus is mainly to follow the testimony of Diogenes Laertius: Diogenes' "utopia" outlawed temples, law courts, gymnasia, weapons, money (perhaps to be replaced by knucklebones), difference in dress between men and women, and perhaps clothes altogether. In place of law and state-sponsored violence, perfect friendship and "free love" will reign, perhaps even to the point of incest and public sex with strangers. Surely only true "dog-philosophers" are capable or deserving of such anarchical happiness, and so Diogenes' republic may have been a "community of the wise", in which only Cynics were citizens. If so, then similar themes were closely revisited by both Zeno, who was said to have written his *Republic* "on the dog's tail" (i.e. under Cynic influence), and by Chrysippus.[1] They were later savaged by Philodemus of Gadara, an Epicurean whose polemical *On the Stoics* portrays the Cynicizing Stoics in the sort of lurid terms that Lucian and Julian used to denigrate Cynics of their times. But Diogenes' own views (one may surmise) may have been more positive: among the virtuous, law and its violence will wither away, so that in a philosophical community there will be no need for courts (all are just and commit no crimes), money (all live in the moment, sharing nature's wealth), gymnasia (all are temperate, fit and healthy already) or temple sacrifices (all are pious and god-like in their own selves).

Furthermore, what is known about the *Republics* of Diogenes and Zeno might be evaluated in a variety of ways. Malcolm Schofield suggests three possibilities: Zeno was a purely antinomian critic of the *status quo*, a visionary of a "community of sages" or a communist. Schofield himself regards Zeno's republic in communist terms, as a city united by "love". But the three possibilities overlap, and the essential ideas of each may be comprehended better under the rubric of "anarchism", at least in the case of Diogenes' republic, given his rejection elsewhere of all coercive *nomoi*. On the other hand, a scholar such as Doyne Dawson may be right to lay more emphasis on poems such as Crates' *Pēra*: the Cynics were not serious political thinkers and before all abstract utopias "preferred the more practical ideal of the city of the wallet" (1992: 150), a sort of "anti-*polis*" that could exist anywhere. Yet if so, one finds anarchists here too. Crates' *Pēra* sings of an anarchist freedom: don't pack – just wander through the door, and see where the road takes you!

Furthermore, like their modern cousins, the Cynic anarchists could engage in "acts of resistance". If the modern anarchist was often demonized as "bomb-toting" and intent on using violence to overthrow inherently violent hierarchies, so too the ancient Cynic could be stereotyped as a wild man who stood on the corner piercing passers-by with his glances, passing remarks to all and sundry, but reserving his bitterest scorn for the elites who parade by in purple and chariots, living unnatural lives, and trampling on the natural equality of man. Thus in Cynic lore, Diogenes attacks Midas and other rich tyrants. In historical fact, Peregrinus, Theagenes, Demonax and others criticized Herodes Atticus, Demetrius vilified successive emperors and other Cynics publicly lashed into Nero, Vespasian, Titus, Antoninus Pius and others, and were repeatedly banished from Rome and Italy as subversives. As we have seen, Alexandria had many Cynics who may well have helped agitate Alexandria's unruly mob to its frequent rioting. Similarly, in a surprising turn of events at a time when the Roman Peace seemed so secure, did Peregrinus help inspire an armed uprising in Achaea? The Cynic "war" against authority is carried on in literature too: Cynics ("literary" or otherwise, we do not know) write *Epistle* after *Cynic Epistle* to kings, tyrants, generals and other powerbrokers, urging them to give up power; Lucian's Cynics are violently harsh towards the rich and the office-holders.[2] But if, before this onslaught, the Athenian democracy were in reality overthrown, the Seleucids toppled from their elephants, or the Roman emperors stripped of their legions and *fasces*, what then? The Cynics' attitude generally seems to have been that with governments dissolved, people would return to nature's "law" of frugality and easygoing humour. Lying in the sun without a care for politics, law suits and wars: this is the *Pēra* of Crates. In this regard, Cynicism, like modern anarchism, has an irrepressible faith in basic human goodness and rejects the cynicism of those for whom such an optimism is hopelessly naive.

Democrats

Anarchism and democracy are closely related in their stress on natural freedom and equality. Democrats, however, tend not to share the anarchist's optimistic belief in the goodness of *all* people. For the typical democrat, the common people are temperate, honest and generous; but there are also many others who are greedy, unfair and factious. In ancient democracies like classical Athens, these undesirable types were suspected of congregating more numerously among the rich and powerful. Democracy was rule by the *dēmos*, that is rule by the poor (as Aristotle insists),[3] and as a result, it was often felt that the rich were not naturally supporters of the democracy, but would be quite willing to call in Spartan or Macedonian warlords to help them "undo the *dēmos*" and institute an exclusive government more sensitive to their interests. Therefore, Athenian democrats of the classical period were often paranoid about aristocratic, oligarchic and tyrannical plots. Any expression of superiority – wearing purple, growing one's hair long, driving a chariot, holding *symposia* in a certain style, consuming fish and other luxuries – might be eyed as a sign of impending treason. Ever wary of the plots of the "few", therefore, the democratic "many" instituted a variety of institutional defences. Many magistrates were appointed by lot and not by elections, which were regarded as less democratic because they could be rigged and because they inherently favoured the rich and well-known. Offices were multiplied. Magistrates had to share power with colleagues. Offices lasted only a year, and during that year, each magistrate had to render an account of his activities to the sovereign People, in the assembly and law courts. Legislation was sometimes passed against marrying foreigners, holding lavish private funerals and other practices that bolstered the power of aristocratic families. And as a last resort there was ostracism: if it sensed danger in any figure, the People could vote to exile him for ten years. All of this served to break up any incipient power clusters, to weaken strong men and great families, and keep sovereignty in the hands of the People as they gathered in their assembly and courts.

All of this is relevant to Cynicism, for the Cynics first appeared in the more democratic environment of classical Greece. Major cities of the first Cynics – Sinope, Athens, Syracuse and even Thebes – had democratic traditions of varying strengths. Moreover, the Greek social environment could be strongly egalitarian. Power was distributed through different cities and authorities, and the cosmopolitan Cynics' own non-attachment to place made them less deferential to local elites. Cities themselves were small and this tended to limit the inequality that could exist between rich and poor. There were inequalities, of course, but when these became serious, faction-fighting and civil war often broke out, especially through the fourth century. This may testify to the fact that Greek democrats were ready to fight for their belief in universal freedom and equality, the two ideas that, as Plato and others write, were the watch-words of democracy. A democracy such as the Athenians' institutionalized them by giving each citizen the rights of *isēgoria* and *parrhēsia* in the assembly. Here each citizen could speak freely, ideally without flattering the rich or influential, or fearing the censure of others: namely, he should speak his mind and give the city the benefit of whatever insights he might have.

Many of these features of a democracy such as Athens' seem to resurface in Cynicism. First, democratic *parrhēsia* becomes the hallmark of the Cynic.[4] He will speak his mind, and will not flatter, sweet-talk or bamboozle. The simple truth is his only theme. Whether his audience wants to hear it or not hardly matters. Let them be shocked by his shamelessness, for what they call shamelessness is in fact the truth and can only do them good. The Cynic *parrhēsiast* therefore prides himself on telling the truth when all others are awed to silence by the authorities or public opinion. This attitude becomes a commonplace among Second Sophistic orators such as Dio Chrysostom, but some of the impetus comes originally from the classical democracies, often *via* Cynicism. In addition, there may be democratic precedents for the Cynics being called "dogs", a name linked to the practice of a rude, barking *parrhēsia*. Democratic leaders sometimes called themselves the "watch-dogs of the people" (Ar. *Eq.* 1017–34, *Vesp.* 894ff [Cleon]; Dem. 25.40 [Aristogeiton]), and Cleon is often pictured snapping at the *dēmos* for their laziness, complacency, stupidity, and other vices (Thuc. 3.37–8).[5] One of the functions of these "watch-dogs" may have been to guard against plots by the subversive rich, and so protect the people while they slept, as it were, in the activities of their private lives. Such protection of the people from domestic injustice is one of the functions of Plato's "guardians", whom he also styles "watch-dogs". It is therefore possible that the Cynics have fastened on to this political metaphor: they too were "watch-dogs" who barked at vice and kept a sharp eye especially on the rich.

Like Cleon, the "dog-philosophers" did not spare the *dēmos* either. But as poor themselves, they might have been regarded as fundamentally friends of the poor, given that they admired the common virtues of frugality (*euteleia*) and "work" (*ponos*), and lived among the people in the streets and marketplaces. And although they do not describe themselves as belonging to any particular city or *dēmos*, their antinomian attitude has an air of democratic egalitarianism. The Cynic as natural democrat is hinted at in many anecdotes. In one, Diogenes admires Harmodius and Aristogeiton: the tyrant-killers, champions of liberty, and heroes of all free Athenians (DL 6.50). Another story has it that when some naughty boy broke Diogenes' *pithos*, the Athenians voted him a second one and had the boy whipped (6.43). If true, the anecdote has powerful democratic resonances: by punishing the boy themselves rather than handing him over to Diogenes for punishment, the Athenians would have been treating the crime essentially as a public one, a crime against the *dēmos* itself, and by magnanimously granting Diogenes another "tub", the Athenians would seem to have been honouring him as a public benefactor. Nor, in fact, did such honours go only to the rich for providing the city with a trireme or cheap grain: the Athenians voted a pension to the descendants of Harmodius and Aristogeiton, for example, when they learned that they were living in poverty. In another anecdote, the Athenians asked Diogenes to be initiated into the Mysteries, at the time a privilege of citizens only (6.39). As for other figures, Crates' nicknames ("good *daimōn*" and "door-opener") suggest a measure of popularity (Jul. *Or.* 6.199c–200b). Many centuries later, Lucian's Demonax seems to have been the most popular person in Athens, which still retained its local democratic traditions, even though ultimate power lay with the Roman proconsul; and Lucian makes Menippus and Micyllus the cobbler best friends. Such evidence is important to remember, as an antidote to the stereotype of the Cynic as the angry, self-righteous lout. If they had been indiscriminately hostile to all their neighbours, they would have been hated in turn and the ordinary people among whom they lived would hardly have tolerated them. But as enemies of wealth, pedigree and snobbishness, they may have been welcomed as champions of equality in the cities of the Hellenistic and Roman periods, when true democracy had become a distant memory.

The democratic populism of some Cynics may be reflected in other ways also. First, as satirists and comedians who make every situation humorous, the Cynics have been compared to the "comic heroes" of Old Comedy.[6] The comic hero is a champion of the ordinary man against all sorts of establishment types, whether politicians, generals or intellectuals. He is a rebel against the status quo, sparking off a period of festive misrule and a return to elemental simplicities by which all pretensions are deflated. In Aristophanes' *Clouds* Strepsiades farts in the sophists' lecture halls, and in *Wasps* Philocleon grabs the flute girls during the aristocrats' stuffy symposium. Analogous here is the celebrated anecdote of Diogenes rushing into Plato's Academy with a plucked chicken crying, "Here is Plato's man" (i.e. a "featherless biped"). So the Cynic champions the virtues and rough sense of the natural man, who has little time for Ideas and essential definitions. Of course, the Cynic goes far beyond common sense when he affirms that his poverty is "wealth" and homelessness "kingship". But like the comic hero with his "great idea", the Cynic overthrows humdrum reality with his paradoxical rhetoric, and goes on to entertain his hearers with a feast of clever and sometimes fantastical ideas.

For Epictetus, the true Cynic is not a dour moralizer but an irrepressible wit; Lucian hoped for more wits among contemporary Cynics, and may have seen himself as continuing Diogenes' tradition of comic wisdom; Nietzsche certainly did, with his own anti-Platonic, *fröhliche Wissenschaft*. In keeping with this, it is a possible that the Athenians actually liked Diogenes for his irreverent and paradoxical humour. When Diogenes claimed to be the only "king", although poor, he may have slyly flattered the Athenian *dēmos*, which on other occasions delighted in being likened to monarchs and kings.[7] If so, then Diogenes' quasi-democratic rhetoric might partly explain honours such as the new *pithos*. Furthermore, he had to have been at least somewhat popular if he was to attract followers from all over, and to be remembered, imitated, even revered long after his death. In a different way, the Cynic virtue of *philanthrōpia* is a quasi-democratic one: the Cynic loves all the people, old and young, rich and poor; he "punishes" only those who would hubristically set themselves up as superior to others (see esp. Luc. *Demon.*; Epict. *Diss* 3.24.64). One might speculate that a Diogenes or Crates might (like Socrates) have presented their philosophical *philanthrōpia* as a kind of "service to the people", a *leitourgia* that is more valuable than the provision of a warship or tragic chorus.[8]

Thus central Cynic practices such as *parrhēsia*, *euteleia*, satire (especially of rich elites), fantastical humour and public antics had a populist flavour and sometimes even definite precedents in democratic institutions such as *isēgoria*, the comic festivals and system of "liturgies". Sometimes, however, it is a matter of emphasis. Cynic *parrhēsia* can be seen alternately as democratic, anarchistic or even regal: only a true king has the power to speak without flattery. So too, the theme of *philanthrōpia* and universal human brotherhood is well loved of optimistic anarchists. In Cynic literature, however, it has a more monarchical tinge, as the philanthropic Cynic prides himself on working selflessly for the people, in the manner of a true "king".

Kings

In fact, the Cynics themselves did not speak of themselves as anarchists or democrats. Diogenes may have written a book entitled *The People of Athens* (DL 6.80) but one imagines that it berated the *dēmos* for its greed, hypocrisy and other vices, perhaps in the style of Dio's speeches to the people of Alexandria and Tarsus. By contrast, many books testify to the Cynics' lasting fascination with kings. To Antisthenes are attributed books entitled *On Law, Cyrus or On Kingship, Cyrus or the Beloved, Cyrus or Scouts*, as well as a *Menexenus or On Ruling*, and an *Archelaus or On Kingship* (6.16, 6.18).[9] Onesicritus wrote about Alexander (6.84). Cynic anecdotes and the *Cynic Epistles* pay many indirect compliments to royalty simply by focusing so much attention on them. Similarly, one of the most typical Cynic conceits was to claim to be the true "king"': Alexander, stand out of my sun! At first sight, this statement would seem ridiculous. How can a half-naked wanderer claim to be the only true king?

The claim does not arise simply from Cynic conceit, however: in making it, the Cynics draw on the long-accepted notion that the king is "the best", superior to others, and therefore qualified to lead. This presupposition is fundamental to Greek political theory and as old as the Homeric poems. For to the basic political question "Who should have power?", Homer's answer would seem to be fairly clear: in the *Iliad*, the kings are the "best of the Achaeans", the strongest and fastest in battle, most eloquent in debate, most far-seeing in counsel, most commanding and "kingly" to their people. Before these mighty figures, the common soldiers are a nameless rabble and if a lowly Thersites dares protest, he is instantly shouted down by all. It seemed an infallible assumption that the "best" should lead, and the "worse" obey. But who are the best? Individuals have different talents, few have them all, and not everyone agrees on which talent is most important. Two general headings seem to become most important, however: Achilles' valour and Odysseus' intelligence. The best king has both: as a "maker of speeches and doer of deeds" (Hom. *Il.* 9.443), he fights in the front ranks where the fighting is thickest, and gives unerring counsel among his peers.

This focus on individual excellence or virtue (*aretē*) made Greek political theory often quite personal in its approach.[10] For the question "Who should rule?" encourages one to concentrate on individual rulers or groups of rulers, rather than on institutions or bureaucratic systems that function regardless of who staffs them. So too, the Homeric king rules mainly owing to personal merit, not because he represents the gods' will and maintains the cosmic balance in his person; nor because he represents the people's will and serves their needs; nor again because his father ruled before him. Those other considerations can, of course, play a role: Agamemnon cannot wholly disregard the will of the army, and he himself rules by hereditary right symbolized by the sceptre of Hephaestus. Or, the religious aura of kingship is evident in the Oedipus myth: Oedipus' crime throws nature out of joint, making fields barren and women sterile, and therefore, by order of Apollo, the king must die, or at least be banished. Such "primitive" notions survived submerged in certain classical institutions: the Athenian king-archon, for instance, presided over sacrilegious homicides and other crimes against the gods. Yet these do not represent the dominant Greek approach to government. The good king is not the gods' puppet, people's representative or hereditary office-holder. Rather, he rules by native right, on the strength of his superior personal virtue.

Such an orientation may partly explain the Greeks' perennial fascination with the kings of heroic myth. It is remarkable that despite being so egalitarian, quarrelsome and envious of superiority, despite being the inventors of democracy, despite the generations of warfare with the Persian monarchs, and the sad experiences under fourth-century tyrants: despite all this, the Greeks never developed a visceral aversion to kings *per se* or even to the principle of one-man rule. Certainly the city-states resisted Philip and even Alexander, hating to become "slaves" of another. But despite this indomitable love of freedom, there was always a romance about kings. The Homeric poems ever cast their spell. The Athenian tragedians returned again and again to the legends of the Houses of Atreus and Oedipus. Kingship and tyranny marked the pinnacle of worldly success and, as we have seen, even the Athenian people enjoyed being called "king".

One can only contrast these rich ambiguities with the blunt univocity of the Romans for whom even the word *rex* was hateful. Even their emperors never called themselves "kings" (although the Greeks did refer to them as *basileis*) and, until Diocletian, continued to veil their power under Augustus' cunning subterfuge, titling themselves *imperatores* and *principes*, as if they were merely "the first among equals". Domitian demanded to be called *Dominus et deus* – god and master (i.e. of slaves) – but he did not ask for the title of king, perhaps remembering Caesar's fate (Suet. *Dom.* 4, 13).

The Greeks' more varied attitudes allowed for the meteoric rise of a philosophical monarchism in the fourth-century BCE. At the time, monarchy was an anomaly in the Greek world: kings from the glorious Homeric past might be admired, but there they should belong, and in the present, only barbarians, Macedonians, Spartans and other uncouth peoples had kings. It was as if kings were somehow unGreek and contrary to Greek political ideals. In the hallowed phrase, a citizen should "rule and be ruled in turn", but to live under a king was simply to be ruled: one became a subject, not a citizen, or, even worse, a "slave" and not free. Yet for all this, in philosophic circles one sees the steady rise in theories of monarchy, which revisit Homeric themes about kings' pre-eminent virtues. Notably Socrates, as he philosophized among the cobblers and tailors of Athens, seems to have theorized his way to the notion of an "art" or "craft of politics", a political *technē*, by whose rational procedures the political craftsman would be able to shape cities with as much expertise as a cobbler shapes leather into shoes (see Xen. *Mem.* 2.1.17, 4.2.11; Pl. *Euthd.* 291c–d, *Plt.* 311c, *Resp.*). A "craftsman" with such expertise would clearly be the best at politics and therefore entitled to most power. Indeed, the true political craftsman would deserve all power. Socrates may well have described his political expert as the true "king", and the political *technē* as a "regal" one. If so, his craft analogies are the immediate precedent to fourth-century theories of philosopher-kings.

Plato, Isocrates, Xenophon, Antisthenes and Aristotle are some of the many fourth-century theorists of kingship, and through the Hellenistic period "On Kingship" would be a common title.[11]

For Alexander's legacy ensured that political philosophy would be largely in thrall to kings. Kings bestrode their dominions like gods, commanding resources and mustering armies on a scale unprecedented for the Greeks. They still paid attention to cities, of course, and cities remained important, but power no longer radiated solely from the old assemblies where citizens "ruled and were ruled in turn". The symbiosis between Hellenistic kings and cities, both old and newly founded, is perhaps reflected in the somewhat ambiguous new political thought that emerges from the philosophical schools. These Hellenistic theories of kingship develop ideas of the fourth-century Socratics, and reworked aspects of the Homeric poems to depict the ideal kings as "living law", "benefactors", "saviours" and "liberators" who, in their virtuous strength, guarantee justice, prosperity and freedom for their subjects. Indeed, the good king becomes representative of the gods, the true and highest ruler of the world. Some Hellenistic kings were spoken of even as gods themselves, such as Demetrius or Antiochus IV, "the visible god", or Ptolemy XII, "the new Dionysus": such ruler cults were adapted by the Roman emperors after them.[12] Philosophical writers in their own way also "divinized" kings by trying to educate them into enlightened philosopher-kings. The ideal recalls Plato but it is equally Cynic and Stoic. Onesicritus, for instance, tried to see Alexander as a "philosopher in arms" (Strabo 15.1.64) and Marcus Aurelius did indeed combine both lives uneasily.

At the same time, however, there was a tendency to exalt the old city-state. Now as kingdoms were expanding, and interconnectedness between regions deepening, the cosmos as a whole often came to be termed a single "city" that comprised both gods and mortals, living and dead. The Roman Empire, which seemed to incorporate most or the best of the inhabited world, could be equated with this world-city: *Roma*, once a city-state on the Tiber but now an empire straddling the Mediterranean, was at once cosmic *urbs* and all-embracing *orbs terrarum*. Rome the city had become an empire "without limit" (*sine fine*) and, as it were, made the whole cosmos Rome. This idea was very widespread and was eventually taken up in Christian literature: pagan Rome for Augustine becomes the City of Man, while as seat of the Church it is *Roma aeterna*, the visible symbol of the *civitas Dei*.

The Cynics too had their part to play in the wide diffusion of ideas like this in the Hellenistic and Roman periods, for in a striking series of formulations, they claimed to be at once "kings", "citizens of themselves", and "citizens of the cosmos". Before turning to their peculiar cosmopolitanism, we focus here briefly on one group of speeches drawing on partially Cynic notions of the ideal king. The first four Orations of Dio Chrysostom masterfully synthesize ideas of Homer, Plato, Aristotle, the Stoics and the Cynics. Most explicitly Cynic are Orations 1 and 4, but all four draw on the common idea that the "true king" is the best and most virtuous. Oration 1 ends with a Dio retelling Prodicus' story of the "Choice of Heracles", with its Cynic contrast of virtue and pleasure, and its idealization of Heracles, *the* Cynic hero. Dio provides a Cynic frame for this retelling, for he said that he heard the future prophesied by an old peasant woman in Elis or Arcadia, "once when I chanced to be wandering in exile" (D. Chr. 1.50). Oration 2 is a dialogue between Alexander and Philip, in which Alexander quotes Homer at length. In Oration 3, Dio makes Socrates his mouthpiece while in Oration 4 (another dialogue) Diogenes gives Alexander a lengthy lesson in the art of kingship. Here Dio imagines what they might have said on that legendary afternoon when Alexander visited Diogenes in the Craneum in Corinth, and was told to stand out of the sun. Of course, Dio relies on his imagination mainly and does not pretend otherwise: "I would like to tell what sorts of things they probably said" (4.3). But given Dio's own experience and respect for Cynicism, the words he attributes to Diogenes should be taken as representative of one set of Cynic ideas; the words given to Socrates seem cut from the same cloth. In addition to these four orations, one can add Dio's Sixth Discourse ("Diogenes or on Tyranny"), in which "Diogenes" condemns the Persian kings as so many tyrants who do not deserve the rights and privileges of kingship, as he does.

If Dio did indeed deliver his four kingship orations to Trajan, then in the course of them the emperor would have heard that the ideal king is distinguished by a host of virtues. He is philanthropic, just, lawful, prudent, temperate, brave and magnanimous. He is not cruel, hubristic, thoughtless, quick to anger or emotionally volatile. He is gentle, mild, kindly, not only to his friends and allies, but to all mankind, for he recognizes all as potential friends. In a word, he is full of love: he loves and is pious towards the gods (1.16) and towards mankind he demonstrates a pre-eminent *philanthrōpia* (1.17). He is a generous benefactor (*euergetēs*), a "shepherd of the people" who looks to their good, not his own (1.12–13, 1.23–4). Here he is like a captain steering a ship, a general ordering an army, a soul unifying a body, a man providing for his family, or the sun overseeing the entire world (3.62–85). Like all these, he is a "lover of toil" (*philo-ponos*, 1.21, 3.55–7, 82 *et al.*), and like the Cynic he actively embraces *ponos*, hardship and all challenges for the good of all: labour is the wages of a king, and only here does he demand to have more than anyone else.[13] This makes him ceaselessly active: "he attends to some matter needing his supervision, he acts promptly where speed is needed, accomplishes something not easy of accomplishment, reviews an army, subdues a province, founds a city, bridges rivers, or builds roads through a country" (3.127). Or alternatively, he goes hunting, the only pastime really appropriate for kings (3.136). In particular, he does not shirk the hardships of campaign, but suffers everything equally with his soldiers (1.28–9). In all he does, he follows the example of Heracles and calls on the assistance of this man-god, who is rightly praised as the "saviour of mankind", for he spent his life working to help others (e.g. 3.6). In turn, his great service for others is reciprocated by a profound respect, which binds them to him as if they were members of the same body (1.32; 3.104–7).

In these sustained exhortations to virtue, it is clear that the by-now ancient Homeric paradigm is still operative. But now besides the old Homeric virtues of prowess and intelligence, gentler qualities are also emphasized. The king is still a "shepherd of the people", but he is a gentle shepherd. Most remarkable of all is Dio's repeated invocation of love: the king loves his companions, his citizens and soldiers (*philetairos, philopolitēs, philostratiōtēs*) (1.28) and he recognizes that *philia* is easily the greatest good (3.86ff.). Of course, such *philia* was not as strong a notion as Christ's love for mankind, and Dio does not argue that the king should sacrifice his life for peoples everywhere. On the other hand, *philia* is a stronger term than our "friendship", more akin to fellow-feeling or affection for one's own kind. In his *Politics*, for instance, Aristotle had discussed the *philia* as the basic human relation: husband and wife, parents and children, friends, fellow-citizens and strangers on a journey all are bound by *philia*, now stronger, now weaker. *Philia* for Aristotle is more basic even than justice and the duty of reciprocity, and without some *philia* there can be no true community. Consequently, Aristotle makes it the highest task of the legislator to increase this natural affection between citizens. Dio's thought is quite Aristotelian here. In order to increase *philia* between citizens, the king should set an example of *philanthrōpia* and strive to be superior to everyone in "love of mankind". *Philanthrōpia* is therefore the highest virtue, and the true king is the most philanthropic. Furthermore, for Dio, this conception of the ideal king is not merely a Greek notion, but stems from nature herself: even wild animals and birds would recognize the king as rightful ruler, if they could (1.14, 4.25); natural societies are monarchical, for each herd has its king-bull and each hive its king-bee (2.66, 3.50).

Dio's speeches are eloquent and polished, but the ideas they contain could be adapted to other contexts too. In particular, they can illuminate the mentality that underlies the Cynics' paradoxical political manifesto. The poor Cynic can claim to be "king" because in his wild, unconventional life he has recovered all the natural virtues: courage, temperance, simplicity, freedom and, most of all, *philanthrōpia*. As "kings" who try to lead people to a life "according to nature", they are acting only in the people's best interest. They alone love mankind, and so in comparison with them, Sardanapallus, Xerxes, Philip, Alexander, Antigonus, Seleucus, Ptolemy, Nero, Vespasian, Domitian and the rest are only gangsters.

Cosmopolitans

Finally, we come to the most controversial of the Cynics' self-descriptions: the claim to be "cosmopolitan". Many passages are of relevance here, but the following two statements are probably the most cited: (i) "When asked from where he came, Diogenes said 'I am a *cosmopolitēs*'" (DL 6.63); and (ii) "The only true commonwealth (Diogenes said), is the 'one in the cosmos'" (6.72). In other passages, Crates' lines emphasize his rootlessness: "My homeland is not one tower, nor one roof, but the citadel and home of the whole world is ready for us to inhabit" (6.98). Crates also claimed that he was a "citizen of Diogenes"; his fatherland was "Dishonour and Poverty unsacked by Fortune" (6.93) and his home was *Pēra*, Travelling Bag, which he carried everywhere. According to Dio Chrysostom, Diogenes

> had no house or hearth of his own as the well-to-do have, but he made the cities his house and used to live there in the public buildings and in the shrines, which are dedicated to the gods, and took for his hearth-stone the wide world, which after all is man's common hearth and nourisher.
>
> (D. Chr. 4.13)

Epictetus' ideal Cynic says:

> I am without a city, without a house, without possessions, without a slave; I sleep on the ground; I have no wife, no children; no little mansion, but only the earth and heavens, and one little cloak. And what do I lack?   (*Discourses* 3.22.47)

Lucian's Diogenes says that he is "from everywhere" and "of the cosmos, a citizen" (Luc. *Vit. auct.* 8). In these and like passages,[14] the Cynic boasts that his home, city and fatherland are not some fixed locale but something more indeterminate and intangible: another Cynic, the Cynic lifestyle, the open road, the wide earth.

Placed in the context of the Cynics' antinomianism, naturalism and cheerful superiority to fortune, Diogenes' claim to be a *cosmopolitēs*, that is, "citizen of the cosmos", does not seem strange or implausible. Yet there are several questions that one may ask. First, did Diogenes or an early Cynic actually use the word, or even invent it? If they did, how did they construe it and what did they mean by claiming to be "cosmopolitans"? The idea seems to look forward to the more properly Stoic doctrine of the brotherhood of all peoples, and the "citizenship" of each person in a single moral community that supersedes all tribal loyalties and all merely political groupings. Indeed, the discovery of the idea of this kind of cosmopolitanism is a revolutionary one. Most historical societies have existed in relative isolation from each other. From this perspective, one is a member of one's group, but everyone outside it is "other": *barbaroi*, *goyim*, Gentiles, heathens, Franks, Huns – generally distrusted, often despised, sometimes hated. In sharp contrast, the cosmopolitan regards all human beings as equal in their humanity, and with a moral claim equal to that of his or her "own" people. Furthermore, cosmopolitan types do not rest content with their "own" culture but actively seek to broaden their experience of humanity, by travelling, learning foreign languages and studying other literatures and histories. The ideal cosmopolitan feels at home in several cultures and welcomes cultural difference for its own sake, quoting Terence's tag as if it were a creed: "I am human and consider nothing human to be alien to me". Moreover, this cosmopolitan creed can inform attitudes towards empire, as when Alexander tried to promote the unity of Greeks and Persians (at least among the elites), when Roman authorities extended citizenship to allies and subject peoples, and when Roman writers promoted the ideal of *humanitas*. Cosmopolitan ideas can inform Christian and Kantian ethics: the Christian imitates Christ in loving all peoples, Jew and Gentile alike; the Kantian speaks of a Kingdom of Ends, in which the inherent dignity of each rational being is respected equally, and no one is treated merely as a means to further ends, or a thing with a market "price" but no moral "value". The concept of cosmopolitanism continues to gain importance in our own time as the world becomes not a "city" as in antiquity, but something potentially even more intimate: a "global village" in which we are all fellow villagers.

Cosmopolitanism, therefore, is a concept that would go on to have an illustrious career. But how much of this did Diogenes anticipate when he used the word *cosmopolitēs*, if indeed he used it? With regard to the word itself, it is a typical Greek amalgamation of two nouns. In form, it is not unusual but it occurs rarely in extant Greek literature, and nowhere before Roman-period authors such as Philo and Diogenes Laertius. But these later writers, in turn, attribute its use to early Cynics (such as Diogenes) and Stoics (such as Chrysippus). It is generally accepted that *cosmopolitēs* was a Cynic coinage, and to this consensus one might add here that this would only be in accord with the linguistic creativity of many Cynic writers.

Assuming then that Diogenes did actually use the word in the late classical period, what did he mean by it? Most scholars have asserted that Diogenes' statement was merely "negative": that when he claimed to be "a citizen of the world" (as it is often translated), Diogenes effectively said "I am not a Sinopean, or an Athenian, or an Elean, or a Theban, or a citizen of any particular *polis*". He did not anticipate Stoic, Roman, Christian, Kantian and other forms of cosmopolitanism. He did not learn foreign languages, or travel to view the pageantry of human customs in their wild variety. Indeed, he scorned this variety as mere deviations from the one true, natural life. In this interpretation, cosmopolitanism (and the closely related *philanthrōpia*, love for all mankind) became a Cynic virtue only later in the more ecumenical culture of the Roman Empire. For it would have been inconceivable for a Greek of the fourth-century to "love mankind" generally and not to follow the Greek custom of looking down on foreign peoples as so many "barbarians". Alexander tried to change this custom, but the Successor kings and Greek elites that ruled in Egypt and Asia tended to revert to traditional prejudice. Given this prevailing cultural chauvinism, was it possible for the early Cynics to be cosmopolitan in any positive sense?

"Yes, in fact it was", interject some scholars who, like John Moles, have dissented from the majority view. From this perspective, there are several reasons to doubt that Cynic cosmopolitanism was merely a form of nay-saying.[15] First, Diogenes' term *cosmopolitēs* is not an alpha-privative, and if Diogenes' point were merely negative, he could easily have said "I am not from any conventional Greek city" or simply "I am without a city (*apolis*)". Indeed, such a formulation is attributed to him in the tragic verses: "I am without a city, without a home, deprived of native land, a beggar, a wanderer who gets his livelihood from day to day" (DL 6.38). Clearly Diogenes' word contains some more positive element. Furthermore, taken in conjunction with other relevant passages, Diogenes' statement can be seen as reflecting an at least incipient affirmation of the brotherhood of mankind. Crates' claims – to be a "citizen of Diogenes", of the Cynic lifestyle and of the Cynic *Pēra* – would make him a citizen of a brotherhood of friends, a "community of the wise" at least. Such a community would not include all mankind, and the Cynic renunciation of custom marks a clear separation between Cynic and non-Cynic. And yet, this division is not an absolute one. By philosophizing on the streets, the Cynics would seem intent on persuading passers-by "to turn dog" (*kynizein*) and join their philosophical pack, or rather, to rejoin the silent majority of mankind: the poor, the country-folk, the "primitives" who live closer to nature. Thus, unlike Epicureans or Gnostics, say, the little band of Cynic "citizens" was not an exclusive sect but seems to have been sometimes driven by the desire to evangelize, as it were. The virtue of *philanthrōpia* inspired them to liberate others from conventional illusions. If so, Diogenes' statement is not unrelated to later, stronger cosmopolitan affirmations among Stoics and others, and cannot be said to be merely "negative".

One might argue further that this "positive" cosmopolitanism was first broached during the earlier, more creative classical period, and inherited by later thinkers, who merely embroidered the theme. Certainly, the idea that a human being is not defined by citizenship in his native *polis* had been entertained for well over a century before Diogenes. Presocratic philosophers made vast speculations about the universe and saw human beings, their cities and empires, as specks within the cosmic whole. The speculative freedom of these creative minds is captured in the anecdote about Anaxagoras. "When someone said to him, 'You don't care about your fatherland', Anaxagoras replied, 'Have some respect! For I do take my fatherland very seriously', and pointed to the sky" (DL 2.7). A more explicitly cosmopolitan saying is attributed to Democritus: "the whole earth is open to the wise man; for the whole cosmos is the fatherland of the good soul" (DK 247). Again, the Sophists were cosmopolitan nearly in our sense of the word: educated, travelling between cities, casting their eyes beyond the Greek world as they learned about foreign ways and theorized about the general relation of human customs to nature (*physis*). Plato's ideal philosopher casts his thoughts beyond the temporal world altogether; his body may be here in Athens, but his soul is not bounded by Athenian territory as it flies up to contemplate all Being (Pl. *Tht.* 173c6–174a). There were also popular images of the unattached intellectual: Thales falling into the well while star-gazing, or Aristophanes' Socrates flying about in a basket as he contemplates the sun. Nor was it only intellectuals who articulated cosmopolitan sentiments. There are fragmentary quotations from the Athenian stage: "The whole sky is thoroughfare for the eagle, and the whole earth is fatherland to the noble man" (Eur. Fr. 1047 [Nauck]); "The good man – even if he live far away and I never see him with my own eyes – I judge him still a friend" (902); "the fertile earth is everywhere home" (777); and "home is wherever one is prospering" (Ar. *Plut.* 1151). Whenever Greeks travelled or were exiled, they might have repeated the sentiment articulated many times in Xenophon's *Anabasis*: "You, my friends, are now my fatherland" (Xen. *An.* 1.3.6, 3.1.5). Such passages suggest that the Cynics coined a word for an idea that was already current, and slanted it to their own perspective.

This perspective was that nature is the source of value, and this brings us to the final point about a "positive" Cynic cosmopolitanism. The English "cosmopolitan" has its own peculiar connotations but, thinking in Greek, one recognizes that the Greek word *cosmopolitēs* is not simply or even primarily political, ethical and cultural in register. Diogenes does not say that he is a "cosmopolitan" or a "citizen of the world", that is, the *human* world. Rather, he says that he is a "citizen of the cosmos". The *cosmos* is not a human construct, but exists beyond human control and even conception. It is an important word in the philosopher's vocabulary, of course, and almost every thinker has theories about the universe's size, structure, duration and the like. But this makes Diogenes' word even more startling. For how one be a *citizen* of the totality and its vast spaces? Can one make the *cosmos* one's *home*? For Aristotle, true citizenship is possible only in the intimacy of the *polis*, for Hegel only in that of the nation-state. In stark contrast, Diogenes implies that only the Cynic wanderer is truly at home anywhere.

Thus, the Cynics' cosmopolitan ideal may take them well beyond the range of typical political discourse, and may be more properly understood in relation to the philosophical goal of finding a harmony between the individual and nature. In the phrase attributed to Democritus, man is a "little cosmos" (DK 34). Plato's *Timaeus* expands the thought to make the human form (soul and body) a mirror of the universe; in the *Republic* too, Socrates' city grows to perfection as a projection of the soul, and therefore becomes a home perfectly designed for human beings, an ideal state. In a different key, Aristotle writes that "the soul (*psychē*) is somehow all things" (*De an.* 431b21), suggesting that for a rational mind, nothing is alien or other, and that the categoreal structure of language and thought mirrors that of nature. For such thinkers, the philosopher is one who strives to recognize, appreciate and even identify with the unity of the cosmos. The world is beautiful and rational: it is a sign of the highest enlightenment to love its beauty everywhere, and when one does, one is radically at home in it. The Cynic too, in his own anti-intellectual way, as he wanders about as homeless as a bird yet also utterly at home everywhere, asserts his own vision of how to find a human place within nature's solitudes. His is the simplest of visions, yet even someone as complex as Nietzsche expressed his admiration for it when he makes his Zarathustra cry out: "Stay true to the earth, O my brothers!" (*Thus Spoke Zarathustra*: "Prologue", §3).

Only the most resolute optimist thinks that human beings can be fully at home in mortality, and one might contrast Cynic optimism with the tragic view of more dualistic thinkers. In the *New Testament*, for example, the word *cosmos* has come to mean "the world" in opposition to God. This eventually makes "citizenship in the cosmos" impossible for the Christian. For as created, the cosmos is good, beautiful and god-like and should be loved as an expression of God's will. But it is not God. Partially good, it is also a "vale of tears": a fallen realm of sin and death that can only strive to return to paradise and the fullness of God. Thus when Matthew asks, "What does it profit a man to gain the world, if he lose his own soul?" (16:26), his word for "world" is *cosmos*. For Augustine, "our heart is restless, Lord, until it rest in Thee" (*Conf.* 1.1), and for later medieval Christianity, the human being is a pilgrim journeying towards a heavenly home. Like Plato's Socrates, the pilgrim is not fully at home *here*. By contrast, Cynics such as Diogenes do claim to be at home here, in *this* sunshine; Lucian's characters express no longings for transcendence but are fully at home in themselves, even as they journey down to Hell.

Cynic cosmopolitanism can sometimes have a further sense that was probably lost on many contemporaries but that may be more immediately appealing now. For us, in an ecological age that sees human beings as "citizens" of an interconnected ecosystem, some stray Cynic comments are striking. Lucian's Demonax said that he was not worried about shipwreck or being eaten by fish, for it would only be just for fish to eat him, since in the past he ate fish himself (Luc. *Demon.* 35). Similarly, Demonax gave orders that when he died, his body should be left unburied, so that he could be "useful" for birds and dogs (66). Diogenes' remarks about the kinship of all materiality (bread, flesh, etc.) (DL 6.73) may look forward to the monism of the Stoics, for whom nature, the cosmos and God are all one, animated by a single "breath".[16] In the Stoic perspective, the human being is just one puff in this cosmic *pneuma* and can come to unity with it only through philosophy. Thus, if the Cynics were "citizens of nature" in a radical sense, stressing the affinity of mankind with animals, they would seem to anticipate, if only vaguely, the more developed theories of the Stoics: in philosophy, differences between self and other breaks down; one sees others as one's friends, brothers, fellow-citizens; one extends one's love to ever greater circles, to foreigners, barbarians and even the most primitive peoples; and ultimately, one loves the cosmos as oneself, recognizing oneself as a strand inextricably woven into the totality. If so, then the Cynics' outlook, if not their explicit statements, are one of the influences that helped shape Stoic formulations such as this:

All things are woven together, and the binding together is sacred, and essentially nothing is alien to anything else. For all things have been arranged together and together they compose the one cosmos. For the cosmos is one, though composed of all things, and God is one, though existing through all things, and substance is one, and law is one, and reason is common to all intelligent living beings, and truth is one.   (Marcus Aurelius, *Med.* 7.9)

Conclusion

Stoics such as Marcus Aurelius obviously engaged in the rough and tumble of politics, and the general Stoic position was that one should be a citizen of the world first, and of Rome or some particular community only second. By this ordering, one would strive to transform a particular city into an image of the cosmic "city", and in so doing feel no essential conflict between the ideal of a self-sufficient, cosmic unity on the one hand, and one's duties to family and fellow citizens on the other. The Cynics did not articulate or even anticipate such a solution, and their responses to political imperatives were more individualistic and irreverent. Particular cities and empires are *not*, in their eyes, an image of some cosmic city but only the product of all-too-human ambition and delusion. The path to "utopia" is not through idealized politics but through the renunciation of normal political activities, indeed the renunciation of all conventional sorts of power. Therefore the Cynic renounces citizenship to become a wanderer; he renounces all Romes for "Attic poverty" and his private city of *Pēra*.

Yet such rhetorical nay-saying has radical political consequences. Paradoxically, the renunciation of politics is itself a political act, and, like Socrates, the ostensibly apolitical Cynic can claim to play the highest political role.[17] Namely, they boast of being "kings", superior in virtue to all others, tougher, smarter, more frugal and more just. For some, the pinnacle of virtue is *philanthrōpia* and as universal kings they love not just one people, but all mankind. Indeed, they love others enough to satirize and mock them. Their *parrhēsia* is a public benefit and this harsh truth-telling makes them at once kings (for only the "best" can undertake such a benefaction), anarchists (for only the free refrain from false flattery), and democratic "watch-dogs" who remain vigilant while the people slumber. Again, in criticizing elites and advocating the end of illegitimate government by the rich and self-interested, they can be seen as either the true, but unrecognized, kings, or as a sort of popular opposition. Most important of all is freedom. Customary political organizations are false, and the Cynic frees himself from them to become a "citizen" of himself, the cosmos, and other Cynics. Thus, as the Cynics wandered from city to city, scorning the jurisdiction of local authorities, they showed themselves as both anarchists and "kings", transcending any positive law. For them, nature is the only law-giver, and so as "citizens of the cosmos" living according to nature's rule, they might look beyond arbitrary human systems to the great community of nature, of all like-minded Cynics and even all living things. Of this "community" they claimed to be citizens: citizens of the cosmos, at home here and everywhere because they were radically at home with their present selves. Anarchists, democrats, cosmopolitans, kings: all of these in a way, but most of all (to adapt Nietzsche's phrase) "free spirits, *very* free spirits".

SIX
Cynic legacies

Free-spirited and varied as Cynicism was in antiquity, its legacy has been even more so. It is a legacy that stretches fairly continuously from Onesicritus to the present day, and over this long span one could point to many figures who partially resemble the ancient Cynics in one or more respects: for embracing poverty, rebelling against a stultifying society, rejecting learning or praising the happiness of simplicity. Depending on one's sympathetic imagination, this group could potentially include many characters: hermits, anchorites, Benedictines, Carthusians and other monks, Franciscans and Dominicans, as well as Jains, *pasupatas*, *Sadhus* and ascetics from other religious traditions; pioneers, explorers, adventurers who sailed out beyond the world's edge; Robin Hood and his merry men, modern anarchists, tramps, hoboes, Beats, hippies, punks, new agers, bohemians and all who those resolutely "do their own thing". If the more closed ancient and medieval societies tended to produce characters who turned inwards to the unexplored mysteries of the self, a more expansive modern society lures its rebels and mystics to turn outwards to the infinite promise of an unexamined world beyond. There is a streak of Cynicism in Mark Twain's Huckleberry Finn, who can never get used to the itchy clothes and praying and stuffy drawing rooms of Aunt Sally's world, so that he runs away, helping Jim escape from slavery, and eventually escaping himself west into "Injun Territory" where "a somebody can still be free".

Because the ideals of freedom and simplicity are perennial ones, partial parallels with Cynicism could be discerned from many times and places. Here, however, we shall discuss briefly some of those whose contact with the Cynics themselves was more direct and deliberate. Our selective list includes the Stoics, early Christian Apologists and Medieval theologians, some Renaissance writers, Shakespeare, a few Enlightenment thinkers, Rousseau and Nietzsche and his postmodern successors. All of these comparisons deserve fuller treatment than is possible here, and there are other colossal figures, such as Erasmus, Rabelais, Montaigne and Foucault, who loom in the background but must be passed by with a mere doff of the cap.

Ancient Stoicism

First in this long line of respondents to the Cynics are the ancient Stoics. As we have seen, Zeno of Citium was a "student" of Crates and an associate of the early Cynics for some twenty years before he diverged to "found" the Stoa. His *Republic* was said to have been "written on the dog's tail" due to its astonishing political vision, and Cynic ideas may have surfaced in Chrysippus' *Republic* too (see Erskine 1990: 14). Even so, Chrysippus as the "second founder of Stoicism" marks a turning point, for owing especially to his work, the school grew into a systematic philosophy embracing logic, physics and ethics. Yet even as it outgrew its Cynic origins, there remained many points of continuity: Cynic opportunism regarding pleasure looks forward to the Stoic doctrine that the things of fortune are "preferred indifferents"; the Cynic claim to be "king" returns in the Stoic paradoxes, while the Stoics add that the sage is also the only true judge, general, pilot and so forth, because he alone has knowledge, while all others are fools; the Cynic "citizen of the cosmos" anticipates the Stoic self who is both radically individualistic yet also radically at one with nature and with the "city" of all gods and human beings; the Cynic adapts himself to every circumstance, while the Stoic welcomes every event as necessary and even claims to "love fate". Most of all, Stoicism ever retained its core Cynic vision of the self-sufficient sage living "according to nature"; Stoics typically add a systematic framework, and the conviction that self-sufficiency is possible only for those who have studied logic and physics, for it is only by understanding nature that one can overcome its seeming otherness. But many thinkers of the "later Stoa", such as Seneca, Epictetus and Marcus Aurelius, retreated from the high intellectualism of predecessors like Chrysippus, and what remains then is that ethical core which can again become closely associated with an ideal Cynicism; Epictetus' sage is the Cynic wanderer, and his first demand (that one distinguish between what one can and cannot control) resembles the Cynics' dichotomy of the self and fortune. Such reversions to the example of the early Zeno are evident earlier also; some continued to regard Cynicism as "the most manly" strain of Stoicism (DL 6.14), while Aristo of Chios (c. 250 BCE) abandoned orthodox Stoic categories such as "preferred indifferents", which seemed too accommodating to customary opinion (6.105, 7.160–64); his severity here, as well as his praise of *ponos* and avoidance of useless erudition, has earned him comparisons with the Cynics.

Early and medieval Christianity

If the resemblances between Cynicism and later Stoicism are striking, more enigmatic are certain family resemblances between Cynicism and early Christianity. These resemblances have been noted and stressed by a number of recent writers (notably F. Gerald Downing, Burton Mack, Leif Vaage and John Crossan). Collectively, these have constructed a theory that discerns Cynicism in the heart of the Christian Gospels themselves: namely, that Jesus was a Cynic. According to this interpretation of ancient evidence, the Galilee of Jesus' time was not a provincial backwater but, on the contrary, almost cosmopolitan, with many non-Jews and Greek speakers, particularly in the large towns such as Tiberias and Sepphoris. Jesus was a carpenter, so one might surmise that he had customers in the market town of Sepphoris,[1] with whom he needed to speak; later, in Jerusalem, he is depicted as speaking with Pontius Pilate directly, without an interpreter, and presumably therefore in Greek. From such considerations one might ask: did Jesus speak Greek in addition to Aramaic (and/or Hebrew)? If so, could he have been influenced somehow by the language of the Cynics? Indeed, Gadara – home to Cynics such as Menippus, Meleager and Oenomaus – was little more than thirty kilometres from Nazareth, and eight kilometres from the Sea of Galilee where so much of Jesus' ministry was conducted. In two of the Synoptic Gospels, the name Gadara is associated with one of Jesus' miracles, for it was in the country "of the Gadarenes" (and/or "Gergenses") that Christ met a madman, who wore no clothes, lived among tombs, and was possessed by the demon "Legion".[2] Christ drove the demons into a herd of pigs, which then rushed "into the sea" and were drowned. Was this daimoniac a Cynic? The Palestinian Talmud *yGittin* depicts the *kinukos* (Hebrew for "Cynic") as a madman who lives in cemeteries, wears rags, throws away his property and the like. In addition, since the area of "Gadara" produced some of the most famous Cynics), some conclude that the man whom Jesus met was indeed a Cynic.[3]

The case for contact between Jesus and Cynicism might seem to gain in credibility when one compares selected ideas and phrases in the Gospels (particularly the Synoptic Gospels) with the language of a Demonax or Dio Chrysostom. The parallels sometimes are uncanny. Do Beatitudes such as "Blessed are the poor, for yours is the kingdom of God" (Luke 6:20) and "the last will be first" (Luke 13:30) echo the Cynics' praise of poverty, their delight in paradox and overturning of customary expectations? When Jesus commands his listeners to give up all they own and follow him (Matthew 19:21), does one hear a Galilean version of a Crates or Monimus throwing their wealth away to follow Diogenes? When Jesus commands love of others, even enemies, can one discern Cynic praise of *philanthrōpia*? When Jesus says that the Kingdom is at hand, and that one should love "one's neighbour" (literally "the person nearby"), is this only a variation on the Cynic advice to attend to what is present? Or when

Jesus says that his kingdom is "not of this world" (John 18:36), are there distant echoes of the Cynics' boast that the virtuous philosopher is king? Could even Jesus' claim to be "son of God" be a refraction of the Cynic half-jest that Diogenes (like Heracles) was "born of Zeus"? In the story of the temptation in the desert, does Satan tempt Jesus as once Vice tempted Heracles, as in Prodicus' allegory "The Choice of Heracles"?

Those who choose such comparisons will find further possible resemblances. Born in a stable in Bethlehem, son of a carpenter, a carpenter himself who sought out fishermen, prostitutes, tax-collectors and other "low" types, Jesus lived on the edges of official society, like the Greek Cynics, who sat in the marketplaces among fish-mongers and cobblers. Cynic *parrhēsiasts* boldly spoke their truths everywhere and in all circumstances, and similarly when Pilate queries his mission, Jesus self-confidently replies, "I have come into the world to be a witness to the truth" (John 18:37). If Cynics were unafraid before local magistrates and Roman emperors, neither did Jesus bow before the Sanhedrin, the aristocratic Sadducees, or before Caiaphas, the high priest of Solomon's Temple. On the contrary, Jesus threw over the money-changers' tables in the temple, and threatened to destroy the temple itself, even during Passover. Like a Cynic renouncing *nomoi* of purification and sacrifice, Jesus rebelled against the external rites of the priestly hierarchy: not worthy is sacrifice at the temple, but rather the widow's mite; not ritual purity, but "the upright heart and pure"; not empty expense, but inner holiness and the turning of the heart. Jesus as quasi-Cynic revolutionary also challenged the Pharisees and the scribes with their legalistic precision and intimidating show of erudition; slavery to the "letter of the law" kills the spirit, and one must cut through the knotted complexity of the Mosaic Code to the two essential things "love God" and "love your neighbour". Sometimes this Cynic Jesus seems even to have rejected the law wholesale, as when he "declares all foods clean", including (it would seem) the pork, shellfish and other meats solemnly forbidden in Deuteronomy and Leviticus. Unafraid to reject such ancient taboos and *typhos*, this "free, *very* free spirit" would also find a language appropriate for his simple gospel of universal love. Therefore (it can be argued), like a Diogenes or Crates avoiding Platonic dialectic for the simpler language of bodily gesture, apophthegms and moral example, Jesus passed over tangled scriptural exegesis for the more direct medium of anecdotes and parables. Perhaps most Cynic of all is the fact that Jesus' parables draw on the wisdom of the natural world. Apart from the crucial reference to God, everything in the parable about the lilies, for example, could be seen in a Cynic light:

> And why take ye thought for raiment? Consider the lilies of the field, how they grow; they toil not, neither do they spin: and yet I say unto you, that even Solomon in all his glory was not arrayed like one of these. Wherefore, if God so clothe the grass of the field, which today is and tomorrow is cast into the oven, shall He not much more clothe you, O ye of little faith? Therefore take no thought, saying, What shall we eat? or, What shall we drink? or, Wherewithal shall we be clothed? (Matthew 6:28–31)[4]

Such possible commonalities are stressed by Downing, Mack, Vaage and others when they conclude emphatically that Cynic influence on Jesus was predominant, and that we should view Jesus not primarily as a Jewish rabbi or prophet, but as an itinerant Cynic. Yet despite many points of seeming resemblance, the "Cynic Jesus" is far from winning universal acceptance. Other perspectives suggest that the hypothesis has been overstated. It is unclear, for example, to what extent Hellenism had penetrated Galilee. Even if Jesus spoke some Greek, it was not his native language and surely he did not speak Greek to Peter the fisherman. Moreover, the depiction of Jesus as a Cynic rebel against *nomos* should not be exaggerated. He may have opposed Pharisaic legalism, questioned laws of diet and purity, "worked" on the Sabbath day and so forth, yet he still recognized the Sabbath as a special day, celebrated Passover as a holy time, and did not quip, like Crates, that for him *every* day was a festival day. Although not a Pharisee, Jesus did argue from scripture, thus showing his respect for a tradition that needed to be reformed, not rejected outright. In fact, his followers regarded him as the fulfilment of that tradition: an Elijah and David come again in a new dispensation. Nor should one rush to conclude that Jesus' ministry was "Cyniclike" simply because it was "itinerant". And even if it was itinerant, Jesus' travels were within Galilee mainly. His longest journey was to Jerusalem; Diogenes wandered much further. Jesus ministered to his own people, and was not an exile or homeless beggar. He preached to large crowds but he did not harangue random passers-by in the cities of Tiberias or Sepphoris. He preached equality before God, but he had twelve close *disciples*, whom he did not try to beat away with a stick, as Antisthenes is said to have beaten Diogenes. He was single (according to traditional accounts at least), yet he insisted vehemently on the sanctity of marriage; contrast both facts with Crates' "dog-marriage", which so epitomizes Cynic contempt for the traditional custom.

Other purported similarities do not support any great weight. Jesus encouraged his followers to renounce wealth as a necessary step for entering his Kingdom: words indeed reminiscent of Cynic language. Yet the Cynics were not the only ancient group to criticize wealth, and Jesus' language of kingship is too culturally complex to be mapped straight onto that of the Cynics, who harked back to Homer's kings rather than to Saul and David. Jesus may have been a "king" of sorts, but he was also called "rabbi", "Son of God", "son of Man", successor to Elijah and the prophets, Messiah, and most of all, *Christos*, the Anointed of the Lord. It would seem strange if Jesus himself had been a Cynic, only to be so utterly transformed and misconstrued by the early Christian writers. Most of all, a Diogenes or Crates may have been quizzical of customary religion, but it seems artificial to find behind the Gospels a Jesus who was not intensely religious, with a religiosity that was wholly unGreek: baptized by John the Baptist, he came to preach not Cynic frugality but the coming of the Kingdom, the resurrection of the body, the forgiveness of sins, and the intimate love of the Father. His *philanthrōpia* is not expressed in Cynic renunciation and truculence, but in healings and the washing of feet. Far from being a water-drinker, Jesus makes wine from water at the wedding at Cana, and at the Last Supper, says "I am the bread and wine of life", thus making human things the highest symbol, vehicle, and even the very stuff of divinity. The Greek Cynics do not speak like this: their ideals are more obvious ones such as self-sufficiency, practical freedom and tricks for enduring fortune. Cynicism may well have touched Jesus in some way, but if so it was only one in a complex nexus of influences.

Early Christians certainly did not overplay the Cynic connection, or even call attention in any way to the possibility. Indeed, scriptural writers (including Paul) never mention Cynics explicitly, and for centuries Christian authors distanced themselves from the shameless, pagan "dogs" of the Greeks. Thus, although some might detect Cynic echoes in Jesus' instructions to the Apostles – to go forth to the cities, carrying "no purse, *pēra*, or shoes, and saluting no-one on the road" (Luke 10:1–16, esp. 10:4) – nevertheless it is a fact that Luke does not name the Cynics outright, as he does name the Stoics and Epicureans (Acts 17:18).

In the second century CE, Christianity had become more than a minor offshoot of Judaism, attracting more pagan converts, as well as the political and intellectual attention of the surrounding pagan population. As a result, Christians began to feel the need to defend their new religion *vis-à-vis* the established order, and the so-called Christian Apologists began to write "apologies" or defences of Christianity, particularly in relation to the different Greek philosophies. These Apologists often mention the Cynics, but mainly in negative terms. Compared to Jesus' ministry to the poor and sick, many Apologists ask, what good did Diogenes ever do by lying in his tub? Whom did Crates help when he threw his money into the sea? Was anyone more shameless than Crates and Hipparchia when they consummated their "dog-marriage" in public? And are not Cynics the worst sort of hypocrites, for although they claim to renounce money, they beg and steal, and although they claim to renounce honour, they in fact seek it with their flashy antics? Beneath their squalid beards, are they not materialists? Behind their shamelessness, are they not utter slaves to the public regard?

Such criticisms (particularly the last one, of *philodoxia*) echo those made by contemporary pagans such as Lucian and Julian. Thus, both camps united in vilifying the Cynics as the "bad boys" of philosophy. And just as an Epictetus and Lucian honour "true" Cynics like Diogenes or Menippus as the greatest champions of philosophy, so the Apologists fasten on them as the epitome and essence of Greek wisdom. That is, the philosophy of the Greeks is so much foolishness, because they do not know God. Even their sages are ignorant of Christ and so their vision of the highest good (it is alleged) must always remain tainted by their unredeemed humanity. That is, the Greeks can never fully escape the sin, and sadness, of pride. The Cynics epitomize this failing because more than all others they seek to escape the lure of honour; yet even in their shamelessness, they gain honour, come to desire it and so become ensnared by it again. Thus human beings cannot by their own efforts escape from the unhappiness of a merely human happiness: the paradoxically shameless pride of the Cynics only demonstrates the folly and misery of man without God.

From our perspective, it might seem strange that the Cynics (rather than Plato or Aristotle) could be taken up as representative of Greek philosophy, yet this tactic would indeed be adopted in Christian literature over several centuries, from Justin Martyr, Tatian, Theophilus of Antioch, Clement of Alexandria and Tertullian in the second century CE, down to Eusebius, Gregory of Nazianzus, Augustine, John Chrysostom, Theodoret, and others, in the third, fourth and fifth centuries. Some quotations from Tatian, Tertullian and Augustine offer a glimpse of this tradition of polemic. In his criticism of the Greek philosophers, Justin's student Tatian begins with none more foolish than Diogenes:

> What noble thing have you [i.e. the Greeks] produced by your pursuit of philosophy? Who of your most eminent men has been free from vain boasting? Diogenes, who made such a parade of his independence with his tub, was seized with a bowel complaint through eating a raw polypus [i.e. octopus], and so lost his life by glutton.
> (*Ad Gr.* 2; trans. Pratten, in Roberts & Donaldson 1868)

After mocking Aristippus, Plato, Aristotle, Heraclitus, Zeno, Empedocles, Pherecydes and Pythagoras in turn, Tatian ends his tirade by returning to the Cynics: "And who would give his approval to the dog-marriage of Crates, and not rather repudiate the wild, bloated language of his ilk?" (3). Later, Tatian rounds on his favourite targets again as godless hypocrites:

> O man competing with the dog, you do not know God, and so have turned to the imitation of an irrational animal. You cry out in public with an assumption of authority, and take upon you to avenge your own self; and if you receive nothing, you indulge in abuse, and philosophy is with you the art of getting money.
>
> (*Ad Gr.* 25; trans. Pratten, in Roberts & Donaldson 1868)

Thus, it is not just Tertullian who would thunder that Athens has "nothing to do with Jerusalem" (*Apology* 46, 50): the theme would be hammered home in some quarters in the effort to establish Christianity as an independent force. Centuries later, when Christianity had become the official religion of the Empire, Augustine would revisit Tatian's polemics in his *City of God*, a whole chapter of which is dedicated to the "most proud shamelessness of the Cynics":

> Even today we see that there are still Cynic philosophers. For these are the ones who not only cover themselves with the *pallium*, but even carry clubs. Still though, none of them dare to do this (i.e. public fornication), for if they did, they would not only be stoned by the people but would be actually spat upon. Thus, human nature is ashamed of this lust, and rightly ashamed. For in the disobedience which by its own prompting masters the genitalia and removes them from the power of the will – here is clear proof of how that first human disobedience has been punished.
>
> (*De civ. D.* 14.20)

Their overall criticisms notwithstanding, Christian writers could also express admiration for some aspects of Cynicism, and often in the very treatises that condemned the Cynics as shameless, vain-glorious atheists. For although the Cynics were "atheists", at least they did not believe in the pagan gods and, with their criticism of pagan customs, they helped prepare the way for the Gospel. Thus, for example, even Tertullian praises Diogenes and Varro ("the Roman Cynic") for exposing the pagan deities (*Apology* 14). Eusebius quotes Oenomaus at length, making his excoriation of the oracles a part of the Christian's education, a moment in the "preparation for the Gospel". Perhaps most enduring here is the admiration of Cynic asceticism as quasi-Christian, as if their renunciation of worldly goods such as wealth and power foreshadowed the holy poverty of Jesus and the Apostles. Thus Origen, for example, singles out Antisthenes, Diogenes and Crates as champions of pagan asceticism and likens them to the Hebrew prophets; even more radically, he implicitly compares them with Christ himself (*C. Cels.* 2.41, 7.7; cf. 6.28). This admiration for the ascetic Cynics is evident in influential writers such as Jerome, Gregory of Nazianzus and others, down even to Dante, who places Diogenes in the first circle of hell, the limbo that holds unfortunate innocents such as the unbaptized and other "virtuous pagans" like Socrates and Plato (*Inferno* 4.130–144). As unworldly mendicants, the Cynics would be cited approvingly by John of Wales, Thomas Aquinas (*Summa Theologiae* II Q.186 A.3) and others when the great controversy arose in the 1200s as to whether a vow of poverty is necessary for a truly religious life. Since then, the ancient Cynics have sometimes been used to recall Christians to the simplicity of the Apostles and early Church. The Cynics are often likened also to the friars, particularly the Franciscans, with their joyful wisdom (*gaya scienza*) and their love for our "brothers and sisters", our fellow creatures, the animals.

Yet, despite partial similarities between ascetic Cynicism and ascetic strains of Christianity, in antiquity the two seem to have occupied very different cultural spaces, too separate for a single person to bridge. The record at least seems to indicate very few who were both Cynics and Christians. By one reckoning, we know of only three such persons, at the most, and they span three centuries: Peregrinus Proteus, Heraclas, and Maximus Hero.[5] Many early

Christians, of course, adopted ascetic ways that might recall the Cynics and so Tatian, despite his anti-pagan polemics, was said to "have practised an utterly Cynic life" (*Elenchos* 10.18).[6] Certainly Cynic *askēsis* must have been one influence on the anchorites, the Desert Fathers, the early monasteries and other Christian ascetics. This aspect of the Cynic legacy would prove very enduring indeed, if Derek Krueger is right in interpreting Leontius's seventh-century *Life of Symeon* as a quasi-Cynic hagiography, and the ascetic Symeon as a sort of Cynic-Christian. According to the *Life*, Symeon was a Syrian Christian and a hermit who one day gave up the anchorite's life, left the desert and rejoined mankind. As soon as he returned to Emesa, however, he began to act strangely. He tied a dead dog to his belt, carrying it everywhere. He lived in a shockingly open way, mocking passers-by, throwing nuts at the women during mass, eating raw meat and lupin-beans, farting continuously and defecating in public places. Krueger's claim is that by narrating (or fabricating) such antics, "Leontius sets up a parallel between Symeon and Diogenes which pervades the entire text" (1996: 105). As a new Diogenes and human "dog", Symeon descends into obscenity, and yet this fall into animality, paradoxically, empowers him to transcend the body itself. Living utterly "according to nature", he transcends nature and becomes Christ-like. It was as if a Cynic-style life were Symeon's Passion, Golgotha and Resurrection: he descended into the full degradation of the body only to be born again out of it, renewed and sanctified, a true "fool of Christ", superior even to the anchorites and monks more familiar in the Syria of the time.

But if it is true that Leontius makes Cynic naturalism a vehicle for Christian sanctity, he would be quite unusual. Christian writers throughout the Middle Ages tend to maintain the old ambiguity towards the Cynics, now praising them as proto-Christians with their voluntary poverty and rejection of idols, now cursing them as "dogs" who seek glory by fornicating in the streets. Even at such a distance, those strange figures from the ancient world continued to fascinate, and as a result the *Cynic Epistles* remained popular, eventually being among the first of printed books, after the Bible.[7] Furthermore, the shameless antics of ancient Cynics made them a useful label for blackening an opponent. The word "Cynic" could be used as an easy insult for those opposed to all right-thinking folk. Thus in their years of contention, Luther and Erasmus would often abuse the other as "a shameless Cynic dog": as handy a put-down as, say, "anti-Christ". Many generations of such mudslinging in books, pamphlets and public debate may be one reason that the resonances of the word "cynic" have gradually changed. The best ideals of ancient Cynicism were forgotten, and only the lewd sensationalism remained: *parrhēsia* degenerated into ranting *effronterie*; self-sufficiency into self-assured contempt for others; frugality into miserliness; solitary freedom into greedy self-interest; simplicity into blunt refusal; and life "according to nature" into a life according to *my* nature and *my* obstinate will. It is remembered that Diogenes scorned Alexander, but not that he praised the sunshine. As the positive aspects of ancient Cynicism are ignored, its negative sides come to the fore. Gradually the modern "cynic" is born, as one who rejects all ideals, denigrates all mankind and can see nothing good anywhere.

Renaissance

Along with such slow linguistic changes were other, more dramatic transformations. In the Middle Ages, Europe was ideally Christendom: a single realm united by a common faith. The Reformation and Wars of Religion effectively ended this, and often even the ideal was forgotten. With the age of exploration, and the rediscovery of more of pagan antiquity from the late-fifteenth century, the intense longing to transcend this imperfect world began gradually to relax. Other, non-religious aspects of antiquity became interesting to more secular readers. With regard to Cynicism in particular, interest drifted away from proto-Christian Cynic asceticism towards other Cynic practices such as social satire, *parrhēsia*, self-sufficiency and radical autonomy. In the Renaissance, a satirical author such as Lucian enjoyed tremendous vogue, and through him the name of Menippus has become firmly stamped onto the genre of "Menippean satire". Lucian's dialogues inspired many emulators and his influence is key to myriad works, such as Erasmus' *Praise of Folly* (1511 CE), the anonymous *Momus* (*c*.1520), Lipsius' *Satyra Menippea* and *Somnium* (1581), Cervantes' *Colloquy of Two Dogs* (1613), Andreae's *Menippus; or, One Hundred Satiric Dialogues* (1617), Hensius' *Cras Credo, Hodie Nihil* (1621), and Cunaeus' *Sardinians on the Slave Block: A Menippean Satire on the People of This Age, Most of Them Badly Educated* (1612). In such works, according to Relihan (1996: 272–3), the traditional duality of Cynicism resurfaces in that Renaissance writers often treat Diogenes as the true Cynic, a noble dog, while Menippus becomes a nasty mutt, a mere scoffer, whose rightful place is in the hell where Lucian put him.

The fame of Menippus was such that in 1639–41 Velazquez painted a "portrait" of him, in the guise of an older, bearded man with hat, high boots and great black coat. He is half turned towards his viewers, and one's gaze is drawn inevitably to the bright, twin-kling eye that seems friendly, distant, quizzical, sardonic, sympathetic and knowing, all at once. Scattered on the floor around his feet are a book, some manuscripts and a jug of water. Velazquez's *Menippus*, along with his *Aesop* were partly intended (like his other portraits of court buffoons and peasants) to remind the Spanish king of the wisdom of the common people. Turning to literature again, the title of Swift's *Tale of a Tub* (1704) recalls Diogenes' *pithos*, and his *Gulliver's Travels* (1726) has been called a "Menippean satire" by the literary critic Northrop Frye (1957: 311–12), who makes "anatomy" (i.e. Menippean satire) one of the four basic literary genres.[8] Other examples of this sort of fantastical, allegorical satire include works such as Rabelais's *Gargantua and Pantagruel* (1532), Fielding's *The History of Tom Jones, a Foundling* (1749), Williams Blake's *An Island in the Moon* (1784), Lewis Carroll's *Alice's Adventures in Wonderland* (1865) and James Joyce's *Finnegans Wake* (1939). Similarly, Mikhail Bakhtin's *The Dialogic Imagination* (1975) detects in ancient Menippean satires a carnivalesque blending of voices that was the first ancestor of the modern, polyphonic novel. Bakhtin's important and suggestive ideas are still influential today, but when "Menippean" satire is detected in works from Chaucer to Kierkegaard, Pynchon, Joyce and Monty Python, one begins to suspect that the notion is being stretched rather far. Certainly, the link with ancient Cynicism has grown very tenuous.

In Shakespeare's *King Lear*, however, one finds a play that is strongly Cynic in orientation, in the ancient sense, as if Shakespeare had deepened the Renaissance fascination with Diogenes and Crates into something far more profound than the typical bandying of praise and blame. Many Cynics tropes appear in *King Lear*: the harmful conventions of dowries and courtly forms; the needlessness of luxury and the simplicity of nature; the ambitious flatterer and truth-telling fool; the nature of kingship, the fate of tyrants and the nakedness of man. The play begins in the company of "gentles" as Goneril and Regan pay their courtly flatteries to Lear and are rewarded richly. Cordelia, by contrast, speaks the truth simply, and is cursed, sent into exile, with just truth as her dowry. As a Cynic might comment, the desire for wealth is here the "mother-city of evils" and from it the tragedy unfolds. Lear cannot forgo his kingly honours. His daughters progressively strip him of his knights and privileges, eventually pushing him out of the house altogether. All but exiled from "civilization", the king stands on the heath during the storm, alone apart from his fool and a stray madman. They creep about looking for a hovel, but Lear in his madness cries defiance at the heavens and at fate. If falling rain is "nature", then external nature cannot be unkind, ungrateful or evil: evil belongs only to the world of human convention and falseness. Therefore he shouts at the storm:

> Rumble thy bellyful! Spit, fire! spout, rain!
> Nor rain, wind, thunder, fire, are my daughters:
> I tax not you, you elements, with unkindness;
> I never gave you kingdom, call'd you children,
> You owe me no subscription: then let fall
> Your horrible pleasure: here I stand, your slave,
> A poor, infirm, weak, and despis'd old man.
>
> (*King Lear* III.ii)

And yet in this despair, his "wits begin to turn". He begins to take an interest in mad Tom (Edgar), whom he questions as a "noble philosopher" and "my philosopher". In fact, he addresses Tom as "good Athenian" and "learned Theban", as if he were speaking with Diogenes or Crates. "What is the cause of thunder?" he asks him but Tom does not reply. "What is your study?", Lear enquires again and seems satisfied when Tom says that he knows "how to prevent the fiend and kill vermin". It is this same Tom who points out, again in Cynic fashion, that "the prince of darkness is a gentleman". Lear too has had enough of gentlemen now. Looking on Tom as the true human being, he is overcome with realization and tears off his clothes in a final act of renunciation:

> Is man no more than this? Consider him well. Thou owest
> the worm no silk, the beast no hide, the sheep no wool,
> the cat no perfume. Ha! Here's three on 's are sophisticated!
> Thou art the thing itself: unaccommodated man is no more
> but such a poor bare, forked animal as thou art. Off, off, you
> lendings! Come, unbutton here.   (III.iv)

He is a broken, half-naked old man; fortune has flung Lear down from the highest heights. And yet, it is in his fall and "exile" that Lear regains his humanity; in his madness, he begins to understand properly. No longer the aloof, arrogant king, he learns a little *philanthrōpia* and delight in elemental things:

> Come on, my boy: how dost, my boy? art cold?
> I am cold myself. Where is this straw, my fellow?
> The art of our necessities is strange,
> That can make vile things precious.   (III.ii)

So Lear learns to love his fool, his bit of food and straw, his Cordelia, his remaining years of life. Now the show of power and wealth are hateful to him. When a farmer's dog barks at a beggar, he says bitterly, "There thou mightst behold the great image of authority: a dog's obeyed in office" (IV.vi).

The Enlightenment, Rousseau and Nietzsche

It is a terrible knowledge that Lear gains, and he gains it through exile, dishonour, loss and the *ponos* of physical hardship: a Cynic's education. When one turns from such thoughts to the jaunty confidence of Enlightenment authors, the contrast can be stark. The Enlightenment motto was *sapere aude*, "dare to know", and a favourite image to complement this brave saying was the image of Diogenes in the marketplace, with his lantern at noon. Light symbolizes knowledge and truth, of course, and in their typical simplifications, Enlightenment polemicists often castigate past generations for not consulting the "natural light of reason", which so brightly illuminates the natural and social worlds. The Enlightenment Diogenes, on the other hand, carries his lantern into the marketplace: he tests ideas by the evidence; he is not daunted by kings, priests, and the guardians of age-old prejudice; he exposes theological humbug and unjustified feudal privilege; he is a hero of Reason; he dares to know, and he dares to tell the truth to people who do not want to know. So Cynic *parrhēsia* was adapted to the agenda of a new age.

Part of the attraction of Diogenes may be that he seemed incompatible with medieval Christianity and hierarchical organizations. Plato and Aristotle had been long associated with Augustinian and Thomistic thought, and with the Church and establishment generally. Their brand of philosophy, with its Ideas and entelechies and primary substances, seemed irremediably tainted by an irrational mysticism that could only favour priestly castes. Diogenes, on the other hand, by mocking Plato's Ideas and recognizing only the testimony of his senses, seemed a sensible, worldly empiricist, an ancestor of Locke, and therefore an appropriate symbol for a new, rational era. Moreover, as political opinion began to drift towards notions of republicanism and popular rule, Diogenes might be taken up as a champion of rational egalitarianism. Nobody is king by birth or divine right. Liberty, equality and the rights of man are as plain as noonday for those who consult "the natural light of reason". Therefore, Diogenes commanding Alexander not to block the sun becomes a potent image of the *philosophes* clearing away the darkness of the *corvée* and other irrational feudal relics. Important authors who explore these and other ideas with explicit reference to Cynicism include the German Christoph Martin Wieland (1733–1813) especially in *The Mad Socrates; or, the Dialoges of Diogenes of Sinope* and *The Private Life of Peregrinus Proteus, the Philosopher*; and the French Denis Diderot (1713–84) whose *Rameau's Nephew* stars a cynical courtier entertaining his interlocutor with a wide-ranging rant in which life is presented as a pantomime where everyone puts on different masks for different occasions, angling for favours from this patron or that.[9]

The "Rameau" who in Diderot is the genius uncle to his cynical nephew may well be modelled on Jean-Jacques Rousseau (1712–78), who was known to Diderot and other contemporaries as "the modern Diogenes". Rousseau himself rarely mentions the Cynics, whom he passes by for the more patriotic virtues of the Spartans and Romans, as in Plutarch's *Lives*. But so eloquently did he criticize human artifice and praise natural goodness in his prize-winning *Discourse on the Arts and Sciences* (1749) that he gained a new reputation almost overnight. According to his sometime friend Friedrich-Melchior Baron von Grimm:

> Up to that point he was a man of compliments, courteous, well-mannered, sweet as honey in his demeanour, and through the use of mannered idioms he became almost tiresome. Suddenly, however, he cloaked himself in the coat of the Cynic and fell into the other extreme …
>
> (quoted in Niehues-Pröbsting 1996: 341)

Rousseau may even have played the Diogenes by missing a meeting with King Louis XV and snubbing royal offers of advancement. Throughout his life, he would be admired as a modern Diogenes, or mocked for it, as when Voltaire vilifies him as "Diogenes' dog bastard" and "Diogenes' monkey". His writings, particularly the two *Discourses*, did advocate a return to Cynic-like values. In the first, the arts, sciences and all the products of a "higher" culture only corrupt people, making them weak, vain, selfish and altogether contemptible in comparison with "primitive" peoples such as the ancient Persians, Scythians or early Romans. In the *Discourse on the Origin of Inequality* (1755), the desire for wealth becomes the root of evil. The first, natural peoples were free, equal, satisfied with their lot, sympathetic towards each other and filled with pity, the basic moral emotion. But when objects first came to be called "mine", then the trouble began: the desire for acquisition grew to a rage, spawning metallurgy, money, wars. Some grew rich, others poor. Governments were instituted, laws passed and soldiers armed, and all to maintain the "haves" in their superiority over the "have-nots". Now the system has become so powerful, Rousseau argues, that nobody lives on the basis of a natural "love of self", but everyone is distracted by *amour propre*, the desire to be honoured and admired by others. It is indeed then in quasi-Cynic fashion that Rousseau seeks to overcome this, praising simplicity over false complexity, nature over culture, instinct over erudition, passion over reason, and authentic spontaneity over calculated self-interest. Very much in the style of an ancient Cynic mocking the Games, Rousseau attacked the theatre in Geneva as a symbol of civilized perversity: better the clean Swiss mountains than the filth of Paris.

Rousseau was also one of the few authors who could awaken Kant from his "dogmatic slumbers".[10] Immanuel Kant (1724–1804) in most ways occupies the antipodes of the typical Cynic: a Pietist-raised professor who spent his life amid books and lectures, regulating his hours with a famous punctuality, and infamously obeying when King Frederick William II ordered him to stop writing publicly about religious matters, his books are known for their dense, technical style. And yet, the Kantian ethics of rational duty bears the impress of the Stoics, and thus, indirectly, of the Cynics. For Kant, natural events are mere phenomena without moral significance, just as for the Stoics they are "indifferent": neither good nor evil. "There is nothing absolutely good in this world, and perhaps out of it, except the good will": the opening salvo of Kant's *Fundamental Principles of the Metaphysics of Morals* has its analogue in *the* central Stoic tenet that there is nothing truly good except virtue, which (as for Kant) is the outward expression of a pure moral reason. But behind Kant's dichotomy between natural phenomena (conceived mechanically) and the moral will, and behind the Stoic dichotomy between the external and the internal, lies the similar dichotomy of the Cynics between fortune and the self. Thus, broadly speaking, the Kantian framework of moral autonomy ultimately echoes the Cynics' elevation of the sage, with his self-sufficient will, over the heteronomous claims of *Tychē*.

In a more distant way, Cynic scepticism regarding metaphysical idealism can be seen as a remote ancestor of the modern reaction against medieval scholasticism that culminates in Kant's three *Critiques*. In the Cynics' legendary mockery of Platonic Ideas can be found, in seed form, something of that stress on the subjective ego that would become the focus of so much modern thought. "*I* think, therefore *I* am", concludes Descartes in his foundational statement, and modern thinking typically begins with subjective reflections: reflection on method, reflection on the mind's capacities and limitations, reflection on the mind's conceptual transformation of a common external world. Cynic scepticism regarding intellectual speculation resonates distantly in the modern stress on the limitations of human perspectives. David Hume and Kant in particular warn against transgressing these limits and entering an arena of metaphysical wrangling: asking questions that cannot be answered, concerning God's existence, the soul's fate, the world's infinity or boundedness and the like. Hume would commit such discussions "to the flames" ([1748] 1972: 165), and while not quite so incendiary, Kant too is severely critical. This trend recalls aspects of the Cynics' scorn for traditional religion, the Mysteries, the Academy, Lyceum and the like. In fact, at crucial moments, Kant actually repeats one of these Cynic anecdotes. In his *Inaugural Address* (1770), Kant alludes to Lucian's *Demonax* where the Cynic compares two wrangling sophists to goat-milkers and sieve-holders:

> Philosophers therefore discuss every form of idle question regarding the locations in the corporeal universe of substances that are immaterial – and of which for that very reason there can be no sensuous intuition nor any possible

spatial representation – or regarding the seat of the soul, and the like. And since the sensuous mixes with the intellectual about as badly as square with round, it frequently happens that the one disputant appears holding a sieve into which the other milks a he-goat.

(Quoted in Kemp Smith 1918: 159–60, trans. Eckoff)

The *Address* inaugurates Kant's "Critical Period", and in it may be anticipations of his characteristic distinction between phenomena and organizing categories, which he would develop fully in the *Critique of Pure Reason*. Indeed, in that *Critique*, he quotes Demonax's similes again with approval, and as if they represented "the ancients" at their best (A58–62/B83–6). These quotations are significant in illustrating how Cynic subjectivism could be used as one ally in the formulation of a modern, human-centred philosophy. In Kant and his ilk, the human self remains inescapably at the centre of its own physical and moral universe, even as it strains to expand that universe. This ultimately secular vision would be developed in one direction by Nietzsche, an author who more than most returned to ancient sources for his modern, yet quasi-Cynic, philosophy.

Nietzsche (1844–1900) first worked as a classical philologist before retiring to nurse his fragile health and focus on his own ideas. An interest in Cynicism spanned his life both before and after this retirement. In his first book as a young professor, *The Birth of Tragedy* (1872), he alludes to Menippean satire and how the Cynic writers adopted a medley of styles. The lack of a consistent style is for the young Nietzsche a proof of the Cynics' Hellenistic "decadence", which he detects and condemns in philosophical literature as early as the Platonic dialogues. In many of his later books, however, Nietzsche himself adopted the "decadent" style, and preferred before all "scientific" treatises a mode of expression that, like the extant Cynic corpus, is distinguished by creative experiment, a plurality of voices and personas (or "masks"), and a variety of rhetorical styles, including anecdotes, aphorisms, riddles, pointed questions, witty answers and polemical "diatribes", as well as paragraphs that trail off like ancient fragments, unfinished but enigmatically suggestive.

One of Nietzsche's reasons for renouncing the grave tones of a nineteenth-century *Professor der klassischen Altertumswissenschaft* was philosophical. Renouncing the cult of "scientific results" just as much as Diogenes had protested against Platonic Ideas, Nietzsche required a fluid mode of expression commensurate with a philosophy of Becoming and his new gospel of "Dionysus".

If "style is the man", then still other aspects of Nietzsche's lifestyle reveal him as a Diogenes of sorts. On retirement from academic life due to health problems, Nietzsche had no further paid employment, lived modestly on a small pension and had no fixed abode, but stayed for a season now in Sils-Maria, now Genoa, now Rapallo, now Nice, now Turin, ever wandering from room to rented room, with his correspondence, his notes, a few books and almost no friends. Thus "exile" – from the Academy, from citizenship in any one country, from the surrounding Christian culture – "made him a philosopher". It also made him a cosmopolitan, or as he would style himself, a "good European". Like Cynic "cosmopolitans" who avoided normal politics yet styled themselves "kings", Nietzsche hated the rising social democratic movements that were dragging the masses into politics, spawning journalists, newspaper readers, politicians and other contemptible little "last men". Yet at the same time, this apolitical Nietzsche yearned for an age of "great politics" (*Größe Politik*) with great passions, great ideas, great leaders more magnificent even than Caesar or Napoleon, and great wars that would dwarf the conflicts of the past. This last idea takes Nietzsche well beyond the ancient Cynics, who deplored the foolishness of war, yet it does represent Nietzsche's extrapolation from that other great theme of Cynicism, *askēsis*. Nietzsche was hard on himself, his students and readers, convinced that there is nothing great without asceticism, suffering, "a little bit of the tub" (*Human, All Too Human*: "Preface", §5). And so in one exhortation to himself and his future disciples, Nietzsche cries, "Let us remain hard, we latest Stoics" (*Beyond Good and Evil*: §227). Slightly more humorous is his parable in which the diamond says to the coal: "my brother, you must become *hard*, for all creatures are hard" (*Thus Spoke Zarathustra*: III.29 and *Twilight of the Idols*: "The Hammer Speaks", adapted by author).

These and other quasi-Cynic moments in Nietzsche's life should be understood from the following vantage point. Like the Cynics, Nietzsche avoided academic, systematic philosophy for a more chaotic, inspirational approach, convinced that it is only when one has "chaos in one's soul" that one can "give birth to a dancing star" (*Thus Spoke Zarathustra*: "Prologue", §5): what is important for both Nietzsche and the Cynics is not ideas and the relations between ideas purely in themselves, but the interplay between ideas and character: ideas shaping the ethos of a civilization, for instance, or a single forceful personality forging world-historical and even seemingly "necessary" ideas. Thus Nietzsche rejects a Platonic realm of Ideas as firmly as did Diogenes. But while Diogenes stressed ethical ideas such as self-sufficiency, the inspirational ideas to which Nietzsche returns often in his intellectual wanderings have a wider range. They include tragic being, the Dionysian, the redemption of life through art, free creativity, the revaluation of values, self-mastery, the *Übermensch*, will-to-power, the death of God, eternal recurrence and love of fate (*amor fati*).

Some of these do have a definite Cynic tinge. Certain individual Nietzschean virtues parallel Cynic ones: personal sovereignty resembles Cynic self-sufficiency and kingship, honesty (*Redlichkeit*) *parrhēsia*, and wickedness (*Bösheit*) shamelessness. More generally, it has been suggested that Nietzsche's demand for a "revaluation of values" (*Umwertung aller Werte*) was directly inspired by the Cynic motto, *paracharattein to nomisma*; like the Cynic replacing *nomos* with nature, the Nietzschean philosopher smashes conventional "idols" in order to set up his new gods and tablets of laws. To promote this ideally destructive–creative philosophy, Nietzsche sought to educate a new aristocracy of radical free-thinkers: "free, *very* free spirits", who, like the Cynics, would have the courage to question all conventional notions of good and evil, including even "indubitable" standards of what is natural, true, and possible. Thus Cynic scepticism is a necessary step towards any new order: "The modern Diogenes. – Before one seeks a human being, one must have found the lantern. Will it have to be the lantern of the cynic?" (*The Wanderer and his Shadow*: §18).

The sceptical "enlightenment" of a modern Diogenes can easily lead to despair, yet Nietzsche hopes that his free spirits will retain the strength to affirm themselves "beyond good and evil", even when all else melts away. Beyond all *nomoi*, these heroic philosophers will live according to their *own* nature, that is, their own indomitable will. Such wills necessarily adopt many masks, and so Nietzsche speaks of them variously as aristocrats, law-givers, heroes, warriors, prophets, priests, Dionysian artists and creators, cosmic dancers: a variety of names that might recall the diversity of Cynic self-descriptions as "kings", "spies", "benefactors" and the like. Nietzsche's vision is indeed a regal one; his noble followers will master their fluctuating thoughts and will to "love fate" to such an extent that they will be able to transform external contingencies into expressions of their own will. This is the final triumph of the will. Nothing remains that is really transcendent: no nature alien to one's own will, no eternal realm, no God or universal truths grounding "objective" facts and values. The Eleatic and Platonic visions of Being are only beautiful dreams, for what is truly real is the will-to-power, which strives for ever more effective, subtle forms of mastery. This is a tragic wisdom but the more one learns it through suffering, the more one may transform it into something blissful. Tragedy is followed by satyr play, then comedy: transcending illusions of an abiding Being, one regains the "innocence of becoming" and becomes like a child at play. Like a Cynic, one can laugh again, and at everything. Or, like Diogenes, one steps into the sunshine; strong enough to reject the gifts of an Alexander, Plato or Christ, one learns to delight in this moment. Thus, in many complex ways, Nietzsche would find much significance in the anecdote of Diogenes and Alexander. Diogenes *was* greater than Alexander the Great: "the highest one can reach on earth [is] Cynicism".[11]

In particular, the highest one can reach (Nietzsche concludes) is *not* holiness or godliness in a Christian sense. Nietzsche is one of the great religious sceptics of modernity, and, like Julian the Apostate trying to enrol Cynics in his war against "the Galilaeans", so Nietzsche can sometimes use Cynicism to rant against the Christian heritage and its Platonic background. In the most important of these moments, Nietzsche revives the ancient *chreia* of Diogenes and his lantern. As for Enlightenment thinkers, this Diogenes dares to know and to bring the highest knowledge to the people. But this knowledge now involves a terrible, tragic wisdom. "God is dead", says Nietzsche's Diogenes, and nothing can stay the same afterwards:

> *The madman.* – Have you not heard of that madman who lit a lantern in the bright morning hours, ran to the market place, and cried incessantly: "I seek God! I seek God!" – As many of those who did not believe in God were standing around just then, he provoked much laughter. Has he got lost? asked one. Did he lose his way like a child? asked another. Or is he hiding? Is he afraid of us? Has he gone on a voyage? Emigrated? – Thus they yelled and laughed. The madman jumped into their midst and pierced them with his eyes. "Whither is God?" he cried. "I will tell you. *We have killed him*—you and I! All of us are his murderers! But how did we do this? How could we drink up the sea? Who gave us the sponge to wipe away the entire horizon? What were we doing when we unchained this earth from its sun? Whither is it moving now? Whither are we moving? Away from all suns? Are we not plunging continually? Backward, sideward, forward, in all directions? Is there still any up or down? Are we not straying as through an infinite nothing? Do we not feel the breath of empty space? Has it not become colder? Is not night continually closing in on us? Do we not need to light lanterns in the morning?"
>
> (*The Gay Science*: §125; trans. Kaufman)

The "madman" is clearly reminiscent of Diogenes, the "mad Socrates", who went into the marketplace when it was fullest (i.e. in the late morning, the "bright morning hours"). But there are significant changes: Nietzsche's Diogenes does not seek "a human being" or "an honest man", but God. The ancient anecdote is extremely short and does not discuss Diogenes' motivations or the spectators' reactions. Nietzsche's madman speaks at length, and is mocked by the onlookers, who (we are told) have already dismissed God, because in their "wretched self-complacency" (*erbärmliches Behagen*) they do not have the greatness of spirit to seek him. The madness of this "Diogenes" is thus not a truly divine madness, yet for Nietzsche it *is* the "highest thing on earth": most follow the lazy crowd, but the madman is restless and creative enough to seek something beyond all human constructs. And the madman does find God, if only the "god within", the will that is fragmented through all things, "Dionysus" that surges forth in every new growth, driving the cosmic chaos into fleeting forms of partial unity. Nietzsche's Zarathustra will revisit this revelation, with some significant additions. In *Thus Spoke Zarathustra*, Zarathustra wanders highest up the mountain. He wanders higher even than the holy hermit, and in those solitary heights, he learns to seek God no longer. He learns instead of the need to "love mankind" (*Thus Spoke Zarathustra*: "Prologue", §2) and so he descends the mountain and wanders from city to city in the spirit of *philanthrōpia*, preaching the truth to a reluctant humanity.

The twentieth century and beyond

Nietzsche cast a long shadow over his philosophical successors and ideas such as his death of God reverberate still. A number of post-modern thinkers have followed Nietzsche in looking to the ancient Cynics as a means of overcoming modern pessimism and loss of faith in Christ and in other "grand narratives" such as the Enlightenment myth of scientific progress, the nationalist myth of a happy, self-contained *Volk*, the Marxist myth of a proletarian utopia, the capitalist myth of a consumerist utopia, and so forth. For postmodern thinkers, there is no centre: no longer are the nation, the Church or God central sources of authority and purpose. In a pluralist, cosmopolitan world, individuals are thrown more on their own resources. The times thus partly recall the Hellenistic period, when the city-state (nation) and its traditions faded in importance, when more people wandered between cities, kingdoms and cultures, and yet before Rome or Christ became the new, dominant law-giver. In such a postmodern culture, it is interesting to see various writers attempting to revive the optimism of ancient Cynicism, or, like Lucian, to dig Menippus up from the grave. Two of these authors who we can touch on only briefly are Peter Sloterdijk and Luis Navia.

In 1983 Sloterdijk published his *Critique of Cynical Reason*, which has become a philosophical bestseller. The title itself is a parody of Kant's *Critique of Pure Reason* and *Critique of Practical Reason*, those monumental tomes of "high" philosophy. Sloterdijk's own critique is of the technocratic, imperialistic and other utilitarian mentalities that treat reason merely as a means to satisfy an array of ignoble passions. Before this harsh, Nietzschean deconstruction, the various grand narratives from both before and after the Enlightenment have been exposed as so many ideological ploys for self-promotion. The result is a general pessimism: *all* grand-narratives, it is felt, are suspect. What can one do? Most endure quietly while the ambitious cynically create new narratives for their own ends, in the conviction that all is will-to-power. In both cases, "cynicism" is at work, defined by Sloterdijk as "enlightened false consciousness" (1987: 5–6) for the cynic knows (is "enlightened") that reigning ideals are contingent and subjective, yet goes on acting according to them regardless ("false consciousness"). The result is internal division, unhappiness, hypocrisy and malaise. Worse, it threatens a return to the sort of totalitarian systems that so idolized the Will, and welcomed any means to a willed end. Cynicism is now dominant in Western life, Sloterdijk concludes after analysing a huge range of cultural phenomena, yet before the gathering gloom, he does not himself despair. All is not lost! There is a saviour for our cynical, disillusioned time and Sloterdijk hails him, not as Plato, Epicurus, Jesus, Nietzsche, Prometheus or Edison (twin torch-bearers for the goddess Technology) but as Diogenes. We must relearn the "lost cheekiness" of the ancient Cynics, Sloterdijk argues. They did not argue with tyrants, but laughed, danced capers and farted at all self-appointed authorities. Such elemental glee and irrepressible laughter cannot be spun into a sinister, grand narrative because it is non-verbal and transcends narrative *per se*. Indeed, it deflates the pretensions of all such narratives in many ways, not least because it points to that which cannot be consciously systematized. The Cynics were thus the perfect rebels: they had no cause because they knew that today's "cause" becomes tomorrow's orthodoxy. They simply startled people back to the body and delight in the present moment, knowing that in the end, before Ideas, creed, party and fatherland, these alone are the real things.[12]

These and other themes return in different modulations with our final modern "Cynic". Navia is one of the leading scholars of ancient Cynicism, yet for all their wide-ranging and detailed scholarship, his writings are not simply academic, but glow with the passionate conviction of a believer. Ancient Cynicism is not for Navia an object of "scientific" curiosity only. It is important for him as the closest approximation to the true ethical philosophy, and the salutary outlook that we in our technological culture now need most. One idea that surfaces regularly in Navia's work is the fear that contemporary human beings have become too dependent – on a system that creates and then panders to unnecessary desires and that increasingly establishes itself as the sole reality. Worse, this system of endless acquisition and consumption harbours terrible violence, both to the natural environment whose dwindling resources support it, and to human beings who are progressively dehumanized, continuously pumped with ideas, beliefs and desires from the outside, and blinded by the swirling *typhos* of media images, advertisements, plastic celebrities and political cant. The only solution is to wage "war" on this system, like an Antisthenes or Diogenes, and thus not in the spirit of mere renunciation. For Navia, the true Cynic criticizes out of a deep moral idealism, and the interpretation of ancient Cynicism as wholly negative is itself a sad reflection on our own moral impoverishment. We have, Navia argues through his scholarship, taken too little thought of the wisdom of the ancient Cynics: live simply, scorn unnecessary desires, do not follow the slavish crowd but speak the truth clearly in righteous war against untruth and, most of all, cultivate the virtue of *philanthrōpia* and learn to love others now, for it is from this that everything else will follow.

Glossary of names

This list is selective. Further information can be found in the *Oxford Classical Dictionary* or the French-language *Dictionnaire des Philosophes Antiques* (Goulet 1994).

Agathobulus of Alexandria (second century CE), famous Cynic who wrote nothing but "taught" Peregrinus, Demonax, and others.

Antisthenes (*c.*445–*c.*365 BCE), half-Athenian teacher of rhetoric, Socratic and possible "founder" of Cynicism, who wrote widely, admired Socrates greatly and may have known Diogenes.

Aristotle of Stagira (384–322 BCE), student of Plato, tutor to Alexander the Great and "Peripatetic" thinker. He founded the Lyceum. He was a contemporary of Diogenes, to whom he seems to refer by his nickname, "the Dog" (*Rh.* 3.10.7). His intellectual philosophy, which makes citizenship in a Greek-style *polis* the highest ethical goal, is often contrasted with Cynic ideas.

Bion of Borysthenes (*c.*335–245 BCE), "many-coloured sophist" who lived a varied life and who studied various philosophies at Athens, including Cynicism. His name is traditionally associated with the satirical "diatribe".

Cercidas of Megalopolis (*c.*290–220 BCE), politician, general and Cynic poet, who invented the meliambic metre and advocated wealth redistribution in vituperative verse.

Crates of Thebes (*c.*360–280 BCE), follower of Diogenes, husband of Hipparchia, teacher of Zeno of Citium and others, and imaginative writer (e.g. of *Pēra*, "Praise of Lentil Soup" and "Hymn to Frugality"). He was nicknamed the "Door-Opener" and is often associated with Cynic *philanthrōpia*.

Demetrius of Corinth (first century CE), lived in Rome as a vocal critic of Caligula, Nero and Vespasian. Exiled in 66 CE after the Pisonian conspiracy (owing to his close friendship with Thrasea Paetus and other members of the "Stoic Opposition"), he defended Egnatius Celer in 70, and was exiled again in 71 by Vespasian. He was the "teacher" of Demonax and was greatly admired by Seneca.

Democritus of Abdera (*c*.460–370 BCE), influential atomist, who is said to have written as widely as Aristotle, but whose works are now fragmentary. His physics were adopted by Epicurus while his ethical fragments have been compared to Cynic ideas, with their praise of *ponos* and *autarkeia*, for instance. Democritus became typecast in later antiquity and especially the Renaissance, as the "laughing philosopher", who (like a Cynic) laughed at the follies of mankind and who had a "twin" in Heraclitus, the "weeping philosopher".

Demonax of Cyprus (*c*.70–170 CE), "student" of Agathobulus, Demetrius, Epictetus and Timocrates, who spent his life in Athens as a public character beloved by the people, and by Lucian, who wrote an almost hagiographical biography of him.

Dio Chrysostom ("the golden-mouthed") of Prusa (*c*.40–112 CE), accomplished orator of the so-called Second Sophistic, who led a wandering, seemingly Cynic life from 82–96 CE after his banishment by the emperor Domitian and before his pardon by Nerva. Thereafter he returned to the public eye, giving speeches in cities across the Greek East and perhaps delivering his four kingship orations to Trajan.

Diogenes Laertius (unknown, perhaps *c*.200 CE), doxographer and writer of *Lives of Philosophers*, in ten books. Book 6 is dedicated to Cynics (Antisthenes, Diogenes, Monimus, Onesicritus, Crates, Metrocles, Hipparchia, Menippus, Menedemus) and Book 7 to Stoics (beginning with Zeno). Bion is classified with the Academics in Book 4 (DL 4.46–58). Despite his reputation as an uncritical compiler of information both useful and useless, he is the single most important source for our knowledge of the Cynics.

Diogenes of Sinope (*c*.412–*c*.323 BCE), son of the banker Hicesias. He left Sinope perhaps owing to financial irregularities (did he or his father deface the city's coins?), moved to mainland Greece and quickly became a legend, nicknamed "the Dog", the quintessence of ancient Cynicism. Many stories are associated with him through antiquity, some of which must have some kernel of historical truth: that he lived sometimes in a *pithos*, that he threw away his last cup, that he masturbated in public, that he refused Alexander's gifts, that he was captured by pirates and sold as a slave to Xeniades of Corinth, and so forth. Notable followers were Crates, Onesicritus and Monimus.

Epictetus of Hierapolis (*c*.55–135 CE), freed slave, pupil of Musonius Rufus, exiled from Italy in 94 CE. He established his own school in Nicopolis, where he became respected as one of the great teachers of Stoicism. His quasi-Cynic ideal is expressed in *Discourses* 3.22.

Epicurus (341–271 BCE), founder of Epicureanism, the main ancient school of hedonism, and a perennial rival to the Stoics. Epicurus recommended simplicity of lifestyle and self-sufficiency as a way to banish pain, but perhaps to discourage any potentially embarrassing comparisons with Cynic equivalents, he denigrated the Cynics as "enemies of Hellas" (DL 10.8) and demanded that the philosopher "not turn dog" (*kyniein*, DL 10.119).

Gorgias of Leontini (*c*.485–380 BCE), one of the greatest Sophists, who mesmerized the Athenians with his rhetoric in 427 BCE, and who was perhaps the teacher of a Callicles (who advocates "might is right" in Plato's *Gorgias*), and of Antisthenes.

Heracles (legendary), son of Zeus and Alcmena, greatest of the Greek heroes, who outwrestled the Nemean Lion, shot down the Stymphalian Birds, retrieved Cerberus from Hades, took Hippolyta's girdle, cleaned the Augean Stables, and completed other celebrated *ponoi* and *aethla*, which he endured at the command of the tyrant Eurystheus and for which he was rewarded immortality. For the hardships he endured voluntarily for mankind, he was adopted by the Cynics (and Stoics) as *the* exemplar of philosophical fortitude, self-sufficiency, voluntary asceticism and *philanthrōpia*. Peregrinus compared his death with that of Heracles, who is said to have died on a pyre on Mount Oeta.

Hipparchia of Maroneia (fourth century BCE), sister of Metrocles, who overcame family objections to marry her beloved Crates, with whom she shared everything. She was famous through antiquity for this "dog-marriage" and for her astonishing free-spiritedness.

Julian "the Apostate" Emperor (331–63 CE; emperor 361–63), a member of the Constantine clan who rejected their Christianity and as emperor laboured to restore pagan religion to dominance. Cynicism forms one part of this essentially Neoplatonic programme and so Julian dedicates two orations (6, 7) to his views of the true nature of Cynicism.

Lucian of Samosata (*c*.120–185 CE), writer of the so-called Second Sophistic, best known for his satiric dialogues, which mix comedy and philosophy (e.g. *Sale of Lives*). He was an admirer of "good" Cynics such as Diogenes, Menippus and Demonax, but the implacable satirist of "bad" contemporary Cynics such as Peregrinus and Theagenes.

Marcus Aurelius (121–80 CE; emperor 161–80), Stoic and last of the "Good Emperors", a philosopher-king whose *Meditations* (in Greek) reveal his admiration for certain Cynics as well as ideals such as *ponos*, *autarkeia*, *parrhēsia* and cosmopolitanism.

Maximus Hero of Alexandria (fourth century CE), one of the very few who was both Cynic and Christian. He was a sometime friend of St Gregory of Nazianzus but schemed to be crowned bishop of Constantinople briefly in 380 CE.

Meleager of Gadara (*c*.135–50 BCE), fellow citizen of Menippus and Oenomaus, composer of Cynic satires (included the "Comparison of Pea- and Lentil-Soup") and of many epigrams, which he included in his famous "Garland" or anthology.

Menippus of Gadara (first half of third century BCE), travelled from his native Syria to Athens where he met Crates. Little is known of his life or work, but the *Sale of Diogenes*, *Symposium*, *Nekyia* and many other works attributed to him would make him one of the most famous and influential Cynic writers. He is often seen as champion of the "serious-funny" style (*to spoudogeloion*), which Lucian loved, as "founder" of the prosi-metric "Menippean satire", which mixes prose and song, as in Seneca's *Apocolocyntosis*, Petronius' *Satyricon*, Boethius' *Consolation of Philosophy*, and many others.

Metrocles of Maroneia (fourth and third centuries BCE), brother of Hipparchia, follower of Crates after unsuccessful stints in the Theophrastus' Lyceum and Xenocrates' Academy.

Monimus of Syracuse (fourth century BCE), slave of a Corinthian banker who "converted" to Cynicism when he heard reports about Diogenes; he started throwing money around his master's table in the marketplace, and was promptly dismissed as mad. He was celebrated for his serio-comic style (as in his "*Paignia* mixed with hidden seriousness"). One of his anti-intellectual sayings, "all conception is *typhos*", became widely quoted, as by Menander (DL 6.83) and Marcus Aurelius (*Med.* 2.15).

Oenomaus of Gadara (second century CE), fellow citizen of Menippus and Meleager, unsparing critic of the ancient oracles in his *Detection of Impostors*, which Eusebius quotes and Julian decries as anti-pagan propaganda.

Onesicritus of Astypalaea (*c*.380–305 BCE), an Aegean-islander who came to admire Diogenes in Athens, before marching East with Alexander and eventually becoming pilot of the royal flagship in India. He continued to admire Cynicism and wrote famously about his embassy to the Indian gymnosophists at Taxila in spring 326 BCE.

Parmeniscus (unknown), writer of *The Cynics' Symposium*, part of which is quoted in Athenaeus' *Deipnosophistae* (4.156c–157d).

Peregrinus of Parium (*c*.100–165 CE), nicknamed "Proteus" for his varied identity and experience: now wealthy citizen of Parium, now Christian leader in Palestine, now Cynic critic of Roman authorities, now imitator of Heracles, committing suicide at the Olympic Games in 165. He was hated by Lucian, whose *On the Death of Peregrinus* is nevertheless our main source of knowledge regarding this complex character.

Petronius, Gaius (first century CE), a little-known figure thought to be Nero's "director of elegance" (*arbiter elegantiae*) and admired now for his *Satyricon*, a "Menippean satire" whose most famous incident is the "Dinner of Trimalchio" (Chapters 26–78), a riotous affair in which one may discern quasi-Cynic elements.

Plato of Athens (*c*.429–347 BCE), reportedly descended from the early Athenian kings, admirer of Socrates, teacher of Aristotle, founder of the Academy and writer of hugely influential dialogues that draw creatively on many philosophical traditions, from Pythagoreanism to Democritus. In the tradition of Cynic *chreiai*, as an idealist, rival Socratic, lecture-giving sophist, flatterer of tyrants, and aristocrat, he is the greatest nemesis of Antisthenes and Diogenes, mocked by them for worrying about Ideas, for not growing his own vegetables, for courting the tyrant Dionysius, for wearing purple, keeping horses and other allegations (e.g. DL 6.7, 58).

Plutarch of Chaeronea (*c*.46–120 CE), influential Platonic philosopher, biographer, essayist, local magistrate and priest of Delphic Apollo, who wrote a lost life of fellow-Boeotian Crates and whose large corpus contains many incidental references to Cynics.

Sallustius of Emesa (late-fifth century CE), Syrian who associated with the Neoplatonist Isidore and is the last known Cynic of antiquity.

Seneca the Younger (*c.* 4 BCE–65 CE), Stoic philosopher, advisor to Nero, admirer of Demetrius and prolific author in whose *Epistulae Morales* and *De Beneficiis* especially can be found many incidental references to the Cynics.

Socrates of Athens (469–399 BCE), son of a sculptor and midwife, "gadfly" of Athens, and icon of philosophy itself, whose dialectical conversations inspired Plato, while his endurance and ascetic frugality impressed Antisthenes, and indirectly influenced later Cynics.

Teles of Megara (second half of third century BCE), Cynic writer who admired Bion above all, and an epitome of whose "diatribes" are anthologized in Stobaeus.

Theagenes of Patras (second century CE), Cynic follower of Peregrinus who accompanied his master to Rome, Elis and Olympia, where he pronounced Peregrinus' funeral oration.

Varro, Marcus Terentius (116–27 BCE), Roman polymath who, amid much else, wrote 150 "Menippean satires" (in Latin) for which he was sometimes called the "Roman Cynic".

Zeno of Citium (*c.*335–263 BCE), reportedly shipwrecked in Athens, where he became a follower of Crates mainly, before founding his own school of Stoicism, named after the "Painted Stoa" in which he liked to philosophize. With its dominant Cynic themes, his *Republic* was said to have been "written on the dog's tail".

Xeniades of Corinth, the man who in Cynic lore and literature is said to have bought Diogenes in a Cretan slave market. He made Diogenes the tutor to his sons, but Diogenes quickly became the *de facto* master. The (true?) incident inspired various books titled "Sale of Diogenes" by Menippus, Hermippus and Eubulus as well as Lucian's *Sale of Lives*.

Glossary of Greek terms

anaideia, shamelessness   The quality of a dog (the Greeks did not tend to praise dogs for loyalty or for being "man's best friend"), and of a Cynic, who does everything publicly, without embarrassment and without care for observers' opinions.

apatheia, lack of or freedom from passion (*pathos*)   The ideal state of the Stoic sage, a near-relative of Epicurean *ataraxia* (inner tranquillity) and of Cynic indifference to external events.

askēsis, training, exercise   For the Cynics it entailed ascetic practices such as sleeping rough, walking barefoot everywhere, enduring heat and cold, and generally living "according to nature" without any artificial aids.

autarkeia, literally "rule over oneself", hence self-sufficiency   The state of not needing anything external; a fundamental ideal of much ancient politics and ethics, and one goal of the Cynic life.

chreia (pl. chreiai), anecdote   Typically featuring an action and saying that together encapsulate the outlook of a famous person. Usually, a philosopher does something, says something, and the reader is left to meditate on the many-fold significance of it all, as with the *chreia* of Diogenes sunning himself and refusing Alexander's offer, or that of him walking into the crowded marketplace with a lamp, saying that he was "looking for a human being". The first known collection of *Chreiai* was by Demetrius of Phalerum (DL 5.81), while Metrocles was the first known to have collected Cynic *chreiai* in particular (DL 6.33). Zeno collected *chreiai* about his teacher Crates (DL 6.91, 7.4). One of the most popular of philosophical and rhetorical forms in later antiquity, the *chreia* makes a comeback in modern writers such as Nietzsche, who stress the interplay of ideas and personality in an authentic life.

diatribē, originally "a means of passing the time", hence (among the talkative Greeks) a conversation, or a philosophical conversation   Eventually it came to mean a feigned conversation in which the (e.g. Cynic) philosopher does all of the talking, asking and answering questions on behalf of an overawed or imaginary inter-locutor. Owing perhaps to Bion's works, it became one of the main literary styles of Cynicism: a sort of heated soliloquy on a stated topic, as the speaker poses questions and answers them in rapid fire, using short punchy sentences and the second-person singular to keep his hearers alert. Teles' fragments, Seneca's *Epistles* and Epictetus' *Discourses* offer examples of a lively "genre" that may recall Cynic street-preaching.

euteleia, frugality   A Cynic virtue about which Crates wrote an encomium and to attain which Diogenes threw away his last cup.

mempsimoiria, fault-finding or literally "blaming fate"   A captious and complaining disposition, often seen as the peculiar fault of luxury lovers. For Bion, this vice is to be avoided above all others (Fr. 16; cf. Kindstrand 1976: 210–11).

nomos (pl. *nomoi*), custom   A practice that becomes habitual in a society, as for example in customs of dress, food, etiquette, religious observance or political organization. Greek Sophists tend to contrast *nomos* and *physis* (nature), and often defend *physis* as a more compelling force and source of law and morals. The Cynics are even more radical critics of *nomoi*: rejecting most (Greek) customs as unnatural and corrupting, they gain a reputation for shamelessness (*anaideia*).

paracharattein to nomisma, to deface the coinage   What Diogenes' father Hecesias is reported to have done in Sinope, and what Diogenes and Cynics claimed to do metaphorically: putting the "coin" (*nomisma*) of custom (*nomos*) out of circula-tion.

paignion (pl. *paignia*), caprices, frolics or play-pieces   Pieces that take some surprising angle or theme, such as Crates' "Praise of Lentil Soup" and "Diary of a Profligate", Parmeniscus' *Cynics' Symposium*, Meleager's "Comparison of Pea and Lentil Soup", Monimus' "*Paignia* Mixed with Hidden Seriousness", Lucian's "Praise of a Fly", Dio's *Encomium of Hair*, Menander the Rhetor's "Praise of Poverty or of Proteus the Cynic", and so forth.

parrhēsia, freedom of speech   Associated first with the assemblies of classical democra-cies, where citizens had the right to speak openly and freely, it becomes one of the Cynic's virtues, as he fearlessly speaks his mind to all hearers, whether crowds or kings. Diogenes calls *parrhēsia* "mankind's most beautiful thing" (DL 6.69). The neo-Cynic Nietzsche often claims to be the only really "honest" philosopher, and the older Foucault admired Cynic *parrhēsiasts* for telling "the truth" to the powerful.

pēra, traveller's bag or sack   Part of the Cynic's typical garb, and the name that Crates gives to his utopia, because it contains no coins but only simple, natural things such as figs and thyme.

philodoxia, love of fame or honour   A standard charge against the Cynics (e.g. DL 6.8, 26, 41; Luc. *De mort. Peregr.* 38); Alexander the Great was sometimes taken as the epitome of it.

pithos, storage jar   The sort of large earthenware container (common in the ancient world) in which Diogenes was said to have lived for a time; often translated as "tub".

ponos, both "work" and "pain"   Related etymologically to the English "pain", it becomes the usual antonym to *hēdonē* (pleasure), and is used specifically by Cynics to describe their hard, ascetic life. Related words are *athlos*, *talaipōria* and *askēsis*.

philanthrōpia, love of mankind   An important Cynic virtue, exemplified by Crates, Demonax, Peregrinus and, later, Nietzsche's Zarathustra. As the true "king", the Cynic claims to promote the good of all mankind, but with his unsparing *parrhēsia* he can be a harsh benefactor, as if in the belief that sometimes one must be cruel to be kind.

spoudogeloion, the serious-funny or serio-comic   A jokey style that masks a serious intent. Aristophanes (the Athenian comic playwright) sometimes describes his work as *spoudogeloion*, and the approach was common to Socrates and Cynic writers such as Crates, Bion, Menippus and Meleager, as well as Cynic-influenced satirists like Lucian. Cf. *paignion*.

typhos, literally, "smoke, vapour"   Used by the Cynics to denote the delirium of popular ideas and conventions. For the Cynics, these are insubstantial "smoke" in comparison with the self and its present experiences, which alone can be known and possessed. One Cynic goal is *atyphia*, complete freedom from *typhos*.

Tychē, Fortune or Chance   Personified as a goddess, especially in the Hellenistic and Roman period, but not worshipped by the Cynics, who rejected her gifts (especially wealth, power and honours) as unpredictable, transient, unimportant and even harmful to one's self-sufficiency, virtue and happiness.

Notes

Introduction

1. It is possible to understand Cynicism as inspired by a single "ruling idea" and different scholars have stressed different ones. For J. F. Kindstrand it is negative freedom (*Bion of Borysthenes: A Collection of the Fragments with Introduction and Commentary* [Uppsala: Acta Universitatis Uppsalensis, 1976], 59–60); for D. Dawson it is *autarkeia* (*Cities of the Gods: Communist Utopias in Greek Thought* [Oxford: Oxford University Press, 1992], 145–6); for M.-O. Goulet-Cazé it is *askēsis* (*L'Ascèse Cynique: Un Commentaire de Diogène Laërce VI 70–71* [Paris: Vrin, 1986], esp. 17–92); and for me previously it was the critique of wealth (*The Greek Praise of Poverty: Origins of Ancient Cynicism* [Notre Dame, IN: University of Notre Dame Press, 2006]). Other studies focus on a plurality of ideas. A. A. Long isolates seven core Cynic "propositions", the first of which is what living "according to nature" brings ("Cynics", in *Encyclopaedia of Ethics*, L. C. Becker & C. B. Becker [eds], vol. 1, 234–6 [New York: Garland, 1992]); Goulet-Cazé looks at "liberty, autonomy, imperturbability, training to endure difficulties and ordeals of all sorts, the rejection of civilization and cosmopolitanism" (in M.-O. Goulet-Cazé & R. Goulet [eds], *Le Cynisme ancien et ses prolongements: Acts du Colloque International du CNRS* [Paris: Presses Universitaires de France, 1993], v); L. Paquet isolates "internal freedom, the spirit of liberty, frankness of speech, criticism of received opinions, the social order and of established power, flight from the world, return to nature, cosmopolitanism (*Les Cyniques grecs: Fragments et témoignages*, 2nd edn [Ottawa: Presses de l'Université d'Ottawa 1975], 11); while according to Navia, "Concepts such as 'a life lived according to nature', rationality, lucidity, self-sufficiency, disciplined asceticism, freedom of speech, shamelessness, indifference, cosmopolitanism, philanthropy, and others, permeate in varying degrees the Cynics' *Weltanschauung*, and constitute, as it were, the foundations of their philosophy" (*Classical Cynicism: A Critical Study* [Westport, CT: Greenwood Press, 1996], ix).

1. Ancient Cynics and their times

1. For phrases like this, see, for example, Luc. *Demon.* 19, 48; Origen *Contra Celsum* 7.7. Cf. Luc. *De mort. Pereg.* 15.4, *Fugitivi* 16; Jul. *Or.* 6.188b.
2. For Cynics in the countryside, see D. Chr. 7, Luc. *Demon.* 1 (Sostratus).
3. Cf. D. R. Dudley: "The period between the death of Vespasian and that of Marcus Aurelius saw Cynicism numerically far stronger than it had ever been before. The fact is reflected in the literature of the period, for the references to the Cynics appear in almost every author from Martial to Lucian" (*A History of Cynicism from Diogenes to the 6th Century AD* [Chicago, IL: Ares, (1937) 1980], 143); and R. MacMullen, *Enemies of the Roman Order: Treason, Unrest, and Alienation in the Empire* (Cambridge, MA: Harvard University Press, 1966), 59–60.
4. Cf. Dudley, *A History of Cynicism*, 95; M.-O. Goulet-Cazé, "Le Cynisme à l'époque impériale", *Aufstieg und Niedergang der römischen Welt* II **36**(4) (1990): 2720–833.
5. See, for example, DL 6.71; D. Chr. 1.59–84; ps.-Heraclitus *Ep.* 4; Luc. *Vit. auct.* 8; ps.-Luc. *Cyn.* 13; Jul. *Or.* 6.187c.
6. See, for example, D. Chr. 3.19, 32.88, 33.14–15 *et al.*, esp. 9.9; R. Höistad, *Cynic Hero and Cynic King: Studies in the Cynic Conception of Man* (Uppsala: C. W. K. Gleerup, 1948), 94–102; S. Swain, *Hellenism and Empire* (Oxford: Clarendon Press, 1996), 201. Cf. Teles on Odysseus' father, Laertes, as a Cynic, as he lives among the pigs in squalor (Stob. 4.44.82).
7. Peter Sloterdijk likens Diogenes to Japanese Zen Masters (*Kritik der zynischen Vernunft* [Frankfurt: Surkamp, 1983], 157).
8. Julian notes Socrates' and Diogenes' shared unconcern for common opinion (*Or.* 6.188d–189a, 6.191a–c). For a "mad" Socrates see: DL 6.54; Ael. *VH* 14.33. For Socrates' irony developing into Cynic mockery (*dérision*), see L. Ucciani, *De l'ironie socratique à la dérision cynique. Éléments pour une critique par les formes exclues* (Paris: Les Belles Lettres, 1993).
9. Dudley, *A History of Cynicism*, 27–8; cf. M.-O. Goulet-Cazé, *Le Kynica du stoïcisme* (Stuttgart: Franz Steiner, 2003) for the part Apollodorus of Seleucia played in this process.
10. On the question of who "founded" Cynicism, see, for example, G. Giannantoni, "Antistene fondatore della scuola cinica?", in *Le Cynisme ancien et ses prolonge-ments*, Goulet-Cazé & Goulet (eds), 15–34, with Navia, *Classical Cynicism*, 16–22. Navia continues to regard Antisthenes as a true Cynic, and this view may find encouragement in Goulet-Cazé's suggestion that Aristotle's reference to "the Dog" may be to Antisthenes, and not to Diogenes as is standardly assumed (R. Bracht Branham & M.-O. Goulet-Cazé [eds], *The Cynics: The Cynic Movement in Antiquity and Its Legacy* [Berkeley, CA: University of California Press, 1996], Appendix B, 414–15).
11. That DL 6.95 refers to Crates' followers is argued in M.-O. Goulet-Cazé, "Une List des disciples de Cratès le cynique en Diogène Laërce 6,95", *Hermes* **114** (1986), 247–52.
12. See, for example, Cercidas of Megalopolis 6.77; cf. Epictetus *Diss.* 3.22.82 (the Cynic is son and servant of Zeus).

13. D. M. Robinson, "Ancient Sinope: Second Part", *American Journal of Philology* **27**(3) (1906), 245–79, has interesting speculation on "The Civilization of Sinope":

    Life at the limit line of civilization is perpetually bringing forward sharp contrasts between the rude and the cultured, the cowardly and the brave, the blunt-minded and the keen. Constant hardship and privation teach such men to scorn delights and luxuries, to increase the catalogue of things they can go without and to write the articles of necessity in the fewest lines. The temper of mind becomes independent, brave, terse, and cynical. That this was the characteristic Sinopean spirit is evident from the quality of literary genius her men developed after being transferred to the congenial soil of Athens. The Sinopean product there was the keen laconic contempt of Diogenes (412–323) and in the new comedy. (*Ibid.*: 258)

14. See H. A. Fischel, "Studies in Cynicism and the Ancient Near East: The Transformation of a *Chria*", in *Religions in Antiquity: Essays in Memory of Erwin Ramsdell Goodenough*, J. Neusner (ed.), 372–411 (Leiden: Brill, 1968), 374; cf. D. Krueger, "The Bawdy and Society: The Shamelessness of Diogenes in Roman Imperial Culture", in *The Cynics*, Bracht Branham & Goulet-Cazé (eds), 222–39, esp. 222–4, on the *chreia* tradition in late antique education.

15. Goya writes this (*No lo encontrarás*) on his lithograph of the searching Diogenes.

16. Stobaeus suggests that Diogenes' Medea was a Cynic: with her philosophical sorcery (i.e. Cynic *ponos* and *askēsis*), she "boiled" flabby people back to youth and vigour (3.655.11–17). The *Thyestes* may have advocated cannibalism (DL 6.73).

17. For scepticism about Diogenes as author see DL 6.73, 80; cf. DL 6.31, 6.48; Jul. *Or.* 6.189b. For the tragedies see DL 6.80. Julian calls the tragedies "much talked of " but asserts that Philiscus wrote them (*Or.* 6.186c, 7.210d).

18. Cf. Dio Chrysostom on the Cynic "kitharists" of Alexandria, who are as mesmerizing as Orpheus of old (32.62–6).

19. Erasmus writes that Diogenes "far surpasses all others with the inexhaustible charm of his words" (cited in S. Matton, "Cynicism and Christianity from the Middle Ages to the Renaissance", in Bracht Branham & Goulet-Cazé, *The Cynics*, 240–64, esp. 250). On Diogenes' wit, cf. DL 6.74.

20. H. Beckby, *Anthologia Graeca* [*AG*], vols 1–4, 2nd edn (Munich: Heimeran, 1965–68), 7.63–8 (poems by Antipater, Honestus, Leonidas, Archias). Cf. *AG* 7.116 (by Diogenes Laertius).

21. In *Epistle of Crates* 33 we learn that Pasicles is to be raised a Cynic. Crates also had a brother Pasicles (DL 6.89).

22. Diogenes Laertius describes them eating and "being together" (a euphemism for intercourse?) in public (DL 6.97).

23. For a complementary passage, see Plut. *Alex.* 64–5. For commentary, see especially C. Muckensturm, "Les Gymnosophistes, étaient-ils des Cyniques modèles?", in *Le Cynisme ancien et ses prolongements*, Goulet-Cazé & Goulet (eds), 225–40.

24. See, for instance, E. N. O'Neill, *Teles: The Cynic Teacher* (Missoula, MT: Scholars Press, 1977), for whom Teles' fragments are the first clear remnants of Cynic diatribes. Kindstrand, on the other hand, hesitates to make the diatribe a "genre" (rather than simply a "popular philosophical dialexis") and to make Bion the first inventor of the diatribe, either as a genre or a conversational style. Yet at the same time,

he concludes that "Bion was probably a well-known exponent of this style which combined rhetorical and Cynical elements ... and he perfected it in order to attract listeners" (*Bion of Borysthenes*, 98). That is, the diatribe style had existed before – as when in Plato's *Apology* Socrates "shadow-boxes", asking and answering questions on behalf of his accusers – but Bion accentuated it and made it all his own.

25. Horace refers to "Bion's talks (*sermones*) and black wit" (*Epist.* 2.2.60); cf. M. Morford, *The Roman Philosophers* (New York: Routledge, 2002), 7.

26. These are known at third-hand, from John Stobaeus, who quotes the epitome that Theodorus made of Teles. The fragments are collected in P. P. Fuentes Gonzáles, *Les Diatribes de Télès: Introduction, texte revu et commentaire des fragments, avec en appendice une traduction espagnole* (Paris: Vrin, 1998), which replaces O. Hense (ed.), *Teletis Reliquiae* (Hildesheim: Olms, [1889] 1969).

27. Cf. M. Noussia, "Literary Models and Teachers of Thought: Crates of Thebes and the Tradition of Parody", in *Beyond the Canon*, M. A. Harder, R. F. Regtuit & G. C. Wakker (eds), 229–48 (Leuven: Peeters, 2006), and D. Clayman, "Philosophers and Philosophy in Greek Epigram", in *Brill's Companion to Hellenistic Epigram Down to Philip*, P. Bing & J. S. Bruss (eds), 497–517 (Leiden: Brill, 2007). On Phoenix of Colophon, see G. A. Gerhard, *Phoinix von Kolophon: Text und Untersuchungen* (Leipzig: Teubner, 1909).

28. For a "Menippus of Sinope", see DL 6.95. Using this and other evidence, Robinson, "Ancient Sinope: Second Part", 259–60, 275–6, argues that Menippus was from Sinope, not Gadara; cf. E. Zeller, "The Cynics", in his *Socrates and the Socratic Schools*, O. J. Reichel (trans.), 285–337 (New York: Russell & Russell, 1962), vol. II, 286 n.3.

29. See J. Relihan, *Ancient Menippean Satire* (Baltimore, MD: Johns Hopkins University Press, 1993), 229 n.7, for various attempts to reconstruct the theme of *Arcesilaus* (mentioned in Ath. 664e=14.85.27), the title of which probably refers to the Arcesilaus who headed the Academy during Menippus' lifetime.

30. In *Dialogues of the Dead*, Lucian pictures Menippus as "Old, bald, with a cloak that allows him loads of light and air, and is patched up with all sorts of colours; always laughing and mocking vain philosophers" (1.2).

31. These nicknames are found in Ath. 4.510, Tert. *Apol.* 14.9 and Tert. *Ad Nat.* 1.10.43, respectively. For these and other details, see Relihan, *Ancient Menippean Satire*, 49–74. Cicero and Aulus Gellius claim that Varro "imitated" or "emulated" but did not copy the Greek original (Cic. *Acad.* 1.2.8; Gell. 2.18; cf. Macrob. *Sat.* 1.11). The title is Varro's own, but later others called the volumes "Cynic Satires" (Gell. *NA* 2.187.7, 13.31.1). Into this massive work of 150 satires, written between 80 and 67 BCE, Varro poured all his linguistic ingenuity and vast learning. Relihan's conclusion is that Varro's work is Menippean because it imitates the universal, reflexive parody of Menippus' own writings:

> Varro, a student of philosophy if not a philosopher, makes fun of matters dear to his own heart as he follows the lead of Menippus, who abused all dogmatic systems and even the Cynicism that presumed to criticize these systems. The self-parody of Menippean satire becomes in Varro's hands the parody of encyclopaedic knowledge. (*Ancient Menippean Satire*, 71–2)

And it is all "fantastically innovative" (*ibid.*, 72). In one satire ("Grave of Menippus"), Menippus is described as "that noble dog of former times". Other satires are titled

"Meleagers", "The Cynic", "The Horse-Cynic" (i.e. Roman senator), "The Cynic Orator", "The Water-Drinking Cynic" (*Hydrokyōn*), and "Cynic's Handbook".

32. From such appearances in Lucian, R. Helm, *Lucien und Menipp* (Leipzig: Teubner, 1906), tries to reconstruct Menippus' own writings, in an attempt that is now not generally accepted.

33. See, for example, Dudley, *A History of Cynicism*, 69; Relihan, *Ancient Menippean Satire*, 39, alluding to J. W. Duff, *Roman Satire: Its Outlook on Social Life* (Berkeley, CA: University of California Press, 1936), who also makes the comparison.

34. Cf. *AG* 7.419.3–4 and the title of his *Menippeae Charites*. This last contained the celebrated "Comparison of Pea- and Lentil-Soup", in the tradition of Crates' "Praise of Lentil Soup".

35. See *Suda*, "Oenomaus", for the first four titles. Julian (*Or.* 7.209b) alludes to Oenomaus' tragedies, his *Against the Oracles* (perhaps the same as Γοήτων Φώρα, *Detection of Imposters*), and to an Αὐτοφωνία τοῦ κυνός.

36. Cf. Plutarch's *On the Decline of the Oracles*, at the start of which the Cynic Didymus jumps up, beats the ground with his staff and curses the oracles for entertaining trivial, selfish questions from any chance-comers. After his outburst, Didymus storms out in disgust (*De def. or.* 413a–d), leaving the learned, and more pious, interlocutors to debate the reasons (material and spiritual) for the oracles' decline.

37. For philosophers in Rome of the first century CE, see J. Toynbee, "Dictators and Philosophers in the First Century AD", *Greece & Rome* **13**(38–9) (1944): 43–58.

38. For these suggestions, see Dudley, *A History of Cynicism*, 135, 141; and M. I. Rostovtzeff, *Social and Economic History of the Roman Empire* (Oxford: Clarendon Press, 1926), 519.

39. Wealthy Romans in the later Republic and early Empire might maintain a "house philosopher" for instruction, advice or even amusement: Cicero kept one Diodotus, and Augustus' philosopher was Arius Didymus; cf. Morford, *The Roman Philosophers*, 6, 17, 134–6.

40. "Cosmus, this man, whom you often see in the inner sanctum of the temple of Pallas and on the threshold of the new temple – this old man with his staff and *pēra* and his grey hair standing up dirty and his foul beard falling onto his chest – whom a wax-coloured cloak covers, as if it were his wife sharing a cheap bed – and to whom the passing mob gives the food he has barked for – do you think, deceived by some false notion, that he is a Cynic? He is not a Cynic, Cosmus. What then? He is a dog."

41. For Peregrinus see C. P. Jones, *Culture and Society in Lucian* (Cambridge, MA: Harvard University Press, 1986), 120, and "Cynisme et sagesse barbare: Le cas de Pérégrinus Proteus", in Goulet-Cazé & Goulet, *Le Cynisme ancien et ses prolongements*, 305–18. For Crescens see Dudley, *A History of Cynicism*, 143.

42. Cf. DL 6.13 for the nickname applied to Antisthenes.

43. For more on Favonius see Plut. *Pomp.* 60.7–8, *Caes.* 41.3 and *Brut.* 34.7.

44. Cf. *Fugitivi* 33 on the punishment of Cantharus, false Cynic.

45. For more historical details on the Stoic Opposition, see Dudley, *A History of Cynicism*, 125–42 (primarily a Roman historian, Dudley's interest in Roman politics is evident in this chapter); cf. Morford, *The Roman Philosophers*, 161–4.

46. Cf. Dudley, *A History of Cynicism*, 125. For the influence of Demetrius, see esp. M. Billerbeck, "La Reception de cynisme à Rome", *L'Antiquité Classique* **51** (1982), 151–

73, published in English as "Greek Cynicism in Imperial Rome", in *Die Kyniker in der modernen Forschung*, M. Billerbeck (ed.), 147–66 (Amsterdam: Grüner, 1991).

47. For such dichotomies see, for example, D. Chr. 32.35–43 (Alexandria), 33.18–30 (Ithaca versus Troy, Sybaris, Tarsus *et al.*), 36.13 (a small but orderly city on a rock versus "mad Ninevah"); Luc. *Nigr.* 12–18 (praising Athens); cf. Luc. *Fugitivi* 24, where false, materialistic Cynics will not be found in Athens, because "they do not need Attic poverty".

48. Lucian refers to hoards of Cynics (*De mort. Peregr.* 3; *Pisc.* 42; *Fugitivi*, 12 and esp. 16); For Cynics in Alexandria see D. Chr. 32.9 and Jul. *Or.* 7.224c–d, 7.225b. For Cynic–Stoic preachers in Rome, see Hor. *Sat.* 2.2.55–62. Cf. Dudley, *A History of Cynicism*, 143.

49. Note how Julian chastises Heraclius for travelling only as far as Italy, too lazy to go on to Gaul (*Or.* 7.223d); or how Augustine writes that "even now Cynic philosophers can be seen", for example, in Africa, Italy (*De civ. D.* 14.20).

50. See, for example, DL 6.8, 6.26; Luc. *Demon.* 48, *De mort. Peregr.* 4, 25; Jul., *Or.* 6.191c–d. Tacitus gives his own variations on the theme when he sneers that in defending Egnatius Celer, Demetrius was acting "ambitiosius quam honestius" – Demetrius who "professed the Cynic sect with a different sort of fame" (*Hist.* 4.40); and when (in a much-quoted maxim) he generalizes from denigrations of Thrasea Paetus that "the lust for glory is the last to be shed by the wise" (*etiam sapientibus cupido gloriae novissima exuitur*; *Hist.* 4.6), even by Stoics and Cynics who claim to be above it.

51. Cf. Simplicius' *Commentary on the Encheiridion*, 53–4, where Diogenes and Heraclitus are praised for being closest to the divine.

52. For Cynics in Lucian, see especially *Sale of Lives, Fisher, Fugitives, Menippus, Icaromenippus, Descent to the Underworld, Dialogues of the Dead* (#1–3, 10–11, 13, 16–18, 20–22, 24–8), *Zeus Cross-Examined, Anacharsis, Demonax, On the Death of Peregrinus* as well as the *Cynicus* (ps.-Luc.).

53. This was no mean achievement: "Athenian politics of the 160s were exceptionally turbulent" (Jones, *Culture and Society in Lucian*, 97). Cf. "[T]he advocacy of harmonious relations … was a characteristic task of Greek intellectuals in the second sophistic period. Cities too often advertised 'concord' (*homonoia*) on their coins with the aim of promoting or celebrating good reciprocal relations" (Swain, *Hellenism and Empire*, 219).

54. By Lucian's time, it seems to have been a common view that the "Brahmans" or "Gymnosophists" customarily burned themselves alive, "ascending a huge pyre and enduring being burnt, not shifting their position or from their place" (Luc. *Fugitivi* 7).

55. See Dudley, *A History of Cynicism*, 176. Cf. D. Chr. 32.8–10, where "so-called philosophers" (probably Cynics) are blamed for recent riots in Alexandria.

56. On this and Peregrinus as agitator, see Jones, *Culture and Society in Lucian*, 124–5; cf. Dudley, *A History of Cynicism*, 176–7. The rebellion is mentioned, obscurely, only in *SHA Ant. Pius.* 5.

57. Despite Lucian's scorn, these may be taken literally, as exercises to teach Peregrinus shamelessness and freedom from fear of convention. Diogenes was said to have shaved half his head (DL 6.33); cf. DL 7.166 on Zeno and Herillus.

58. Cf. Gell *NA* 8.3 and Jones, *Culture and Society in Lucian*, 131–2 for non-Lucianic references to Peregrinus.
59. Morford writes: "Of the Stoics, he [Marcus] is closest to Epictetus. He quotes him frequently" (*The Roman Philosophers*, 233).
60. Cf. 7.238c–d, where Julian links Cynic cosmopolitanism and being a "citizen of the cosmos" with the Stoic sage's identification with Nature as a totality, and with his own Neoplatonic notions of piety – another remarkable piece of syncretism.
61. Julian tells a story of how Diogenes once reproved a young man and hit him with his stick, because the rascal had farted in public (*Or.* 6.197b–c). This was a "most dignified" response, according to Julian. This may be to take the story in the wrong spirit, however, if it belongs with the many other anecdotes that depict Diogenes' surprising reversals of expectations. That is, the point of the anecdote may be that Diogenes reprimands the young man not for farting *per se*, but for usurping the Cynics' "royal" privilege for such acts of shamelessness: he was not yet worthy of this great honour. Compare the story of Diogenes and Dionysius in Plut. *Tim.* 14–15 esp. 15.8–10 (cf. my *The Greek Praise of Poverty*, 70–71).

2. Renunciation of custom

1. This is just a suggestion. One explanation, mentioned by Diogenes Laertius, is that the Cynic folds his cloak because he had to sleep in it too (DL 6.22) – an obscure statement.
2. For Socrates going around barefoot see, for example, Pl. *Symp.* 173b, 174a, 220b; *Phaedr.* 229a; cf. DL 2.28. For barefoot Cynics see, for example, DL 6.31, 6.34 (through snow); D. Chr. 10.8, 66.25; Luc. *Icar.* 31.9; ps.-Luc. *Cyn.* 1.3, 14.1, 17.3. For the barefoot commoner see, for example, Pl. *Resp.* 372a–b; Luc. *Catapl.* 15.7, 20.15 (the poor cobbler Micyllus, fast friends with Cyniscus). Plato writes of man being naturally barefoot (*Prot.* 321c; *Symp.* 203d [of *Eros*, symbolic of resourceful, suffering mankind]).
3. Cf. stories told of Antisthenes (DL 6.10) and Diogenes' remark that pedigree, honour and the like are only *prokosmēmata kakias*, "coverings for evil" (DL 6.72). The notion that clothes (and perfume) are deceitful is not Cynic alone; see, for instance, the reaction of Herodotus' Ethiopians to Persian gifts (*Hist.* 3.22).
4. This was a clever argument, since Roman policy was to leave their subjects a measure of internal autonomy: thus, Demonax counsels that the Cynics be allowed their traditional "customs" and freedoms.
5. Near contemporaries Musonius Rufus and Dio Chrysostom also abhorred depilation as akin to the unnatural practice of homosexuality (e.g. Epict. *Diss.* 1.16.9–12; D. Chr. 33.52–64). For discussion and further references see Swain, *Hellenism and Empire*, 215–16.
6. For temples, porticoes and gymnasia see, for example, DL 6.22; D. Chr. 6.14; Stob. 3.1.98 (Diogenes sleeping in the Athenian Parthenon). The metaphor regarding temples is readily suggestible in Greek, as *naos* means dwelling-place, and the temple was treated as a house for the deity. For Cynics sleeping in baths see, for example, Stob. 3.1.98, and for the open air see Luc. *Demon.* 1.13; *Anach.* 16. For Diogenes' *pithos* see DL 6.23; cf. *Ep. Diog.* 16 [Malherbe].

7. For details of the Cynics' diet see, for example, DL 6.25 (figs, olives), 6.44 (no work needed), 6.58 (growing vegetables), 6.85 (Crates' *Pēra*), DL 6.105, Stobaeus 3.1.98; Cass. Dio 6.12–13. Cf. O. Lovejoy & G. Boas, *Primitivism and Related Ideas in Antiquity* (New York: Octagon Books, [1935] 1965), 133–4.

8. Ath. 4.44–51. In the torrent of conversation, it is noted that Homer was a Syrian like Meleager, that Homeric heroes do not eat fish (later regarded often as a luxurious food), that Orestes broke his fast by slurping lentil soup, and that one of the sisters of wise Odysseus was named "Lentil". The inference is that Homer's "sons of the Achaeans" also ate lentils – in the style of the heroic Cynics. It is also high Stoic dogma that only the sage knows how to cook lentils properly for he follows Zeno's wise precept: "To the lentils, add a twelfth part of coriander".

9. On hunger being the best sauce see, for example, Xen. *Mem.* 2.1.30; Bion Fr. 17 (with Kindstrand, *Bion of Borysthenes*, 216–17); D. Chr. 6.12; Jul. *Or.* 6.203a.

10. Cynic opportunism regarding good food (and other "goods") may anticipate the Stoic doctrine of "preferred indifferents": indifferent to luxuries, the Stoic does not hunt them out, but if they are to hand, he will "prefer" to take them than to leave them. The Cynic lives in the moment and avoids the trouble of getting luxuries, but if they are at hand, he applies his principle of "using what is present". This may be the sense of Bion's statement that "he would not even stretch forth his finger for pleasure" – not (one surmises) because pleasure is bad, but because stretching is too much trouble.

11. Cf. D. Chr. 8.33, where "Diogenes" calls Prometheus a sophist, enchained to opinion and *typhos* until freed by Heracles.

12. Cf. Plut. *Mor.* 956b, 995d; Luc. *Vit. auct.* 10; and esp. Jul. *Or.* 6.181a, 190d–193c. For eating raw camel see Leontius' *Life of Symeon* (158), in D. Krueger, *Symeon the Holy Fool: Leontius' Life and the Late Antique City* (Berkeley, CA: University of California Press, 1996).

13. Cf. Dio Chrysostom, who writes of wine as a luxury (4.110, 7.1.52, 11.42) and who pictures Diogenes drinking flowing water, not Thasian wine (6.12). See also Luc. *Fugitivi* 20; ps.-Luc. *Cyn.* 5, *et al.*

14. Cf. Augustine *De civ. D.* 14.20 for the claim that Diogenes had sex in public, a claim perhaps ultimately inspired by the *kynogamia* of Hipparchia and Crates (DL 6.97), and the promiscuity allegedly promoted in the ideal republics of Diogenes and Zeno.

15. Cf. *Epp. Diog.* 35, 42, 46; D. Chr. 6.16–20; Ath. 4.14.

16. Such a line of thought might explain some of the severely misogynistic comments of some Cynics, such as in DL 6.51 (women like weasels), 6.52.

17. Cf. the anecdote in DL 6.62.

18. For Dio's "hatred of homosexuality" as unnatural, unGreek, unpatriotic and some-times a metaphor for "slavery" to Rome, see particularly his speeches to the Tarsians (D. Chr. 33–4) and Swain, *Hellenism and Empire*, 213–15. Swain writes: "The only favourable allusion to homosexuality [in Dio's corpus] is Epaminondas' establish-ment of the so-called 'sacred band' at Or. xxii. 2; but Epaminondas is something of special case for Dio" (*ibid.*: 215, n.101).

19. For example, Hes. *Op.* 754; Ar. *Nub.* 991, 1043–6. According to legend, the hardy Spartans bathed in the cold Eurotas.

20. Cf. Nigrinus criticizing baths in Rome (Luc. *Nigr.* 34).

21. This is also attributed to Antisthenes (DL 6.3). Cf. Diogenes, who said that for a young man it is too early to marry, and for an old man, too late (6.54).

22. Cf. Diogenes' unconventional view that marriage be based on mutual consent, not material concerns: "he thought nothing to be marriage, except when a man persuades a woman to live with him willingly" (DL 6.72).

23. Dawson (*Cities of the Gods*, 156 n.38) detects an insinuation of promiscuity when the Cynic courtesan is called a "dog-fly" in Ath. 4.157a.

24. So the gymnosophists said to Alexander, according to Arrian (*Anab.* 7.1.5–6).

25. Note Bracht Branham's insight: "Cynicism is the only philosophical movement in antiquity to make freedom a central value" ("Diogenes' Rhetoric and the *Invention of Cynicism*", in Bracht Branham & Goulet-Cazé, *The Cynics*, 81–104, esp. 104).

26. Cf. the last words of Diogenes' favourite quotation: "without city, home, fatherland, having no obol, drachma, and *no slave*" (Jul. *Or.* 6.195b; cf. DL 6.38).

27. For Cynics' positive attitudes to labour see A. C. Bayonas, "Travail manuel et esclavage d'après les Cyniques", *Rendiconti dell'Istituto Lombardo* **100** (1966), 383–8; R. F. Hock, "Simon the Shoemaker as an Ideal Cynic", *Greek, Roman and Byzantine Studies* **17** (1976), 41–53 reprinted in Billerbeck, *Die Kyniker in der modernen Forschung*, 259–71; and H. Schulz-Falkenthal, "Zum Arbeitsethos der Kyniker", *Wissenschaftliche Zeitschrift der Martin Luther Universität* **29** (1980), 91–101, reprinted in Billerbeck, *Die Kyniker in der modernen Forschung*, 287–302.

28. See also Bion Fr. 34–6, with Kindstrand, *Bion of Borysthenes*, 241–55; Stobaeus, 3.93.35; *Ep. Diog.* 50 [Malherbe]; ps.-Luc. *Cyn.* 15 (desire for money and for more are cause of "seditions and wars and conspiracies and murders"); cf. H. Niehues-Pröbsting, *Der Kynismus des Diogenes und der Begriff des Zynismus* (Munich: Wilhelm Fink, 1979), 43–63.

29. See also Philostr. *V S* 2.563.1; and Gell. *NA* 9.2, where Herodes lashes out at a begging philosopher.

30. See, for example, Barry Baldwin, who (augmenting Rostovtzeff, *Social and Economic History*) argues that Lucian's dialogues are evidence for an underlying social discontent in the second century, and that the Cynic protest against inequality was "rooted in practical politics and actual participation in social revolutionary movements and goes far beyond the repetition of mere ethical clichés generally ascribed to it" ("Lucian as Social Satirist", *Classical Quarterly* **11**[2] [1961], 199–208, esp. 199). If so, Gibbon's famous conclusion – "If a man were called to fix the period in the history of the world, during which the condition of the human race was most happy and prosperous, he would, without hesitation, name that which elapsed from the death of Domitian to the accession of Commodus" (*The History of the Decline and Fall of the Roman Empire* [Harmondsworth: Penguin, 2000], 83) – might be too rosy.

31. On the basic agreement of Cynics and Stoics regarding externals as "indifferents", see DL 6.105.

32. The discussion in Kindstrand, *Bion of Borysthenes*, 64–7, is representative of the confusion caused by this misleading dichotomy between hedonism and asceticism.

33. For the explanation, see D. Chr. 32.97–8 (with Ar. *Pax* 1–18).

34. That wealth belongs to fortune is an "extremely common" idea (Kindstrand, *Bion of Borysthenes*, 246); cf. K. J. Dover, *Greek Popular Morality* (Indianapolis, IN: Hackett, 1994), 174ff. Cf. *AG* 9.74; Horace, *Sat.* 2.2.133–5.

35. For example, Luc. *Catapl.* 7 and *Dial. mort.* 1.1, 2.3.

36. See also similar arguments attributed by Seneca to Bion and Demetrius (*Ben.* 7.4, 7.7).

37. See Plut. *De tranq. Anim.* 466e; cf. 477c3–6, *Tim.* 15. Cf. Pl. *Symp.* 216d–e on Socrates; my *The Greek Praise of Poverty*, 68–71, 193. Note also that the later Nietzsche often speaks of himself as a (Cynic?) "buffoon".

38. For a seemingly programmatic statement, ambiguously praising athletic training, see DL 6.70. For various critics of the Games, including Lucian's *Anacharsis* see R. Bracht Branham, *Unruly Eloquence: Lucian and the Comedy of Traditions* (Cambridge, MA: Harvard University Press, 1989), 85–8. Most of all, see Dio Chrysostom's ninth oration, "Diogenes or the Isthmian Discourse", which depicts Diogenes at the Isthmian Games, triumphing over the world (cf. D. Chr. 8.6–11).

39. Most typically Greek city-states had a population of 1000–5000 people (D. B. Nagle, *The Household as the Foundation of Aristotle's Polis* [Cambridge: Cambridge University Press, 2006]).

40. Plut. *Regum et Imperatorum Apophthegmata, Antigonus* 15.182e; Sen. *Ben.* 2.17.1 See also DL 6.43 on Philip, 6.38 on Alexander, 6.44 on Perdiccas, whom Diogenes would rank no higher than a beetle or spider, and 6.57 on Craterus. Sometimes the stories become ridiculous caricatures, as when one Cynic starts bickering with Alexander and then whacks him on the head with his staff (Artem. 4.33), as if Alexander would have endured that!

41. Cf. Nietzsche's phrase "human, all-too-human".

42. Cf. my *The Greek Praise of Poverty*, Ch. 3, for classical philosophers' critique of war.

43. For Cynic rhetoric of "invincibility", cf. my *The Greek Praise of Poverty*, 137–9.

44. See H. Erbse, "*Plutarchs Schrift Περὶ Δεισιδαιμονίας*", *Hermes* **80** (1952), 296–314, esp. 299–300. Cf. Bion Fr. 29 with Kindstrand, *Bion of Borysthenes*, 231–2.

45. The remark is attributed also to Diagoras of Melos, "the atheist" (Hipparchia may have known Theodorus, another atheist: see DL 6.98).

46. So Goulet-Cazé concludes: "The Mysteries became an extremely widespread institution in the Hellenistic Age. There were Orphic Mysteries, Mysteries of Demeter and of Kore at Eleusis, Mysteries of Dionysus, of Isis and Osiris in Egypt, Mysteries of Attis in Phrygia, of Adonis in Syria, and of the Cabiri in Samothrace" ("Religion and the Early Cynics", in Bracht Branham & Goulet-Cazé, *The Cynics*, 47–80, esp. 57, summarizing M. P. Nilsson, *Geschichte der griechischen Religion*, vols I–II (Munich: C. H. Beck, 1974), 2.90–113.

47. This passage may not be fully representative of Antisthenes' position towards religion; see Goulet-Cazé & Goulet, *Le Cynisme ancien et ses prolongements*, 117–59.

48. Cf. Delphian Apollo's oracle to Socrates: Pl. *Ap.* 20e–21a; DL 2.38.

49. For a similar conclusion, see Goulet-Cazé, "Religion and the Early Cynics", 79–80. On the later trend to idealize Cynicism, see M. Billerbeck, "The Ideal Cynic from Epictetus to Julian", in Bracht Branham & Goulet-Cazé, *The Cynics*, 205–21.

50. On the association of Diogenes and others with famous atheists such as Diagoras of Melos and Theodorus, see M. Winiarczyk, "Diagoras von Melos und Diogenes

von Sinope", *Eos* **64** (1976), 177–84, and "Theodoros ὁ Ἄθεος und Diogenes von Sinope", *Eos* **69** (1981), 37–42.

51. On whistling, see DL 6.27. On eating beans, see DL 6.48, 6.86, 6.94. On farting, see, for example, DL. 2.117, 6.48, 6.94, 6.20 and 6.80 (attributed to Diogenes is a book titled *Pordalos*, roughly translated as *The Farter*); Epict. *Diss.* 3.22.80; Jul. *Or.* 6.202b. On urinating, see DL 6.46. On defecating (the literal meaning of *apopatein*, "to go off the path", epitomizes the Cynics' antinomian behaviour), see D. Chr. 8.35–6; Jul. *Or.* 6.202b; cf. Krueger, *Symeon the Holy Fool*, ch. 6. On masturbating, see DL 6.46, 6.69; *Epp. Diog.* 35, 42, 44; D. Chr. 6.16–20; Ath. 4.145ff. On carrying a broken wine jar, tuna, lentils, cheese and so on, see DL 6.35–6, 7.3 (of Zeno).

52. The Greek *mainesthai*, like the English "to be mad", has the sense both of "to be insane", and "to be angry". In 33.37, Dio Chrysostom imagines a rude city in which everyone always points with the middle finger. For the gesture, cf. Juvenal 10.53 and the scholion on Ar. *Nub.* 653.

53. Note that Gorgias, alleged intellectual ancestor of Cynicism, was the first to use *homoioteleuton* (a form of rhyme) generously. Bion seems to have loved it too (examples in Kindstrand, *Bion of Borysthenes*, 34).

54. The word appears here in a learned discussion of types of wine. Did Meleager compliment a city that drank no wine?

55. For example, DL 6.43; Epict. *Diss.* 3.22; Secund. *Sentent.* 7 Cf. "We two alone [i.e. Lear and Cordelia] will sing like birds i' the cage/… And take upon's the mystery of things,/ As if we were God's spies' (Shakespeare, *King Lear* V.iii).

56. See J. L. Moles, "Cynic Cosmopolitanism", in Bracht Branham & Goulet-Cazé, *The Cynics*, 105–20, esp. 115 n.58, for many of these labels, to which I have added a few others. Most culturally specific is the *sophronistes*, a "superintendent of the youth in the gymnasia" (H. G. Liddell, R. Scott & H. S. Jones, *A Greek–English Lexicon*, 9th edn. [Oxford: Clarendon Press, 1968]), and more generally, a moral inspector who ensured that the youth, women, drinkers in the *symposium* and so on were *sophron*, self-restrained.

57. Given the poetic innovations of Cynics such as Crates and Cercidas, prosody might not have been regarded as uselessly intellectual, pace Relihan, *Ancient Menippean Satire*, who implies that Cynics would avoid technical discussions of metre. For the reference to Varro, see Caesius Bassus, *De Metris* 6.261.

58. For possible Cynic influence on Timon, see A. A. Long, "Timon of Phlius: Pyrrhonist and Satirist", *Proceedings of the Cambridge Philological Society* **24** (1978), 68–91. Cynic influence may have even affected the moralizing historian Theopompus: see G. Murray, "Theopompus, or the Cynic as Historian", in his *Greek Studies*, 149–70 (Oxford: Clarendon Press, 1946).

59. Note, however, that Demonax teased those who cultivated pure classical Attic: if you ask them a question today, they speak as if they were living in the time of Agamemnon (Luc. *Demon.* 26).

60. Cf. "Corpses, you know, should be thrown out quicker than dung" (Heraclitus Fr. 96 [DK]).

61. For the Cynic belief that there is nothing after death see Kindstrand, *Bion of Borysthenes*, 286–8.

3. A life according to nature

1. Cf. ps.-Luc., *Cyn.* 5. See Krueger, *Symeon the Holy Fool*, Ch. 6, for many references. A scholar like Kindstrand sees only negativity in Cynicism: "If we are to find a single concept to characterize the Cynics, I think that freedom would be the obvious choice ... This freedom means a complete independence from everything – external circumstances, state, family, friends and even the gods. Therefore this freedom proves to be of a mainly negative character; it is essentially freedom from things" (*Bion of Borysthenes*, 59–60). But this overlooks positive notions such as self-sufficiency, individual autonomy, the natural life and its elemental pleasures, and even the *philanthrōpia* that may develop from it. Contrast Kindstrand with Dawson:

   > Their most fundamental postulate seems to be *autarkeia*; but *autarkeia* often seems to imply something much less negative than we convey by the usual translation "self-sufficiency." It seems to carry also the connotation of "spontaneity." *Autarkeia* freed the Cynic from all motives of exploiting others; and left him or her free to help others, which only the free are qualified to do. It was only necessary to achieve freedom through the *askēsis*, and then to follow one's impulses ... Cynicism was based on the theory, or rather the intuitive assumption that human life reduced to absolute simplicity is absolutely altruistic. One who had learned that the easy and pleasant way of life was to live for the present could not help but spread this message to those around, by example and by precept. (*Cities of the Gods*, 145–6)

2. Cf. Arist. *Rh.* 1355a16 and Julian's Aristotelian language in *Or.* 7.207b. Dio Chrysostom speaks of the desire to learn as distinctly Greek (36.16, 26).

3. An exception is Antisthenes' two volumes "On Nature" (DL 6.17), but Antisthenes, again, was more catholic in his intellectual interests than typical Cynics.

4. For a survey of the Sophistic criticism of traditional religion, see W. Jaeger, *The Theology of the Early Greek Philosophers*, E. S. Robinson (trans.) (Oxford: Clarendon Press, 1936), 172–90. Note that according to Philodemus of Gadara, Antisthenes claimed that there are many gods by custom, but only one by nature: a controversial statement that has led some to regard him as a proto-monotheist.

5. "Diogenes said that fish are wiser than human beings: for when they need to release their seed, they go out and rub themselves on something rough" (D. Chr. 6.18). Cf. Crates' lines: "Fasting quenches desire, and if you cannot fast, then hang yourself" (DL 6.86; *Anth. Pal.* 9.497; Jul. *Or.* 6.198d).

6. See, for instance, DL 6.33, 6.35–6, 7.3; Luc. *De mort. Peregr.* 17; Epict. *Diss.* 3.15.11–12 for practices whose purpose may have been to strengthen the mind (*gnōmē*, *psychē*) as implied in DL 6.70 and Strabo 15.1.65 (quoted above).

7. For the motto χρῶ τοῖς παροῦσιν, see, for example, D. Chr. 30.33; Plut. 16.606d; Epict. *Diss.* 4.4.45; Luc. *Tox.* 34; cf. Kindstrand, *Bion of Borysthenes*, 65–6, 218–19.

8. Cf. Nietzsche for ideas about the momentary, unhistorical life of animals and the conclusion that "the happiness of the animal, like that of the full Cynic *(des vollendeten Zynikers)*, is living proof of the rightness of Cynicism" (*Use and Abuse of History*, §1).

9. Antisthenes wrote much on the Persian Cyrus the Great (DL 6.2, 16, 18). The nomadic Scythians lived across the Black Sea from Sinope, and north of Bion's Borysthenes (DL 4.55). Possessing little, carrying their homes with them as they rode across the great Eurasian steppe, these wanderers were reputed to be unconquerable and at times were admired as "noble savages". Lucian and certain *Cynic Epistles* make the Scythian Anacharsis representative of the natural man, and Cynics as early as Diogenes may have admired Anacharsis as a Cynic of sorts (see R. P. Martin, "The Scythian Accent: Anacharsis and the Cynics", in Bracht Branham & Goulet-Cazé, *The Cynics*, 136–55, esp. 154–5). For the Getae, see D. Chr. 6. On the Gymnosophists, see Onesicritus (e.g. in Strabo 15.1.64–5); Luc. *Fugitivi* 6. On the Spartans see, for example, Arist. *Rhet.* 1411a24, DL 6.39. For Dio Chrysostom, simple poor people like these were the happiest and best of all the people he met (D. Chr. 7, esp. 7.65–76, 7.81–103), and recall Micyllus the cobbler in Lucian's *Descent to the Underworld* (e.g. Catapl. 25).

10. For the Cynics' claimed primitivism, see Luc. *Fugitivi* 17; *Ep. Diog.* 32.3 [Malherbe]; D. Chr. 8.33, 10.16. Scholars disagree on how to interpret such claims, in particular the extent to which Diogenes and others advocated "natural" cannibalism, incest and unrestrained promiscuity.

4. Chance, fate, fortune and the self

1. Cf. DL 6.6, on how philosophy taught Antisthenes "to be able to converse with himself".

2. In some schemes, *Lachesis* controls the past, *Clōthō* the present and *Atropos* the future, as in Pl. *Resp.* 617c. For Fate as a "spinner", see e.g. Hom. *Il.* 24.209–10, *Od.* 7.197–8.

3. For the oracle at Praeneste, see Cic. *Div.* 2.85–6.

4. See Nilsson, *Geschichte der griechischen Religion*, II.200–210, and a brief synopsis in Goulet-Cazé, "Religion and the Early Cynics", 55.

5. Polybius writes: "what makes my work distinctive, and what is astonishing in our times is this – that *Tychē* has turned almost all the affairs of the world in one direction, forced them to incline to one and the same goal" (1.4.1), that is, the unification of Mediterranean lands under Roman rule. But *Tychē* elsewhere in Polybius can refer to chance occurrences, not providence: thus his use of this "mercurial" term only reflects the confusion of popular semantics (cf. F. W. Walbank, *Polybius, Rome and the Hellenistic World: Essays and Reflections* [Cambridge: Cambridge University Press, 2002], 182–3). Similarly, in his *De Fortuna Romanorum*, Plutarch relates the story that when *Tychē* entered Rome, she threw away her sandals, wings and rolling "unstable globe", for she intended never to abandon this city as she had abandoned the Assyrians, Persians, Macedonians, Carthaginians before (317f). Treatises titled "On Fortune" were common: see e.g. Plutarch's *De Fortuna* and *De Fortuna Alexandri*, Dio Chrysostom's three speeches "On Fortune" (63–5), and works attributed to Aristippus, Demetrius of Phalerum, the Stoic Sphaerus and others.

6. Various guesses of its identity have included Cumae, Naples and Puteoli.

7. Varro includes the same detail in the *Eumenides* of his *Menippean Satires* (Fr. 143), where a Cynic hosts a symposium and regales the guests in ways perhaps similar to Trimalchio (so Relihan, *Ancient Menippean Satire*, 67).

8. Cf. DL 2.27; Desmond, *The Greek Praise of Poverty*, 38–40; Goulet-Cazé, "Religion and the Early Cynics", 61–4.

9. Cf. "By far the best is he who knows all things by himself; but good also is the man who obeys a sensible speaker" (Hes. *Op*. 293–7).

10. For images of the Cynic as solitary or alienated see D. Chr. 4.14, 8.7–11, 8.26, 9.4–7; Jul. *Or*. 6.190d.

11. Hippias tried to demonstrate his self-sufficiency by appearing at the Olympic festival with products all of his own making: he had made his own ring and seal ring, strigil, oil flask, shoes, cloak, tunic and belt, as well as his own prose pieces, epic, tragic and dithyrambic poems, and, finally, his own amazing memory system (Pl. *Hp. mi.* 368).

12. For man as the "dream of a shadow", see Pind. *Pyth.* 8.95; "straw", Leonidas of Tarentum (in *AG* 7.472); "dust and shadow", Horace *Carm*. 4.7; and the "quintessence of dust", Shakespeare, *Hamlet* II.ii.

13. Cf. Menippus' mockery of Mausolus of Caria for his huge mausoleum: "When Aeacus measures out each person's space, the biggest he gives is no bigger than a foot's breath" (Luc. *Nec.* 17).

14. Cf. Epictetus: "you are not flesh or hair, but moral purpose" (*Diss.* 3.1.40); "Like timber to the carpenter, and leather-hides to the cobbler, so my mind is the matter with which I must work. My task is the right use of impressions. My little body is nothing to me; its parts are nothing to me" (3.22.20).

15. On the Cynic as warrior see, for example, DL 6.12–13, 6.38; Stob. 2.8.21; cf. Cic. *Nat. D.* 3.83, 3.86 and D. Chr. 63.18 on "arrows of Fortune". For the Cynic as fortress see, for example, DL 6.13; Cic. *Paradoxa Stoicorum* 27; Luc. *Fugitivi* 15. For Marcus Aurelius as a rock, see *Med.* 4.49; cf. Matthew 16:18. On "the god within", see, for example, D. Chr. 4.139; M. Aur. *Med.* 2.13, 2.17, 3.5–6, 3.16, 12.26; Jul. *Or.* 4.6; Max. Tyr. 36.1.

16. Bion calls Fortune "a poetess" who now gives one the role of a king, now that of a wanderer or exile: the good person will, like a good actor, play his allotted part (Stob. 3.1.98, 4.44.82).

17. Parmeniscus here adapts a tragic line, replacing *kakos* (bad) with *phakos* (lentil).

5. Anarchists, democrats, cosmopolitans, kings

1. See DL 7.32–4, 131; Dawson, *Cities of the Gods*, 111–59; "Epicurean and Stoic Political Thought", in *The Cambridge History of Greek and Roman Political Thought*, C. J. Rowe & M. Schofield (eds), 415–34 (Cambridge: Cambridge University Press, 2000), esp. 443–6; Goulet-Cazé, *Le Kynica du stoïcisme*. Speculation about Diogenes' *Republic* is based mainly on speculation about Zeno's, and is therefore doubly hazardous. The consensus, however, is that DL 6.72 "represents a coherent and close summary of Diogenes *Politeia*" (J. L. Moles, "The Cynics", in Rowe & Schofield, *The Cambridge History*, 415–34, esp. 426), and that both *Republics* represent a reaction to Plato's statist utopia.

2. See, for example, Lucian's *Cataplus*, where a Cynic who was nailed up for criticizing the tyrant Megapenthes has his final revenge in the underworld when he beats him with his stick (13.24–8).

3. Cf. "It must be remembered that for the Greeks democracy did not mean, as for modern thinkers, a system of government in which every person and every point of view was permitted to express itself freely; it meant a system of government by the masses and for the masses. The few, the rich aristocrats, were not disenfranchised, but political power rested with the masses, who used it for their own advantage" (M. Hammond, *City-State and World State in Greek and Roman Political Theory until Augustus* [Cambridge, MA: Harvard University Press, 1951], 12).

4. Cf. Theophrastus' *Characters* 28.6 on the association of (Cynic?) abuse (*kakologia*) and *parrhēsia* with democracy and freedom.

5. Cf. D. Chr. 32 ("To the Alexandrians") and 33 ("To the Tarsians") for the politically beneficial mixture of *parrhēsia* and abuse (*loidoria*).

6. For ancient comparisons of the two, see D. Chr. 32.5–6 (alluding to the *parodos*); M. Aur. *Med.* 11.6.2; Jul. *Or.* 7.204a–b.

7. See, for example, Ar. *Eq.* 164–77, 1333; Xen. *Symp.* 4.29–32; cf. Arist. *Pol.* 1274a5–21; D. Chr. 32.25–9, of Alexandrians; my *The Greek Praise of Poverty*, 57–9.

8. Some (e.g. Navia, Moles) regard *philanthrōpia* as a central Cynic virtue, evident in Crates, Diogenes and even Antisthenes, and not a later development (e.g. Moles, "Cynic Cosmopolitanism", 114–17). Note also how Socrates converses with everyone regardless of background and how he presents himself as public benefactor in Pl. *Ap.* 36d–37a.

9. Antisthenes' "Cyrus" is probably Cyrus II ("the Great") of Persia, whom Xenophon lionized in his *Cyropaedia*.

10. The focus on individual excellence is reflected also in the trope of the wise legislator who in a single act of political creation gives a people their whole way of life: such was the legendary wisdom of a Lycurgus, Charondas, Solon or later the Romans' Numa. Cf. Hammond, *City-State and World State*, 11–12, 18.

11. Note Aristotle's praise of monarchy and aristocracy in *Pol.* 1248a3–17 (in which he alludes approvingly to Antisthenes' fable of the lion and the hares). Only fragments of the treatises "On Kingship" by Diotogenes and ps.-Ekphrantus remain as representatives of a very popular genre.

12. See R. Balot, *Greek Political Thought* (Oxford: Blackwell, 2006), 269–76, for a survey of Hellenistic ideologies of kingship.

13. Such statements are reflected in the voluntary *ponos* of a Hadrian, Marcus Aurelius and Julian (see e.g. 259b–264a of the *Letter to Themistius* attributed to him).

14. Other passages include: Epict. *Diss.* 3.22.45–8, 3.24.64–6; Plut. *De Alex. fort.* 6.329a–d, 10.332b–c; ps.-Luc. *Cyn.* 15; Jul. *Or.* 6.201c, 7.238b–c; Max. Tyr. 36.4–5; Teles in Stob. 3.40.8; ps.-Heraclitus *Ep.* 5.2, 36.9.2, 4, 7; *AP* 7.417 (Meleager).

15. "The answers suggested by the majority of modern scholars – 'I am a citizen of no polis' and 'There is no good government' – are … intolerably bland" (Moles, "Cynic Cosmopolitanism", 110); and "The Cynics did not bequeath to the Stoics a purely negative concept ('we reject the city') to which the latter added the positive value: rather, Cynic cosmopolitanism already contained all the essential positive qualities which the Stoics endowed with a fuller exposition, and which

they integrated into a fully developed physical system" (Moles, "The Cynics", 443).

16. Moles comments: "We seem here to be verging on the idea (which would have very important consequences) that the universe is a unified physical organism" ("Cynic Cosmopolitanism", 112). Indeed, the idea of the world as a single, living animal is a crucial one for Stoic monism.

17. Socrates never went to court before he was seventy (Pl. *Ap*. 32b), and nor did he engage much in customary political activities, yet he claimed to be the only true political man in Athens (Pl. *Grg*. 521d). The same paradox of being at once an apolitical cosmopolitan and a prophet of *Größe Politik* is important for the neo-Cynical Nietzsche.

6. Cynic legacies

1. Sepphoris was some six kilometres from Nazareth, and was the traditional birth-place of Anna and Joachim, Mary's parents.

2. Where exactly the miracle occurred is a controversial question. One interpretation is that it took place in "the country of the Gergenses" (Matthew 8:28–34), in the village of Gergesa near the Sea of Galilee, but when Mark and Luke were composing for audiences unfamiliar with such a local place, they opted to refer to the bigger, and better-known Gadara (Luke 8:26–39; Mark 5:1–20).

3. According to Galen and Aëtius of Amida, those who suffer from the type of madness called *kynanthrōpia* ("dog-humanness") can be recognized by their ten-dency to lurk about cemeteries at night (Galen 19.719; Aëtius 6.11). For these and other references concerning the Hebrew word *kinukos*, see M. Luz, "A Description of the Greek Cynic in the Jerusalem Talmud", *Journal for the Study of Judaism* **20** (1989), 49–60.

4. Cf. possible parallels in D. Chr. 10.16 and Jul. *Or*. 6.181c.

5. See F. G. Downing, "Cynics and Early Christianity", in Goulet-Cazé & Goulet, *Le Cynisme ancien et ses prolongements*, 281–304, esp. 284ff., citing Luc. *De mort. Peregr*. 11–16 (for Peregrinus), Eusebius *Hist. eccl.* 6.3.2 (for Heraklas) and Gregory Nazianzus, *Discourse* 25–6 and *De vita sua* 2.1 (for Maximus), although one should note that Eusebius does not explicitly state that Heraklas was a Cynic. On the other hand, Maximus was installed briefly, by stealth, and to huge con-troversy, as Bishop of Constantinople in 380 CE: his Cynic's mane of hair was cut for the ceremony (Gregory, *De Vita Sua*, 915–23), although it is unclear what his "Cynicism" really entailed. Cf. Jones, "Cynisme et sagesse barbare", on Peregrinus as Christian, and on the public enmity between Justin Martyr and Crescens the Cynic.

6. Gregory of Nazianzus continued to admire the Cynics despite being betrayed by one, his friend and follower Maximus. For more details on "the image of the Cynics among the Greek Fathers" and particularly the "assimilation du cynisme à l'hellénisme", see D. Dorival, "L'image des Cyniques chez les Pères grecs", in Goulet-Cazé & Goulet, *Le Cynisme ancien et ses prolongements*, 419–43.

7. The *Letters of Crates*, for instance, were published in 1471 in Paris. In 1542 Erasmus'

Apophthegmes (*Apophthegmatum ex optimis utriusque linguae scriptoribus*) was published in London, with many Cynic sayings included in its 231 items.

8. Frye takes his cue from the title of Robert Burton's *The Anatomy of Melancholy* (1621). Cf. A. Weiss, "An Anatomy of Anatomy", *Drama Review* **41**(1) (1999), 137–44.

9. For Niehues-Pröbsting, *Rameau's Nephew* is "the fundamental book of modern cynicism" ("The Modern Reception of Cynicism: Diogenes in the Enlightenment", in Bracht Branham & Goulet-Cazé, *The Cynics*, 329–65, esp. 350).

10. While it was Hume who Kant claimed helped wake him from his "dogmatic slumbers", Rousseau exercised a significant influence on the younger Kant, and the high esteem in which Kant continued to hold him is reflected in the fact that the only portrait that hung in his house was one of Rousseau.

11. Nietzsche, *Ecce Homo*, "Why I Write Such Good Books", §3. Cf. Nieuhues-Pröbsting, *Der Kynismus des Diogenes*, 353–63; and H. D. Betz, "Jesus and the Cynics: Survey and Analysis of a Hypothesis", *Journal of Religion* **74**(4) (1994), 453–75, esp. 465–70, for the view that Nietzsche's Jesus is a neo-Cynic, proto-Nietzschean whose Beatitudes look forward to Nietzsche's "innocence of becoming" but not to the ascetic dualism of a Paul or Augustine.

12. For Sloterdijk's ideal of Cynic cheekiness, see *Kritik der zynischen Vernunft*, esp. 101–33.

Guide to further reading

Ancient texts

Collections

The standard scholarly collection, including a great variety of Cynic and related material in the original languages, is G. Giannantoni, *Socratis et Socraticorum Reliquiae* (Naples: Bibliopolis, 1990). L. Paquet, *Les Cyniques grecs: Fragments et témoignages*, 2nd edn (Ottawa: Presses de l'Université d'Ottawa, 1988) is also useful, containing Orations 4, 6 and 9–10 of Dio, along with much other material in the original languages (and French translation). There is also G. Luck, *Die Weisheit der Hunde: Texte der antiken Kyniker in deutscher Übersetzung mit Erläuterungen* (Stuttgart: Alfred Kröner, 1997), a collection of 784 Cynic extracts, translated into German with commentary. More limited but useful also, with its Greek selections, English translation and discussion is O. Lovejoy & G. Boas, *Primitivism and Related Ideas in Antiquity* (New York: Octagon Books, [1935] 1965), especially pages 117–52 on "Cynic Primitivism".

Many relevant authors can be consulted in the Loeb Classical Library, notably: Crates in J. M. Edmonds (trans.), *Elegy and Iambus, Being the Remains of all the Greek Elegiac and Iambic Poets from Callinus to Crates* (Cambridge, MA: Harvard University Press, 1931); Cercidas in A. D. Knox (trans.), *Herodes, Cercidas, and the Greek Choliambic Poets* (London: Heinemann, 1929) and J. Rusten & I. C. Cunningham (eds), *Characters. Mimes. Cercidas and the Choliambic Poets* (Cambridge, MA: Harvard University Press, 1993); and Epictetus, Julian and Lucian.

There are other important scholarly collections of individual Cynic authors, notably: F. D. Caizzi, *Antisthenis fragmenta* (Milan: Istituto Editoriale Cisalpino, 1966) for Antisthenes; J. F. Kindstrand, *Bion of Borysthenes: A Collection of the Fragments with Introduction and Commentary* (Uppsala: Acta Universitatis Uppsalensis, 1976) for Bion; A. J. Malherbe, *The Cynic Epistles: A Study Edition* (Missoula, MT: Scholars Press, 1977) and E. Müseler, *Die Kynikerbriefe* (Paderborn: Schoningh, 1994) for the Cynic Epistles;

and P. P. Fuentes Gonzáles, *Les Diatribes de Télès: Introduction, texte revu et commentaire des fragments, avec en appendice une traduction espagnole* (Paris: Vrin, 1998) and O. Hense (ed.), *Teletis Reliquiae* (Hildesheim: Olms, [1889] 1969) for Teles.

Source criticism

For work that sifts Cynic notions from other (especially Stoic) material from sources such as Dio Chrysostom and Diogenes Laertius, see: K. von Fritz, "Quellenuntersuchung zu Leben und Philosophie des Diogenes von Sinope", *Philologos*, Supplement **18**(2) (Leipzig: Dietrich, 1926); M.-O. Goulet-Cazé, *L'Ascèse Cynique: Un Commentaire de Diogène Laërce VI 70–71* (Paris: Vrin, 1986), "Le Livre VI de Diogène Laërce: Analyse de sa structure et réflexions méthodologiques", *Aufstieg und Niedergang der römischen Welt* II **36**(6) (1992), 3880–4048 and *Le Kynica du stoïcisme* (Stuttgart: Franz Steiner, 2003); and J. Mansfeld, "Diogenes Laertius on Stoic Philosophy", *Elenchos* 7 (1986), 295–382.

On the *chreia* tradition, see: G. Rudberg, "Zur Diogenes Tradition", *Symbolae Osloenses* **14** (1935), 22–43 and "Zum Diogenes-Typus", *Symbolae Osloenses* **15** (1936), 1–18, both reprinted in M. Billerbeck (ed.), *Die Kyniker in der modernen Forschung* (Amsterdam: Grüner, 1991), 107–26 and 127–43, respectively; H. A. Fischel, "Studies in Cynicism and the Ancient Near East: The Transformation of a *Chria*", in *Religions in Antiquity: Essays in Memory of Erwin Ramsdell Goodenough*, J. Neusner (ed.), 372–411 (Leiden: Brill, 1968); J. F. Kindstrand, "Diogenes Laertius and the *Chreia* Tradition", *Elenchos* 7 (1986), 217–43; and D. Krueger, "The Life of Symeon the Fool and the Cynic Tradition", *Journal of Early Christian Studies* 1 (1993), 423–42, and *Symeon the Holy Fool: Leontius' Life and the Late Antique City* (Berkeley, CA: University of California Press, 1996).

General surveys of ancient Cynicism

D. R. Dudley, *A History of Cynicism from Diogenes to the 6th Century AD* (Chicago: Ares, [1937] 1980), H. D. Rankin, *Sophists, Socratics and Cynics* (London: Croom Helm, 1983) and L. E. Navia, *Classical Cynicism: A Critical Study* (Westport, CT: Greenwood Press, 1996) give good overviews, while R. Höistad, *Cynic Hero and Cynic King: Studies in the Cynic Conception of Man* (Uppsala: C. W. K. Gleerup, 1948) is somewhat more specialized; see also Lovejoy & Boas, *Primitivism and Related Ideas in Antiquity*, for an intelligent discussion within the wider context of ancient primitivist ideas. H. Niehues-Pröbsting, *Der Kynismus des Diogenes und der Begriff des Zynismus* (Munich: Wilhelm Fink, 1979) treats both ancient and modern material. F. Sayre, *The Greek Cynics* (Baltimore, MD: J. H. Furst, 1948) is polemically judgemental but clear.

Ready information on individual figures can be found in R. Goulet (ed.), *Dictionnaire des Philosophes Antiques* (Paris: CNRS Éditions, 1994) and the third edition of the *Oxford Classical Dictionary*. Billerbeck, *Die Kyniker in der modernen Forschung*, gathers together a wide spectrum of articles from the nineteenth and twentieth centuries, while the range of more recent scholarship is best represented by the collections of articles in M.-O. Goulet-Cazé & R. Goulet (eds), *Le Cynisme ancien et ses prolongements: Acts du*

Colloque International du CNRS (Paris: Presses Universitaires de France, 1993): these are mostly in French but several have been translated into English and reprinted in R. Bracht Branham & M.-O. Goulet-Cazé (eds), *The Cynics: The Cynic Movement in Antiquity and Its Legacy* (Berkeley, CA: University of California Press, 1996). Many of these articles are referenced individually below and in the bibliography. On the distinction between ancient Cynicism (*der Kynismus*) and cynicism (*der Zynismus*), see especially Niehues-Pröbsting, *Der Kynismus des Diogenes*.

Many other surveys are useful for cultural and philosophical background. W. K. C. Guthrie, *A History of Greek Philosophy, Vol. 3: The Sophists and Socrates* (Cambridge: Cambridge University Press, 1969) is part of his highly regarded *History of Greek Philosophy*, and contains short discussions of Antisthenes and the Cynics (pp. 209–19, 304–11, 247–9). Nor should one forget the great history of Greek philosophy by the nineteenth-century German scholar E. Zeller, *Philosophie der Griechen in ihrer geschichtlichen Entwicklung*, vols I–III (Tübingen: L.F. Fues, 1856–68), and his intelligent discussion of the Cynics in "The Cynics", in his *Socrates and the Socratic Schools*, O. J. Reichel (trans.), 285–337 (New York: Russell & Russell, 1962). For Hellenistic philosophies, see A. A. Long & D. Sedley, *The Hellenistic Philosophers*, vols 1–2 (Cambridge: Cambridge University Press, 1987).

1. Ancient Cynics and their times

Proto-Cynics

On the possible influence of Democritus' ideas on Cynics, see: F. W. Lenz, "Ἔθος δευτέρη φύσις: A New Fragment of Democritus?", *Transactions and Proceedings of the American Philological Association* 72 (1942), 214–31; Z. Stewart, "Democritus and the Cynics", *Harvard Studies in Classical Philology* 63 (1958), 179–91; O. Temkin, *Hippocrates in a World of Pagans and Christians* (Baltimore, MD: Johns Hopkins University Press, 1991), 61ff.; and M. Gigante, *Cinismo e Epicureismo* (Naples: Bibliopolis, 1992), reprinted in abbreviated form in Goulet-Cazé & Goulet (eds), *Le Cynisme ancien et ses prolongements*, 159–222. For various similarities between Heraclitus and the Cynics, see J. F. Kindstrand, "The Cynics and Heraclitus", *Eranos* 82 (1984), 149–78. On Cynics and heroes Heracles and Odysseus, see Höistad, *Cynic Hero and Cynic King*, Ch.1; cf. A. J. Malherbe, "Antisthenes and Odysseus, and Paul at War", *Harvard Theological Review* 76(2) (1983), 143–73, which is reproduced in his *Paul and the Popular Philosophers* (Philadelphia, PA: Fortress Press, 1989), 67–77.

For broader explorations of classical Greek precedents for Cynicism, see Höistad, *Cynic Hero and Cynic King*, and my *The Greek Praise of Poverty: Origins of Ancient Cynicism* (Notre Dame, IN: University of Notre Dame Press, 2006). A. Gladisch, *Einleitung in das Verständniss der Weltgeschichte* (Posen: J. J. Heine, 1841) was one of the first resolute attempts to pinpoint Eastern precedents for ancient philosophies. More recent works that treat the Cynics in particular are T. McEvilley, "Early Greek Philosophy and Madhyamika", *Philosophy East and West* 31 (1981), 141–64, and *The Shape of Ancient Thought: Comparative Studies in Greek and Indian Philosophies* (New York: Allworth, 2002). For specific comparisons of the *pasupatas* and Cynics, see: D. Ingalls, "Cynics and

Pasupatas: The Seeking of Dishonor", *Harvard Theological Review* **55** (1962), 281–98; A. Syrkin, "The Salutary Descent", *Numen* **35** (1988), 1–23, 213–37; M. Hulin, "Doctrines et comportements 'cyniques' dans certaines sects hindoues anciennes et contemporaines", in Goulet-Cazé & Goulet, *Le Cynisme ancien et ses prolongements*, 557–70; and McEvilley, *The Shape of Ancient Thought*, 225–35. Cf. C. Muckensturm, "Les Gymnosophistes, étaient-ils des Cyniques modèles?", in Goulet-Cazé & Goulet, *Le Cynisme ancien et ses prolongements*, 225–40.

For an argument that Socratic irony fathered Cynic mockery, see L. Ucciani, *De l'ironie socratique à la dérision cynique. Éléments pour une critique par les formes exclues* (Paris: Les Belles Lettres, 1993). For Simon the shoemaker, legendary "Cynic" companion of Socrates, see R. F. Hock, "Simon the Shoemaker as an Ideal Cynic", *Greek, Roman and Byzantine Studies* **17** (1976), 41–53, reprinted in Billerbeck, *Die Kyniker in der modernen Forschung*, 259–71.

On Antisthenes generally, see the book-length studies H. D. Rankin, *Antisthenes Sokratikos* (Amsterdam: Hakkert, 1986) and L. E. Navia, *Antisthenes of Athens: Setting the World Aright* (Westport, CT: Greenwood Press, 2001); cf. F. D. Caizzi, "Antistene", *Studi Urbinati* **I** (1964), 25–76, L. E. Navia, *The Socratic Presence: A Study of the Sources* (New York: Garland, 1993) and S. Prince, "Socrates, Antisthenes, and the Cynics", in *A Companion to Socrates*, S. Ahbel-Rappe & R. Kamtekar (eds), 75–92 (Oxford: Blackwell, 2005). For Antisthenes' probable association with the Cynosarges gymnasium, see M. F. Billot, "Antisthène et le Cynosarges dans l'Athènes de Ve et IVe siècles", in Goulet-Cazé & Goulet, *Le Cynisme ancien et ses prolongements*, 69–116, and "Le Cynosarges: Histoire, myths et archéologie", in Goulet, *Dictionnaire des Philosophes Antiques*, vol. 2, 917–66. On Antisthenes' anti-Platonic logic and epistemology, see H. D. Rankin, "That it is Impossible to say 'Not' and Related Topics in Antisthenes", *International Logic Review* **10** (1979), 51–98, A. Brancacci, *Oikeios logos: La filosofia del linguaggio di Antistene* (Naples: Bibliopolis, 1990) and Navia, *Antisthenes of Athens*, 53–64. For the argument that Antisthenes' Cynic ideas were a major influence on Plato and Xenophon, see K. Joël, *Der echte und der Xenophontische Sokrates* (Berlin: R. Gaertner, 1893) and, on a more limited scale, S. Rappe, "Father of the Dogs? Tracking the Cynics in Plato's *Euthydemus*", *Classical Philology* **95**(3) (2000), 282–303. Karl Popper alludes to Joël's hypothesis in his *Open Society and its Enemies, vol. 1* (London: Routledge & Kegan Paul, 1945), where he argues that Plato betrayed the "great generation" and the moral authority of Socrates. Against Plato, Popper sets Antisthenes as a champion of cosmopolitan, free-thinking egalitarianism, a proponent of physical labour, and critic of slavery. See G. J. de Vries, *Antisthenes Redivivus: Popper's Attack on Plato* (Amsterdam: North-Holland, 1952) for one cogent response.

From many works debating whether Antisthenes or Diogenes was the first Cynic, see for instance K. von Fritz, "Antistene e Diogene. Le loro relazioni reciproche e la lora importanza per la setta cinica", in Billerbeck, *Die Kyniker in der modernen Forschung*, 59–72, and especially G. Giannantoni, "Antistene fondatore della scuola cinica?", in Goulet-Cazé & Goulet, *Le Cynisme ancien et ses prolongements*, 15–34; cf. Bracht Branham & Goulet-Cazé, *The Cynics*, Appendix B.

Classical Cynicism

For Diogenes, see M.-O. Goulet-Cazé, D. Gutas & M. C. Hellman, "Diogène de Sinope, surnommé le Chien", in Goulet, *Dictionnaire des Philosophes Antiques*, vol. 2, 812–23, and the book-length study L. E. Navia, *Diogenes: The Man in the Tub* (Westport, CT: Greenwood Press, 1995). On Diogenes, his father and the controversy about "defacing the coins", compare C. T. Seltman, "Diogenes of Sinope, Son of the Banker Hikesias", in *Transactions of the International Numismatic Congress*, J. Allan, H. Mattingley & E. S. G. Robinson (eds), 121 (London: Bernard Quaritch, 1936), Dudley, *A History of Cynicism*, 20–22, and H. Bannert, "Numismatisches zur Biographie und Lehre des Hundes Diogenes", *Litterae Numismaticae Vindobonenses* 1 (1979), 49–63. For Crates as writer, see M. Noussia, "Literary Models and Teachers of Thought: Crates of Thebes and the Tradition of Parody", in *Beyond the Canon*, M. A. Harder, R. F. Regtuit & G. C. Wakker (eds), 229–48 (Leuven: Peeters, 2006).

Hellenistic Cynicism

On the Cynics' literary imagination and influence in the Hellenistic and Roman periods, see: G. A. Gerhard, *Phoinix von Kolophon: Text und Untersuchungen* (Leipzig: Teubner, 1909); Dudley, *A History of Cynicism*, 110–16; G. Murray, "Theopompus, or the Cynic as Historian", in his *Greek Studies*, 149–70 (Oxford: Clarendon Press, 1946); S. Follet, "Les Cyniques dans la poésie épigrammatique à l'époque impériale", in Goulet-Cazé & Goulet, *Le Cynisme ancien et ses prolongements*, 359–80; J. Hammerstädt, "Le Cynisme littéraire à l'époque impériale", in Goulet-Cazé & Goulet, *Le Cynisme ancien et ses prolongements*, 399–418; Noussia, "Literary Models and Teachers of Thought"; and D. Clayman, "Philosophers and Philosophy in Greek Epigram", in *Brill's Companion to Hellenistic Epigram Down to Philip*, P. Bing & J. S. Bruss (eds), 497–517 (Leiden: Brill, 2007). For more general surveys of Hellenistic literature, see also T. Gelzer, "Transformations", and P. Parsons, "Identifies in Diversity", both in *Images and Ideologies: Self-definition in the Hellenistic World*, A. Bulloch, E. Gruen, A. A. Long & A. Stewart (eds), 130–51 and 152–71, respectively (Berkeley, CA: University of California Press, 1993).

On Onesicritus, see especially T. S. Brown, *Onesicritus: A Study in Hellenistic Historiography* (New York: Ares, [1949] 1981). On Onesicritus and the gymnosophists, see Muckensturm, "Les Gymnosophistes", and R. Stoneman, "Naked Philosophers: The Brahmans in the Alexander Historians and the Alexander Romance", *Journal of Hellenic Studies* 115 (1995), 99–114. For Cercidas, see M.-O. Goulet-Cazé & J. L. López Cruces, "Cercidas de Mégalopolis", in Goulet, *Dictionnaire des Philosophes Antiques*, vol. 2, 269–81. Kindstrand, *Bion of Borysthenes*, is a far-ranging commentary on Bion and Cynicism generally. On Teles and the diatribe, see Gonzáles, *Les Diatribes de Télès*, as well as E. N. O'Neill's older commentary, *Teles: The Cynic Teacher* (Missoula, MT: Scholars Press, 1977); cf. A. C. van Geytenbeek, *Musonius Rufus and Greek Diatribe* (Assen: Van Gorcum, 1963).

On the diatribe in relation to St Paul and Judaeo-Christian wisdom literature, see: J. M. Reese, *Hellenistic Influence in the Book of Wisdom and its Consequences* (Rome: Biblical Institute Press, 1970); S. K. Stowers, *The Diatribe and Paul's Letters to the Romans* (Chico,

CA: Scholars Press, 1981); and T. Schmeller, *Paulus und die "Diatribe": Eine vergleichende Stilinterpretation* (Munster: Aschendorff, 1987). The seminal work is R. Bultmann, *Der Stil der paulinischen Predigt und die kynisch-stoische Diatribe* (Göttingen: Vandenhoeck & Ruprecht, 1910).

On the tradition of "Menippean satire", see: E. P. Kirk, *Menippean Satire: An Annotated Catalogue of Texts and Criticism* (New York: Garland, 1980) and J. Relihan, *Ancient Menippean Satire* (Baltimore, MD: Johns Hopkins University Press, 1993). J. Relihan, "Menippus in Antiquity and the Renaissance", in Bracht Branham & Goulet-Cazé, *The Cynics*, 265–93, tracks the figure of Menippus from antiquity into Renaissance literature. On Meleager's cosmopolitan, trilingual epitaph, see M. Luz, "Salam, Meleager!", *Studi Italiani di Filologia Classica* 6 (1988), 222–31. J. Hammerstädt, Γοήτων φῶρα: *Die Orakelkritik des Kyniker Oenomaus* (Frankfurt: Athenaeum, 1988) is an informative commentary on Oenomaus. For the possible identification of Oenomaus of Gadara with the Jewish philosopher, Abnimos ha-Gadi, see S. J. Bastomsky, "Abnimos and Oenomaus: A Question of Identity", *Apeiron* 8 (1974), 57–61.

Cynicism and the Romans

For background on philosophy in Roman settings, see: M. T. Griffin & J. Barnes (eds), *Philosophia Togata I: Essays on Philosophy and Roman Society* (Oxford: Clarendon Press, 1997); E. Rawson, *Intellectual Life in the Late Roman Republic* (Baltimore, MD: Johns Hopkins University Press, 1985) and *Roman Culture and Society* (Oxford: Clarendon Press, 1991); and M. Morford, *The Roman Philosophers* (New York: Routledge, 2002). Concerning later Hellenism and the Romans, see: G. W. Bowersock, *Greek Sophists in the Roman Empire* (Oxford: Clarendon Press, 1969); G. Anderson, *The Second Sophistic: A Cultural Phenomenon in the Roman Empire* (London: Routledge, 1993); and S. Swain, *Hellenism and Empire* (Oxford: Clarendon Press, 1996).

For a thorough overview of Cynicism under the Roman principate, see M.-O. Goulet-Cazé, "Le Cynisme à l'époque impériale", *Aufstieg und Niedergang der römischen Welt* II 36(4) (1990), 2720–833; cf. M. Billerbeck, "La Reception de cynisme à Rome", *L'Antiquité Classique* 51 (1982), 151–73, published in English as "Greek Cynicism in Imperial Rome", in Billerbeck, *Die Kyniker in der modernen Forschung*, 147–66, and D. Krueger, "The Bawdy and Society: The Shamelessness of Diogenes in Roman Imperial Culture", in Bracht Branham & Goulet-Cazé, *The Cynics*, 222–39.

For Cynics and other philosophers as "enemies of the Roman [imperial] order", see the lively book by R. MacMullen, *Enemies of the Roman Order: Treason, Unrest, and Alienation in the Empire* (Cambridge, MA: Harvard University Press, 1966), 46–94. For the dynamic of the "philosophical opposition" in the Flavian period, see B. F. Harris, "Stoic and Cynic under Vespasian", *Prudentia* 11 (1977), 105–14. M. T. Griffin, "Cynicism and the Romans: Attraction and Repulsion", in Bracht Branham & Goulet-Cazé, *The Cynics*, 190–204 (originally published as "Le Mouvement cynique et les Romains: attraction et répulsion", in Goulet-Cazé & Goulet, *Le Cynisme ancien et ses prolongements*, 241–58) explains Roman ambivalence towards the Cynics.

For Demetrius, see M. Billerbeck, *Der Kyniker Demetrius: Ein Beitrag zur Geschichte der frühkaiserzeitlichen Popularphilosophie* (Leiden: Brill, 1979). For Musonius Rufus, see C. Lutz (ed. and trans.), *Musonius Rufus: "The Roman Socrates"* (New Haven, CT: Yale University, 1947) and A. Jagu, *Musonius Rufus, Entretiens et fragments* (Hildesheim: Olms, 1979). For Demetrius' controversial defense of Celer, see J. F. Kindstrand, "Demetrius the Cynic", *Philologus* **124** (1980), 83–98, and J. L. Moles, "'Honestius quam ambitiosius?' An Exploration of the Cynic's Attitude toward Moral Corruption in His Fellow Men", *Journal of Hellenic Studies* **103** (1983), 103–23.

On Epictetus, see especially A. A. Long, *Epictetus: A Stoic and Socratic Guide to Life* (Oxford: Clarendon Press, 2002). On the emergence of ideal Cynic piety from Epictetus to Julian, see M. Billerbeck, "The Ideal Cynic from Epictetus to Julian", in Bracht Branham & Goulet-Cazé, *The Cynics*, 205–21, originally published as "Le Cynisme idéalisé d'Épictète à Julien", in Goulet-Cazé & Goulet, *Le Cynisme ancien et ses prolongements*, 219–338.

For Lucian, see: C. Robinson, *Lucian and his influence in Europe* (London: Duckworth, 1979); Niehues-Pröbsting, *Der Kynismus des Diogenes*, 195–213, on Lucian as a "literary Cynic"; J. Hall, *Lucian's Satire* (New York: Arno Press, 1981); C. P. Jones, *Culture and Society in Lucian* (Cambridge, MA: Harvard University Press, 1986); R. Bracht Branham, *Unruly Eloquence: Lucian and the Comedy of Traditions* (Cambridge, MA: Harvard University Press, 1989); and J. A. Francis, *Subversive Virtue: Asceticism and Authority in the Second-Century Pagan World* (University Park, PA: Pennsylvania State University Press, 1995), 53–82. J. Bernays, *Lucian und die Kyniker* (Berlin: Hertz, 1879) is the seminal work for Cynicism in Lucian.

For Dio Chrysostom, see C. P. Jones, *The Roman World of Dio Chrysostom* (Cambridge, MA: Harvard University Press, 1978) and S. Swain (ed.), *Dio Chrysostom: Politics, Letters, and Philosophy* (Oxford: Oxford University Press, 2000); cf. F. Jouan, "Le Diogène de Dion Chrysostome", in Goulet-Cazé & Goulet, *Le Cynisme ancien et ses prolongements*, 381–98. On the complex figure of Peregrinus and his changing relation to Cynicism, see: H. M. Hornsby, "The Cynicism of Peregrinus Proteus", *Hermathena* **48** (1933), 65–84, reprinted in Billerbeck, *Die Kyniker in der modernen Forschung*, 167–81; Jones, *Culture and Society in Lucian*, and "Cynisme et sagesse barbare: Le cas de Pérégrinus Proteus", in Goulet-Cazé & Goulet, *Le Cynisme ancien et ses prolongements*, 305–18; and J. König, "The Cynic and Christian Lives of Lucian's Peregrinus", in *The Limits of Ancient Biography*, B. McGing & J. Mossman (eds), 227–54 (Swansea: Classical Press of Wales, 2006).

On Marcus Aurelius generally, see A. S. L. Farquharson, *Marcus Aurelius: His Life and his World* (Oxford: Blackwell, 1952) and R. B. Rutherford, *The Meditations of Marcus Aurelius* (Oxford: Oxford University Press, 1989). G. Rudberg, "Diogenes the Cynic and Marcus Aurelius", *Eranos* **47** (1949), 7–12, deals with Marcus and Cynic *parrhēsiasts* (in the tradition of Attic Old Comedy).

For full studies of Julian, see: G. W. Bowersock, *Julian the Apostate* (Cambridge, MA: Harvard University Press, 1978); P. Athanassiadi-Fowden, *Julian and Hellenism: An Intellectual Biography* (London: Routledge, 1992); J. Bouffartigue, *L' Empereur Julien et la culture de son temps* (Paris: Institut d'Études augustiniennes, 1992); and especially R. Smith, *Julian's Gods: Religion and Philosophy in the Thought and Action of Julian* (London: Routledge, 1995), 49–90. For an Italian-language commentary on his Oration 6, see C. Prato & D. Micalella, *Giuliano Imperatore contro I Cinici ignoranti. Edizione critica, traduzione e commento* (Lecce: Università degli Studi, 1988). On Sallustius, last of the known Cynics, see R. Asmus, "Der kyniker Sallustius bei Damascius", *Neue Jahrbücher für klassische Altertum* **13** (1910), 504–22.

2. Renunciation of custom

Background information on Greek society and customs can be found in, for instance, R. Garland, *The Greek Way of Life: From Conception to Old Age* (Ithaca, NY: Cornell University Press, 1992) and *Daily Life of the Ancient Greeks* (Westport, CT: Greenwood Press, 1998). J. Ferguson, *Moral Values in the Ancient World* (London: Methuen, 1958) is informative on a variety of ethical concepts through antiquity (e.g. cardinal virtues, *philanthrōpia*), while K. J. Dover, *Greek Popular Morality* (Indianapolis, IN: Hackett, 1994) is the standard work on moral attitudes of the classical period.

The following are a few studies on specific themes: B. R. Voss, "Die Keule der Kyniker", *Hermes* **95** (1967), 441–6, on the association of the Cynics' staff with Heracles' club; A. C. Bayonas, "Travail manuel et esclavage d'après les Cyniques", *Rendiconti dell'Istituto Lombardo* **100** (1966), 383–8, and H. Schulz-Falkenthal, "Zum Arbeitsethos der Kyniker", *Wissenschaftliche Zeitschrift der Martin Luther Universität* **29** (1980), 91–101, reprinted in Billerbeck, *Die Kyniker in der modernen Forschung*, 287–302, on Cynics' attitudes to work and slavery; my *The Greek Praise of Poverty* on the Cynic and classical Greek criticisms of wealth; M.-O. Goulet-Cazé, "Religion and the Early Cynics", in Bracht Branham & Goulet-Cazé, *The Cynics*, 47–80 (originally published as "Les Premiers Cyniques et la religion", in Goulet-Cazé & Goulet, *Le Cynisme ancien et ses prolongements*, 117–58) on early Cynics' scepticism towards Greek religion; R. Bracht Branham, "Diogenes' Rhetoric and the *Invention* of Cynicism", in Bracht Branham & Goulet-Cazé, *The Cynics*, 81–104 (originally published in Goulet-Cazé & Goulet, *Le Cynisme ancien et ses prolongements*, 445–74), among others, on Cynic literary inventiveness; and F. D. Caizzi, "Τῦφος. Contributo alla storia di un concetto", *Sandalion* **3** (1980), 53–66, reprinted in Billerbeck, *Die Kyniker in der modernen Forschung*, 273–85, on *typhos*.

3. A life according to nature

Lovejoy & Boas, *Primitivism and Related Ideas in Antiquity*, 447–56, survey sixty-six uses of the word *physis*, while F. Heinimann, *Nomos und Physis: Herkunft und Bedeutung einer Antithese im griechischen Denken des 5. Jahrhunderts* (Basel: Reinhardt, 1945) focuses on its opposition to *nomos* in the Sophistic period. J. Annas, *The Morality of Happiness* (Oxford: Oxford University Press, 1995), 133–220, discusses ethical naturalism as the standard approach of ancient ethicists. On the Cynics' simple conception of "nature", see H. Schulz-Falkenthal, "Κατὰ φύσιν: Bemerkungen zum Ideal des naturgemäßen Lebens bei den 'älteren' Kynikern", *Wissenschaftliche Zeitschrift der Martin-Luther-Universität, Halle-Wittenberg* **26** (1977), 51–60. Nietzsche (*Beyond Good and Evil*, §9) comments cynically on the (Stoic) motto of "living according to nature".

4. Chance, fate, fortune and the self

On Greek views of *Tychē*, see M. P. Nilsson, *Geschichte der griechischen Religion* (Munich: C. H. Beck, 1974), II.200–10. For Roman *Fortuna*, see J. Champeaux, *Fortuna: Recherches sur le culte de la Fortune à Rome et dans le monde romain des origines à la mort de César* (Rome: École Française de Rome, 1982). C. Gill (ed.), *Personality in Greek Epic, Tragedy, and Philosophy* (Oxford: Oxford University Press, 1996) and *The Structured Self in Hellenistic and Roman Thought* (Oxford: Oxford University Press, 2006) and R. Sorabji, *Self: Ancient and Modern Insights about Individuality, Life, and Death* (Chicago, IL: University of Chicago Press, 2006) explore various ancient (although not Cynic) concepts of the self. For a different approach (touching on Cynic writers also), see M. Foucault, *The Hermeneutics of the Subject: Lectures at the College de France 1981–1982* (Basingstoke: Palgrave Macmillan, 2005). A. N. M. Rich, "The Cynic Conception of αὐτάρκεια", *Mnemosyne* **9** (1956), 23–29, reprinted in Billerbeck, *Die Kyniker in der modernen Forschung*, 233–39, discusses Cynic *autarkeia*.

5. Anarchists, democrats, cosmopolitans, kings

For general surveys of Greek political thought, from differing perspectives, see: E. Barker, *Greek Political Theory* (London: Methuen, [1918] 1970); A. T. Sinclair, *A History of Greek Political Theory* (London: Routledge, 1951); M. Hammond, *City-State and World State in Greek and Roman Political Theory until Augustus* (Cambridge, MA: Harvard University Press, 1951); R. Balot, *Greek Political Thought* (Oxford: Blackwell, 2006); and especially C. Rowe & M. Schofield (eds), *The Cambridge History of Greek and Roman Political Thought* (Cambridge: Cambridge University Press, 2000). More specific to Cynic politics are: D. Dawson, *Cities of the Gods: Communist Utopias in Greek Thought* (Oxford: Oxford University Press, 1992), 111–52; J. L. Moles, "The Cynics and Politics", in *Justice and Generosity: Studies in Hellenistic Social and Political Philosophy*, A. Laks & M. Schofield (eds), 129–58 (Cambridge: Cambridge University Press, 1995) and "The Cynics", in Rowe & Schofield, *The Cambridge History*, 415–34. On Diogenes' *Republic* and its relation to Zeno's, see: A. Chroust, "The Ideal Polity of the Early Stoics: Zeno's *Republic*", *Review of Politics* **27**(2) (1965), 173–83; H. C. Baldry, "Zeno's Ideal State", *Journal of Hellenic Studies* **79** (1959), 3–15; A. Erskine, *The Hellenistic Stoa: Political Action and Thought* (Princeton, NJ: Princeton University Press, 1990); M. Schofield, *The Stoic Idea of the City* (Cambridge: Cambridge University Press, 1991), 22–56, and "Epicurean and Stoic Political Thought", in Rowe & Schofield, *The Cambridge History*, 435–56, esp. 443–6; Dawson, *Cities of the Gods*, 111–52; T. Dorandi, "La Politeia de Diogène de Sinope et quelques remarques sur sa pensée politique", in Goulet-Cazé & Goulet, *Le Cynisme ancien et ses prolongements*, 57–68; and Goulet-Cazé, "Cynicism and the Romans".

On the early Zeno as a proto-anarchist, see P. Kropotkin, "Anarchism", in *Encyclopaedia Britannica*, 11th edn (Cambridge: Cambridge University Press, 1910) and "Modern Science and Anarchism", in *Kropotkin's Revolutionary Pamphlets*, 145–94 (Whitefish, MT: Kessinger, [1913] 2005); cf. M. Nettlau, *A Short History of Anarchism* (London: Freedom Press, 1996) on anarchism generally. MacMullen, *Enemies of the*

Roman Order, and Francis, *Subversive Virtue*, treat the Cynics as anarchistic critics of Rome. For assimilation of Cynicism to modern communism (and the Left generally), see C. W. Goettling, "Diogenes der Cyniker oder die Philosophie des griechischen Proletariats", in *Gesammelte Abhandlungen aus dem klassischen Altertume* (Halle, 1851), 51–277, reprinted in Billerbeck, *Die Kyniker in der modernen Forschung*, 31–57, and G. Rieger, *Diogenes als Lumpensammler: Materialen zu einer Gestalt der französischen Literatur des 19. Jahhunderts* (Munich: Wilhelm Fink, 1982).

From a large bibliography on all aspects of the Athenian democracy, see especially: A. H. M. Stockton, *Athenian Democracy* (Baltimore, MD: Johns Hopkins University Press, 1986); J. Ober, *Mass and Élite in Democratic Athens* (Princeton, NJ: Princeton University Press, 1989); and M. H. Hansen, *The Athenian Democracy in the Age of Demosthenes: Structure, Principles and Ideology* (Oxford: Blackwell, 1991). A. Zimmern, *The Greek Commonwealth* (New York: Modern Library, 1956) remains an enjoyable and insightful introduction; cf. M. H. Hansen, *Polis: An Introduction to the Ancient Greek City-State* (Oxford: Oxford University Press, 2006) for the *polis* generally. For thematic parallels between Athenian democratic ideology and Cynicism, see my *The Greek Praise of Poverty*.

For political background and kingship ideology post-Alexander, see: A. Bulloch, E. Gruen, A. A. Long & A. Stewart, *Images and Ideologies: Self-definition in the Hellenistic World* (Berkeley, CA: University of California Press, 1993); G. Shipley, *The Greek World after Alexander, 323–30 BC* (London: Routledge, 2000), 59–108 ("Kings and Cities"); and D. Hahm, "Kings and Constitutions: Hellenistic Theories", in Rowe & Schofield, *The Cambridge History*, 457–76. Höistad, *Cynic Hero and Cynic King*, and J. L. Moles, "The Fourth Kingship Oration of Dio Chrysostom", *Classical Antiquity* **2**(2) (1983), 251–78, and "The Kingship Orations of Dio Chrysostom", *Papers of the Leeds International Latin Seminar, Sixth Volume,* F. Cairns & M. Heath (eds), 297–375 (Leeds: Francis Cairns, 1990) study Dio's vision of the ideal king.

Some influential discussions touching on the Cynics "negative" cosmopolitanism are: W. W. Tarn, "Alexander the Great and the Unity of Mankind", *British Academy Proceedings* **19** (1933), 123–66; E. Badian, "Alexander the Great and the Unity of Mankind", *Historia* **7** (1958), 425–44; and H. C. Baldry, *The Unity of Mankind in Greek Thought* (Cambridge: Cambridge University Press, 1965), 101–12; cf. Schofield, *The Stoic Idea of the City*, 141–5. On the other hand, J. L. Moles, "Cynic Cosmopolitanism", in Bracht Branham & Goulet-Cazé, *The Cynics*, 105–20, originally published as "Le Cosmopolitisme cynique", in Goulet-Cazé & Goulet, *Le Cynisme ancien et ses prolongements*, 259–80, argues for a "positive" Cynic cosmopolitanism.

6. Cynic legacies

For the Cynics and Stoicism, see J. M. Rist, *Stoic Philosophy* (Cambridge: Cambridge University Press, 1969). More specifically on Aristo are: M. Schofield, "Ariston of Chios and the Unity of Virtue", *Ancient Philosophy* **4** (1984), 83–95; A. A. Long, *Hellenistic Philosophy: Stoics, Epicureans, Skeptics* (Berkeley, CA: University of California Press, 1986), 189–99; and J. I. Porter, "The Philosophy of Aristo of Chios", in Bracht Branham & Goulet-Cazé, *The Cynics*, 156–89.

For Hellenistic influence on the Judaeo-Christian cultures, see: H. Chadwick, *Early Christian Thought and the Classical Tradition* (Oxford: Oxford University Press, 1966); R. Wallace & W. Williams, *The Three Worlds of Paul of Tarsus* (London: Routledge, 1998); E. Ferguson, *Background of Christian Origins* (Grand Rapids, MI: Eerdmans, 1993); and S. Liebermann, *Hellenism in Jewish Palestine* (New York: JTS Press, 1994). For parallels between Dio and the New Testament, see G. Mussies, *Dio Chrysostom and the New Testament* (Leiden: Brill, 1972).

For the thesis that Jesus was primarily a Cynic, see especially: F. G. Downing, *Cynics and Christian Origins* (Edinburgh: T&T Clark, 1992) and "Cynics and Early Christianity", in Goulet-Cazé & Goulet, *Le Cynisme ancien et ses prolongements*, 281–304; L. Vaage, *Galilean Upstarts: Jesus' First Followers According to Q* (Valley Forge, PA: Trinity Press International, 1994); B. L. Mack, *The Lost Gospel: the Book of Q and Christian Origins* (New York: HarperCollins, 1993); J. D. Crossan, *The Historical Jesus: The Life of a Mediterranean Jewish Peasant* (San Francisco, CA: Harper San Francisco, 1991) and *Jesus: A Revolutionary Biography* (New York: HarperCollins, 1993). H. D. Betz, "Jesus and the Cynics: Survey and Analysis of a Hypothesis", *Journal of Religion* 74(4) (1994), 453–75, and P. R. Eddy, "Jesus as Diogenes? Reflections on the Cynic Jesus Thesis", *Journal of Biblical Literature* 115(3) (1996), 449–69, provide useful and critical surveys of such scholarship. B. Witherington, *The Jesus Quest: The Third Search for the Jew of Nazareth* (Downers Grove, IL: Intervarsity Press, 1993), 58–92, and *Jesus the Sage* (Minneapolis, MN: Augsburg Fortress, 1994), 117–45, are very critical; more diplomatic but equally dismissive is J. P. Meier, who acknowledges some similarities between Jesus and the Cynics but warns against "making much out of little" (*A Marginal Jew. Rethinking the Historical Jesus: Companions and Competitors*, vol. III [New Haven, CT: Yale University Press, 2001], 90–91, n.22).

For a classicist's perspective, see J. L. Moles, "Cynic Influence upon First-century Judaism and Early Christianity?", in *The Limits of Ancient Biography*, B. McGing & J. Mossman (eds), 81–116 (Swansea: University of Wales Press, 2006). Malherbe, *Paul and the Popular Philosophers*, collects many of his insightful articles on Cynic and Stoic elements in Paul. For the Cynics as viewed by the Patristics, see D. Dorival, "L'image des Cyniques chez les Pères grecs", in Goulet-Cazé & Goulet, *Le Cynisme ancien et ses prolongements*, 419–43, and D. Krueger, "Diogenes the Cynic among the Fourth-Century Fathers", *Vigiliae Christianae* 47(1) (1993), 29–49. Focusing on St Gregory of Nazianzus are R. Asmus, "Gregorius von Nazianz und sein Verhältnis zum Kynismus", *Theologische Studien und Kritiken* 67 (1894), 314–39, reprinted in Billerbeck, *Die Kyniker in der modernen Forschung*, 185–205, and R. R. Ruether, *Gregory of Nazianzus: Rhetor and Philosopher* (Oxford: Oxford University Press, 1969).

For surveys of Cynicism in the Middle Ages, see: G. Boas, *Primitivism and Related Ideas in the Middle Ages* (Baltimore, MD: Johns Hopkins University Press, [1946] 1997), 87–126; D. Kinney, "Heirs of the Dog: Cynic Selfhood in Mediaeval and Renaissance Culture", in Bracht Branham & Goulet-Cazé, *The Cynics*, 294–328; and S. Matton, "Cynicism and Christianity from the Middle Ages to the Renaissance", in Bracht Branham & Goulet-Cazé, *The Cynics*, 240–64. M. Clément, *Le Cynisme à la renaissance d'Érasme à Montaigne* (Geneva: Droz, 2005) and H. Roberts, *Dogs' Tales: Representations of Ancient Cynicism in French Renaissance Texts* (Amsterdam: Rodopi, 2006) focus on the French Renaissance, with much material on Rabelais, Erasmus and Montaine. On the Renaissance, see also

J. Lievsay, "Some Renaissance Views of Diogenes the Cynic", in *Joseph Quincy Adams: Memorial Studies*, J. McManaway, G. Dawson & E. Willoughby (eds), 447–55 (Washington, DC: Folger Shakespeare Library, 1948) and R. Esclapez, "Montaigne et les philosophes cyniques", *Bulletin de la Société des Amis de Montaigne* **5/6** (1986), 59–76, as well as M. Bakhtin, *Rabelais and his World*, H. Iswolsky (trans.) (Bloomington, IN: Indiana University Press, [1968] 1984), an influential study of the period generally.

On Cynics and Shakespeare's *King Lear*, see: E. M. M. Taylor, "Lear's Philosophers", *Shakespeare Quarterly* **6**(3) (1955), 364–5; J. Donawerth, "Diogenes the Cynic and Lear's Definition of Man, *King Lear* III.iv.101–109", *English Language Notes* **15** (1977), 10–14; F. G. Butler, "Who are King Lear's Philosophers? An Answer with some Help from Erasmus", *English Studies* **67** (1986), 511–24; S. Doloff, "'Let Me Talk with this Philosopher': The Alexander/Diogenes Paradigm in *King Lear*", *Huntington Library Quarterly* **54**(3) (1991), 253–5; and R. Soellner, *Shakespeare's Patterns of Self-Knowledge* (Columbus, OH: Ohio State University Press, 1972), 300–302. A. von Mattyasovsky-Lates, "Stoics and Libertines: Philosophical Themes in the Art of Caravaggio, Poussin, and their Contemporaries", PhD dissertation, Columbia University (1988) looks at how Cynicism and Stoicism are presented by Caravaggio, Poussin and other artists.

On Diogenes among the eighteenth-century *philosophes*, particularly Rousseau and Diderot, see J. Starobinski, "Diogenes dans *Le Neveu de Rameau*", *Stanford French Review* **8** (1984), 147–65; on Diderot, see especially D. O'Gorman, *Diderot the Satirist: Le Neveu de Rameau and Related Works: An Analysis* (Toronto: University of Toronto Press, 1971). On Diogenes as Enlightenment hero and revolutionary, see K. Herding, "Diogenes als Bürgerheld", *Boreas* **5** (1982), 232–54. On Wieland, Rousseau and Diderot, see H. Niehues-Pröbsting, "The Modern Reception of Cynicism: Diogenes in the Enlightenment", in Bracht Branham & Goulet-Cazé, *The Cynics*, 329–65, originally published as "Die Kynismus-Rezeption der Moderne: Diogenes in der Aufklärung", in Goulet-Cazé & Goulet, *Le Cynisme ancien et ses prolongements*, 519–55. Kant's allusion to Demonax is noted in D. S. Robinson, "Kant and Demonax – A Footnote to the History of Philosophy", *Philosophy and Phenomenological Research* **10**(3) (1950), 374–9. For Nietzsche as "neo-Cynic", see: Niehues-Pröbsting, *Der Kynismus des Diogenes*, 250–77; Betz, "Jesus and the Cynics"; and R. Bracht Branham, "Nietzsche's Cynicism: Uppercase or Lowercase?", *Nietzscheforschung* **10** (2003); cf. A. McIntyre, *The Sovereignty of Joy: Nietzsche's Vision of Grand Politics* (Toronto: University of Toronto Press, 1997) and R. J. White, *Nietzsche and the Problem of Sovereignty* (Champaign, IL: University of Illinois Press, 1997) on Nietzschean "sovereignty".

The most important work in the twentieth century is Peter Sloterdijk's *Kritik der zynischen Vernunft* (Frankfurt: Surkamp, 1983), published in English as *Critique of Cynical Reason*, M. Eldred (trans.) (Minneapolis, MN: University of Minnesota Press, 1987). Sloterdijk's thesis that a cynical modern world needs to return to some form of the ancient Cynics' mischievous humour is echoed in different ways by M. Onfray, *Cynismes: Portrait du philosophe en chien* (Paris: Grasset, 1990) and Navia, *Classical Cynicism*. For the later Foucault's interest in Cynicism (especially *parrhēsia*), see T. R. Flynn, "Foucault and the Politics of Postmodernity", *Noûs* **23** (1989), 187–98, and "Foucault as Parrhesiast: His Last Course at the Collège de France (1984)", in *The Final Foucault*, J. Bernauer & D. Rasmussen (eds), 102–18 (Cambridge, MA: MIT Press, 1991). See also Niehues-Pröbsting, *Der Kynismus des Diogenes*, 278–92, on Cynicism and psychoanalysis.

Bibliography

Alonso-Nuñez, J. M. 1984. "L'empereur Julien et les Cyniques". *Les Études Classiques* **52**: 254–9.

Attridge, H. W. 1976. *First-Century Cynicism in the Epistles of Heraclitus*. Missoula, MT: Scholars Press.

Baldwin, B. 1961. "Lucian as Social Satirist". *Classical Quarterly* **11**(2): 199–208.

Balot, R. 2006. *Greek Political Thought*. Oxford: Blackwell.

Bayonas, A. C. 1966. "Travail manuel et esclavage d'après les Cyniques". *Rendiconti dell'Istituto Lombardo* **100**: 383–8.

Beckby, H. 1965–68. *Anthologia Graeca*, vols 1–4, 2nd edn. Munich: Heimeran. [*AG*]

Betz, H. D. 1994. "Jesus and the Cynics: Survey and Analysis of a Hypothesis". *Journal of Religion* **74**(4): 453–75.

Billerbeck, M. (ed.) 1978. *Epiktet: Vom Kynismus*. Leiden: Brill.

Billerbeck, M. 1982. "La Reception de cynisme à Rome". *L'Antiquité Classique* **51**: 151–73; published in English as "Greek Cynicism in Imperial Rome", in Billerbeck (1991), 147–66.

Billerbeck, M. (ed.) 1991. *Die Kyniker in der modernen Forschung*. Amsterdam: Grüner.

Billerbeck, M. 1996. "The Ideal Cynic from Epictetus to Julian". See Bracht Branham & Goulet-Cazé (1996), 205–21. Originally published as "Le Cynisme idéalisé d'Épictète à Julien", in Goulet-Cazé & Goulet (1993), 219–338.

Bouffartigue, J. 1993. "Le Cynisme dans le cursus philosophique au IVe siècle". See Goulet-Cazé & Goulet (1993), 339–58.

Bracht Branham, R. 1989. *Unruly Eloquence: Lucian and the Comedy of Traditions*. Cambridge, MA: Harvard University Press.

Bracht Branham, R. 1996. "Diogenes' Rhetoric and the *Invention* of Cynicism". See Bracht Branham & Goulet-Cazé (1996), 81–104. Originally published in Goulet-Cazé & Goulet (1993), 445–74.

Bracht Branham, R. & M.-O. Goulet-Cazé (eds) 1996. *The Cynics: The Cynic Movement in Antiquity and Its Legacy*. Berkeley, CA: University of California Press.

Clayman, D. 2007. "Philosophers and Philosophy in Greek Epigram". In *Brill's Companion to Hellenistic Epigram Down to Philip*, P. Bing & J. S. Bruss (eds), 497–517. Leiden: Brill.

Dawson, D. 1992. *Cities of the Gods: Communist Utopias in Greek Thought*. Oxford: Oxford University Press.

Desmond, W. 2006. *The Greek Praise of Poverty: Origins of Ancient Cynicism*. Notre Dame, IN: University of Notre Dame Press.

Diels, H. & W. Kranz 1952. *Die Fragmente der Vorsokratiker*, 6th edn. Berlin: Weidmann. [DK]

Dorival, D. 1993. "L'image des Cyniques chez les Pères grecs". See Goulet-Cazé & Goulet (1993), 419–43.

Dover, K. J. 1994. *Greek Popular Morality*. Indianapolis, IN: Hackett.

Downing, F. G. 1993. "Cynics and Early Christianity". See Goulet-Cazé & Goulet (1993), 281–304.

Dudley, D. R. [1937] 1980. *A History of Cynicism from Diogenes to the 6th Century AD*. Chicago, IL: Ares.

Duff, J. W. 1936. *Roman Satire: Its Outlook on Social Life*. Berkeley, CA: University of California Press.

Emeljanow, V. E. 1968. *The Letters of Diogenes*, PhD dissertation, Stanford University.

Erbse, H. 1952. "*Plutarchs Schrift Περὶ Δεισιδαιμονίας*". *Hermes* **80**: 296–314.

Erskine, A. 1990. *The Hellenistic Stoa: Political Action and Thought*. Princeton, NJ: Princeton University Press.

Fischel, H. A. 1968. "Studies in Cynicism and the Ancient Near East: The Transformation of a *Chria*". In *Religions in Antiquity: Essays in Memory of Erwin Ramsdell Goodenough*, J. Neusner (ed.), 372–411. Leiden: Brill.

Foucault, M. 1986. *The Care of the Self: The History of Sexuality, vol. 3*, R. Hurley (trans.). New York: Vintage.

Frye, N. 1957. *The Anatomy of Criticism*. Princeton, NJ: Princeton University Press.

Fuentes Gonzáles, P. P. 1998. *Les Diatribes de Télès: Introduction, texte revu et commentaire des fragments, avec en appendice une traduction espagnole*. Paris: Vrin.

Gerhard, G. A. 1909. *Phoinix von Kolophon: Text und Untersuchungen*. Leipzig: Teubner.

Giangrande, L. 1972. *The Use of Spoudaiogeloion in Greek and Roman Literature*. The Hague: Mouton.

Giannantoni, G. 1993. "Antistene fondatore della scuola cinica?". See Goulet-Cazé & Goulet (1993), 15–34.

Gibbon, E. [1776, 1781, 1788] 2000. *The History of the Decline and Fall of the Roman Empire*. Harmondsworth: Penguin.

Goulet-Cazé, M.-O. 1986a. *L'Ascèse Cynique: Un Commentaire de Diogène Laërce VI 70–71*. Paris: Vrin.

Goulet-Cazé, M.-O. 1986b. "Une List des disciples de Cratès le cynique en Diogène Laërce 6,95". *Hermes* **114**: 247–52.

Goulet-Cazé, M.-O. 1990. "Le Cynisme à l'époque impériale". *Aufstieg und Niedergang der römischen Welt* II **36**(4): 2720–833.

Goulet-Cazé, M.-O. 1996. "Religion and the Early Cynics". See Bracht Branham & Goulet-Cazé (1996), 47–80. Originally published as "Les Premiers Cyniques et la religion", in Goulet-Cazé & Goulet (1993), 117–58.

Goulet-Cazé, M.-O. 2003. *Le Kynica du stoïcisme*. Stuttgart: Franz Steiner.

Goulet-Cazé, M.-O. & R. Goulet (eds) 1993. *Le Cynisme ancien et ses prolongements: Acts du Colloque international du CNRS*. Paris: Presses Universitaires de France.

Goulet-Cazé, M.-O. & M. C. Hellman 1994. "Antisthène". In *Dictionnaire des Philosophes Antiques*, R. Goulet (ed.), vol. 1, 245–54. Paris, CNRS Éditions.

Goulet, R. (ed.) 1994. *Dictionnaire des Philosophes Antiques*. Paris: CNRS Éditions.

Hammerstädt, J. 1990. "Der Kyniker Oenomaus von Gadara". *Aufstieg und Niedergang der römischen Welt* II **36**(4): 2834–65.

Hammond, M. 1951. *City-State and World State in Greek and Roman Political Theory until Augustus*. Cambridge, MA: Harvard University Press.

Helm, R. 1906. *Lucien und Menipp*. Leipzig: Teubner.

Hense, O. (ed.) [1889] 1969. *Teletis Reliquiae*. Hildesheim: Olms.

Hock, R. F. 1976. "Simon the Shoemaker as an Ideal Cynic". *Greek, Roman and Byzantine Studies* **17**: 41–53; reprinted in Billerbeck (1991), 259–71.

Höistad, R. 1948. *Cynic Hero and Cynic King: Studies in the Cynic Conception of Man*. Uppsala: C. W. K. Gleerup.

Hulin, M. 1993. "Doctrines et comportements 'cyniques' dans certaines sects hindoues anciennes et contemporaines". See Goulet-Cazé & Goulet (1993), 557–70.

Hume, D. 1972. *Enquiries Concerning Human Understanding and Concerning the Principles of Morals*, 3rd edn, L. A. Selby-Bigge & P. H. Nidditch (ed.). Oxford: Clarendon Press.

Ingalls, D. 1962, "Cynics and Pasupatas: The Seeking of Dishonor". *Harvard Theological Review* **55**: 281–98.

Jaeger, W. 1936. *The Theology of the Early Greek Philosophers*, E. S. Robinson (trans.). Oxford: Clarendon Press.

Jones, C. P. 1986. *Culture and Society in Lucian*. Cambridge, MA: Harvard University Press.

Jones, C. P. 1993. "Cynisme et sagesse barbare: Le cas de Pérégrinus Proteus". See Goulet-Cazé & Goulet (1993), 305–18.

Kassel, R. (ed.) 1998. *Poetae Comici Graeci: Menander*. New York: De Gruyter.

Keats, J. 2007. "Ode to a Nightingale". In his *Selected Poems*, 193–5. Harmondsworth: Penguin.

Kemp Smith, N. 1918. *A Commentary to Kant's Critique of Pure Reason*. London: Macmillan.

Kindstrand, J. F. 1976. *Bion of Borysthenes: A Collection of the Fragments with Introduction and Commentary*. Uppsala: Acta Universitatis Uppsalensis.

Kindstrand, J. F. 1994. "Bion de Borysthène". In *Dictionnaire des Philosophes Antiques*, R. Goulet (ed.), vol. 1, 108–12. Paris: CNRS Éditions.

Kropotkin, P. 1910. "Anarchism". In *Encyclopaedia Britannica*, 11th edn. London.

Kropotkin, P. [1913] 2005. "Modern Science and Anarchism". In *Kropotkin's Revolutionary Pamphlets*, 145–94. Whitefish, MT: Kessinger.

Krueger, D. 1996a. "The Bawdy and Society: The Shamelessness of Diogenes in Roman Imperial Culture". See Bracht Branham & Goulet-Cazé (1996), 222–39.

Krueger, D. 1996b. *Symeon the Holy Fool: Leontius' Life and the Late Antique City*. Berkeley, CA: University of California Press.

Liddell, H. G., R. Scott & H. S. Jones 1968. *A Greek–English Lexicon*, 9th edn. Oxford: Clarendon Press.

Long, A. A. 1978. "Timon of Phlius: Pyrrhonist and Satirist". *Proceedings of the Cambridge Philological Society* **24**: 68–91.

Long, A. A. 1992. "Cynics". In *Encyclopaedia of Ethics*, L. C. Becker & C. B. Becker (eds), vol. 1, 234–6. New York: Garland.

Lovejoy, O. & G. Boas [1935] 1965. *Primitivism and Related Ideas in Antiquity*. New York: Octagon Books.

Luz, M. 1989. "A Description of the Greek Cynic in the Jerusalem Talmud". *Journal for the Study of Judaism* **20**: 49–60.

Mack, B. L. 1998. *A Myth of Innocence: Mark and Christian Origins*. Minneapolis, MN: Augsburg Fortress Press.

MacMullen, R. 1966. *Enemies of the Roman Order: Treason, Unrest, and Alienation in the Empire*. Cambridge, MA: Harvard University Press.

Malherbe, A. J. 1968. "The Beasts at Ephesus". *Journal of Biblical Literature* **87**(1): 71–80.

Malherbe, A. J. 1970. "'Gentle as a Nurse': The Cynic Background to 1 Thessalonians 2". *Novum Testamentum* **12**: 203–17.

Malherbe, A. J. 1977. *The Cynic Epistles: A Study Edition*. Missoula, MT: Scholars Press.

Malherbe, A. J. 1978. "Ps.-Heraclitus, Ep. 4: The Divinization of the Wise Man". *Zeitschrift für Antikes Christentum (JAC)* **21**: 42–64.

Malherbe, A. J. 1982. "Self-definition among Epicureans and Stoics". In *Jewish and Christian Self-definition*, B. F. Meyers & E. P. Sanders (eds), 46–59. Philadelphia, PA: Fortress Press.

Malherbe, A. J. 1987. *Paul and the Thessalonians*. Philadelphia, PA: Fortress Press.

Martin, R. P. 1996. "The Scythian Accent: Anacharsis and the Cynics". See Bracht Branham & Goulet-Cazé (1996), 136–55.

Mejer, J. 1978. *Diogenes Laertius and his Hellenistic Background*. Wiesbaden: Steiner.

Matton, S. 1996. "Cynicism and Christianity from the Middle Ages to the Renaissance". See Bracht Branham & Goulet-Cazé (1996), 240–64.

McCarthy, B. P. (ed.) 1934. "Lucian and Menippus". *Yale Classical Studies* **4**: 1–55.

Meilland, J. M. 1983. "L'Anti-intellectualisme de Diogène le Cynique". *Revue de Théologie et de Philosophie* **3**: 233–46.

Moles, J. L. 1978. "The Career and Conversion of Dio Chrysostom". *Journal of Hellenic Studies* **98**: 79–100.

Moles, J. L. 1996. "Cynic Cosmopolitanism". See Bracht Branham & Goulet-Cazé (1996), 105–20. Originally published as "Le Cosmopolitisme cynique", in Goulet-Cazé & Goulet (1993), 259–80.

Moles, J. L. 2000. "The Cynics". In *The Cambridge History of Greek and Roman Political Thought*, C. J. Rowe & M. Schofield (eds), 415–34. Cambridge: Cambridge University Press.

Morford, M. 2002. *The Roman Philosophers*. New York: Routledge.

Mras, K. 1914. "Varros Menippeische Satiren und die Philosophie". *Neues Jahrbuch für Philologie* **33**: 390–420.

Muckensturm C. 1993. "Les Gymnosophistes, étaient-ils des Cyniques modèles?" See Goulet-Cazé & Goulet (1993), 225–40.

Murray, G. 1946. "Theopompus, or the Cynic as Historian". In his *Greek Studies*, 149–70. Oxford: Clarendon Press.

Nagle, D. B. 2006. *The Household as the Foundation of Aristotle's Polis*. Cambridge: Cambridge University Press.

Nakhov, I. M. 1981. *The Philosophy of the Cynics*. Moscow: Nuaka.

Nauck, A. (ed.) 1964. *Tragicorum Graecorum Fragmenta*. Hildesheim: Olms.

Navia, L. E. 1995. *The Philosophy of Cynicism: An Annotated Bibliography*. Westport, CT: Greenwood Press.

Navia, L. E. 1996. *Classical Cynicism: A Critical Study*. Westport, CT: Greenwood Press.

Niehues-Pröbsting, H. 1979. *Der Kynismus des Diogenes und der Begriff des Zynismus*. Munich: Wilhelm Fink.

Niehues-Pröbsting, H. 1996. "The Modern Reception of Cynicism: Diogenes in the Enlightenment". See Bracht Branham & Goulet-Cazé (1996), 329–65. Originally published as "Die Kynismus-Rezeption der Moderne: Diogenes in der Aufklärung", in Goulet-Cazé & Goulet (1993), 519–55.

Nietzsche, F. 1966. *Werke in Drei Bänden*. Munich: Carl Hanser.

Nietzsche, F. 1974. *The Gay Science*, W. Kaufmann (trans.). New York: Vintage.

Nilsson, M. P. 1974. *Geschichte der griechischen Religion*, vols I–II. Munich: C. H. Beck.

Noussia, M. 2006. "Literary Models and Teachers of Thought: Crates of Thebes and the Tradition of Parody". In *Beyond the Canon*, M. A. Harder, R. F. Regtuit & G. C. Wakker (eds), 229–48. Leuven: Peeters.

O'Neill, E. N. 1977. *Teles: The Cynic Teacher*. Missoula, MT: Scholars Press.

Paquet, L. 1988. *Les Cyniques grecs: Fragments et témoignages*, 2nd edn. Ottawa: Presses de l'Université d'Ottawa.

Parsons, P. 1993. "Identifies in Diversity". In *Images and Ideologies: Self-definition in the Hellenistic World*, A. Bulloch, E. Gruen, A. A. Long and A. Stewart (eds), 152–71. Berkeley, CA: University of California Press.

Poe, E. A. 2006. *The Portable Edgar Allan Poe*, J. G. Kennedy (ed.). Harmondsworth: Penguin.

Race, W. H. 1997. *Pindar: Olympian Odes. Pythian Odes*. Loeb Classical Library. Cambridge, MA: Harvard University Press.

Rahn, H. 1959. "Die Frömmigkeit der Kyniker". *Paideuma* 7: 280-092; reprinted in Billerbeck (1991), 241–57.

Relihan, J. 1993. *Ancient Menippean Satire*. Baltimore, MD: Johns Hopkins University Press.

Relihan, J. 1996. "Menippus in Antiquity and the Renaissance". See Bracht Branham & Goulet-Cazé (1996), 265–93.

Roberts, A. & J. Donaldson (eds) 1868. *Translations of the Writings of the Fathers down to AD 325, Vol. III: Tatian, Theophilus and the Clementine Recognitions* (Edinburgh: T. & T. Clark).

Roberts, H. 2004. "Cynic Shamelessness in Late Sixteenth-Century French Texts. *Modern Language Review* **99**(3): 595–607.

Robinson, D. M. 1906a. "Ancient Sinope: First Part". *American Journal of Philology* 27(2): 125–53.

Robinson, D. M. 1906b. "Ancient Sinope: Second Part". *American Journal of Philology* 27(3): 245–79.

Rostovtzeff, M. I. 1926. *Social and Economic History of the Roman Empire*. Oxford: Clarendon Press.

Sayre, F. 1938. *Diogenes of Sinope: A Study of Greek Cynicism*. Baltimore, MD: J. H. Furst.

Sayre, F. 1948. *The Greek Cynics*. Baltimore, MD: J. H. Furst.

Schofield, M. 1991. *The Stoic Idea of the City*. Cambridge: Cambridge University Press.

Schofield, M. 2000. "Epicurean and Stoic Political Thought". In *The Cambridge History of Greek and Roman Political Thought*, C. J. Rowe & M. Schofield (eds), 435–56. Cambridge: Cambridge University Press.

Schulz-Falkenthal, H. 1980. "Zum Arbeitsethos der Kyniker". *Wissenschaftliche Zeitschrift der Martin Luther Universität* **29**: 91–101; reprinted in Billerbeck (1991), 287–302.

Sloterdijk, P. 1983. *Kritik der zynischen Vernunft*. Frankfurt: Surkamp. Published in English as *Critique of Cynical Reason*, M. Eldred (trans.) (Minneapolis, MN: University of Minnesota Press, 1987).

Stewart, Z. 1958. "Democritus and the Cynics". *Harvard Studies in Classical Philology* **63**: 179–91.

Swain, S. 1996. *Hellenism and Empire*. Oxford: Clarendon Press.

Syrkin, A. 1988. "The Salutary Descent". *Numen* **35**: 1–23, 213–37.

Temkin, O. 1991. *Hippocrates in a World of Pagans and Christians*. Baltimore, MD: Johns Hopkins University Press.

Toynbee, J. 1944. "Dictators and Philosophers in the First Century AD". *Greece & Rome* **13**(38–9): 43–58.

Ucciani, L. 1993. *De l'ironie socratique à la dérision cynique. Éléments pour une critique par les formes exclues*. Paris: Les Belles Lettres.

Vaage, L. 1987. *Q: The Ethos and Ethics of an itinerant Intelligence*. PhD dissertation, Claremont Graduate University, California.

Voss, B. R. 1967. "Die Keule der Kyniker". *Hermes* **95**: 441–6.

Walbank, F. W. 2002. *Polybius, Rome and the Hellenistic World: Essays and Reflections*. Cambridge: Cambridge University Press.

Weber, T. & R. G. Khouri 1989. *Umm Qais, Gadara of the Decapolis*. Amman: Economic Press.

Weiss, A. 1999. "An Anatomy of Anatomy". *Drama Review* **41**(1): 137–44.

Wilson, W. T. 1991. *Love Without Pretense: Romans 12.9–21 and Hellenistic-Jewish Wisdom*. Tübingen: Mohr-Siebeck.

Wimbush, L. 1990. *Ascetic Behavior in Greco-Roman Antiquity: A Sourcebook*. Minneapolis, MN: Augsburg Fortress.

Winiarczyk, M. 1976. "Diagoras von Melos und Diogenes von Sinope". *Eos* **64**: 177–84.

Winiarczyk, M. 1981. "Theodoros ὁ Ἄθεος und Diogenes von Sinope". *Eos* **69**: 37–42.

Xenakis, J. 1973. "Hippies and Cynics". *Inquiry* **16**: 1–15.

Zeller, E. 1962. "The Cynics". In his *Socrates and the Socratic Schools*, O. J. Reichel (trans.), 285–337. New York: Russell & Russell.

Index

Page numbers in italics indicate more important discussions